Python Network Programming Cookbook

Second Edition

Overcome real-world networking challenges

Pradeeban Kathiravelu
Dr. M. O. Faruque Sarker

Packt>

BIRMINGHAM - MUMBAI

Python Network Programming Cookbook

Second Edition

First published: March 2014

Second edition: August 2017

Production reference: 1080817

Published by Packt Publishing Ltd.
Livery Place
35 Livery Street
Birmingham
B3 2PB, UK.

ISBN 978-1-78646-399-9

www.packtpub.com

Credits

Authors
Pradeeban Kathiravelu
Dr. M. O. Faruque Sarker

Reviewers
Dr. S. Gowrishankar
Michael Bright

Commissioning Editor
Kartikey Pandey

Acquisition Editor
Rahul Nair

Content Development Editor
Abhishek Jadhav

Technical Editor
Mohd Riyan Khan

Copy Editors
Safis Editing
Juliana Nair

Project Coordinator
Judie Jose

Proofreader
Safis Editing

Indexer
Aishwarya Gangawane

Graphics
Kirk D'Penha

Production Coordinator
Aparna Bhagat

About the Author

Pradeeban Kathiravelu is an open source evangelist. He is a Ph.D. researcher at INESC-ID Lisboa/Instituto Superior Tecnico, Universidade de Lisboa, Portugal, and Universite Catholique de Louvain, Belgium. He is a Fellow of Erasmus Mundus Joint Degree in Distributed Computing (EMJD-DC), researching a software-defined approach to quality of service and data quality in multi-tenant clouds.

Pradeeban holds a master of science degree, Erasmus Mundus European Master in Distributed Computing (EMDC), from Instituto Superior Tecnico, Portugal and KTH Royal Institute of Technology, Sweden. He also holds a first class bachelor of science in engineering (Hons) degree, majoring in computer science and engineering, from the University of Moratuwa, Sri Lanka. His research interests include Software-Defined Networking (SDN), distributed systems, cloud computing, web services, big data in biomedical informatics, Network Functions Virtualizations (NFV), and data mining. He is very interested in free and open source software development and has been an active participant in the Google Summer of Code (GSoC) program since 2009, as a student and as a mentor.

Pradeeban has published several conference papers and co-authored a few book chapters. He has also worked on *OpenDaylight Cookbook* and *Learning OpenDaylight* as a technical reviewer. *Python Network Programming Cookbook, Second Edition* (2017) is his first book as an author, and he is quite excited about it.

I would like to thank my readers for the interest in the book. Please feel free to contact me if you need any assistance in the topics or the recipes, beyond what we have discussed in the book. I would like to thank the entire editorial team at Packt, including Abhishek Jadhav, Rahul Nair, and Mohd Riyan Khan. I would like to extend my thanks to the Linux Foundation for their open source projects on softwarization of networks and systems. I would like to thank my friends and colleagues who helped me in various ways. I would like to thank Prof. Luís Veiga (INESC-ID Lisboa), my MSc and Ph.D. advisor, for sharing his wisdom and encouragement throughout my stay in Instituto Superior Técnico. I would like to thank him for being my mentor since 2012. I would also like to thank Prof. Ashish Sharma (Emory University, Atlanta) for his guidance and motivation.

My special thanks go to my loving wife, Juejing Gu. This book would not be a reality without her continuous support and creative suggestions. Her tireless efforts helped me always be on time without missing the deadlines.
I would like to thank my mom, Selvathie Kathiravelu, for her support.

Dr. M. O. Faruque Sarker is a software architect based in London, UK, where he has been shaping various Linux and open source software solutions, mainly on cloud computing platforms, for commercial companies, educational institutions, and multinational consultancies. Over the past 10 years, he has been leading a number of Python software development and cloud infrastructure automation projects. In 2009, he started using Python, where he was responsible for shepherding a fleet of miniature E-puck robots at the University of South Wales, Newport, UK. Later, he honed his Python skills, and he was invited to work on the Google Summer of Code (2009/2010) programs for contributing to the BlueZ and Tahoe-LAFS open source projects. He is the author of *Python Network Programming Cookbook* and *Learning Python Network Programming* both by *Packt Publishing*.

He received his Ph.D. in multi-robot systems from the University of South Wales. He is currently working at University College London. He takes an active interest in cloud computing, software security, intelligent systems, and child-centric education. He lives in East London with his wife, Shahinur, and daughter, Ayesha.

All praises and thanks to Allah, the God who is the Merciful and the Beneficent. I would not be able to finish this book without the help of God. I would like to thank everyone who has contributed to the publication of this book, including the publisher, technical reviewers, editors, my family and friends for their sacrifice of time, encouraging words, and smiles, especially my wife Shahinur Rijuani for her love and support in my work. I also thank the readers who have patiently been waiting for this book and who have given me lots of valuable feedback.

About the Reviewers

Dr. S. Gowrishankar is currently working as an associate professor in the Department of Computer Science and Engineering at Dr. Ambedkar Institute of Technology, Bengaluru, Karnataka, India.

He received his Ph.D. in Engineering from Jadavpur University, Kolkata, West Bengal, India in 2010, MTech in software engineering and BE in computer science and engineering from Visvesvaraya Technological University (VTU), Belagavi, Karnataka, India in the year 2005 and 2003 respectively.

From 2011 to 2014 he worked as a senior research scientist and tech lead at Honeywell Technology Solutions, Bengaluru, Karnataka, India.

He has published several papers in various reputed international journals and conferences. He is serving as an editor and reviewer for various prestigious international journals. He is also a member of IEEE, ACM, CSI, and ISTE.

He has delivered many keynote addresses and invited talks throughout India on a variety of subjects related to computer science and engineering. He was instrumental in organizing several conferences, workshops, and seminars. He has also served on the panel of a number of academic bodies of universities and autonomous colleges as a BOS and BOE member.

His current research interests are mainly focused on data science, including its technical aspects as well as its applications and implications. Specifically, he is interested in the applications of Machine Learning, Data Mining, and Big Data Analytics in Healthcare.

I would like to acknowledge my earnest gratitude to my wife, Roopa K M, for her constant source of support and encouragement throughout this assignment. I'm truly thankful to almighty God for having her in my life and give her my deepest expression of love and appreciation.

Michael Bright, RHCE/RHCSA, is a solution architect working in the HPE EMEA Customer Innovation Center.

He has strong experience across Cloud and Container technologies (Docker, Kubernetes, AWS, GCP, Azure) as well as NFV/SDN.

Based in Grenoble, France, he runs a Python user group and is a co-organizer of the Docker and FOSS Meetup groups. He has a keen interest in Container, Orchestration, and Unikernel technologies on which he has presented and run training tutorials in several conferences.
He has presented many times on subjects diverse as NFV, Docker, Container Orchestration, Unikernels, Jupyter Notebooks, MongoDB, and Tmux.

Michael has a wealth of experience across pure research, R&D and pre-sales consulting roles.

www.PacktPub.com

For support files and downloads related to your book, please visit `www.PacktPub.com`.

Did you know that Packt offers eBook versions of every book published, with PDF and ePub files available? You can upgrade to the eBook version at `www.PacktPub.com`and as a print book customer, you are entitled to a discount on the eBook copy. Get in touch with us at `service@packtpub.com` for more details.

At `www.PacktPub.com`, you can also read a collection of free technical articles, sign up for a range of free newsletters and receive exclusive discounts and offers on Packt books and eBooks.

`https://www.packtpub.com/mapt`

Get the most in-demand software skills with Mapt. Mapt gives you full access to all Packt books and video courses, as well as industry-leading tools to help you plan your personal development and advance your career.

Why subscribe?

- Fully searchable across every book published by Packt
- Copy and paste, print, and bookmark content
- On demand and accessible via a web browser

Customer Feedback

Thanks for purchasing this Packt book. At Packt, quality is at the heart of our editorial process. To help us improve, please leave us an honest review on this book's Amazon page at https://www.amazon.com/dp/1786463997.

If you'd like to join our team of regular reviewers, you can e-mail us at customerreviews@packtpub.com. We award our regular reviewers with free eBooks and videos in exchange for their valuable feedback. Help us be relentless in improving our products!

I dedicate this book to the world, in memory of my dad, Kanapathipillai Kathiravelu.

Table of Contents

Preface

It has been more than 3 years since *Python Network Programming Cookbook* was first published. In this second edition, we extend our book to discuss the recent advancements in the networking industry and network softwarization. The widespread use of Software-Defined Networking (SDN), Network Functions Virtualization (NFV), and orchestration have been addressed in detail in the latter chapters while the first eight chapters were taken from the first edition, improved with a few new recipes based on the feedback from the readers.

This book is an exploratory guide to network programming in Python. It has touched a wide range of networking protocols such as TCP/UDP, HTTP/HTTPS, FTP, SMTP, POP3, IMAP, and CGI. With the power and interactivity of Python, it brings joy and fun to develop various scripts for performing real-world tasks on network and system administration, web application development, interacting with your local and remote network, low-level network packet capture and analysis, and so on. The primary focus of this book is to give you a hands-on experience on the topics covered. So, this book covers less theory, but it is packed with practical materials.

This book is written with a DevOps mindset, where a developer is also more or less in charge of operation, that is, deploying the application and managing various aspects of it, such as remote server administration, monitoring, scaling-up, and optimizing for better performance. This book introduces you to a bunch of open-source, third-party Python libraries, which are ideal to be used in various use cases. We elaborate in detail the configurations of complex networking systems with helpful hints to ensure that the reader can follow them without getting stuck.

We hope you will enjoy the recipes presented in this book and extend them to make them even more powerful and enjoyable.

What this book covers

Chapter 1, *Sockets, IPv4, and Simple Client/Server Programming*, introduces you to Python's core networking library with various small tasks and enables you to create your first client-server application.

Chapter 2, *Multiplexing Socket I/O for Better Performance*, discusses various useful techniques for scaling your client/server applications with default and third-party libraries.

Chapter 3, *IPv6, Unix Domain Sockets, and Network Interfaces*, focuses more on administering your local machine and looking after your local area network.

Chapter 4, *Programming with HTTP for the Internet*, enables you to create a mini command-line browser with various features such as submitting web forms, handling cookies, managing partial downloads, compressing data, and serving secure content over HTTPS.

Chapter 5, *Email Protocols, FTP, and CGI Programming*, brings you the joy of automating your FTP and e-mail tasks such as manipulating your Gmail account, and reading or sending emails from a script or creating a guest book for your web application. We learn to write email clients with SMTP and POP3.

Chapter 6, *Programming Across Machine Boundaries*, gives you a taste of automating your system administration and deployment tasks over SSH. You can run commands, install packages, or set up new websites remotely from your laptop.

Chapter 7, *Working with Web Services – XML-RPC, SOAP, and REST*, introduces you to various API protocols such as XML-RPC, SOAP, and REST. You can programmatically ask any website or web service for information and interact with them. For example, you can search for products on Amazon or Google.

Chapter 8, *Network Monitoring and Security*, introduces you to various techniques for capturing, storing, analyzing, and manipulating network packets. This encourages you to go further to investigate your network security issues using concise Python scripts.

Chapter 9, *Network Modeling*, introduces you to the world of network simulations and emulations. You learn to simulate networks with NS-3, and emulate networking systems with Mininet and its extensions.

Chapter 10, *Getting Started with SDN*, discusses the enterprise SDN controllers, configuring them to use in Software-Defined Networks. We learn to develop SDN visually with MiniEdit, and configure the networks with OpenDaylight, ONOS, Floodlight, Ryu, and POX controllers.

Chapter 11, *Authentication, Authorization, and Accounting (AAA)*, introduces how the networks are secured, and discusses configuring LDAP clients with Python, accounting aspects of the network, and authentication and access of network services.

Chapter 12, *Open and Proprietary Networking Solutions*, discusses in detail, configuring large-scale enterprise networking projects, including a few projects from Cisco, Juniper, VMware, and the Linux Foundation.

Chapter 13, *NFV and Orchestration – A Larger Ecosystem*, discusses configuring complex NFV and orchestration systems of the Linux Foundation, such as OPNFV, DPDK, SNAS.io, Dronekit, and PNDA. We elaborate the use of Python in these complex systems.

Chapter 14, *Programming the Internet*, presents you various Python libraries for BGP protocol and implementations developed for the internet scale. We learn to use and benchmark libraries such as exabgp and yabgp, and also discuss the looking glass implementations with Python.

What you need for this book

You need a working PC or laptop, preferably with a modern Linux operating system. The installation instructions are written and tested on Ubuntu 16.04 LTS and would work on any recent Debian-based Linux operating system without modification. We developed for Python 3. However, we have maintained backward-compatibility with Python 2 in our recipes as much as we can. On the other hand, some open source projects used in this book do not yet support Python 3. So, ideally, you will need both Python 2 and Python 3 to test all the recipes in this book.

Most of the recipes in this book will run on other platforms such as Windows and Mac OS with some changes in the configuration steps. Some of the recipes require two or more computers in a cluster to test the distributed systems. You may use Amazon Web Services (AWS) to initiate a cluster inside a single placement group to test these recipes.

You also need a working internet connection to install the third-party software libraries mentioned with respective recipes. If you do not have a stable or continuous internet connection, you can download the third-party libraries and install them in one go. However, it is highly recommended to test some of these recipes with the internet connection, as it would make the configuration task minimal and more interesting, than having to download a bulk of software in bunch. Moreover, testing the application in an AWS cluster would certainly require the internet connectivity.

The following is a list of the Python third-party libraries with their download URLs:

- ntplib: `https://pypi.python.org/pypi/ntplib/`
- diesel: `https://pypi.python.org/pypi/diesel/`
- nmap: `https://pypi.python.org/pypi/python-nmap`
- scapy: `https://pypi.python.org/pypi/scapy`
- netifaces: `https://pypi.python.org/pypi/netifaces/`

- netaddr: https://pypi.python.org/pypi/netaddr
- pyopenssl: https://pypi.python.org/pypi/pyOpenSSL
- pygeocoder: https://pypi.python.org/pypi/pygocoder
- pyyaml: https://pypi.python.org/pypi/PyYAML
- requests: https://pypi.python.org/pypi/requests
- feedparser: https://pypi.python.org/pypi/feedparser
- paramiko: https://pypi.python.org/pypi/paramiko/
- fabric: https://pypi.python.org/pypi/Fabric
- supervisor: https://pypi.python.org/pypi/supervisor
- xmlrpclib: https://pypi.python.org/pypi/xmlrpclib
- SOAPpy: https://pypi.python.org/pypi/SOAPpy
- bottlenose: https://pypi.python.org/pypi/bottlenose
- construct: https://pypi.python.org/pypi/construct/
- libpcap: https://pypi.python.org/pypi/pcap
- setup tools: https://pypi.python.org/pypi/setuptools
- exabgp: https://pypi.python.org/pypi/exabgp
- traixroute: https://pypi.python.org/pypi/traixroute
- dronekit: https://pypi.python.org/pypi/dronekit
- dronekit-sitl: https://pypi.python.org/simple/dronekit-sitl/
- ryu: https://pypi.python.org/pypi/ryu
- Flask: https://pypi.python.org/pypi/Flask
- smtpd: https://pypi.python.org/pypi/secure-smtpd
- twisted: https://pypi.python.org/pypi/Twisted
- tornado: https://pypi.python.org/pypi/tornado
- dnspython: https://pypi.python.org/pypi/dnspython
- ldap3: https://pypi.python.org/pypi/ldap3
- Eve: https://pypi.python.org/pypi/Eve
- RequestsThrottler: https://pypi.python.org/pypi/RequestsThrottler
- PyNSXv: https://pypi.python.org/pypi/pynsxv
- vmware-nsx: https://pypi.python.org/pypi/vmware-nsx

Other software needed to run some recipes are as follows:

- postfix: http://www.postfix.org/
- openssh server: http://www.openssh.com/
- mysql server: http://downloads.mysql.com/
- apache2: http://httpd.apache.org/download.cgi/
- virtualenv: https://virtualenv.pypa.io/
- filezilla: https://filezilla-project.org/
- vsftpd: https://security.appspot.com/vsftpd.html
- telnetd: telnetd.sourceforge.net/
- curl: https://curl.haxx.se/
- NS-3: https://www.nsnam.org/ns-3-26/download/
- Mininet: mininet.org/
- Ansible: https://www.ansible.com/
- Git: https://git-scm.com/
- aptitude: https://www.openhub.net/p/aptitude
- Node-ws / wscat: https://www.npmjs.com/package/wscat
- MaxiNet: https://github.com/MaxiNet/MaxiNet/
- Mininet-WiFi: https://github.com/intrig-unicamp/mininet-wifi
- ContainerNet: https://github.com/containernet/containernet.git
- Ant: ant.apache.org/
- Maven: https://maven.apache.org/
- OpenDaylight: https://www.opendaylight.org/downloads
- ONOS: https://wiki.onosproject.org/display/ONOS/Downloads
- Floodlight: http://www.projectfloodlight.org/download/
- POX: http://github.com/noxrepo/pox
- libnl-3-dev: https://packages.debian.org/sid/libnl-3-dev
- libnl-genl-3-dev: https://packages.debian.org/sid/libnl-genl-3-dev
- libnl-route-3-dev: https://packages.debian.org/sid/libnl-route-3-dev
- pkg-config: https://www.freedesktop.org/wiki/Software/pkg-config/
- python-tz: pytz.sourceforge.net/
- libpcap-dev: https://packages.debian.org/libpcap-dev
- libcap2-dev: https://packages.debian.org/jessie/libcap2-dev

- wireshark: https://www.wireshark.org/
- Juniper Contrail: http://www.juniper.net/support/downloads/?p=contrail #sw
- OpenContrail Controller: https://github.com/Juniper/contrail-controller
- Contrail Server Manager: https://github.com/Juniper/contrail-server-man ager.git
- VMWare NSX for vSphere 6.3.2: https://my.vmware.com/group/vmware/detail s?downloadGroup=NSXV_632_OSS&productId=417
- OPNFV Compass: https://wiki.opnfv.org/display/compass4nfv/Compass4n fv
- OPNFV SDNVPN: https://wiki.opnfv.org/display/sdnvpn/SDNVPN+project +main+page
- libpcap-dev: https://packages.debian.org/libpcap-dev
- DPDK: http://dpdk.org/download
- SNAS.io: http://www.snas.io/
- pnda.io: http://pnda.io/
- bgperf: https://github.com/pradeeban/bgperf.git
- swig: www.swig.org/
- yabgp: https://github.com/smartbgp/yabgp
- Virtualbox: https://www.virtualbox.org/wiki/VirtualBox
- Vagrant: https://www.vagrantup.com/
- RED PNDA: https://github.com/pndaproject/red-pnda
- Apache ZooKeeper: https://zookeeper.apache.org/
- Apache Cassandra: http://cassandra.apache.org/
- RabbitMQ: https://www.rabbitmq.com/
- pyIOSXR: https://github.com/fooelisa/pyiosxr
- Cisco Spark API: https://github.com/CiscoDevNet/ciscosparkapi

Who this book is for

If you are a network programmer, system/network administrator, or a web application developer, this book is ideal for you. You should have a basic familiarity with the Python programming language and TCP/IP networking concepts. However, if you are a novice, you will develop an understanding of the concepts as you progress with this book. This book will serve as supplementary material for developing hands-on skills in any academic course on network programming.

Sections

In this book, you will find several headings that appear frequently (Getting ready, How to do it…, How it works…, There's more…, and See also). To give clear instructions on how to complete a recipe, we use these sections as follows:

Getting ready

This section tells you what to expect in the recipe, and describes how to set up any software or any preliminary settings required for the recipe.

How to do it…

This section contains the steps required to follow the recipe.

How it works…

This section usually consists of a detailed explanation of what happened in the previous section.

There's more…

This section consists of additional information about the recipe in order to make the reader more knowledgeable about the recipe.

See also

This section provides helpful links to other useful information for the recipe.

Conventions

In this book, you will find a number of text styles that distinguish between different kinds of information. Here are some examples of these styles and an explanation of their meaning. Code words in text, database table names, folder names, filenames, file extensions, pathnames, dummy URLs, user input, and Twitter handles are shown as follows: "If you need to know the IP address of a remote machine you can use the built-in library function `gethostbyname()`" A block of code is set as follows:

```
def test_socket_timeout():
    s = socket.socket(socket.AF_INET, socket.SOCK_STREAM)
```

```
print "Default socket timeout: %s" %s.gettimeout()
s.settimeout(100)
print "Current socket timeout: %s" %s.gettimeout()
```

Any command-line input or output is written as follows:

```
$ python 2_5_echo_server_with_diesel.py --port=8800
[2013/04/08 11:48:32] {diesel} WARNING:Starting diesel <hand-rolled
select.epoll>
```

New terms and **important words** are shown in bold.

Warnings or important notes appear like this.

Tips and tricks appear like this.

Reader feedback

Feedback from our readers is always welcome. Let us know what you think about this book-what you liked or disliked. Reader feedback is important for us as it helps us develop titles that you will really get the most out of. To send us general feedback, simply e-mail feedback@packtpub.com, and mention the book's title in the subject of your message. If there is a topic that you have expertise in and you are interested in either writing or contributing to a book, see our author guide at www.packtpub.com/authors .

Customer support

Now that you are the proud owner of a Packt book, we have a number of things to help you to get the most from your purchase.

Downloading the example code

You can download the example code files for this book from your account at `http://www.p acktpub.com`. If you purchased this book elsewhere, you can visit `http://www.packtpub.c om/support`and register to have the files e-mailed directly to you. You can download the code files by following these steps:

1. Log in or register to our website using your e-mail address and password.
2. Hover the mouse pointer on the **SUPPORT** tab at the top.
3. Click on **Code Downloads & Errata**.
4. Enter the name of the book in the **Search** box.
5. Select the book for which you're looking to download the code files.
6. Choose from the drop-down menu where you purchased this book from.
7. Click on **Code Download**.

You can also download the code files by clicking on the **Code Files** button on the book's webpage at the Packt Publishing website. This page can be accessed by entering the book's name in the **Search** box. Please note that you need to be logged in to your Packt account. Once the file is downloaded, please make sure that you unzip or extract the folder using the latest version of:

- WinRAR / 7-Zip for Windows
- Zipeg / iZip / UnRarX for Mac
- 7-Zip / PeaZip for Linux

The code bundle for the book is also hosted on GitHub at `https://github.com/PacktPubl ishing/Python-Network-Programming-Cookbook-Second-Edition`. We also have other code bundles from our rich catalog of books and videos available at `https://github.com/P acktPublishing/`. Check them out!

Downloading the color images of this book

We also provide you with a PDF file that has color images of the screenshots/diagrams used in this book. The color images will help you better understand the changes in the output. You can download this file from `https://www.packtpub.com/sites/default/files/downloads/PythonNetworkProgramming CookbookSecondEdition_ColorImages.pdf`.

Errata

Although we have taken every care to ensure the accuracy of our content, mistakes do happen. If you find a mistake in one of our books-maybe a mistake in the text or the code-we would be grateful if you could report this to us. By doing so, you can save other readers from frustration and help us improve subsequent versions of this book. If you find any errata, please report them by visiting http://www.packtpub.com/submit-errata, selecting your book, clicking on the **Errata Submission Form** link, and entering the details of your errata. Once your errata are verified, your submission will be accepted and the errata will be uploaded to our website or added to any list of existing errata under the Errata section of that title. To view the previously submitted errata, go to https://www.packtpub.com/books/content/support and enter the name of the book in the search field. The required information will appear under the **Errata** section.

Piracy

Piracy of copyrighted material on the Internet is an ongoing problem across all media. At Packt, we take the protection of our copyright and licenses very seriously. If you come across any illegal copies of our works in any form on the Internet, please provide us with the location address or website name immediately so that we can pursue a remedy. Please contact us at copyright@packtpub.com with a link to the suspected pirated material. We appreciate your help in protecting our authors and our ability to bring you valuable content.

Questions

If you have a problem with any aspect of this book, you can contact us at questions@packtpub.com, and we will do our best to address the problem.

1
Sockets, IPv4, and Simple Client/Server Programming

In this chapter, we will cover the following recipes:

- Printing your machine's name and IPv4 address
- Retrieving a remote machine's IP address
- Converting an IPv4 address to different formats
- Finding a service name, given the port and protocol
- Converting integers to and from host to network byte order
- Setting and getting the default socket timeout
- Handling socket errors gracefully
- Modifying a socket's send/receive buffer size
- Changing a socket to the blocking/non-blocking mode
- Reusing socket addresses
- Printing the current time from the internet time server
- Writing an SNTP client
- Writing a simple TCP echo client/server application
- Writing a simple UDP echo client/server application

Introduction

This chapter introduces Python's core networking library through some simple recipes. Python's socket module has both class-based and instances-based utilities. The difference between a class-based and instance-based method is that the former doesn't need an instance of a socket object. This is a very intuitive approach. For example, in order to print your machine's IP address, you don't need a socket object. Instead, you can just call the socket's class-based methods. On the other hand, if you need to send some data to a server application, it is more intuitive that you create a socket object to perform that explicit operation. The recipes presented in this chapter can be categorized into three groups as follows:

- In the first few recipes, the class-based utilities have been used in order to extract some useful information about host, network, and any target service.
- After that, some more recipes have been presented using the instance-based utilities. Some common socket tasks, including manipulating the socket timeout, buffer size, and blocking mode has been demonstrated.
- Finally, both class-based and instance-based utilities have been used to construct some clients, which perform some practical tasks, for example, synchronizing the machine time with an internet server or writing a generic client/server script.

You can use these demonstrated approaches to write your own client/server application.

Printing your machine's name and IPv4 address

Sometimes, you need to quickly discover some information about your machine, for example, the hostname, IP address, number of network interfaces, and so on. This is very easy to achieve using Python scripts.

Getting ready

You need to install Python on your machine before you start coding. Python comes preinstalled in most of the Linux distributions. For Microsoft Windows operating systems, you can download binaries from the Python website: `http://www.python.org/download/`.

Currently, Python 3.x is released in addition to Python 2.x. Many of the current Linux distributions and macOS versions are still shipping Python 2 by default. However, some ship both of them.

Download the relevant installer for your operating system and the relevant version based on whether your operating system is 32 bit or 64 bit.

You may consult the documentation of your operating system to check and review your Python setup. After installing Python on your machine, you can try opening the Python interpreter from the command line by typing python. This will show the interpreter prompt, >>>, which should be similar to the following output:

```
~$ python
Python 2.7.12 (default, Nov 19 2016, 06:48:10)
[GCC 5.4.0 20160609] on linux2
Type "help", "copyright", "credits" or "license" for more information.
>>>
```

How to do it...

In the latter versions of Ubuntu since Ubuntu 14.04, Python 3 can be executed by typing python3:

```
~$ python3
Python 3.5.2 (default, Nov 17 2016, 17:05:23)
[GCC 5.4.0 20160609] on linux
Type "help", "copyright", "credits" or
"license" for more information.
>>>
```

Similarly, to be specific about which version you prefer to use, you may type python2 to execute Python 2 as well:

```
~$ python2
Python 2.7.12 (default, Nov 19 2016, 06:48:10)
[GCC 5.4.0 20160609] on linux2
Type "help", "copyright", "credits" or "license" for more information.
>>>
```

There are a few changes in Python 3 that made some code written for Python 2 incompatible with Python 3. When you write network applications, try to follow the Python 3 best practices as these changes and improvements are back ported to the latter versions of Python 2. Thus, you may be fine by running the latest versions of Python 2 such as Python 2.7. However, some code developed focusing on Python 2 may not run on Python 3.

The following recipes in this chapter are written in Python 3. However, please keep in mind that a few network projects and modules may have been developed for Python 2. In that case, you will either have to port the application to Python 3 or use Python 2 depending on your requirements.

As this recipe is very short, you can try this in the Python interpreter interactively.

First, we need to import the Python `socket` library with the following command:

```
>>> import socket
```

Then, we call the `gethostname()` method from the `socket` library and store the result in a variable as follows:

```
>>> host_name = socket.gethostname()
>>> print "Host name: %s" %host_name
Host name: llovizna
>>> print "IP address: %s"
%socket.gethostbyname(host_name)
IP address: 127.0.1.1
```

The entire activity can be wrapped in a free-standing function, `print_machine_info()`, which uses the built-in socket class methods.

We call our function from the usual Python __main__ block. During runtime, Python assigns values to some internal variables such as __name__. In this case, __name__ refers to the name of the calling process. When running this script from the command line, as shown in the following command, the name will be __main__. But it will be different if the module is imported from another script. This means that, when the module is called from the command line, it will automatically run our `print_machine_info` function; however, when imported separately, the user will need to explicitly call the function.

Listing 1.1 shows how to get our machine info, as follows:

```
#!/usr/bin/env python
# Python Network Programming Cookbook,
    Second Edition -- Chapter - 1
# This program is optimized for Python 2.7.12
    and Python 3.5.2.
```

```
# It may run on any other version with/without
  modifications.
    import socket
    def print_machine_info():
        host_name = socket.gethostname()
        ip_address = socket.gethostbyname(host_name)
        print ("Host name: %s" %host_name)
        print ("IP address: %s" %ip_address)
    if __name__ == '__main__':
        print_machine_info()
```

In order to run this recipe, you can use the provided source file from the command line as follows:

$ python 1_1_local_machine_info.py

On my machine, the following output is shown:

Host name: llovizna
IP address: 127.0.1.1

The hostname is what you assigned to your computer when you configured your operating system. This output will be different on your machine depending on the system's host configuration. Here hostname indicates where the Python interpreter is currently executing.

Please note that the programs in this book are run with both versions 2 and 3. We avoid mentioning python3 and python2 in commands, as they are too specific to some distributions and assumes that a specific version is installed. You may run any of the programs in either version by using python2 or python3 accordingly.

How it works...

The import socket statement imports one of Python's core networking libraries. Then, we use the two utility functions, gethostname() and gethostbyname(host_name). You can type help(socket.gethostname) to see the online help information from within the command line. Alternatively, you can type the following address in your web browser at http://docs.python.org/3/library/socket.html. You can refer to the following code:

```
gethostname(...)
    gethostname() -> string
    Return the current host name.
gethostbyname(...)
    gethostbyname(host) -> address
    Return the IP address (a string of the form
    '255.255.255.255') for a host.
```

The first function takes no parameter and returns the current or localhost name. The second function takes a single `hostname` parameter and returns its IP address.

Retrieving a remote machine's IP address

Sometimes, you need to translate a machine's hostname into its corresponding IP address, for example, a quick domain name lookup. This recipe introduces a simple function to do that.

How to do it...

If you need to know the IP address of a remote machine, you can use a built-in library function, `gethostbyname()`. In this case, you need to pass the remote hostname as its parameter.

In this case, we need to call the `gethostbyname()` class function. Let's have a look at this short code snippet.

Listing 1.2 shows how to get a remote machine's IP address as follows:

```python
#!/usr/bin/env python
# Python Network Programming Cookbook, Second Edition
    -- Chapter - 1
# This program is optimized for Python 2.7.12 and
    Python 3.5.2.
# It may run on any other version with/without
    modifications.
import socket
def get_remote_machine_info():
    remote_host = 'www.python.org'
    try:
        print ("IP address of %s: %s" %(remote_host,
        socket.gethostbyname(remote_host)))
    except socket.error as err_msg:
        print ("%s: %s" %(remote_host, err_msg))
if __name__ == '__main__':
    get_remote_machine_info()
```

If you run the preceding code it gives the following output:

```
$ python 1_2_remote_machine_info.py
IP address of www.python.org: 151.101.36.223
```

How it works...

This recipe wraps the `gethostbyname()` method inside a user-defined function called `get_remote_machine_info()`. In this recipe, we introduced the notion of exception handling. As you can see, we wrapped the main function call inside a `try-except` block. This means that, if some error occurs during the execution of this function, this error will be dealt with by this `try-except` block.

For example, let's change the `remote_host` value and replace `https://www.python.org/` with something non-existent, for example, `www.pytgo.org`:

```python
#!/usr/bin/env python
# Python Network Programming Cookbook,
  Second Edition -- Chapter - 1
# This program is optimized for Python 2.7.12 and
  Python 3.5.2.
# It may run on any other version with/without
  modifications.
    import socket
    def get_remote_machine_info():
        remote_host = 'www.pytgo.org'
        try:
            print ("IP address of %s: %s" %
                (remote_host,
            socket.gethostbyname(remote_host)))
        except socket.error as err_msg:
            print ("%s: %s" %(remote_host, err_msg))
    if __name__ == '__main__':
        get_remote_machine_info()
```

Now run the following command:

```
$ python 1_2_remote_machine_info.py
www.pytgo.org: [Errno -2] Name or service not known
```

The `try-except` block catches the error and shows the user an error message that there is no IP address associated with the hostname, `www.pytgo.org`.

Converting an IPv4 address to different formats

When you would like to deal with low-level network functions, sometimes, the usual string notation of IP addresses are not very useful. They need to be converted to the packed 32-bit binary formats.

How to do it...

The Python `socket` library has utilities to deal with the various IP address formats. Here, we will use two of them: `inet_aton()` and `inet_ntoa()`.

Let us create the `convert_ip4_address()` function, where `inet_aton()` and `inet_ntoa()` will be used for the IP address conversion. We will use two sample IP addresses, `127.0.0.1` and `192.168.0.1`.

Listing 1.3 shows `ip4_address_conversion` as follows:

```python
#!/usr/bin/env python
# Python Network Programming Cookbook,
  Second Edition -- Chapter - 1
# This program is optimized for Python 2.7.12 and
  Python 3.5.2.
# It may run on any other version with/without
  modifications.
  import socket
  from binascii import hexlify
  def convert_ip4_address():
      for ip_addr in ['127.0.0.1', '192.168.0.1']:
          packed_ip_addr = socket.
                             inet_aton(ip_addr)
          unpacked_ip_addr = socket.inet_ntoa
                             (packed_ip_addr)
          print ("IP Address: %s => Packed: %s,
                 Unpacked: %s" %(ip_addr,
                 hexlify(packed_ip_addr),
                 unpacked_ip_addr))
  if __name__ == '__main__':
      convert_ip4_address()
```

Now, if you run this recipe, you will see the following output:

```
$ python 1_3_ip4_address_conversion.py
IP Address: 127.0.0.1 => Packed: 7f000001, Unpacked:
127.0.0.1
IP Address: 192.168.0.1 => Packed: c0a80001, Unpacked: 192.168.0.1
```

How it works...

In this recipe, the two IP addresses have been converted from a string to a 32-bit packed format using a `for-in` statement. Additionally, the Python `hexlify` function is called from the `binascii` module. This helps to represent the binary data in a hexadecimal format.

Finding a service name, given the port and protocol

If you would like to discover network services, it may be helpful to determine what network services run on which ports using either the TCP or UDP protocol.

Getting ready

If you know the port number of a network service, you can find the service name using the `getservbyport()` socket class function from the socket library. You can optionally give the protocol name when calling this function.

How to do it...

Let us define a `find_service_name()` function, where the `getservbyport()` socket class function will be called with a few ports, for example, `80`, `25`. We can use Python's `for-in` loop construct.

Listing 1.4 shows `finding_service_name` as follows:

```
#!/usr/bin/env python
# Python Network Programming Cookbook, Second Edition -- Chapter - 1
# This program is optimized for Python 2.7.12 and Python 3.5.2.
# It may run on any other version with/without modifications.
```

```
import socket

def find_service_name():
    protocolname = 'tcp'
    for port in [80, 25]:
        print ("Port: %s => service name: %s" %(port,
socket.getservbyport(port, protocolname)))
    print ("Port: %s => service name: %s" %(53, socket.getservbyport(53,
'udp')))
if __name__ == '__main__':
    find_service_name()
```

If you run this script, you will see the following output:

```
$ python 1_4_finding_service_name.py
Port: 80 => service name: http
Port: 25 => service name: smtp
Port: 53 => service name: domain
```

This indicates that `http`, `smtp`, and `domain` services are running on the ports 80, 25, and 53 respectively.

How it works...

In this recipe, the `for-in` statement is used to iterate over a sequence of variables. So for each iteration, we use one IP address to convert them in their packed and unpacked format.

Converting integers to and from host to network byte order

If you ever need to write a low-level network application, it may be necessary to handle the low-level data transmission over the wire between two machines. This operation requires some sort of conversion of data from the native host operating system to the network format and vice versa. This is because each one has its own specific representation of data.

How to do it...

Python's `socket` library has utilities for converting from a network byte order to host byte order and vice versa. You may want to become familiar with them, for example, `ntohl()`/`htonl()`.

Let us define the `convert_integer()` function, where the `ntohl()`/`htonl()` socket class functions are used to convert IP address formats.

Listing 1.5 shows `integer_conversion` as follows:

```python
#!/usr/bin/env python
# Python Network Programming Cookbook, Second Edition -- Chapter - 1
# This program is optimized for Python 2.7.12 and Python 3.5.2.
# It may run on any other version with/without modifications.

import socket

def convert_integer():
    data = 1234
    # 32-bit
    print ("Original: %s => Long  host byte order: %s, Network byte order:
%s" %(data, socket.ntohl(data), socket.htonl(data)))
    # 16-bit
    print ("Original: %s => Short  host byte order: %s, Network byte order:
%s" %(data, socket.ntohs(data), socket.htons(data)))

if __name__ == '__main__':
    convert_integer()
```

If you run this recipe, you will see the following output:

```
$ python 1_5_integer_conversion.py
Original: 1234 => Long  host byte order: 3523477504,
Network byte order: 3523477504
Original: 1234 => Short  host byte order: 53764,
Network byte order: 53764
```

How it works...

Here, we take an integer and show how to convert it between network and host byte orders. The `ntohl()` socket class function converts from the network byte order to host byte order in a long format. Here, n represents network and h represents host; l represents long and s represents short, that is, 16-bit.

Setting and getting the default socket timeout

Sometimes, you need to manipulate the default values of certain properties of a `socket` library, for example, the socket timeout.

How to do it...

You can make an instance of a `socket` object and call a `gettimeout()` method to get the default timeout value and the `settimeout()` method to set a specific timeout value. This is very useful in developing custom server applications.

We first create a `socket` object inside a `test_socket_timeout()` function. Then, we can use the `getter/setter` instance methods to manipulate timeout values.

Listing 1.6 shows `socket_timeout` as follows:

```
#!/usr/bin/env python
# Python Network Programming Cookbook, Second Edition -- Chapter - 1
# This program is optimized for Python 2.7.12 and Python 3.5.2.
# It may run on any other version with/without modifications.


import socket

def test_socket_timeout():
    s = socket.socket(socket.AF_INET, socket.SOCK_STREAM)
    print ("Default socket timeout: %s" %s.gettimeout())
    s.settimeout(100)
    print ("Current socket timeout: %s" %s.gettimeout())
if __name__ == '__main__':
    test_socket_timeout()
```

After running the preceding script, you can see how this modifies the default socket timeout as follows:

```
$ python 1_6_socket_timeout.py
Default socket timeout: None
Current socket timeout: 100.0
```

How it works...

In this code snippet, we have first created a `socket` object by passing the socket family and socket type as the first and second arguments of the socket constructor. Then, you can get the socket timeout value by calling `gettimeout()` and alter the value by calling the `settimeout()` method. The timeout value passed to the `settimeout()` method can be in seconds (non-negative float) or `None`. This method is used for manipulating the blocking-socket operations. Setting a timeout of `None` disables timeouts on socket operations.

Handling socket errors gracefully

In any networking application, it is very common that one end is trying to connect, but the other party is not responding due to networking media failure or any other reason. The Python `socket` library has an elegant method of handing these errors via the `socket.error` exceptions. In this recipe, a few examples are presented.

How to do it...

Let us create a few try-except code blocks and put one potential error type in each block. In order to get a user input, the `argparse` module can be used. This module is more powerful than simply parsing command-line arguments using `sys.argv`. In the try-except blocks, put typical socket operations, for example, create a `socket` object, connect to a server, send data, and wait for a reply.

The following recipe illustrates the concepts in a few lines of code.

Listing 1.7 shows `socket_errors` as follows:

```
#!/usr/bin/env python
# Python Network Programming Cookbook, Second Edition -- Chapter - 1
# This program is optimized for Python 2.7.12 and Python 3.5.2.
# It may run on any other version with/without modifications.

import sys
import socket
import argparse


def main():
    # setup argument parsing
    parser = argparse.ArgumentParser(description='Socket Error Examples')
```

```python
    parser.add_argument('--host', action="store", dest="host",
                                                required=False)
    parser.add_argument('--port', action="store", dest="port", type=int,
                                                required=False)
    parser.add_argument('--file', action="store", dest="file",
                                                required=False)
    given_args = parser.parse_args()
    host = given_args.host
    port = given_args.port
    filename = given_args.file
    # First try-except block -- create socket
    try:
        s = socket.socket(socket.AF_INET, socket.SOCK_STREAM)
    except socket.error as e:
        print ("Error creating socket: %s" % e)
        sys.exit(1)
    # Second try-except block -- connect to given host/port
    try:
        s.connect((host, port))
    except socket.gaierror as e:
        print ("Address-related error connecting to
                server: %s" % e)
        sys.exit(1)
    except socket.error as e:
        print ("Connection error: %s" % e)
        sys.exit(1)
    # Third try-except block -- sending data
    try:
        msg = "GET %s HTTP/1.0\r\n\r\n" % filename
        s.sendall(msg.encode('utf-8'))
    except socket.error as e:
        print ("Error sending data: %s" % e)
        sys.exit(1)
    while 1:
        # Fourth tr-except block -- waiting
          to receive
          data from remote host
        try:
            buf = s.recv(2048)
        except socket.error as e:
            print ("Error receiving data: %s" % e)
            sys.exit(1)
        if not len(buf):
            break
        # write the received data
        sys.stdout.write(buf.decode('utf-8'))
if __name__ == '__main__':
    main()
```

How it works...

In Python, passing command-line arguments to a script and parsing them in the script can be done using the `argparse` module. This is available in Python 2.7. For earlier versions of Python, this module is available separately in **Python Package Index (PyPI)**. You can install this via `easy_install` or `pip`.

In this recipe, three arguments are set up—a hostname, port number, and filename. The usage of this script is as follows:

```
$ python 1_7_socket_errors.py --host=<HOST>
  --port=<PORT> --file=<FILE>
In the preceding recipe, msg.encode('utf-8')
encodes the message into UTF-8, and
buf.decode('utf-8') decodes the received UTF-8
format.
```

If you try the preceding recipe with a non-existent host, this script will print an address error as follows:

```
$ python 1_7_socket_errors.py
  --host=www.pytgo.org --port=8080
  --file=1_7_socket_errors.py
Address-related error connecting to
server: [Errno -2] Name or service not known
```

If there is no service on a specific port and if you try to connect to that port, then this will throw a connection timeout error as follows:

```
$ python 1_7_socket_errors.py
  --host=www.python.org --port=8080
  --file=1_7_socket_errors.py
```

This will return the following error since the host, `www.python.org`, is not listening on port 8080:

```
Connection error: [Errno 110] Connection timed out
```

However, if you send an arbitrary request as a correct request to a correct port, the error may not be caught at the application level. For example, running the following script returns no error, but the HTML output tells us what's wrong with this script:

```
$ python 1_7_socket_errors.py
  --host=www.python.org --port=80
  --file=1_7_socket_errors.py
HTTP/1.1 500 Domain Not Found
Server: Varnish
```

```
Retry-After: 0
content-type: text/html
Cache-Control: private, no-cache
connection: keep-alive
Content-Length: 179
Accept-Ranges: bytes
Date: Thu, 01 Jun 2017 22:02:24 GMT
Via: 1.1 varnish
Connection: close
<html>
<head>
<title>Fastly error: unknown domain </title>
</head>
<body>
Fastly error: unknown domain: . Please check that this domain has been
added to a service.</body></html>
```

In the preceding example, four try-except blocks have been used. All blocks use `socket.error` except for the second block, which uses `socket.gaierror`. This is used for address-related errors. There are two other types of exceptions—`socket.herror` is used for legacy C API, and if you use the `settimeout()` method in a socket, `socket.timeout` will be raised when a timeout occurs on that socket.

Modifying a socket's send/receive buffer sizes

The default socket buffer size may not be suitable in many circumstances. In such circumstances, you can change the default socket buffer size to a more suitable value.

How to do it...

Let us manipulate the default socket buffer size using a socket object's `setsockopt()` method.

First, define two constants: `SEND_BUF_SIZE`/`RECV_BUF_SIZE` and then wrap a socket instance's call to the `setsockopt()` method in a function. It is also a good idea to check the value of the buffer size before modifying it. Note that we need to set up the send and receive buffer size separately.

Listing 1.8 shows how to modify socket send/receive buffer sizes as follows:

```python
#!/usr/bin/env python
# Python Network Programming Cookbook, Second Edition -- Chapter - 1
# This program is optimized for Python 2.7.12 and Python 3.5.2.
# It may run on any other version with/without modifications.

import socket

SEND_BUF_SIZE = 4096
RECV_BUF_SIZE = 4096

def modify_buff_size():
    sock = socket.socket( socket.AF_INET, socket.SOCK_STREAM )
    # Get the size of the socket's send buffer
    bufsize = sock.getsockopt(socket.SOL_SOCKET, socket.SO_SNDBUF)
    print ("Buffer size [Before]:%d" %bufsize)
    sock.setsockopt(socket.SOL_TCP,
                    socket.TCP_NODELAY, 1)
    sock.setsockopt(
            socket.SOL_SOCKET,
            socket.SO_SNDBUF,
            SEND_BUF_SIZE)
    sock.setsockopt(
            socket.SOL_SOCKET,
            socket.SO_RCVBUF,
            RECV_BUF_SIZE)
    bufsize = sock.getsockopt(socket.SOL_SOCKET, socket.SO_SNDBUF)
    print ("Buffer size [After]:%d" %bufsize)

if __name__ == '__main__':
    modify_buff_size()
```

If you run the preceding script, it will show the changes in the socket's buffer size. The following output may be different on your machine depending on your operating system's local settings:

```
$ python 1_8_modify_buff_size.py
Buffer size [Before]:16384
Buffer size [After]:8192
```

How it works...

You can call the `getsockopt()` and `setsockopt()` methods on a socket object to retrieve and modify the socket object's properties respectively. The `setsockopt()` method takes three arguments: `level`, `optname`, and `value`. Here, `optname` takes the option name and `value` is the corresponding value of that option. For the first argument, the needed symbolic constants can be found in the socket module (`SO_*etc.`).

Changing a socket to the blocking/non-blocking mode

By default, TCP sockets are placed in a blocking mode. This means the control is not returned to your program until some specific operation is complete. If you call the `connect()` API, the connection blocks your program until the operation is complete. On many occasions, you don't want to keep your program waiting forever, either for a response from the server or for any error to stop the operation. For example, when you write a web browser client that connects to a web server, you should consider a stop functionality that can cancel the connection process in the middle of this operation. This can be achieved by placing the socket in the non-blocking mode.

How to do it...

Let us see what options are available under Python. In Python, a socket can be placed in the blocking or non-blocking mode. In the non-blocking mode, if any call to API, for example, `send()` or `recv()`, encounters any problem, an error will be raised. However, in the blocking mode, this will not stop the operation. We can create a normal TCP socket and experiment with both the blocking and non-blocking operations.

To manipulate the socket's blocking nature, we should create a socket object first.

We can then call `setblocking(1)` to set up blocking or `setblocking(0)` to unset blocking. Finally, we bind the socket to a specific port and listen for incoming connections.

Listing 1.9 shows how the socket changes to blocking or non-blocking mode as follows:

```
#!/usr/bin/env python
# Python Network Programming Cookbook, Second Edition -- Chapter - 1
# This program is optimized for Python 2.7.12 and Python 3.5.2.
# It may run on any other version with/without modifications.

import socket

def test_socket_modes():
    s = socket.socket(socket.AF_INET,
                      socket.SOCK_STREAM)
    s.setblocking(1)
    s.settimeout(0.5)
    s.bind(("127.0.0.1", 0))
    socket_address = s.getsockname()
    print ("Trivial Server launched on
            socket: %s" %str(socket_address))
    while(1):
        s.listen(1)
if __name__ == '__main__':
    test_socket_modes()
```

If you run this recipe, it will launch a trivial server that has the blocking mode enabled as shown in the following command:

```
$ python 1_9_socket_modes.py
Trivial Server launched on
socket: ('127.0.0.1', 51410)
```

How it works...

In this recipe, we enable blocking on a socket by setting the value 1 in the setblocking() method. Similarly, you can unset the value 0 in this method to make it non-blocking.

This feature will be reused in some later recipes, where its real purpose will be elaborated.

Reusing socket addresses

You want to run a socket server always on a specific port even after it is closed intentionally or unexpectedly. This is useful in some cases where your client program always connects to that specific server port. So, you don't need to change the server port.

How to do it...

If you run a Python socket server on a specific port and try to rerun it after closing it once, you won't be able to use the same port. It will usually throw an error like the following command:

```
Traceback (most recent call last):
    File "1_10_reuse_socket_address.py",
    line 40, in <module>
        reuse_socket_addr()
    File "1_10_reuse_socket_address.py",
    line 25, in reuse_socket_addr
        srv.bind( ('', local_port) )
    File "<string>", line 1, in bind
    socket.error: [Errno 98] Address
    already in use
```

The remedy to this problem is to enable the socket reuse option, SO_REUSEADDR.

After creating a socket object, we can query the state of address reuse, say an old state. Then, we call the setsockopt() method to alter the value of its address reuse state. Then, we follow the usual steps of binding to an address and listening for incoming client connections.

In the preceding example, when you close the Python script with *Ctrl + C*, you notice an exception:

```
^CTraceback (most recent call last):File "1_9_socket_modes.py", line 20, in
<module>
test_socket_modes()
File "1_9_socket_modes.py", line 17, in test_socket_modes
s.listen(1)
KeyboardInterrupt
```

This indicates that there was a keyboard interrupt in the execution.

In this example, we catch the KeyboardInterrupt exception so that if you issue *Ctrl + C*, then the Python script gets terminated without showing any exception message.

Listing 1.10 shows how to reuse socket addresses as follows:

```
#!/usr/bin/env python
# Python Network Programming Cookbook, Second Edition -- Chapter - 1
# This program is optimized for Python 2.7.12 and Python 3.5.2.
# It may run on any other version with/without modifications.

import socket
```

```
import sys

def reuse_socket_addr():
    sock = socket.socket( socket.AF_INET, socket.SOCK_STREAM )

    # Get the old state of the SO_REUSEADDR option
    old_state = sock.getsockopt(socket.SOL_SOCKET,
                                socket.SO_REUSEADDR )
    print ("Old sock state: %s" %old_state)

    # Enable the SO_REUSEADDR option
    sock.setsockopt( socket.SOL_SOCKET,
                     socket.SO_REUSEADDR, 1 )
    new_state = sock.getsockopt(
        socket.SOL_SOCKET, socket.SO_REUSEADDR )
    print ("New sock state: %s" %new_state)

    local_port = 8282
    srv = socket.socket(socket.AF_INET,
                        socket.SOCK_STREAM)
    srv.setsockopt(socket.SOL_SOCKET,
                   socket.SO_REUSEADDR, 1)
    srv.bind( ('', local_port) )
    srv.listen(1)
    print ("Listening on port: %s " %local_port)
    while True:
        try:
            connection, addr = srv.accept()
            print ('Connected by %s:%s'
                   % (addr[0], addr[1]))
        except KeyboardInterrupt:
            break
        except socket.error as msg:
            print ('%s' % (msg,))

if __name__ == '__main__':
    reuse_socket_addr()
```

The output from this recipe will be similar to the outcomes produced here, by executing the program:

```
$ python 1_10_reuse_socket_address.py
Old sock state: 0
New sock state: 1
Listening on port: 8282
```

How it works...

You may run this script from one console window and try to connect to this server from another console window by typing `telnet localhost 8282`.

You will see an output printed in the program window as your telnet connects to it:

Connected by 127.0.0.1:46584

Here the host and port will defer based on the telnet instance that you are sending this request from.

After you close the server program, you can rerun it again on the same port. However, if you comment out the line that sets the SO_REUSEADDR, the server will not run for the second time.

Printing the current time from the internet time server

Many programs rely on the accurate machine time, such as the `make` command in UNIX. Your machine time may be different and need synchronizing with another time server in your network.

Getting ready

In order to synchronize your machine time with one of the internet time servers, you can write a Python client for that. For this, `ntplib` will be used. Here, the client/server conversation will be done using **Network Time Protocol** (**NTP**). If `ntplib` is not installed on your machine, you can get it from `PyPI` with the following command using `pip` or `easy_install`:

```
$ pip install ntplib
```

If `pip` is not installed on your computer, first install it before executing the preceding command. In Debian-based Linux distributions such as Ubuntu, this can be installed by:

```
$ sudo apt install python-pip
```

Note that you will need to install `pip` for Python 3 separately if you are running it along side Python 2, as typically Python 2 is set as the default version:

```
$ sudo apt-get install python3-pip
```

Similarly, `ntplib` needs to be installed for `python3-pip` (also called `pip3`) separately:

```
$ pip3 install ntplib
```

It is a good idea to upgrade `pip` to the latest version if you are running an outdated version, by issuing the following command:

```
$ pip install --upgrade pip
```

or:

```
$ pip3 install --upgrade pip
```

If Python 2 and Python 3 are installed alongside in your computer then use `pip3`.

I am using the `pip` version 9.0.1, for both Python 2 and Python 3. This is the latest version at the time of writing.

How to do it...

We create an instance of `NTPClient` and then we call the `request()` method on it by passing the NTP server address.

Listing 1.11 shows how to print the current time from the internet time server as follows:

```python
#!/usr/bin/env python
# Python Network Programming Cookbook,
  Second Edition -- Chapter - 1
# This program is optimized for Python 2.7.12
  and Python 3.5.2.
# It may run on any other version with/without
  modifications.
import ntplib
from time import ctime
def print_time():
    ntp_client = ntplib.NTPClient()
    response = ntp_client.request('pool.ntp.org')
    print (ctime(response.tx_time))
if __name__ == '__main__':
    print_time()
```

In my machine, this recipe shows the following output:

```
$ python 1_11_print_machine_time.py
Fri Jun  2 16:01:35 2017
```

How it works...

Here, an NTP client has been created and an NTP request has been sent to one of the internet NTP servers, `pool.ntp.org`. The `ctime()` function is used for printing the response.

Writing an SNTP client

Unlike the previous recipe, sometimes, you don't need to get the precise time from the NTP server. You can use a simpler version of NTP called simple network time protocol.

How to do it...

Let us create a plain SNTP client without using any third-party library.

Let us first define two constants: `NTP_SERVER` and `TIME1970`. `NTP_SERVER` is the server address to which our client will connect, and `TIME1970` is the reference time on January 1, 1970 (also called *Epoch*). You may find the value of the Epoch time or convert to the Epoch time at `http://www.epochconverter.com/`. The actual client creates a UDP socket (`SOCK_DGRAM`) to connect to the server following the UDP protocol. The client then needs to send the SNTP protocol data (`'\x1b' + 47 * '\0'`) in a packet. Our UDP client sends and receives data using the `sendto()` and `recvfrom()` methods.

When the server returns the time information in a packed array, the client needs a specialized `struct` module to unpack the data. The only interesting data is located in the 11th element of the array. Finally, we need to subtract the reference value, `TIME1970`, from the unpacked value to get the actual current time.

Listing 1.12 shows how to write an SNTP client as follows:

```
#!/usr/bin/env python
# Python Network Programming Cookbook,
  Second Edition -- Chapter - 1
# This program is optimized for Python 2.7.12
  and Python 3.5.2.
```

```
# It may run on any other version with/without
  modifications.
import socket
import struct
import sys
import time
NTP_SERVER = "0.uk.pool.ntp.org"
TIME1970 = 2208988800
def sntp_client():
    client = socket.socket( socket.AF_INET,
                            socket.SOCK_DGRAM )
    data = '\x1b' + 47 * '\0'
    client.sendto( data.encode('utf-8'),
                   ( NTP_SERVER, 123 ))
    data, address = client.recvfrom( 1024 )
    if data:
        print ('Response received
                        from:', address)
    t = struct.unpack( '!12I', data )[10]
    t -= TIME1970
    print ('\tTime=%s' % time.ctime(t))
if __name__ == '__main__':
    sntp_client()
```

This recipe prints the current time from the internet time server received with the SNTP protocol as follows:

```
$ python 1_12_sntp_client.py
('Response received from:',
('192.146.137.13', 123))
        Time=Sat Jun  3 14:45:45 2017
```

How it works...

This SNTP client creates a socket connection and sends the protocol data. After receiving the response from the NTP server (in this case, 0.uk.pool.ntp.org), it unpacks the data with struct. Finally, it subtracts the reference time, which is January 1, 1970, and prints the time using the ctime() built-in method in the Python time module.

Writing a simple TCP echo client/server application

After testing with basic socket APIs in Python, let us create a TCP socket server and client now. Here, you will have the chance to utilize your basic knowledge gained in the previous recipes.

How to do it...

In this example, a server will echo whatever it receives from the client. We will use the Python `argparse` module to specify the TCP port from a command line. Both the server and client script will take this argument.

First, we create the server. We start by creating a TCP socket object. Then, we set the reuse address so that we can run the server as many times as we need. We bind the socket to the given port on our local machine. In the listening stage, we make sure we listen to multiple clients in a queue using the backlog argument to the `listen()` method. Finally, we wait for the client to be connected and send some data to the server. When the data is received, the server echoes back the data to the client.

Listing 1.13a shows how to write a simple TCP echo client/server application as follows:

```python
#!/usr/bin/env python
# Python Network Programming Cookbook,
   Second Edition -- Chapter - 1
# This program is optimized for Python 2.7.12
   and Python 3.5.2.
# It may run on any other version with/without
   modifications.
import socket
import sys
import argparse
host = 'localhost'
data_payload = 2048
backlog = 5
def echo_server(port):
    """ A simple echo server """
    # Create a TCP socket
    sock = socket.socket(socket.AF_INET,
                    socket.SOCK_STREAM)
    # Enable reuse address/port
    sock.setsockopt(socket.SOL_SOCKET,
                socket.SO_REUSEADDR, 1)
```

```python
    # Bind the socket to the port
    server_address = (host, port)
    print ("Starting up echo server  on %s
                 port %s" % server_address)
    sock.bind(server_address)
    # Listen to clients, backlog argument
      specifies the max no.
      of queued connections
    sock.listen(backlog)
    while True:
        print ("Waiting to receive message
                 from client")
        client, address = sock.accept()
        data = client.recv(data_payload)
        if data:
            print ("Data: %s" %data)
            client.send(data)
            print ("sent %s bytes back
                     to %s" % (data, address))
        # end connection
        client.close()
 if __name__ == '__main__':
     parser = argparse.ArgumentParser
     (description='Socket Server Example')
     parser.add_argument('--port',
     action="store", dest="port", type=int,
                         required=True)
     given_args = parser.parse_args()
     port = given_args.port
     echo_server(port)
```

On the client side code, we create a client socket using the port argument and connect to the server. Then, the client sends the message, Test message. This will be echoed to the server, and the client immediately receives the message back in a few segments. Here, two try-except blocks are constructed to catch any exception during this interactive session.

Listing 1-13b shows the TCP echo client as follows:

```python
#!/usr/bin/env python
# Python Network Programming Cookbook,
   Second Edition -- Chapter - 1
# This program is optimized for Python 2.7.12
   and Python 3.5.2.
# It may run on any other version with/without modifications.

import socket
import sys
```

```python
import argparse

host = 'localhost'

def echo_client(port):
    """ A simple echo client """
    # Create a TCP/IP socket
    sock = socket.socket(socket.AF_INET, socket.SOCK_STREAM)
    # Connect the socket to the server
    server_address = (host, port)
    print ("Connecting to %s port %s" % server_address)
    sock.connect(server_address)
    # Send data
    try:
        # Send data
        message = "Test message. This will be
                    echoed"
        print ("Sending %s" % message)
        sock.sendall(message.encode('utf-8'))
        # Look for the response
        amount_received = 0
        amount_expected = len(message)
        while amount_received < amount_expected:
            data = sock.recv(16)
            amount_received += len(data)
            print ("Received: %s" % data)
    except socket.error as e:
        print ("Socket error: %s" %str(e))
    except Exception as e:
        print ("Other exception: %s" %str(e))
    finally:
        print ("Closing connection to the server")
        sock.close()
if __name__ == '__main__':
    parser = argparse.ArgumentParser
            (description='Socket Server Example')
    parser.add_argument('--port', action="store",
dest="port", type=int, required=True)
    given_args = parser.parse_args()
    port = given_args.port
    echo_client(port)
```

How it works...

In order to see the client/server interactions, launch the following server script in one console:

```
$ python 1_13a_echo_server.py --port=9900
Starting up echo server  on localhost port 9900
Waiting to receive message from client
```

Now, run the client from another Terminal as follows:

```
$ python 1_13b_echo_client.py --port=9900
Connecting to localhost port 9900
Sending Test message. This will be echoed
Received: Test message. Th
Received: is will be echoe
Received: d
Closing connection to the server
```

Upon receiving the message from the client, the server will also print something similar to the following message:

```
Data: Test message. This will be echoed
sent Test message. This will be echoed
bytes back to ('127.0.0.1', 42961)
Waiting to receive message from client
```

Writing a simple UDP echo client/server application

As we have developed a simple TCP server and client in the previous recipe, we will now look at how to develop the same with UDP.

How to do it...

This recipe is similar to the previous one, except this one is with UDP. The method recvfrom() reads the messages from the socket and returns the data and the client address.

Listing 1.14a shows how to write a simple UDP echo client/server application as follows:

```python
#!/usr/bin/env python
# Python Network Programming Cookbook,
  Second Edition -- Chapter - 1
# This program is optimized for Python 2.7.12
  and Python 3.5.2.
# It may run on any other version with/without
  modifications.

import socket
import sys
import argparse

host = 'localhost'
data_payload = 2048

def echo_server(port):
    """ A simple echo server """
    # Create a UDP socket
    sock = socket.socket(socket.AF_INET,
                         socket.SOCK_DGRAM)

    # Bind the socket to the port
    server_address = (host, port)
    print ("Starting up echo server
            on %s port %s" % server_address)

    sock.bind(server_address)

    while True:
        print ("Waiting to receive message
                from client")
        data, address = sock.
                        recvfrom(data_payload)
        print ("received %s bytes
                from %s" % (len(data), address))
        print ("Data: %s" %data)
        if data:
            sent = sock.sendto(data, address)
            print ("sent %s bytes back
                    to %s" % (sent, address))


if __name__ == '__main__':
    parser = argparse.ArgumentParser
            (description='Socket Server Example')
    parser.add_argument('--port', action="store", dest="port", type=int,
```

```
required=True)
    given_args = parser.parse_args()
    port = given_args.port
    echo_server(port)
```

On the client side code, we create a client socket using the port argument and connect to the server, as we did in the previous recipe. Then, the client sends the message, `Test message`. `This will be echoed`, and the client immediately receives the message back in a few segments.

Listing 1-14b shows the echo client as follows:

```python
#!/usr/bin/env python
# Python Network Programming Cookbook, Second Edition -- Chapter - 1
# This program is optimized for Python 2.7.12 and Python 3.5.2.
# It may run on any other version with/without modifications.

import socket
import sys
import argparse

host = 'localhost'
data_payload = 2048

def echo_client(port):
    """ A simple echo client """
    # Create a UDP socket
    sock = socket.socket(socket.AF_INET,
                          socket.SOCK_DGRAM)

    server_address = (host, port)
    print ("Connecting to %s port %s" % server_address)
    message = 'This is the message.  It will be
              repeated.'

    try:

        # Send data
        message = "Test message. This will be
                  echoed"
        print ("Sending %s" % message)
        sent = sock.sendto(message.encode
                ('utf-8'), server_address)

        # Receive response
        data, server = sock.recvfrom(data_payload)
        print ("received %s" % data)
```

```
    finally:
        print ("Closing connection to the server")
        sock.close()

if __name__ == '__main__':
    parser = argparse.ArgumentParser
            (description='Socket Server Example')
    parser.add_argument('--port', action="store", dest="port", type=int,
required=True)
    given_args = parser.parse_args()
    port = given_args.port
    echo_client(port)
```

Downloading the example code

Detailed steps to download the code bundle are mentioned in the Preface of this book. The code bundle for the book is also hosted on GitHub at: `htt ps://github.com/PacktPublishing/Python-Network-Programming-Coo kbook-Second-Edition`. We also have other code bundles from our rich catalog of books and videos available at: `https://github.com/PacktPubl ishing/`. Check them out!

How it works...

In order to see the client/server interactions, launch the following server script in one console:

```
$ python 1_14a_echo_server_udp.py --port=9900
Starting up echo server on localhost port 9900
Waiting to receive message from client
```

Now, run the client from another terminal as follows:

```
$ python 1_14b_echo_client_udp.py --port=9900
Connecting to localhost port 9900
Sending Test message. This will be echoed
received Test message. This will be echoed
Closing connection to the server
```

Upon receiving the message from the client, the server will also print something similar to the following message:

```
received 33 bytes from ('127.0.0.1', 43542)
Data: Test message. This will be echoed
sent 33 bytes back to ('127.0.0.1', 43542)
Waiting to receive message from client
```

2
Multiplexing Socket I/O for Better Performance

In this chapter, we will cover the following recipes:

- Using ForkingMixIn in your socket server applications
- Using ThreadingMixIn in your socket server applications
- Writing a chat server using select.select
- Multiplexing a web server using select.epoll
- Multiplexing an echo server using Diesel concurrent library

Introduction

This chapter focuses on improving the socket server performance using a few useful techniques. Unlike the previous chapter, here we consider multiple clients that will be connected to the server and the communication can be asynchronous. The server does not need to process the request from clients in a blocking manner; this can be done independently of each other. If one client takes more time to receive or process data, the server does not need to wait for that. It can talk to other clients using separate threads or processes.

In this chapter, we will also explore the `select` module that provides the platform-specific I/O monitoring functions. This module is built on top of the select system call of the underlying operating system's kernel. For Linux, the manual page is located at `http://man7.org/linux/man-pages/man2/select.2.html` and can be checked to see the available features of this system call. Since our socket server would like to interact with many clients, `select` can be very helpful to monitor non-blocking sockets. There are some third-party Python libraries that can also help us to deal with multiple clients at the same time. We have included one sample recipe using Diesel concurrent library.

Although, for the sake of brevity, we will be using two or few clients, readers are free to extend the recipes of this chapter and use them with tens and hundreds of clients.

Using ForkingMixIn in your socket server applications

You have decided to write an asynchronous Python socket server application. The server will not block in processing a client request. So the server needs a mechanism to deal with each client independently.

Python `SocketServer` class comes with two utility classes: `ForkingMixIn` and `ThreadingMixIn`. The `ForkingMixIn` class will spawn a new process for each client request. This class is discussed in this section. The `ThreadingMixIn` class will be discussed in the next section. For more information, you can refer to the relevant Python 2 documentation at `http://docs.python.org/2/library/socketserver.html` and Python 3 documentation at `https://docs.python.org/3/library/socketserver.html`.

How to do it...

Let us rewrite our echo server, previously described in `Chapter 1`, *Sockets, IPv4, and Simple Client/Server Programming*. We can utilize the subclasses of the `SocketServer` class family. It has ready-made TCP, UDP, and other protocol servers. We can create a `ForkingServer` class inherited from `TCPServer` and `ForkingMixIn`. The former parent will enable our `ForkingServer` class to do all the necessary server operations that we did manually before, such as creating a socket, binding to an address, and listening for incoming connections. Our server also needs to inherit from `ForkingMixIn` to handle clients asynchronously.

The `ForkingServer` class also needs to set up a request handler that dictates how to handle a client request. Here our server will echo back the text string received from the client. Our request handler class, `ForkingServerRequestHandler`, is inherited from the `BaseRequestHandler` provided with the `SocketServer` library.

We can code the client of our echo server, `ForkingClient`, in an object-oriented fashion. In Python, the constructor method of a class is called `__init__()`. By convention, it takes a self-argument to attach attributes or properties of that particular class. The `ForkingClient` echo server will be initialized at `__init__()` and sends the message to the server at the `run()` method respectively.

If you are not familiar with **object-oriented programming** (**OOP**) at all, it might be helpful to review the basic concepts of OOP while attempting to grasp this recipe.

In order to test our `ForkingServer` class, we can launch multiple echo clients and see how the server responds back to the clients.

Listing 2.1 shows a sample code using `ForkingMixIn` in a socket server application as follows:

```python
#!/usr/bin/env python
# Python Network Programming Cookbook, Second Edition -- Chapter - 2
# This program is optimized for Python 3.5.2.
# It may run on any other version with/without modifications.
# To make it run on Python 2.7.x, needs some changes due to API
differences.
# begin with replacing "socketserver" with "SocketServer" throughout the
program.
# See more: http://docs.python.org/2/library/socketserver.html
# See more: http://docs.python.org/3/library/socketserver.html


import os
import socket
import threading
import socketserver


SERVER_HOST = 'localhost'
SERVER_PORT = 0 # tells the kernel to pickup a port dynamically
BUF_SIZE = 1024
ECHO_MSG = 'Hello echo server!'


class ForkedClient():
    """ A client to test forking server"""
    def __init__(self, ip, port):
```

```python
        # Create a socket
        self.sock = socket.socket(socket.AF_INET, socket.SOCK_STREAM)
        # Connect to the server
        self.sock.connect((ip, port))
    def run(self):
        """ Client playing with the server"""
        # Send the data to server
        current_process_id = os.getpid()
        print ('PID %s Sending echo message to the server : "%s"' %
                (current_process_id, ECHO_MSG))

        sent_data_length = self.sock.send(bytes(ECHO_MSG, 'utf-8'))

        print ("Sent: %d characters, so far..." %sent_data_length)
        # Display server response
        response = self.sock.recv(BUF_SIZE)
        print ("PID %s received: %s" % (current_process_id, response[5:]))
    def shutdown(self):
        """ Cleanup the client socket """
        self.sock.close()
class ForkingServerRequestHandler(socketserver.BaseRequestHandler):
    def handle(self):
        # Send the echo back to the client

        #received = str(sock.recv(1024), "utf-8")
        data = str(self.request.recv(BUF_SIZE), 'utf-8')

        current_process_id = os.getpid()
        response = '%s: %s' % (current_process_id, data)
        print ("Server sending response [current_process_id: data] = [%s]"
                %response)
        self.request.send(bytes(response, 'utf-8'))
        return


class ForkingServer(socketserver.ForkingMixIn,
                    socketserver.TCPServer,
                    ):
    """"Nothing to add here, inherited everything necessary from parents"""
    pass


def main():
    # Launch the server
    server = ForkingServer((SERVER_HOST, SERVER_PORT),
                            ForkingServerRequestHandler)
    ip, port = server.server_address # Retrieve the port number
    server_thread = threading.Thread(target=server.serve_forever)
    server_thread.setDaemon(True) # don't hang on exit
```

```
    server_thread.start()
    print ("Server loop running PID: %s" %os.getpid())
    # Launch the client(s)

    client1 =  ForkedClient(ip, port)
    client1.run()

    print("First client running")
    client2 =  ForkedClient(ip, port)
    client2.run()

    print("Second client running")

    # Clean them up
    server.shutdown()
    client1.shutdown()
    client2.shutdown()
    server.socket.close()


if __name__ == '__main__':
    main()
```

How it works...

An instance of `ForkingServer` is launched in the main thread, which has been daemonized to run in the background. Now, the two clients have started interacting with the server.

If you run the script, it will show the following output:

```
$ python 2_1_forking_mixin_socket_server.py
Server loop running PID: 26479
PID 26479 Sending echo message to the server :
 "Hello echo server!"
Sent: 18 characters, so far...
Server sending response [current_process_id: data] = [26481: Hello echo
server!]
PID 26479 received: b': Hello echo server!'
First client running
PID 26479 Sending echo message to the server : "Hello echo server!"
Sent: 18 characters, so far...
Server sending response [current_process_id: data] = [26482: Hello echo
server!]
PID 26479 received: b': Hello echo server!'
Second client running
```

The server port number might be different in your machine since this is dynamically chosen by the operating system kernel.

Using ThreadingMixIn in your socket server applications

Perhaps you prefer writing a multi-threaded application over a process-based one due to any particular reason, for example, sharing the states of that application across threads, avoiding the complexity of inter-process communication, or something else. In such a situation, if you want to write an asynchronous network server using `SocketServer` library, you will need `ThreadingMixIn`.

Getting ready

By making a few minor changes to our previous recipe, you can get a working version of socket server using `ThreadingMixIn`.

How to do it...

As seen in the previous socket server based on `ForkingMixIn`, `ThreadingMixIn` socket server will follow the same coding pattern of an echo server except for a few things. First, our `ThreadedTCPServer` will inherit from `TCPServer` and `TheadingMixIn`. This multi-threaded version will launch a new thread when a client connects to it. Some more details can be found at `http://docs.python.org/2/library/socketserver.html`.

The request handler class of our socket server, `ForkingServerRequestHandler`, sends the echo back to the client from a new thread. You can check the thread information here. For the sake of simplicity, we put the client code in a function instead of a class. The client code creates the client socket and sends the message to the server.

Listing 2.2 shows a sample code on the echo socket server using `ThreadingMixIn` as follows:

```
#!/usr/bin/env python
# Python Network Programming Cookbook, Second Edition -- Chapter - 2
# This program is optimized for Python 3.5.2.
# It may run on any other version with/without modifications.
# To make it run on Python 2.7.x, needs some changes due to API
```

```
differences.
# begin with replacing "socketserver" with "SocketServer" throughout the
program.
# See more: http://docs.python.org/2/library/socketserver.html
# See more: http://docs.python.org/3/library/socketserver.html

import os
import socket
import threading
import socketserver

SERVER_HOST = 'localhost'
SERVER_PORT = 0 # tells the kernel to pickup a port dynamically
BUF_SIZE = 1024


def client(ip, port, message):
    """ A client to test threading mixin server"""
    # Connect to the server
    sock = socket.socket(socket.AF_INET, socket.SOCK_STREAM)
    sock.connect((ip, port))
    try:
        sock.sendall(bytes(message, 'utf-8'))
        response = sock.recv(BUF_SIZE)
        print ("Client received: %s" %response)
    finally:
        sock.close()


class ThreadedTCPRequestHandler(socketserver.BaseRequestHandler):
    """ An example of threaded TCP request handler """
    def handle(self):
        data = self.request.recv(1024)
        cur_thread = threading.current_thread()
        response = "%s: %s" %(cur_thread.name, data)
        self.request.sendall(bytes(response, 'utf-8'))

class ThreadedTCPServer(socketserver.ThreadingMixIn,
socketserver.TCPServer):
    """Nothing to add here, inherited everything necessary from parents"""
    pass


if __name__ == "__main__":
    # Run server
    server = ThreadedTCPServer((SERVER_HOST, SERVER_PORT),
                                ThreadedTCPRequestHandler)
    ip, port = server.server_address # retrieve ip address
```

```
# Start a thread with the server -- one  thread per request
server_thread = threading.Thread(target=server.serve_forever)
# Exit the server thread when the main thread exits
server_thread.daemon = True
server_thread.start()
print ("Server loop running on thread: %s"  %server_thread.name)
# Run clients
client(ip, port, "Hello from client 1")
client(ip, port, "Hello from client 2")
client(ip, port, "Hello from client 3")
# Server cleanup
server.shutdown()
```

How it works...

This recipe first creates a server thread and launches it in the background. Then it launches three test clients to send messages to the server. In response, the server echoes back the message to the clients. In the `handle()` method of the server's request handler, you can see that we retrieve the current thread information and print it. This should be different in each client connection.

In this client/server conversation, the `sendall()` method has been used to guarantee the sending of all data without any loss:

```
$ python 2_2_threading_mixin_socket_server.py
Server loop running on thread: Thread-1
Client received: b"Thread-2: b'Hello from client 1'"
Client received: b"Thread-3: b'Hello from client 2'"
Client received: b"Thread-4: b'Hello from client 3'"
```

Writing a chat server using select.select

Launching a separate thread or process per client may not be viable in any larger network server application where several hundred or thousand clients are concurrently connected to the server. Due to the limited available memory and host CPU power, we need a better technique to deal with a large number of clients. Fortunately, Python provides the `select` module to overcome this problem.

How to do it...

We need to write an efficient chat server that can handle several hundred or a large number of client connections. We will use the select() method from the select module that will enable our chat server and client to do any task without blocking a send or receive a call all the time.

Let us design this recipe such that a single script can launch both client and server with an additional --name argument. Only if --name=server is passed from the command line, the script will launch the chat server. Any other value passed to the --name argument, for example, client1, client2, will launch a chat client. Let's specify our chat server port number from the command line using the --port argument. For a larger application, it may be preferable to write separate modules for the server and client.

Listing 2.3 shows an example of chat application using select.select as follows:

```python
#!/usr/bin/env python
# Python Network Programming Cookbook, Second Edition -- Chapter - 2
# This program is optimized for Python 2.7.12 and Python 3.5.2.
# It may run on any other version with/without modifications.

import select
import socket
import sys
import signal
import pickle
import struct
import argparse

SERVER_HOST = 'localhost'
CHAT_SERVER_NAME = 'server'

# Some utilities
def send(channel, *args):
    buffer = pickle.dumps(args)
    value = socket.htonl(len(buffer))
    size = struct.pack("L",value)
    channel.send(size)
    channel.send(buffer)

def receive(channel):
    size = struct.calcsize("L")
    size = channel.recv(size)
    try:
        size = socket.ntohl(struct.unpack("L", size)[0])
    except struct.error as e:
```

```
        return ''
buf = ""
while len(buf) < size:
    buf = channel.recv(size - len(buf))
return pickle.loads(buf)[0]
```

The `send()` method takes one named argument channel and positional argument `*args`. It serializes the data using the `dumps()` method from the `pickle` module. It determines the size of the data using the `struct` module. Similarly, `receive()` takes one named argument `channel`.

Now we can code the `ChatServer` class as follows:

```
class ChatServer(object):
    """ An example chat server using select """
    def __init__(self, port, backlog=5):
        self.clients = 0
        self.clientmap = {}
        self.outputs = [] # list output sockets
        self.server = socket.socket(socket.AF_INET, socket.SOCK_STREAM)
        self.server.setsockopt(socket.SOL_SOCKET, socket.SO_REUSEADDR, 1)
        self.server.bind((SERVER_HOST, port))
        print ('Server listening to port: %s ...' %port)
        self.server.listen(backlog)
        # Catch keyboard interrupts
        signal.signal(signal.SIGINT, self.sighandler)
    def sighandler(self, signum, frame):
        """ Clean up client outputs"""
        # Close the server
        print ('Shutting down server...')
        # Close existing client sockets
        for output in self.outputs:
            output.close()
        self.server.close()

    def get_client_name(self, client):
        """ Return the name of the client """
        info = self.clientmap[client]
        host, name = info[0][0], info[1]
        return '@'.join((name, host))
```

Now the main executable method of the `ChatServer` class should look like the following code:

```
def run(self):
    inputs = [self.server, sys.stdin]
    self.outputs = []
```

```python
running = True
while running:
    try:
        readable, writeable, exceptional = select.
        select(inputs, self.outputs, [])
    except select.error as e:
        break

    for sock in readable:
        if sock == self.server:
            # handle the server socket
            client, address = self.server.accept()
            print ("Chat server: got connection %d from %s" %
                    (client.fileno(), address))
            # Read the login name
            cname = receive(client).split('NAME: ')[1]
            # Compute client name and send back
            self.clients += 1
            send(client, 'CLIENT: ' + str(address[0]))
            inputs.append(client)
            self.clientmap[client] = (address, cname)
            # Send joining information to other clients
            msg = "\n(Connected: New client (%d) from %s)" %
                    (self.clients, self.get_client_name(client))
            for output in self.outputs:
                send(output, msg)
            self.outputs.append(client)

        elif sock == sys.stdin:
            # handle standard input
            junk = sys.stdin.readline()
            running = False
        else:
            # handle all other sockets
            try:
                data = receive(sock)
                if data:
                    # Send as new client's message...
                    msg = '\n#[' + self.get_client_name(sock)
                            + ']>>' + data
                    # Send data to all except ourself
                    for output in self.outputs:
                        if output != sock:
                            send(output, msg)
                else:
                    print ("Chat server: %d hung up"
                            % sock.fileno())
                    self.clients -= 1
```

```
                                    sock.close()
                                    inputs.remove(sock)
                                    self.outputs.remove(sock)

                                    # Sending client leaving information to others
                                    msg = "\n(Now hung up: Client from %s)" %
                                            self.get_client_name(sock)
                                    for output in self.outputs:
                                            send(output, msg)
                            except socket.error as e:
                                # Remove
                                inputs.remove(sock)
                                self.outputs.remove(sock)
                    self.server.close()
```

The chat server initializes with a few data attributes. It stores the count of clients, map of each client, and output sockets. The usual server socket creation also sets the option to reuse an address so that there is no problem restarting the server again using the same port. An optional backlog argument to the chat server constructor sets the maximum number of queued connections to listen to the server.

An interesting aspect of this chat server is to catch the user interrupt, usually via keyboard, using the `signal` module. So a signal handler `sighandler` is registered for the interrupt signal (`SIGINT`). This signal handler catches the keyboard interrupt signal and closes all output sockets where data may be waiting to be sent.

The main executive method of our chat server `run()` performs its operation inside a `while` loop. This method registers with a select interface where the input argument is the chat server socket, `stdin`. The output argument is specified by the server's output socket list. In return, `select` provides three lists: readable, writable, and exceptional sockets. The chat server is only interested in readable sockets where some data is ready to be read. If that socket indicates to itself, then that will mean a new client connection has been established. So the server retrieves the client's name and broadcasts this information to other clients. In another case, if anything comes from the input arguments, the chat server exits. Similarly, the chat server deals with the other client's socket inputs. It relays the data received from any client to others and also shares their joining/leaving information.

The chat client code class should contain the following code:

```
    class ChatClient(object):
        """ A command line chat client using select """

        def __init__(self, name, port, host=SERVER_HOST):
            self.name = name
            self.connected = False
```

```
        self.host = host
        self.port = port
        # Initial prompt
        self.prompt='[' + '@'.join((name,
socket.gethostname().split('.')[0]))
                        + ']> '
        # Connect to server at port
        try:
            self.sock = socket.socket(socket.AF_INET, socket.SOCK_STREAM)
            self.sock.connect((host, self.port))
            print ("Now connected to chat server@ port %d" % self.port)
            self.connected = True
            # Send my name...
            send(self.sock,'NAME: ' + self.name)
            data = receive(self.sock)
            # Contains client address, set it
            addr = data.split('CLIENT: ')[1]
            self.prompt = '[' + '@'.join((self.name, addr)) + ']> '
        except socket.error as e:
            print ("Failed to connect to chat server
                    @ port %d" % self.port)
            sys.exit(1)

    def run(self):
        """ Chat client main loop """
        while self.connected:
            try:
                sys.stdout.write(self.prompt)
                sys.stdout.flush()
                # Wait for input from stdin and socket
                readable, writeable,exceptional = select.select
                                            ([0, self.sock], [],[])
                for sock in readable:
                    if sock == 0:
                        data = sys.stdin.readline().strip()
                        if data: send(self.sock, data)
                    elif sock == self.sock:
                        data = receive(self.sock)
                        if not data:
                            print ('Client shutting down.')
                            self.connected = False
                            break
                        else:
                            sys.stdout.write(data + '\n')
                            sys.stdout.flush()
            except KeyboardInterrupt:
                print (" Client interrupted. """)
                self.sock.close()
```

```
        break
```

The chat client initializes with a name argument and sends this name to the chat server upon connecting. It also sets up a custom prompt [name@host]>. The executive method of this client run() continues its operation as long as the connection to the server is active. In a manner similar to the chat server, the chat client also registers with select(). If anything in readable sockets is ready, it enables the client to receive data. If the sock value is 0 and there's any data available then the data can be sent. The same information is also shown in stdout or, in our case, the command-line console. Our main method should now get command-line arguments and call either the server or client as follows:

```
if __name__ == "__main__":
    parser = argparse.ArgumentParser(description='Socket Server
                                              Example with Select')
    parser.add_argument('--name', action="store", dest="name",
                                              required=True)
    parser.add_argument('--port', action="store", dest="port",
                                      type=int, required=True)
    given_args = parser.parse_args()
    port = given_args.port
    name = given_args.name
    if name == CHAT_SERVER_NAME:
        server = ChatServer(port)
        server.run()
    else:
        client = ChatClient(name=name, port=port)
        client.run()
```

We would like to run this script thrice: once for the chat server and twice for two chat clients. For the server, we pass –name=server and port=8800. For client1, we change the name argument --name=client1 and for client2, we put --name=client2. Then from the client1 value prompt we send the message "Hello from client 1", which is printed in the prompt of the client2. Similarly, we send "hello from client 2" from the prompt of the client2, which is shown in the prompt of the client1.

The output for the server is as follows:

```
$ python 2_3_chat_server_with_select.py --name=server --port=8800
Server listening to port: 8800 ...
Chat server: got connection 4 from ('127.0.0.1', 59254)
Chat server: got connection 5 from ('127.0.0.1', 59256)
```

The output for `client1` is as follows:

```
$ python 2_3_chat_server_with_select.py --name=client1 --port=8800
Now connected to chat server@ port 8800
[client1@127.0.0.1]>
(Connected: New client (2) from client2@127.0.0.1)
[client1@127.0.0.1]> Hello from client1
[client1@127.0.0.1]>
#[client2@127.0.0.1]>>hello from client2
[client1@127.0.0.1]>
```

The output for `client2` is as follows:

```
$ python 2_3_chat_server_with_select.py --name=client2 --port=8800
Now connected to chat server@ port 8800
[client2@127.0.0.1]>
#[client1@127.0.0.1]>>Hello from client1
[client2@127.0.0.1]> hello from client2
[client2@127.0.0.1]>
```

The whole interaction is shown in the following screenshot:

Chat Server and Clients

How it works...

At the top of our module, we defined two utility functions: `send()` and `receive()`.

The chat server and client use these utility functions, which were demonstrated earlier. The details of the chat server and client methods were also discussed earlier.

Multiplexing a web server using select.epoll

Python's `select` module has a few platform-specific, networking event management functions. On a Linux machine, `epoll` is available. This will utilize the operating system kernel that will poll network events and let our script know whenever something happens. This sounds more efficient than the previously mentioned `select.select` approach.

How to do it...

Let's write a simple web server that can return a single line of text to any connected web browser.

The core idea is during the initialization of this web server, we should make a call to `select.epoll()` and register our server's file descriptor for event notifications. In the web server's executive code, the socket event is monitored as follows:

```
Listing 2.4 Simple web server using select.epoll
#!/usr/bin/env python
# Python Network Programming Cookbook, Second Edition -- Chapter - 2
# This program is optimized for Python 2.7.12 and Python 3.5.2.
# It may run on any other version with/without modifications.


import socket
import select
import argparse

SERVER_HOST = 'localhost'

EOL1 = b'\n\n'
EOL2 = b'\n\r\n'
SERVER_RESPONSE  = b"""HTTP/1.1 200 OK\r\nDate: Mon, 1 Apr 2013 01:01:01
GMT\r\nContent-Type: text/plain\r\nContent-Length: 25\r\n\r\n
Hello from Epoll Server!"""
```

```python
class EpollServer(object):
    """ A socket server using Epoll"""
    def __init__(self, host=SERVER_HOST, port=0):
        self.sock = socket.socket(socket.AF_INET, socket.SOCK_STREAM)
        self.sock.setsockopt(socket.SOL_SOCKET, socket.SO_REUSEADDR, 1)
        self.sock.bind((host, port))
        self.sock.listen(1)
        self.sock.setblocking(0)
        self.sock.setsockopt(socket.IPPROTO_TCP, socket.TCP_NODELAY, 1)
        print ("Started Epoll Server")
        self.epoll = select.epoll()
        self.epoll.register(self.sock.fileno(), select.EPOLLIN)
    def run(self):
        """Executes epoll server operation"""
        try:
            connections = {}; requests = {}; responses = {}
            while True:
                events = self.epoll.poll(1)
                for fileno, event in events:
                    if fileno == self.sock.fileno():
                        connection, address = self.sock.accept()
                        connection.setblocking(0)
                        self.epoll.register(connection.fileno(),
                        select.EPOLLIN)
                        connections[connection.fileno()] = connection
                        requests[connection.fileno()] = b''
                        responses[connection.fileno()] = SERVER_RESPONSE
                    elif event & select.EPOLLIN:
                        requests[fileno] += connections[fileno].recv(1024)
                        if EOL1 in requests[fileno] or EOL2
                        in requests[fileno]:
                            self.epoll.modify(fileno, select.EPOLLOUT)
                            print('-'*40 + '\n' + requests[fileno].decode()
                                  [:-2])
                    elif event & select.EPOLLOUT:
                        byteswritten = connections[fileno].
                                      send(responses[fileno])
                        responses[fileno] = responses[fileno]
                                      [byteswritten:]
                        if len(responses[fileno]) == 0:
                            self.epoll.modify(fileno, 0)
                            connections[fileno].shutdown(socket.SHUT_RDWR)
                    elif event & select.EPOLLHUP:
                        self.epoll.unregister(fileno)
                        connections[fileno].close()
                        del connections[fileno]
        finally:
            self.epoll.unregister(self.sock.fileno())
```

```
                self.epoll.close()
                self.sock.close()


    if __name__ == '__main__':
        parser = argparse.ArgumentParser(description='Socket Server
                                            Example with Epoll')
        parser.add_argument('--port', action="store", dest="port",
                                            type=int, required=True)
        given_args = parser.parse_args()
        port = given_args.port
        server = EpollServer(host=SERVER_HOST, port=port)
        server.run()
```

If you run this script and access the web server from your browsers, such as Google Chrome or Mozilla Firefox, by entering `http://localhost:8800/`, the following output will be shown in the console:

```
$ python 2_4_simple_web_server_with_epoll.py --port=8800
Started Epoll Server
----------------------------------------
GET / HTTP/1.1
Host: localhost:8800
Connection: keep-alive
Upgrade-Insecure-Requests: 1
User-Agent: Mozilla/5.0 (X11; Linux x86_64) AppleWebKit/537.36 (KHTML, like
Gecko) Chrome/58.0.3029.110 Safari/537.36
Accept:
text/html,application/xhtml+xml,application/xml;q=0.9,image/webp,*/*;q=0.8
DNT: 1
Accept-Encoding: gzip, deflate, sdch, br
Accept-Language: en-US,en;q=0.8
----------------------------------------
GET /favicon.ico HTTP/1.1
Host: localhost:8800
Connection: keep-alive
User-Agent: Mozilla/5.0 (X11; Linux x86_64) AppleWebKit/537.36 (KHTML, like
Gecko) Chrome/58.0.3029.110 Safari/537.36
Accept: image/webp,image/*,*/*;q=0.8
DNT: 1
Referer: http://localhost:8800/
Accept-Encoding: gzip, deflate, sdch, br
Accept-Language: en-US,en;q=0.8
```

You will also be able to see the following line in your browser:

```
Hello from Epoll Server!
```

The following screenshot shows the scenario:

Simple Web Server: Terminal and Browser

How it works...

In our `EpollServer` web server's constructor, a socket server is created and bound to a localhost at a given port. The server's socket is set to the non-blocking mode (`setblocking(0)`). The `TCP_NODELAY` option is also set so that our server can exchange data without buffering (as in the case of an SSH connection). Next, the `select.epoll()` instance is created and the socket's file descriptor is passed to that instance to help monitoring.

In the `run()` method of the web server, it starts receiving the socket events. These events are denoted as follows:

- `EPOLLIN`: This socket reads events
- `EPOLLOUT`: This socket writes events

In the case of a server socket, it sets up the response SERVER_RESPONSE. When the socket has any connection that wants to write data, it can do that inside the EPOLLOUT event case. The EPOLLHUP event signals an unexpected close to a socket that is due to the internal error conditions.

Multiplexing an echo server using Diesel concurrent library

Sometimes you need to write a large custom networking application that wants to avoid repeated server initialization code that creates a socket, binds to an address, listens, and handles basic errors. There are numerous Python networking libraries out there to help you remove boiler-plate code. Here, we can examine such a library called Diesel.

Getting ready

Diesel uses a non-blocking technique with co-routines to write networking severs efficiently. As stated on the website, Diesel's core is a tight event loop that uses epoll to deliver nearly flat performance out to 10,000 connections and beyond. Here, we introduce Diesel with a simple echo server. You also need Diesel library 3.0 or any later version. You can do that with pip command:

```
$ pip install diesel
```

If you encounter some issues in installing, make sure you have the dependencies installed. The following command should fix most of these errors:

```
$ sudo apt-get install build-essential libssl-dev libffi-dev python-dev
```

You may need to run as a super-user depending on your operating systems configurations, since diesel installs some critical dependencies such as the cryptography module that requires admin privileges to install.

Diesel has some dependency issues in Python 3. Installing and getting it to work is easier with Python 2.

You may install `diesel` as follows:

```
$ sudo su
# pip install diesel
```

This will display the logs as follows while installing `diesel`:

```
Collecting diesel
Requirement already satisfied: http-parser>=0.7.12 in
/usr/local/lib/python3.5/dist-packages (from diesel)
Requirement already satisfied: flask in /usr/local/lib/python3.5/dist-
packages (from diesel)
Requirement already satisfied: greenlet in /usr/local/lib/python3.5/dist-
packages (from diesel)
Requirement already satisfied: twiggy in /usr/local/lib/python3.5/dist-
packages (from diesel)
Requirement already satisfied: dnspython in /usr/local/lib/python3.5/dist-
packages (from diesel)
Collecting pyopenssl (from diesel)\
Using cached pyOpenSSL-17.0.0-py2.py3-none-any.whl
Requirement already satisfied: Werkzeug>=0.7 in
/usr/local/lib/python3.5/dist-packages (from flask->diesel)
Requirement already satisfied: Jinja2>=2.4 in /usr/lib/python3/dist-
packages (from flask->diesel)
Requirement already satisfied: itsdangerous>=0.21 in
/usr/local/lib/python3.5/dist-packages (from flask->diesel)
Requirement already satisfied: click>=2.0 in /usr/local/lib/python3.5/dist-
packages (from flask->diesel)
Requirement already satisfied: six>=1.5.2 in /usr/lib/python3/dist-packages
(from pyopenssl->diesel)
Collecting cryptography>=1.7 (from pyopenssl->diesel)
Using cached cryptography-1.9.tar.gz
Requirement already satisfied: MarkupSafe in /usr/lib/python3/dist-packages
(from Jinja2>=2.4->flask->diesel)
Requirement already satisfied: idna>=2.1 in /usr/local/lib/python3.5/dist-
packages (from cryptography>=1.7->pyopenssl->diesel)
Requirement already satisfied: asn1crypto>=0.21.0 in
/usr/local/lib/python3.5/dist-packages (from
cryptography>=1.7->pyopenssl->diesel)
Requirement already satisfied: cffi>=1.7 in /usr/local/lib/python3.5/dist-
packages (from cryptography>=1.7->pyopenssl->diesel)
Requirement already satisfied: pycparser in /usr/local/lib/python3.5/dist-
packages (from cffi>=1.7->cryptography>=1.7->pyopenssl->diesel)
Building wheels for collected packages: cryptography
Running setup.py bdist_wheel for cryptography ... done
Stored in directory:
/root/.cache/pip/wheels/ff/a5/ef/186bb4f6a89ef0bb8373bf53e5c9884b96722f0857
bd3111b8
```

```
Successfully built cryptography
Installing collected packages: cryptography, pyopenssl, diesel
Found existing installation: cryptography 1.2.3
Uninstalling cryptography-1.2.3:
Successfully uninstalled cryptography-1.2.3
Successfully installed cryptography-1.9 diesel-3.0.24 pyopenssl-17.0.0
```

How to do it...

In the Python Diesel framework, applications are initialized with an instance of the `Application()` class and an event handler is registered with this instance. Let's see how simple it is to write an echo server.

Listing 2.5 shows the code on the echo server example using Diesel as follows:

```python
#!/usr/bin/env python
# Python Network Programming Cookbook, Second Edition -- Chapter - 2
# This program is optimized for Python 2.7.12.
# It will work with Python 3.5.2 once the depedencies for diesel are sorted
out.
# It may run on any other version with/without modifications.
# You also need diesel library 3.0 or a later version.
# Make sure to install the dependencies beforehand.

import diesel
import argparse

class EchoServer(object):
    """ An echo server using diesel"""

    def handler(self, remote_addr):
        """Runs the echo server"""
        host, port = remote_addr[0], remote_addr[1]
        print ("Echo client connected from: %s:%d" %(host, port))
        while True:
            try:
                message = diesel.until_eol()
                your_message = ': '.join(['You said', message])
                diesel.send(your_message)
            except Exception as e:
                print ("Exception:",e)

def main(server_port):
    app = diesel.Application()
    server = EchoServer()
    app.add_service(diesel.Service(server.handler, server_port))
```

```
        app.run()


if __name__ == '__main__':
    parser = argparse.ArgumentParser(description='Echo server
                                    example with Diesel')
    parser.add_argument('--port', action="store", dest="port",
                                    type=int, required=True)
    given_args = parser.parse_args()
    port = given_args.port
    main(port)
```

If you run this script, the server will show the following output:

```
$ python 2_5_echo_server_with_diesel.py --port=8800
[2017/06/04 13:37:36] {diesel} WARNING|Starting diesel <hand-rolled
select.epoll>
Echo client connected from: 127.0.0.1:57506
```

On another console window, another telnet client can be launched and the echoing message to our server can be tested as follows:

```
$ telnet localhost 8800
Trying 127.0.0.1...
Connected to localhost.
Escape character is '^]'.
Hello Diesel server ?
You said: Hello Diesel server ?
```

The following screenshot illustrates the interaction of the Diesel chat server:

Chat Server and Telnet

How it works...

Our script has taken a command-line argument for `--port` and passed this to the `main()` function where our Diesel application has been initialized and run.

Diesel has a notion of service where an application can be built with many services. `EchoServer` has a `handler()` method. This enables the server to deal with individual client connections. The `Service()` method takes the `handler` method and a port number to run that service.

Inside the `handler()` method, we determine the behavior of the server. In this case, the server is simply returning the message text.

If we compare this code with `Chapter 1`, *Sockets, IPv4, and Simple Client/Server Programming*, in the *Writing a simple echo client/server application* recipe (*listing 1.13a*), it is very clear that we do not need to write any boiler-plate code and hence it's very easy to concentrate on high-level application logic.

3

IPv6, Unix Domain Sockets, and Network Interfaces

In this chapter, we will cover the following topics:

- Forwarding a local port to a remote host
- Pinging hosts on the network with ICMP
- Waiting for a remote network service
- Enumerating interfaces on your machine
- Finding the IP address for a specific interface on your machine
- Finding whether an interface is up on your machine
- Detecting inactive machines on your network
- Performing a basic IPC using connected sockets (socketpair)
- Performing IPC using Unix domain sockets
- Finding out if your Python supports IPv6 sockets
- Extracting an IPv6 prefix from an IPv6 address
- Writing an IPv6 echo client/server

Introduction

This chapter extends the use of Python's `socket` library with a few third-party libraries. It also discusses some advanced techniques, for example, the asynchronous `ayncore` module from the Python standard library. This chapter also touches upon various protocols, ranging from an ICMP ping to an IPv6 client/server.

In this chapter, a few useful Python third-party modules have been introduced by some example recipes. For example, the network packet capture library, `Scapy`, is well known among Python network programmers.

A few recipes have been dedicated to explore the IPv6 utilities in Python including an IPv6 client/server. Some other recipes cover Unix domain sockets.

Forwarding a local port to a remote host

Sometimes, you may need to create a local port forwarder that will redirect all traffic from a local port to a particular remote host. This might be useful to enable proxy users to browse a certain site while preventing them from browsing some others.

How to do it...

Let us create a local port forwarding script that will redirect all traffic received at port 8800 to the Google home page (`http://www.google.com`). We can pass the local and remote host as well as port number to this script. For the sake of simplicity, let's only specify the local port number as we are aware that the web server runs on port 80.

Listing 3.1 shows a port forwarding example, as follows:

```
#!/usr/bin/env python
# Python Network Programming Cookbook, Second Edition -- Chapter - 3
# This program is optimized for Python 2.7.12 and Python 3.5.2.
# It may run on any other version with/without modifications.


import argparse

LOCAL_SERVER_HOST = 'localhost'
REMOTE_SERVER_HOST = 'www.google.com'
BUFSIZE = 4096

import asyncore
import socket

class PortForwarder(asyncore.dispatcher):
    def __init__(self, ip, port, remoteip,remoteport,backlog=5):
        asyncore.dispatcher.__init__(self)
        self.remoteip=remoteip
        self.remoteport=remoteport
        self.create_socket(socket.AF_INET,socket.SOCK_STREAM)
```

```
                self.set_reuse_addr()
                self.bind((ip,port))
                self.listen(backlog)

        def handle_accept(self):
            conn, addr = self.accept()
            print ("Connected to:",addr)
            Sender(Receiver(conn),self.remoteip,self.remoteport)

    class Receiver(asyncore.dispatcher):
        def __init__(self,conn):
            asyncore.dispatcher.__init__(self,conn)
            self.from_remote_buffer=''
            self.to_remote_buffer=''
            self.sender=None

        def handle_connect(self):
            pass

        def handle_read(self):
            read = self.recv(BUFSIZE)
            self.from_remote_buffer += read

        def writable(self):
            return (len(self.to_remote_buffer) > 0)

        def handle_write(self):
            sent = self.send(self.to_remote_buffer)
            self.to_remote_buffer = self.to_remote_buffer[sent:]

        def handle_close(self):
            self.close()
            if self.sender:
                self.sender.close()

    class Sender(asyncore.dispatcher):
        def __init__(self, receiver, remoteaddr,remoteport):
            asyncore.dispatcher.__init__(self)
            self.receiver=receiver
            receiver.sender=self
            self.create_socket(socket.AF_INET, socket.SOCK_STREAM)
            self.connect((remoteaddr, remoteport))
        def handle_connect(self):
            pass
        def handle_read(self):
            read = self.recv(BUFSIZE)
            self.receiver.to_remote_buffer += read
        def writable(self):
```

```
                return (len(self.receiver.from_remote_buffer) > 0)
        def handle_write(self):
            sent = self.send(self.receiver.from_remote_buffer)
            self.receiver.from_remote_buffer = self.receiver.
              from_remote_buffer[sent:]
        def handle_close(self):
            self.close()
            self.receiver.close()


    if __name__ == "__main__":
        parser = argparse.ArgumentParser(description='Stackless
                Socket Server Example')
        parser.add_argument('--local-host', action="store",
        dest="local_host", default=LOCAL_SERVER_HOST)
        parser.add_argument('--local-port', action="store",
        dest="local_port", type=int, required=True)
        parser.add_argument('--remote-host', action="store",
        dest="remote_host",  default=REMOTE_SERVER_HOST)
        parser.add_argument('--remote-port', action="store",
        dest="remote_port", type=int, default=80)
        given_args = parser.parse_args()
        local_host, remote_host = given_args.local_host,
        given_args.remote_host
        local_port, remote_port = given_args.local_port,
        given_args.remote_port
        print ("Starting port forwarding local %s:%s => remote
        %s:%s" % (local_host, local_port, remote_host, remote_port))
        PortForwarder(local_host, local_port, remote_host, remote_port)
        asyncore.loop()
```

If you run this script, it will show the following output:

```
$ python 3_1_port_forwarding.py --local-port=8800
Starting port forwarding local localhost:8800 => remote www.google.com:80
```

Now, open your browser and visit `http://localhost:8800`. This will take you to the Google home page and the script will print something similar to the following command:

```
('Connected to:', ('127.0.0.1', 37236))
```

The following screenshot shows the forwarding of a local port to a remote host:

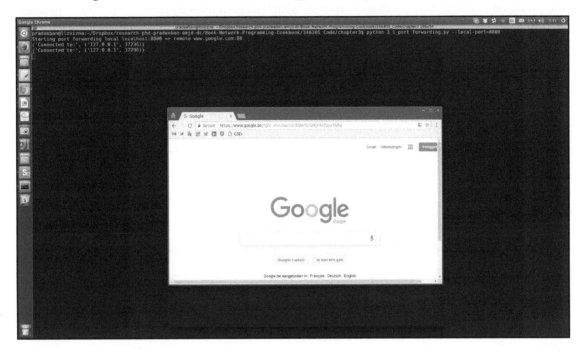

Port Forwarding to Remote Host

How it works...

We created a port forwarding class, `PortForwarder` subclassed, from `asyncore.dispatcher`, which wraps around the `socket` object. It provides a few additional helpful functions when certain events occur, for example, when the connection is successful or a client is connected to a server socket. You have the choice of overriding the set of methods defined in this class. In our case, we only override the `handle_accept()` method.

Two other classes have been derived from `asyncore.dispatcher`. The `Receiver` class handles the incoming client requests and the `Sender` class takes this `Receiver` instance and processes the sent data to the clients. As you can see, these two classes override the `handle_read()`, `handle_write()`, and `writeable()` methods to facilitate the bi-directional communication between the remote host and local client.

In summary, the `PortForwarder` class takes the incoming client request in a local socket and passes this to the `Sender` class instance, which in turn uses the `Receiver` class instance to initiate a bi-directional communication with a remote server in the specified port.

Pinging hosts on the network with ICMP

An ICMP ping is the most common type of network scanning you have ever encountered. It is very easy to open a command-line prompt or Terminal and type `ping www.google.com`. How difficult is that from inside a Python program? This recipe shows you an example of a Python ping.

Getting ready

You need the superuser or administrator privilege to run this recipe on your machine.

How to do it...

You can lazily write a Python script that calls the system ping command-line tool, as follows:

```
import subprocess
import shlex

command_line = "ping -c 1 www.google.com"
args = shlex.split(command_line)
try:
        subprocess.check_call(args,stdout=subprocess.PIPE,\
stderr=subprocess.PIPE)
    print ("Google web server is up!")
except subprocess.CalledProcessError:
    print ("Failed to get ping.")
```

However, in many circumstances, the system's ping executable may not be available or may be inaccessible. In this case, we need a pure Python script to do that ping. Note that this script needs to be run as a superuser or administrator.

Listing 3.2 shows the ICMP ping, as follows:

```
#!/usr/bin/env python
# Python Network Programming Cookbook -- Chapter - 3
# This program is optimized for Python 3.5.2.
```

```
# Instructions to make it run with Python 2.7.x is given below.
# It may run on any other version with/without modifications.

import os
import argparse
import socket
import struct
import select
import time


ICMP_ECHO_REQUEST = 8 # Platform specific
DEFAULT_TIMEOUT = 2
DEFAULT_COUNT = 4


class Pinger(object):
    """ Pings to a host -- the Pythonic way"""
    def __init__(self, target_host, count=DEFAULT_COUNT,
                    timeout=DEFAULT_TIMEOUT):
        self.target_host = target_host
        self.count = count
        self.timeout = timeout


    def do_checksum(self, source_string):
        """  Verify the packet integrity """
        sum = 0
        max_count = (len(source_string)/2)*2
        count = 0
        while count < max_count:

            # To make this program run with Python 2.7.x:
            # val = ord(source_string[count + 1])*256 +
            #           ord(source_string[count])
            # ### uncomment the above line, and comment
            #       out the below line.
            val = source_string[count + 1]*256 + source_string[count]
            # In Python 3, indexing a bytes object returns an integer.
            # Hence, ord() is redundant.

            sum = sum + val
            sum = sum & 0xffffffff
            count = count + 2
        if max_count<len(source_string):
            sum = sum + ord(source_string[len(source_string) - 1])
            sum = sum & 0xffffffff
        sum = (sum >> 16)  +  (sum & 0xffff)
```

```
        sum = sum + (sum >> 16)
        answer = ~sum
        answer = answer & 0xffff
        answer = answer >> 8 | (answer << 8 & 0xff00)
        return answer
    def receive_pong(self, sock, ID, timeout):
        """
        Receive ping from the socket.
        """
        time_remaining = timeout
        while True:
            start_time = time.time()
            readable = select.select([sock], [], [], time_remaining)
            time_spent = (time.time() - start_time)
            if readable[0] == []: # Timeout
                return
            time_received = time.time()
            recv_packet, addr = sock.recvfrom(1024)
            icmp_header = recv_packet[20:28]
            type, code, checksum, packet_ID, sequence = struct.unpack(
                "bbHHh", icmp_header
            )
            if packet_ID == ID:
                bytes_In_double = struct.calcsize("d")
                time_sent = struct.unpack("d", recv_packet[28:28 +
                                          bytes_In_double])[0]
                return time_received - time_sent
            time_remaining = time_remaining - time_spent
            if time_remaining <= 0:
                return
```

We need a `send_ping()` method that will send the data of a ping request to the target host. Also, this will call the `do_checksum()` method for checking the integrity of the ping data, as follows:

```
    def send_ping(self, sock,  ID):
        """
        Send ping to the target host
        """
        target_addr  =  socket.gethostbyname(self.target_host)
        my_checksum = 0
        # Create a dummy heder with a 0 checksum.
        header = struct.pack("bbHHh", ICMP_ECHO_REQUEST, 0,
                             my_checksum, ID, 1)
        bytes_In_double = struct.calcsize("d")
        data = (192 - bytes_In_double) * "Q"
        data = struct.pack("d", time.time()) +
               bytes(data.encode('utf-8'))
```

```
# Get the checksum on the data and the dummy header.
my_checksum = self.do_checksum(header + data)
header = struct.pack(
    "bbHHh", ICMP_ECHO_REQUEST, 0,
    socket.htons(my_checksum), ID, 1
)
packet = header + data
sock.sendto(packet, (target_addr, 1))
```

Let us define another method called `ping_once()` that makes a single ping call to the target host. It creates a raw ICMP socket by passing the ICMP protocol to `socket()`. The exception handling code takes care if the script is not run by a superuser or if any other socket error occurs. Let's take a look at the following code:

```
def ping_once(self):
    """
    Returns the delay (in seconds) or none on timeout.
    """
    icmp = socket.getprotobyname("icmp")
    try:
        sock = socket.socket(socket.AF_INET,
                             socket.SOCK_RAW, icmp)
    except socket.error as e:
        if e.errno == 1:
            # Not superuser, so operation not permitted
            e.msg +=  "ICMP messages can only be sent
                        from root user processes"
            raise socket.error(e.msg)
    except Exception as e:
        print ("Exception: %s" %(e))
    my_ID = os.getpid() & 0xFFFF
    self.send_ping(sock, my_ID)
    delay = self.receive_pong(sock, my_ID, self.timeout)
    sock.close()
    return delay
```

The main executive method of this class is `ping()`. It runs a for loop inside, which the `ping_once()` method is called count times and receives a delay in the ping response in seconds. If no delay is returned, that means the ping has failed. Let's take a look at the following code:

```
def ping(self):
    """
    Run the ping process
    """
    for i in range(self.count):
        print ("Ping to %s..." % self.target_host,)
```

```
        try:
            delay  =  self.ping_once()
        except socket.gaierror as e:
            print ("Ping failed. (socket error: '%s')" % e[1])
            break
        if delay  ==  None:
            print ("Ping failed. (timeout within %ssec.)"
                    % self.timeout)
        else:
            delay  =  delay * 1000
            print ("Get pong in %0.4fms" % delay)

if __name__ == '__main__':
    parser = argparse.ArgumentParser(description='Python ping')
    parser.add_argument('--target-host', action="store",
dest="target_host", required=True)
    given_args = parser.parse_args()
    target_host = given_args.target_host
    pinger = Pinger(target_host=target_host)
    pinger.ping()
```

This script shows the following output. This has been run with the superuser privilege:

```
$ sudo python 3_2_ping_remote_host.py --target-host=www.google.com
Ping to www.google.com...
Get pong in 27.0808ms
Ping to www.google.com...
Get pong in 17.3445ms
Ping to www.google.com...
Get pong in 33.3586ms
Ping to www.google.com...
Get pong in 32.3212ms
```

How it works...

A `Pinger` class has been constructed to define a few useful methods. The class initializes with a few user-defined or default inputs, which are as follows:

- `target_host`: This is the target host to ping
- `count`: This is how many times to do the ping
- `timeout`: This is the value that determines when to end an unfinished ping operation

The `send_ping()` method gets the DNS hostname of the target host and creates an `ICMP_ECHO_REQUEST` packet using the `struct` module. It is necessary to check the data integrity of the method using the `do_checksum()` method. It takes the source string and manipulates it to produce a proper checksum. On the receiving end, the `receive_pong()` method waits for a response until the timeout occurs or receives the response. It captures the ICMP response header and then compares the packet ID and calculates the delay in the request and response cycle.

Waiting for a remote network service

Sometimes, during the recovery of a network service, it might be useful to run a script to check when the server is online again.

How to do it...

We can write a client that will wait for a particular network service forever or for a timeout. In this example, by default, we would like to check when a web server is up in localhost. If you specified some other remote host or port, that information will be used instead.

Listing 3.3 shows waiting for a remote network service, as follows:

```python
#!/usr/bin/env python
# Python Network Programming Cookbook, Second Edition -- Chapter - 3
# This program is optimized for Python 2.7.12 and Python 3.5.2.
# It may run on any other version with/without modifications.

import argparse
import socket
import errno
from time import time as now

DEFAULT_TIMEOUT = 120
DEFAULT_SERVER_HOST = 'localhost'
DEFAULT_SERVER_PORT = 80

class NetServiceChecker(object):
    """ Wait for a network service to come online"""
    def __init__(self, host, port, timeout=DEFAULT_TIMEOUT):
        self.host = host
        self.port = port
        self.timeout = timeout
        self.sock = socket.socket(socket.AF_INET, socket.SOCK_STREAM)
```

```python
    def end_wait(self):
        self.sock.close()

    def check(self):
        """ Check the service """
        if self.timeout:
            end_time = now() + self.timeout
        while True:
            try:
                if self.timeout:
                    next_timeout = end_time - now()
                    if next_timeout < 0:
                        return False
                    else:
                        print ("setting socket next timeout %ss"
                                %round(next_timeout))
                        self.sock.settimeout(next_timeout)
                self.sock.connect((self.host, self.port))
            # handle exceptions
            except socket.timeout as err:
                if self.timeout:
                    return False
            except socket.error as err:
                print ("Exception: %s" %err)
            else: # if all goes well
                self.end_wait()
                return True

if __name__ == '__main__':
    parser = argparse.ArgumentParser(description='Wait for
            Network Service')
    parser.add_argument('--host', action="store", dest="host",
    default=DEFAULT_SERVER_HOST)
    parser.add_argument('--port', action="store", dest="port",
    type=int, default=DEFAULT_SERVER_PORT)
    parser.add_argument('--timeout', action="store", dest="timeout",
    type=int, default=DEFAULT_TIMEOUT)
    given_args = parser.parse_args()
    host, port, timeout = given_args.host, given_args.port,
                        given_args.timeout
    service_checker = NetServiceChecker(host, port, timeout=timeout)
    print ("Checking for network service %s:%s ..." %(host, port))
    if service_checker.check():
        print ("Service is available again!")
```

If a web server is running on your machine, this script will show the following output:

```
$ python 3_3_wait_for_remote_service.py
Waiting for network service localhost:80 ...
setting socket next timeout 120.0s
Service is available again!
```

If you do not have a web server already running in your computer, make sure to install one such as **Apache 2** web server:

```
$ sudo apt install apache2
```

Now, stop the Apache process:

```
$ sudo /etc/init.d/apache2 stop
```

It will print the below message while stopping the service.

```
[ ok ] Stopping apache2 (via systemctl): apache2.service.
```

Run this script, and start Apache again.

```
$ sudo /etc/init.d/apache2 start
[ ok ] Starting apache2 (via systemctl): apache2.service.
```

The output pattern will be different for a different machine. On my machine, the following output pattern was found:

```
Exception: [Errno 103] Software caused connection abort
setting socket next timeout 119.0s
Exception: [Errno 111] Connection refused
setting socket next timeout 119.0s
Exception: [Errno 103] Software caused connection abort
setting socket next timeout 119.0s
Exception: [Errno 111] Connection refused
setting socket next timeout 119.0s
And finally when Apache2 is up again, the following log is printed:
Service is available again!
```

The following screenshot shows the waiting for an active Apache web server process:

Waiting for Apache2 Process

How it works...

The preceding script uses the `argparse` module to take the user input and process the hostname, port, and timeout, which is how long our script will wait for the desired network service. It launches an instance of the `NetServiceChecker` class and calls the `check()` method. This method calculates the final end time of waiting and uses the socket's `settimeout()` method to control each round's end time, that is `next_timeout`. It then uses the socket's `connect()` method to test if the desired network service is available until the socket timeout occurs. This method also catches the socket timeout error and checks the socket timeout against the timeout values given by the user.

Enumerating interfaces on your machine

If you need to list the network interfaces present on your machine, it is not very complicated in Python. There are a couple of third-party libraries out there that can do this job in a few lines. However, let's see how this is done using a pure socket call.

Getting ready

You need to run this recipe on a Linux box. To get the list of available interfaces, you can execute the following command:

```
$ /sbin/ifconfig
```

How to do it...

Listing 3.4 shows how to list the networking interfaces, as follows:

```python
#!/usr/bin/env python
# Python Network Programming Cookbook, Second Edition -- Chapter - 3
# This program is optimized for Python 2.7.12 and Python 3.5.2.
# It may run on any other version with/without modifications.

import sys
import socket
import fcntl
import struct
import array

SIOCGIFCONF = 0x8912 #from C library sockios.h
STUCT_SIZE_32 = 32
STUCT_SIZE_64 = 40
PLATFORM_32_MAX_NUMBER =  2**32
DEFAULT_INTERFACES = 8


def list_interfaces():
    interfaces = []
    max_interfaces = DEFAULT_INTERFACES
    is_64bits = sys.maxsize > PLATFORM_32_MAX_NUMBER
    struct_size = STUCT_SIZE_64 if is_64bits else STUCT_SIZE_32
    sock = socket.socket(socket.AF_INET, socket.SOCK_DGRAM)
    while True:
        bytes = max_interfaces * struct_size
        interface_names = array.array('B', b'\0' * bytes)
        sock_info = fcntl.ioctl(
            sock.fileno(),
            SIOCGIFCONF,
            struct.pack('iL', bytes, interface_names.buffer_info()[0])
        )
        outbytes = struct.unpack('iL', sock_info)[0]
        if outbytes == bytes:
            max_interfaces *= 2
```

```
        else:
            break
    namestr = interface_names.tostring()
    for i in range(0, outbytes, struct_size):
        interfaces.append((namestr[i:i+16].split(b'\0', 1)
                          [0]).decode('ascii', 'ignore'))
    return interfaces


if __name__ == '__main__':
    interfaces = list_interfaces()
    print ("This machine has %s network interfaces: %s." %(len(interfaces),
interfaces))
```

The preceding script will list the network interfaces, as shown in the following output:

```
$ python 3_4_list_network_interfaces.py
This machine has 2 network interfaces: ['lo', 'wlo1'].
```

How it works...

This recipe code uses a low-level socket feature to find out the interfaces present on the system. The single `list_interfaces()` method creates a socket object and finds the network interface information from manipulating this object. It does so by making a call to the `fnctl` module's `ioctl()` method. The `fnctl` module interfaces with some Unix routines, for example, `fnctl()`. This interface performs an I/O control operation on the underlying file descriptor socket, which is obtained by calling the `fileno()` method of the `socket` object.

The additional parameter of the `ioctl()` method includes the `SIOCGIFADDR` constant defined in the C `socket` library and a data structure produced by the `struct` module's `pack()` function. The memory address specified by a data structure is modified as a result of the `ioctl()` call. In this case, the `interface_names` variable holds this information. After unpacking the `sock_info` return value of the `ioctl()` call, the number of network interfaces is increased twice if the size of the data suggests it. This is done in a while loop to discover all interfaces if our initial interface count assumption is not correct.

The names of interfaces are extracted from the string format of the `interface_names` variable. It reads specific fields of that variable and appends the values in the interfaces' list. At the end of the `list_interfaces()` function, this is returned.

Finding the IP address for a specific interface on your machine

Finding the IP address of a particular network interface may be needed from your Python network application.

Getting ready

This recipe is prepared exclusively for a Linux box. There are some Python modules specially designed to bring similar functionalities on Windows and macOS platforms. For example, see `http://sourceforge.net/projects/pywin32/` for Windows-specific implementation.

How to do it...

You can use the `fnctl` module to query the IP address on your machine.

Listing 3.5 shows us how to find the IP address for a specific interface on your machine, as follows:

```
#!/usr/bin/env python
# Python Network Programming Cookbook, Second Edition -- Chapter - 3
# This program is optimized for Python 2.7.12 and Python 3.5.2.
# It may run on any other version with/without modifications.

import argparse
import sys
import socket
import fcntl
import struct
import array


def get_ip_address(ifname):
    s = socket.socket(socket.AF_INET, socket.SOCK_DGRAM)
    return socket.inet_ntoa(fcntl.ioctl(
        s.fileno(),
        0x8915,  # SIOCGIFADDR
        struct.pack(b'256s', bytes(ifname[:15], 'utf-8'))
    )[20:24])

if __name__ == '__main__':
```

```
    parser = argparse.ArgumentParser(description='Python
                                  networking utils')
    parser.add_argument('--ifname', action="store",
                        dest="ifname", required=True)
    given_args = parser.parse_args()
    ifname = given_args.ifname
    print ("Interface [%s] --> IP: %s" %(ifname, get_ip_address(ifname)))
```

The output of this script is shown in one line, as follows:

```
$ python 3_5_get_interface_ip_address.py --ifname=lo
Interface [lo] --> IP: 127.0.0.1
```

In the preceding execution, make sure to use an existing interface, as printed in the previous recipe. In my computer, I got the output previously for `3_4_list_network_interfaces.py`:

```
This machine has 2 network interfaces: ['lo', 'wlo1'].
```

If you use a non-existing interface, an error will be printed.

For example, I do not have eth0 interface right now. So the output is:

```
$ python3 3_5_get_interface_ip_address.py --ifname=eth0
Traceback (most recent call last):
File "3_5_get_interface_ip_address.py", line 27, in <module>
  print ("Interface [%s] --> IP: %s" %(ifname, get_ip_address(ifname)))
  File "3_5_get_interface_ip_address.py", line 19, in get_ip_address
  struct.pack(b'256s', bytes(ifname[:15], 'utf-8'))
OSError: [Errno 19] No such device
```

How it works...

This recipe is similar to the previous one. The preceding script takes a command-line argument: the name of the network interface whose IP address is to be known. The `get_ip_address()` function creates a `socket` object and calls the `fnctl.ioctl()` function to query on that object about IP information. Note that the `socket.inet_ntoa()` function converts the binary data to a human-readable string in a dotted format as we are familiar with it.

Finding whether an interface is up on your machine

If you have multiple network interfaces on your machine, before doing any work on a particular interface, you would like to know the status of that network interface, for example, if the interface is actually up. This makes sure that you route your command to active interfaces.

Getting ready

This recipe is written for a Linux machine. So, this script will not run on a Windows or macOS host. In this recipe, we use **Nmap**, a famous network scanning tool. You can find more about Nmap from its website http://nmap.org/.

Install Nmap in your computer. For Debian-based systems, the command is:

```
$ sudo apt-get install nmap
```

You also need the python-nmap module to run this recipe. This can be installed by pip, as follows:

```
$ pip install python-nmap
```

How to do it...

We can create a socket object and get the IP address of that interface. Then, we can use any of the scanning techniques to probe the interface status.

Listing 3.6 shows the detect network interface status, as follows:

```
#!/usr/bin/env python
# Python Network Programming Cookbook, Second Edition -- Chapter - 3
# This program is optimized for Python 2.7.12 and Python 3.5.2.
# It may run on any other version with/without modifications.


import argparse
import socket
import struct
import fcntl
import nmap
```

```
SAMPLE_PORTS = '21-23'

def get_interface_status(ifname):
    sock = socket.socket(socket.AF_INET, socket.SOCK_DGRAM)
    ip_address = socket.inet_ntoa(fcntl.ioctl(
        sock.fileno(),
        0x8915, #SIOCGIFADDR, C socket library sockios.h
        struct.pack(b'256s', bytes(ifname[:15], 'utf-8'))
    )[20:24])
    nm = nmap.PortScanner()
    nm.scan(ip_address, SAMPLE_PORTS)
    return nm[ip_address].state()
if __name__ == '__main__':
    parser = argparse.ArgumentParser(description='Python
                                     networking utils')
    parser.add_argument('--ifname', action="store", dest="ifname",
                        required=True)
    given_args = parser.parse_args()
    ifname = given_args.ifname
    print ("Interface [%s] is: %s" %(ifname, get_interface_status(ifname)))
```

If you run this script to inquire the status of the eth0 status, it will show something similar to the following output:

```
$ python 3_6_find_network_interface_status.py --ifname=lo
Interface [lo] is: up
```

How it works...

The recipe takes the interface's name from the command line and passes it to the `get_interface_status()` function. This function finds the IP address of that interface by manipulating a UDP `socket` object.

This recipe needs the Nmap third-party module. We can install that PyPI using the `pip install` command. The Nmap scanning instance, `nm`, has been created by calling `PortScanner()`. An initial scan to a local IP address gives us the status of the associated network interface.

Detecting inactive machines on your network

If you have been given a list of IP addresses of a few machines on your network and you are asked to write a script to find out which hosts are inactive periodically, you would want to create a network scanner type program without installing anything on the target host computers.

Getting ready

This recipe requires installing the `Scapy` library (> 2.2), which can be obtained at
`http://www.secdev.org/projects/scapy/files/scapy-latest.zip`.

At the time of writing, the default `Scapy` release works with Python 2, and does not support Python 3. You may download the `Scapy` for Python 3 from `https://pypi.python.org/pyp`
`i/scapy-python3/0.20`.

How to do it...

We can use `Scapy`, a mature network-analyzing, third-party library, to launch an ICMP scan. Since we would like to do it periodically, we need Python's `sched` module to schedule the scanning tasks.

Listing 3.7 shows us how to detect inactive machines, as follows:

```
#!/usr/bin/env python
# Python Network Programming Cookbook, Second Edition -- Chapter - 3
# This program is optimized for Python 2.7.12 and Python 3.5.2.
# It may run on any other version with/without modifications.
# Requires scapy-2.2.0 or higher for Python 2.7.
# Visit: http://www.secdev.org/projects/scapy/files/scapy-latest.zip
# As of now, requires a separate bundle for Python 3.x.
# Download it from: https://pypi.python.org/pypi/scapy-python3/0.20


import argparse
import time
import sched
from scapy.all import sr, srp, IP, UDP, ICMP, TCP, ARP, Ether

RUN_FREQUENCY = 10
```

```
    scheduler = sched.scheduler(time.time, time.sleep)


def detect_inactive_hosts(scan_hosts):
    """
    Scans the network to find scan_hosts are live or dead
    scan_hosts can be like 10.0.2.2-4 to cover range.
    See Scapy docs for specifying targets.
    """
    global scheduler
    scheduler.enter(RUN_FREQUENCY, 1, detect_inactive_hosts,
                    (scan_hosts, ))
    inactive_hosts = []
    try:
        ans, unans = sr(IP(dst=scan_hosts)/ICMP(), retry=0, timeout=1)
        ans.summary(lambda r : r.sprintf("%IP.src% is alive"))
        for inactive in unans:
            print ("%s is inactive" %inactive.dst)
            inactive_hosts.append(inactive.dst)
        print ("Total %d hosts are inactive" %(len(inactive_hosts)))
    except KeyboardInterrupt:
        exit(0)


if __name__ == "__main__":
    parser = argparse.ArgumentParser(description='Python
                                    networking utils')
    parser.add_argument('--scan-hosts', action="store",
    dest="scan_hosts", required=True)
    given_args = parser.parse_args()
    scan_hosts = given_args.scan_hosts
    scheduler.enter(1, 1, detect_inactive_hosts, (scan_hosts, ))
    scheduler.run()
```

The output of this script will be something like the following command:

```
$ sudo python 3_7_detect_inactive_machines.py --scan-hosts=10.0.2.2-4
Begin emission:
.*...Finished to send 3 packets.
.
Received 6 packets, got 1 answers, remaining 2 packets
10.0.2.2 is alive
10.0.2.4 is inactive
10.0.2.3 is inactive
Total 2 hosts are inactive
Begin emission:
*.Finished to send 3 packets.
Received 3 packets, got 1 answers, remaining 2 packets
```

```
10.0.2.2 is alive
10.0.2.4 is inactive
10.0.2.3 is inactive
Total 2 hosts are inactive
```

How it works...

The preceding script first takes a list of network hosts, `scan_hosts`, from the command line. It then creates a schedule to launch the `detect_inactive_hosts()` function after a one-second delay. The target function takes the `scan_hosts` argument and calls `Scapy` library's `sr()` function.

This function schedules itself to rerun after every 10 seconds by calling the `schedule.enter()` function once again. This way, we run this scanning task periodically.

The `Scapy` library's `sr()` scanning function takes an IP, protocol, and some scan-control information. In this case, the `IP()` method passes `scan_hosts` as the destination hosts to scan, and the protocol is specified as ICMP. This can also be TCP or UDP. We do not specify a retry and one-second timeout to run this script faster. However, you can experiment with the options that suit you.

The scanning `sr()` function returns the hosts that answer and those that don't as a tuple. We check the hosts that don't answer, build a list, and print that information.

Performing a basic IPC using connected sockets (socketpair)

Sometimes, two scripts need to communicate some information between themselves via two processes. In Unix/Linux, there's a concept of connected socket, of `socketpair`. We can experiment with this here.

Getting ready

This recipe is designed for a Unix/Linux host. Windows/macOS is not suitable for running this one.

How to do it...

We use a `test_socketpair()` function to wrap a few lines that test the socket's `socketpair()` function.

List 3.8 shows an example of `socketpair`, as follows:

```python
#!/usr/bin/env python
# Python Network Programming Cookbook, Second Edition -- Chapter - 3
# This program is optimized for Python 3.5.2.
# It may run on any other version with/without modifications.
# To make it run on Python 2.7.x, needs some changes due to API
differences.
# Follow the comments inline to make the program work with Python 2.

import socket
import os

BUFSIZE = 1024

def test_socketpair():
    """ Test Unix socketpair"""
    parent, child = socket.socketpair()
    pid = os.fork()
    try:
        if pid:
            print ("@Parent, sending message...")
            child.close()

            parent.sendall(bytes("Hello from parent!", 'utf-8'))
            # Comment out the above line and uncomment
              the below line for Python 2.7.
            # parent.sendall("Hello from parent!")

            response = parent.recv(BUFSIZE)
            print ("Response from child:", response)
            parent.close()
        else:
            print ("@Child, waiting for message from parent")
            parent.close()
            message = child.recv(BUFSIZE)
            print ("Message from parent:", message)

            child.sendall(bytes("Hello from child!!", 'utf-8'))
            # Comment out the above line and
              uncomment the below line for Python 2.7.
            # child.sendall("Hello from child!!")
```

```
            child.close()
    except Exception as err:
        print ("Error: %s" %err)


if __name__ == '__main__':
    test_socketpair()
```

The output from the preceding script is as follows:

```
$ python 3_8_ipc_using_socketpairs.py
@Parent, sending message...
@Child, waiting for message from parent
Message from parent: b'Hello from parent!'
Response from child: b'Hello from child!!'
```

How it works...

The `socket.socketpair()` function simply returns two connected `socket` objects. In our case, we can say that one is a parent and another is a child. We fork another process via a `os.fork()` call. This returns the process ID of the parent. In each process, the other process' socket is closed first and then a message is exchanged via a `sendall()` method call on the process's socket. The try-except block prints any error in case of any kind of exception.

Performing IPC using Unix domain sockets

Unix domain sockets (UDS) are sometimes used as a convenient way to communicate between two processes. As in Unix, everything is conceptually a file. If you need an example of such an IPC action, this can be useful.

How to do it...

We launch a UDS server that binds to a filesystem path, and a UDS client uses the same path to communicate with the server.

Listing 3.9a shows a Unix domain socket server, as follows:

```
#!/usr/bin/env python
# Python Network Programming Cookbook, Second Edition -- Chapter - 3
# This program is optimized for Python 2.7.12 and Python 3.5.2.
# It may run on any other version with/without modifications.
```

```python
import socket
import os
import time

SERVER_PATH = "/tmp/python_unix_socket_server"
def run_unix_domain_socket_server():
    if os.path.exists(SERVER_PATH):
        os.remove( SERVER_PATH )
    print ("starting unix domain socket server.")
    server = socket.socket( socket.AF_UNIX, socket.SOCK_DGRAM )
    server.bind(SERVER_PATH)
    print ("Listening on path: %s" %SERVER_PATH)
    while True:
        datagram = server.recv( 1024 )
        if not datagram:
            break
        else:
            print ("-" * 20)
            print (datagram)
        if "DONE" == datagram:
            break
    print ("-" * 20)
    print ("Server is shutting down now...")
    server.close()
    os.remove(SERVER_PATH)
    print ("Server shutdown and path removed.")

if __name__ == '__main__':
    run_unix_domain_socket_server()
```

Listing 3.9b shows a UDS client, as follows:

```python
#!/usr/bin/env python
# Python Network Programming Cookbook, Second Edition -- Chapter - 3
# This program is optimized for Python 3.5.2.
# It may run on any other version with/without modifications.
# To make it run on Python 2.7.x, needs some changes due to API
differences.
# Follow the comments inline to make the program work with Python 2.


import socket
import sys

SERVER_PATH = "/tmp/python_unix_socket_server"

def run_unix_domain_socket_client():
    """ Run "a Unix domain socket client """
```

```
    sock = socket.socket(socket.AF_UNIX, socket.SOCK_DGRAM)
    # Connect the socket to the path where the server is listening
    server_address = SERVER_PATH
    print ("connecting to %s" % server_address)
    try:
        sock.connect(server_address)
    except socket.error as msg:
        print (msg)
        sys.exit(1)
    try:
        message = "This is the message.  This will be echoed back!"
        print  ("Sending [%s]" %message)

        sock.sendall(bytes(message, 'utf-8'))
        # Comment out the above line and uncomment
            the below line for Python 2.7.
        # sock.sendall(message)

        amount_received = 0
        amount_expected = len(message)
        while amount_received < amount_expected:
            data = sock.recv(16)
            amount_received += len(data)
            print ("Received [%s]" % data)
    finally:
        print ("Closing client")
        sock.close()

if __name__ == '__main__':
    run_unix_domain_socket_client()
```

The server output is as follows:

```
$ python 3_9a_unix_domain_socket_server.py
starting unix domain socket server.
Listening on path: /tmp/python_unix_socket_server
--------------------
This is the message.  This will be echoed back!
```

The client output is as follows:

```
$ python 3_9b_unix_domain_socket_client.py
connecting to /tmp/python_unix_socket_server
Sending [This is the message.  This will be echoed back!]
```

How it works...

A common path is defined for a UDS client/server to interact. Both the client and server use the same path to connect and listen to.

In a server code, we remove the path if it exists from the previous run of this script. It then creates a Unix datagram socket and binds it to the specified path. It then listens for incoming connections. In the data processing loop, it uses the recv() method to get data from the client and prints that information on screen.

The client-side code simply opens a Unix datagram socket and connects to the shared server address. It sends a message to the server using sendall(). It then waits for the message to be echoed back to itself and prints that message.

Finding out if your Python supports IPv6 sockets

IP version 6 or IPv6 is increasingly adopted by the industry to build newer applications. In case you would like to write an IPv6 application, the first thing you'd like to know is if your machine supports IPv6. This can be done from the Linux/Unix command line, as follows:

```
$ cat /proc/net/if_inet6
00000000000000000000000000000001 01 80 10 80       lo
fe80000000000000642a57c2e51932a2 03 40 20 80     wlo1
```

From your Python script, you can also check if the IPv6 support is present on your machine, and Python is installed with that support.

Getting ready

For this recipe, use pip to install a Python third-party library, netifaces, as follows:

```
$ pip install netifaces
```

How to do it...

We can use a third-party library, `netifaces`, to find out if there is IPv6 support on your machine. We can call the `interfaces()` function from this library to list all interfaces present in the system.

Listing 3.10 shows the Python IPv6 support checker, as follows:

```python
#!/usr/bin/env python
# Python Network Programming Cookbook, Second Edition -- Chapter - 3
# This program is optimized for Python 2.7.12 and Python 3.5.2.
# It may run on any other version with/without modifications.
# This program depends on Python module netifaces => 0.8

import socket
import argparse
import netifaces as ni


def inspect_ipv6_support():
    """ Find the ipv6 address"""
    print ("IPV6 support built into Python: %s" %socket.has_ipv6)
    ipv6_addr = {}
    for interface in ni.interfaces():
        all_addresses = ni.ifaddresses(interface)
        print ("Interface %s:" %interface)

        for family,addrs in all_addresses.items():
            fam_name = ni.address_families[family]
            print ('  Address family: %s' % fam_name)
            for addr in addrs:
                if fam_name == 'AF_INET6':
                    ipv6_addr[interface] = addr['addr']
                print ('    Address  : %s' % addr['addr'])
                nmask = addr.get('netmask', None)
                if nmask:
                    print ('    Netmask  : %s' % nmask)
                bcast = addr.get('broadcast', None)
                if bcast:
                    print ('    Broadcast: %s' % bcast)
    if ipv6_addr:
        print ("Found IPv6 address: %s" %ipv6_addr)
    else:
        print ("No IPv6 interface found!")

if __name__ == '__main__':
    inspect_ipv6_support()
```

The output from this script will be as follows:

```
$ python 3_10_check_ipv6_support.py
IPV6 support built into Python: True
Interface lo:
  Address family: AF_PACKET
    Address  : 00:00:00:00:00:00
  Address family: AF_INET
    Address  : 127.0.0.1
    Netmask  : 255.0.0.0
  Address family: AF_INET6
    Address  : ::1
    Netmask  : ffff:ffff:ffff:ffff:ffff:ffff:ffff:ffff/128
Interface enp2s0:
  Address family: AF_PACKET
    Address  : 9c:5c:8e:26:a2:48
    Broadcast: ff:ff:ff:ff:ff:ff
  Address family: AF_INET
    Address  : 130.104.228.90
    Netmask  : 255.255.255.128
    Broadcast: 130.104.228.127
  Address family: AF_INET6
    Address  : 2001:6a8:308f:2:88bc:e3ec:ace4:3afb
    Netmask  : ffff:ffff:ffff:ffff::/64
    Address  : 2001:6a8:308f:2:5bef:e3e6:82f8:8cca
    Netmask  : ffff:ffff:ffff:ffff::/64
    Address  : fe80::66a0:7a3f:f8e9:8c03%enp2s0
    Netmask  : ffff:ffff:ffff:ffff::/64
Interface wlp1s0:
  Address family: AF_PACKET
    Address  : c8:ff:28:90:17:d1
    Broadcast: ff:ff:ff:ff:ff:ff
Found IPv6 address: {'lo': '::1', 'enp2s0':
'fe80::66a0:7a3f:f8e9:8c03%enp2s0'}
```

How it works...

The IPv6 support checker function, `inspect_ipv6_support()`, first checks if Python is built with IPv6 using `socket.has_ipv6`. Next, we call the `interfaces()` function from the `netifaces` module. This gives us the list of all interfaces. If we call the `ifaddresses()` method by passing a network interface to it, we can get all the IP addresses of this interface. We then extract various IP-related information, such as protocol family, address, netmask, and broadcast address. Then, the address of a network interface has been added to the `IPv6_address` dictionary if its protocol family matches `AF_INET6`.

Extracting an IPv6 prefix from an IPv6 address

In your IPv6 application, you need to dig out the IPv6 address for getting the prefix information. Note that the upper 64-bits of an IPv6 address are represented from a global routing prefix plus a subnet ID, as defined in RFC 3513. A general prefix (for example, /48) holds a short prefix based on which a number of longer, more specific prefixes (for example, /64) can be defined. A Python script can be very helpful in generating the prefix information.

How to do it...

We can use the netifaces and netaddr third-party libraries to find out the IPv6 prefix information for a given IPv6 address.

Make sure to have netifaces and netaddr installed in your system:

```
$ pip install netaddr
```

The program is as follows:

```python
#!/usr/bin/env python
# Python Network Programming Cookbook, Second Edition -- Chapter - 3
# This program is optimized for Python 2.7.12 and Python 3.5.2.
# It may run on any other version with/without modifications.
# This program depends on Python modules netifaces and netaddr.

import socket
import netifaces as ni
import netaddr as na

def extract_ipv6_info():
    """ Extracts IPv6 information"""
    print ("IPv6 support built into Python: %s" %socket.has_ipv6)
    for interface in ni.interfaces():
        all_addresses = ni.ifaddresses(interface)
        print ("Interface %s:" %interface)
        for family,addrs in all_addresses.items():
            fam_name = ni.address_families[family]

            for addr in addrs:
                if fam_name == 'AF_INET6':
                    addr = addr['addr']
                    has_eth_string = addr.split("%eth")
```

```
            if has_eth_string:
                addr = addr.split("%eth")[0]
            try:
                print ("    IP Address: %s"
                %na.IPNetwork(addr))
                print ("    IP Version: %s"
                %na.IPNetwork(addr).version)
                print ("    IP Prefix length: %s"
                %na.IPNetwork(addr).prefixlen)
                print ("    Network: %s"
                %na.IPNetwork(addr).network)
                print ("    Broadcast: %s"
                %na.IPNetwork(addr).broadcast)
            except Exception as e:
                print ("Skip Non-IPv6 Interface")


if __name__ == '__main__':
    extract_ipv6_info()
```

The output from this script is as follows:

```
$ python 3_11_extract_ipv6_prefix.py
IPv6 support built into Python: True
Interface lo:
    IP Address: ::1/128
    IP Version: 6
    IP Prefix length: 128
    Network: ::1
    Broadcast: ::1
Interface enp2s0:
    IP Address: 2001:6a8:308f:2:88bc:e3ec:ace4:3afb/128
    IP Version: 6
    IP Prefix length: 128
    Network: 2001:6a8:308f:2:88bc:e3ec:ace4:3afb
    Broadcast: 2001:6a8:308f:2:88bc:e3ec:ace4:3afb
    IP Address: 2001:6a8:308f:2:5bef:e3e6:82f8:8cca/128
    IP Version: 6
    IP Prefix length: 128
    Network: 2001:6a8:308f:2:5bef:e3e6:82f8:8cca
    Broadcast: 2001:6a8:308f:2:5bef:e3e6:82f8:8cca
Skip Non-IPv6 Interface
Interface wlp1s0:
```

How it works...

Python's `netifaces` module gives us the network interface IPv6 address. It uses the `interfaces()` and `ifaddresses()` functions for doing this. The `netaddr` module is particularly helpful to manipulate a network address. It has a `IPNetwork()` class that provides us with an address, IPv4 or IPv6, and computes the prefix, network, and broadcast addresses. Here, we find this information class instance's `version`, `prefixlen`, and `network` and `broadcast` attributes.

Writing an IPv6 echo client/server

You need to write an IPv6 compliant server or client and wonder what could be the differences between an IPv6 compliant server or client and its IPv4 counterpart.

How to do it...

We use the same approach as writing an echo client/server using IPv6. The only major difference is how the socket is created using IPv6 information.

Listing 12a shows an IPv6 echo server, as follows:

```python
#!/usr/bin/env python
# Python Network Programming Cookbook, Second Edition -- Chapter - 3
# This program is optimized for Python 2.7.12 and Python 3.5.2.
# It may run on any other version with/without modifications.

import argparse
import socket
import sys

HOST = 'localhost'

def echo_server(port, host=HOST):
    """Echo server using IPv6 """
    for result in socket.getaddrinfo(host, port, socket.AF_UNSPEC,
socket.SOCK_STREAM, 0, socket.AI_PASSIVE):
        af, socktype, proto, canonname, sa = result
        try:
            sock = socket.socket(af, socktype, proto)
        except socket.error as err:
            print ("Error: %s" %err)
        try:
```

```
                sock.bind(sa)
                sock.listen(1)
                print ("Server lisenting on %s:%s" %(host, port))
            except socket.error as msg:
                sock.close()
                continue
            break
            sys.exit(1)
        conn, addr = sock.accept()
        print ('Connected to', addr)
        while True:
            data = conn.recv(1024)
            print ("Received data from the client: [%s]" %data)
            if not data: break
            conn.send(data)
            print ("Sent data echoed back to the client: [%s]" %data)
        conn.close()


if __name__ == '__main__':
    parser = argparse.ArgumentParser(description='IPv6 Socket
            Server Example')
    parser.add_argument('--port', action="store", dest="port",
                        type=int, required=True)
    given_args = parser.parse_args()
    port = given_args.port
    echo_server(port)
```

Listing 12b shows an IPv6 echo client, as follows:

```
#!/usr/bin/env python
# Python Network Programming Cookbook, Second Edition -- Chapter - 3
# This program is optimized for Python 2.7.12 and Python 3.5.2.
# It may run on any other version with/without modifications.

import argparse
import socket
import sys

HOST = 'localhost'
BUFSIZE = 1024


def ipv6_echo_client(port, host=HOST):
    for res in socket.getaddrinfo(host, port, socket.AF_UNSPEC,
socket.SOCK_STREAM):
        af, socktype, proto, canonname, sa = res
        try:
            sock = socket.socket(af, socktype, proto)
        except socket.error as err:
```

```
                print ("Error:%s" %err)
            try:
                sock.connect(sa)
            except socket.error as msg:
                sock.close()
                continue
        if sock is None:
            print ('Failed to open socket!')
            sys.exit(1)
        msg = "Hello from ipv6 client"
        print ("Send data to server: %s" %msg)
        sock.send(bytes(msg.encode('utf-8')))
        while True:
            data = sock.recv(BUFSIZE)
            print ('Received from server', repr(data))
            if not data:
                break
        sock.close()

    if __name__ == '__main__':
        parser = argparse.ArgumentParser(description='IPv6 socket
                                        client example')
        parser.add_argument('--port', action="store", dest="port",
                            type=int, required=True)
        given_args = parser.parse_args()
        port = given_args.port
        ipv6_echo_client(port)
```

The server output is as follows:

```
$ python 3_12a_ipv6_echo_server.py --port=8800
Server lisenting on localhost:8800
('Connected to', ('127.0.0.1', 56958))
Received data from the client: [Hello from ipv6 client]
Sent data echoed back to the client: [Hello from ipv6 client]
```

The client output is as follows:

```
$ python 3_12b_ipv6_echo_client.py --port=8800
Send data to server: Hello from ipv6 client
('Received from server', "'Hello from ipv6 client'")
```

The following screenshot indicates the server and client output:

IPv6 Echo Server and Client

How it works...

The IPv6 echo server first determines its IPv6 information by calling
`socket.getaddrinfo()`. Notice that we passed the `AF_UNSPEC` protocol for creating a
TCP socket. The resulting information is a tuple of five values. We use three of them,
address family, socket type, and protocol, to create a server socket. Then, this socket is
bound with the socket address from the previous tuple. It then listens to the incoming
connections and accepts them. After a connection is made, it receives data from the client
and echoes it back.

On the client-side code, we create an IPv6-compliant client socket instance and send the
data using the `send()` method of that instance. When the data is echoed back, the `recv()`
method is used to get it back.

4
Programming with HTTP for the Internet

In this chapter, we will cover the following topics:

- Downloading data from an HTTP server
- Serving HTTP requests from your machine
- Extracting cookie information after visiting a website
- Submitting web forms
- Sending web requests through a proxy server
- Checking whether a web page exists with the HEAD request
- Spoofing Mozilla Firefox in your client code
- Saving bandwidth in web requests with the HTTP compression
- Writing an HTTP fail-over client with resume and partial downloading
- Writing a simple HTTPS server code with Python and OpenSSL
- Building asynchronous network applications with Twisted
- Building asynchronous network applications with Tornado
- Building concurrent applications with Tornado Future

Introduction

This chapter explains Python HTTP networking library functions with a few third-party libraries. For example, the `requests` library deals with the HTTP requests in a nicer and cleaner way. The `OpenSSL` library is used in one of the recipes to create an SSL-enabled web server.

Many common HTTP protocol features have been illustrated in a few recipes, for example, the web form submission with `POST`, manipulating header information, use of compression, and so on.

Downloading data from an HTTP server

You would like to write a simple HTTP client to fetch some data from any web server using the native HTTP protocol. This can be the very first steps towards creating your own HTTP browser.

How to do it...

Let us access `https://www.python.org/` with our *Pythonic minimal browser*.

You may need to install `urllib` module for the relevant Python versions:

```
$ sudo pip2 install urllib
```

Listing 4.1 explains the following code for a simple HTTP client:

```
#!/usr/bin/env python
# Python Network Programming Cookbook -- Chapter - 4
# This program requires Python 3.5.2 or any later version
# It may run on any other version with/without modifications.
#
# Follow the comments inline to make it run on Python 2.7.x.

import argparse

import urllib.request
# Comment out the above line and uncomment the below for Python 2.7.x.
#import urllib2

REMOTE_SERVER_HOST = 'http://www.cnn.com'
```

```
class HTTPClient:

    def __init__(self, host):
        self.host = host

    def fetch(self):
        response = urllib.request.urlopen(self.host)
        # Comment out the above line and uncomment the below for
          Python 2.7.x.
        #response = urllib2.urlopen(self.host)

        data = response.read()
        text = data.decode('utf-8')
        return text

if __name__ == "__main__":
    parser = argparse.ArgumentParser(description='HTTP Client Example')
    parser.add_argument('--host', action="store",
     dest="host",  default=REMOTE_SERVER_HOST)

    given_args = parser.parse_args()
    host = given_args.host
    client = HTTPClient(host)
    print (client.fetch())
```

This recipe will by default fetch a page from `http://www.cnn.com`. You can run this recipe with or without the `host` argument. You may choose to fetch any specific web page by passing the URL as an argument. If this script is executed, it will show the following output:

```
$  python 4_1_download_data.py --host=http://www.python.org
<!doctype html>
<!--[if lt IE 7]>    <html class="no-js ie6 lt-ie7 lt-ie8 lt-ie9">
<![endif]-->
<!--[if IE 7]>      <html class="no-js ie7 lt-ie8 lt-ie9">
<![endif]-->
<!--[if IE 8]>      <html class="no-js ie8 lt-ie9">
<![endif]-->
<!--[if gt IE 8]><!--><html class="no-js" lang="en" dir="ltr">  <!--
<![endif]-->

<head>
    <meta charset="utf-8">
    <meta http-equiv="X-UA-Compatible" content="IE=edge">

    <link rel="prefetch" href="//ajax.googleapis.com/ajax/libs/
                                jquery/1.8.2/jquery.min.js">

    <meta name="application-name" content="Python.org">
```

```
<meta name="msapplication-tooltip" content="The official
home of the Python Programming Language">
<meta name="apple-mobile-web-app-title" content="Python.org">
<meta name="apple-mobile-web-app-capable" content="yes">
<meta name="apple-mobile-web-app-status-bar-style" content="black">

<meta name="viewport" content="width=device-width, initial-scale=1.0">
<meta name="HandheldFriendly" content="True">
<meta name="format-detection" content="telephone=no">
<meta http-equiv="cleartype" content="on">
```

. . . .

The following is the screenshot of the program:

Download Data from an HTTP Server

This recipe will also work for any page in the sites. Not just the home page:

```
$ python 4_1_download_data.py --host=https://www.python.org/downloads/
<!doctype html>
<!--[if lt IE 7]>    <html class="no-js ie6 lt-ie7 lt-ie8 lt-ie9">
<![endif]-->
<!--[if IE 7]>       <html class="no-js ie7 lt-ie8 lt-ie9">
<![endif]-->
```

```
<!--[if IE 8]>          <html class="no-js ie8 lt-ie9">
<![endif]-->
<!--[if gt IE 8]><!--><html class="no-js" lang="en" dir="ltr">  <!--
<![endif]-->

. . .
    <title>Download Python | Python.org</title>
. . . .
```

If you run this recipe with an invalid path, it will show the following server response:

```
$ python 4_1_download_data.py --host=https://www.python.org/downloads222/
Traceback (most recent call last):
File "4_1_download_data.py", line 39, in <module>
print (client.fetch())
File "4_1_download_data.py", line 24, in fetch
response = urllib.request.urlopen(self.host)
File "/usr/lib/python3.5/urllib/request.py", line 163, in urlopen return
opener.open(url, data, timeout)
File "/usr/lib/python3.5/urllib/request.py", line 472, in open response =
meth(req, response)
File "/usr/lib/python3.5/urllib/request.py", line 582, in http_response
'http', request, response, code, msg, hdrs)
File "/usr/lib/python3.5/urllib/request.py", line 510, in error
return self._call_chain(*args)
File "/usr/lib/python3.5/urllib/request.py", line 444, in _call_chain
result = func(*args)
File "/usr/lib/python3.5/urllib/request.py", line 590, in
http_error_default
raise HTTPError(req.full_url, code, msg, hdrs, fp)
urllib.error.HTTPError: HTTP Error 404: OK
```

How it works...

This recipe defines an `urllib.request` module that fetches data from the remote host. `urllib.request.urlopen()` opens the given web page and fetches it. Since it comes with Python 3, it does not support Python 2. However, you may install and use `urllib` for Python 2 as we elaborated before.

Serving HTTP requests from your machine

You would like to create your own web server. Your web server should handle client requests and send a simple hello message.

How to do it...

Python ships with a very simple web server that can be launched from the command line as follows:

```
$ python -m SimpleHTTPServer 8080
```

This will launch an HTTP web server on port 8080. You can access this web server from your browser by typing http://localhost:8080. This will show the contents of the current directory from where you run the preceding command. If there is any web server index file, for example, index.html, inside that directory, your browser will show the contents of index.html. However, if you like to have full control over your web server, you need to launch your customized HTTP server.

Listing 4.2 gives the following code for the custom HTTP web server:

```python
#!/usr/bin/env python
# Python Network Programming Cookbook -- Chapter - 4
# This program requires Python 3.5.2 or any later version
# It may run on any other version with/without modifications.
#
# Follow the comments inline to make it run on Python 2.7.x.


import argparse
import sys

from http.server import BaseHTTPRequestHandler, HTTPServer
# Comment out the above line and uncomment the below for Python 2.7.x.
#from BaseHTTPServer import BaseHTTPRequestHandler, HTTPServer

DEFAULT_HOST = '127.0.0.1'
DEFAULT_PORT = 8800


class RequestHandler(BaseHTTPRequestHandler):
    """ Custom request handler"""
    def do_GET(self):
        """ Handler for the GET requests """
        self.send_response(200)
        self.send_header('Content-type','text/html')
        self.end_headers()
        # Send the message to browser
        self.wfile.write("Hello from server!")
        return

class CustomHTTPServer(HTTPServer):
```

```
        "A custom HTTP server"
        def __init__(self, host, port):
            server_address = (host, port)
            HTTPServer.__init__(self, server_address, RequestHandler)

    def run_server(port):
        try:
            server= CustomHTTPServer(DEFAULT_HOST, port)
            print ("Custom HTTP server started on port: %s" % port)
            server.serve_forever()
        except Exception as err:
            print ("Error:%s" %err)
        except KeyboardInterrupt:
            print ("Server interrupted and is shutting down...")
            server.socket.close()


    if __name__ == "__main__":
        parser = argparse.ArgumentParser(description='Simple HTTP Server
                Example')
        parser.add_argument('--port', action="store",
         dest="port", type=int, default=DEFAULT_PORT)
        given_args = parser.parse_args()
        port = given_args.port
        run_server(port)
```

The following screenshot shows a simple HTTP server:

Serving HTTP Request from the Machine

If you run this web server and access the URL from a browser, this will send the one line text **Hello from server!** to the browser, as follows:

```
$ python 4_2_simple_http_server.py --port=8800
Custom HTTP server started on port: 8800
localhost - - [18/Apr/2013 13:39:33] "GET / HTTP/1.1" 200 -
localhost - - [18/Apr/2013 13:39:33] "GET /favicon.ico HTTP/1.1" 200
```

How it works...

In this recipe, we created the `CustomHTTPServer` class inherited from the `HTTPServer` class. In the constructor method, the `CustomHTTPServer` class sets up the server address and port received as a user input. In the constructor, our web server's `RequestHandler` class has been set up. Every time a client is connected, the server handles the request according to this class.

The `RequestHandler` defines the action to handle the client's `GET` request. It sends an HTTP `header` (code `200`) with a success message Hello from server! using the `write()` method.

Extracting cookie information after visiting a website

Many websites use cookies to store their various information on to your local disk. You would like to see this cookie information and perhaps log in to that website automatically using cookies.

How to do it...

Let us try to pretend to log in to a popular code-sharing website, `https://bitbucket.org/`. We would like to submit the login information on the login page, `https://bitbucket.org/account/signin/?next=/`. The following screenshot shows the login page:

Log in to BitBucket

So, we note down the form element IDs and decide which fake values should be submitted. We access this page the first time, and the next time, we access the home page to observe what cookies have been set up.

Listing 4.3 explains extracting cookie information as follows:

```
#!/usr/bin/env python
# Python Network Programming Cookbook -- Chapter - 4
# This program requires Python 3.5.2 or any later version
# It may run on any other version with/without modifications.
#
# Follow the comments inline to make it run on Python 2.7.x.

import http.cookiejar
# Comment out the above line and uncomment the below for Python 2.7.x.
#import cookielib

import urllib

# Uncomment the below line for Python 2.7.x.
#import urllib2


ID_USERNAME = 'id_username'
ID_PASSWORD = 'id_password'
USERNAME = 'you@email.com'
PASSWORD = 'mypassword'
```

```
LOGIN_URL = 'https://bitbucket.org/account/signin/?next=/'
NORMAL_URL = 'https://bitbucket.org/'

def extract_cookie_info():
    """ Fake login to a site with cookie"""
    # setup cookie jar

    cj = http.cookiejar.CookieJar()
    # Comment out the above line and uncomment the below for Python 2.7.x.
    #cj = cookielib.CookieJar()

    login_data = urllib.parse.urlencode({ID_USERNAME : USERNAME,
                ID_PASSWORD : PASSWORD}).encode("utf-8")
    # Comment out the above line and uncomment the below for Python 2.7.x.
    #login_data = urllib.urlencode({ID_USERNAME : USERNAME,
                                    ID_PASSWORD : PASSWORD})

    # create url opener

    opener = urllib.request.
    build_opener(urllib.request.HTTPCookieProcessor(cj))
    # Comment out the above line and uncomment the below for Python 2.7.x.
    #opener = urllib2.build_opener(urllib2.HTTPCookieProcessor(cj))

    resp = opener.open(LOGIN_URL, login_data)

    # send login info
    for cookie in cj:
        print ("----First time cookie: %s --> %s"
          %(cookie.name, cookie.value))
    print ("Headers: %s" %resp.headers)

    # now access without any login info
    resp = opener.open(NORMAL_URL)
    for cookie in cj:
        print ("++++Second time cookie: %s --> %s"
                %(cookie.name, cookie.value))
    print ("Headers: %s" %resp.headers)

if __name__ == '__main__':
    extract_cookie_info()
```

Running this recipe results in the following output:

```
$ python 4_3_extract_cookie_information.py
----First time cookie: bb_session --> aed58dde1228571bf60466581790566d
Headers: Server: nginx/1.2.4
Date: Sun, 05 May 2013 15:13:56 GMT
```

```
Content-Type: text/html; charset=utf-8
Content-Length: 21167
Connection: close
X-Served-By: bitbucket04
Content-Language: en
X-Static-Version: c67fb01467cf
Expires: Sun, 05 May 2013 15:13:56 GMT
Vary: Accept-Language, Cookie
Last-Modified: Sun, 05 May 2013 15:13:56 GMT
X-Version: 14f9c66ad9db
ETag: "3ba81d9eb350c295a453b5ab6e88935e"
X-Request-Count: 310
Cache-Control: max-age=0
Set-Cookie: bb_session=aed58dde1228571bf60466581790566d; expires=Sun, 19-
May-2013 15:13:56 GMT; httponly; Max-Age=1209600; Path=/; secure
Strict-Transport-Security: max-age=2592000
X-Content-Type-Options: nosniff
++++Second time cookie: bb_session --> aed58dde1228571bf60466581790566d
Headers: Server: nginx/1.2.4
Date: Sun, 05 May 2013 15:13:57 GMT
Content-Type: text/html; charset=utf-8
Content-Length: 36787
Connection: close
X-Served-By: bitbucket02
Content-Language: en
X-Static-Version: c67fb01467cf
Vary: Accept-Language, Cookie
X-Version: 14f9c66ad9db
X-Request-Count: 97
Strict-Transport-Security: max-age=2592000
X-Content-Type-Options: nosniff
```

How it works...

We have used Python's cookielib and set up a CookieJar and cj. The login data has been encoded using urllib.urlencode. urllib2 has a build_opener() method, which takes the predefined CookieJar with an instance of HTTPCookieProcessor() and returns a URL opener. We call this opener twice: once for the login page and once for the home page of the website. It seems that only one cookie, bb_session, was set with the set-cookie directive present in the page header. More information about cookielib can be found on the official Python documentation site at http://docs.python.org/2/library/cookielib.html. Cookielib has been replaced by http.cookiejar in Python 3. You may find more information on this at https://docs.python.org/3/library/http.cookiejar.html.

Submitting web forms

During web browsing, we submit web forms many times in a day. Now, you would like do that using the Python code.

Getting ready

This recipe uses a third-party Python module called `requests`. You can install the compatible version of this module by following the instructions from `http://docs.python-requests.org/en/latest/user/install/`. For example, you can use `pip` to install requests from the command line as follows:

```
$ pip install requests
```

How to do it...

Let us submit some fake data to register with `https://twitter.com/`. Each form submission has two methods: `GET` and `POST`. The less sensitive data, for example, search queries, are usually submitted by `GET` and the more sensitive data is sent via the `POST` method. Let us try submitting data with both of them.

Listing 4.4 explains the submit web forms, as follows:

```python
#!/usr/bin/env python
# Python Network Programming Cookbook -- Chapter - 4
# This program requires Python 3.5.2 or any later version
# It may run on any other version with/without modifications.
#
# Follow the comments inline to make it run on Python 2.7.x.


import requests
import urllib

# Uncomment the below line for Python 2.7.x.
#import urllib2

ID_USERNAME = 'signup-user-name'
ID_EMAIL = 'signup-user-email'
ID_PASSWORD = 'signup-user-password'
USERNAME = 'username'
EMAIL = 'you@email.com'
PASSWORD = 'yourpassword'
```

```
SIGNUP_URL = 'https://twitter.com/account/create'


def submit_form():
    """Submit a form"""
    payload = {ID_USERNAME : USERNAME,
               ID_EMAIL    : EMAIL,
               ID_PASSWORD : PASSWORD,}
    # make a get request
    resp = requests.get(SIGNUP_URL)
    print ("Response to GET request: %s" %resp.content)
    # send POST request
    resp = requests.post(SIGNUP_URL, payload)
    print ("Headers from a POST request response: %s" %resp.headers)


if __name__ == '__main__':
    submit_form()
```

If you run this script, you will see the following output:

```
$ python 4_4_submit_web_form.py
Response to GET request: <?xml version="1.0" encoding="UTF-8"?>
    <hash>
      <error>This method requires a POST.</error>
      <request>/account/create</request>
    </hash>
Headers from a POST request response: {'status': '200 OK', 'content-
length': '21064', 'set-cookie': '_twitter_sess=BAh7CD--
d2865d40d1365eeb2175559dc5e6b99f64ea39ff; domain=.twitter.com;
path=/; HttpOnly', 'expires': 'Tue, 31 Mar 1981 05:00:00 GMT',
'vary': 'Accept-Encoding', 'last-modified': 'Sun, 05 May 2013
15:59:27 GMT', 'pragma': 'no-cache', 'date': 'Sun, 05 May 2013
15:59:27 GMT', 'x-xss-protection': '1; mode=block', 'x-transaction':
'a4b425eda23b5312', 'content-encoding': 'gzip', 'strict-transport-
security': 'max-age=631138519', 'server': 'tfe', 'x-mid':
'f7cde9a3f3d111310427116adc90bf3e8c95e868', 'x-runtime': '0.09969',
'etag': '"7af6f92a7f7b4d37a6454caa6094071d"', 'cache-control': 'no-
cache, no-store, must-revalidate, pre-check=0, post-check=0', 'x-
frame-options': 'SAMEORIGIN', 'content-type': 'text/html;
charset=utf-8'}
```

How it works...

This recipe uses a third-party module, requests. It has convenient wrapper methods, get() and post(), which do the URL encoding of data and submit forms properly.

In this recipe, we created a data payload with a USERNAME, PASSWORD, and EMAIL for creating the Twitter account. When we first submit the form with the GET method, the Twitter website returns an error saying that the page only supports POST. After we submit the data with POST, the page processes it. We can confirm this from the header data.

Sending web requests through a proxy server

You would like to browse web pages through a proxy. If you have configured your browser with a proxy server and that works, you can try this recipe. Otherwise, you can use any of the public proxy servers available on the internet.

Getting ready

You need to have access to a proxy server. You can find a free proxy server by searching on Google or on any other search engine. Here, for the sake of demonstration, we have used 165.24.10.8.

How to do it...

Let us send our HTTP request through a public domain proxy server.

Listing 4.5 explains proxying web requests across a proxy server as follows:

```
#!/usr/bin/env python
# Python Network Programming Cookbook -- Chapter - 4
# This program requires Python 3.5.2 or any later version
# It may run on any other version with/without modifications.
#
# Follow the comments inline to make it run on Python 2.7.x.

import urllib.request, urllib.parse, urllib.error
# Comment out the above line and uncomment the below for Python 2.7.x.
#import urllib
```

```
URL = 'https://www.github.com'
PROXY_ADDRESS = "165.24.10.8:8080" # By Googling free proxy server


if __name__ == '__main__':

    proxy = urllib.request.ProxyHandler({"http" : PROXY_ADDRESS})
    opener = urllib.request.build_opener(proxy)
    urllib.request.install_opener(opener)
    resp = urllib.request.urlopen(URL)
    # Comment out the above 4 lines and uncomment the below
        for Python 2.7.x.
    #resp = urllib.urlopen(URL, proxies = {"http" : PROXY_ADDRESS})

    print ("Proxy server returns response headers: %s " %resp.headers)
```

If you run this script, it will show the following output:

```
$ python 4_5_proxy_web_request.py
Proxy server returns response headers: Server: GitHub.com
Date: Thu, 22 Jun 2017 14:26:52 GMT
Content-Type: text/html; charset=utf-8
Transfer-Encoding: chunked
Connection: close
Status: 200 OK
Cache-Control: no-cache
Vary: X-PJAX
X-UA-Compatible: IE=Edge,chrome=1
Set-Cookie: logged_in=no; domain=.github.com; path=/; expires=Mon, 22 Jun
2037 14:26:52 -0000; secure; HttpOnly
Set-Cookie:
_gh_sess=eyJzZXNzaW9uX2lkIjoiNzNiODUwNjg1M2M1ZWQ3NjQxZmE2ODI5NTY5Y2UxNmUiLC
JsYXN0X3JlYWRfZnJvbV9yZXBsaWNhcyI6MTQ5ODE0MTYxMjA2NCwiX2NzcmZfdG9rZW4iOiJmd
1M1ME5oUGUyUU1hS0pVVQ29EZnlTL1Bab0pZOHM1Z1pBT2JoUUhYL1NRPSJ9-
-9db8c2d5bd3e75a1ec5250192094de38937398f8; path=/; secure; HttpOnly
X-Request-Id: 88704a9ed7378c7d930cdff660739693
X-Runtime: 0.033159
Content-Security-Policy: default-src 'none'; base-uri 'self'; block-all-
mixed-content; child-src render.githubusercontent.com; connect-src 'self'
uploads.github.com status.github.com collector.githubapp.com api.github.com
www.google-analytics.com github-cloud.s3.amazonaws.com github-production-
repository-file-5c1aeb.s3.amazonaws.com github-production-upload-manifest-
file-7fdce7.s3.amazonaws.com github-production-user-
asset-6210df.s3.amazonaws.com wss://live.github.com; font-src assets-
cdn.github.com; form-action 'self' github.com gist.github.com; frame-
ancestors 'none'; img-src 'self' data: assets-cdn.github.com
identicons.github.com collector.githubapp.com github-cloud.s3.amazonaws.com
*.githubusercontent.com; media-src 'none'; script-src assets-
```

```
cdn.github.com; style-src 'unsafe-inline' assets-cdn.github.com
Strict-Transport-Security: max-age=31536000; includeSubdomains; preload
Public-Key-Pins: max-age=5184000; pin-
sha256="WoiWRyIOVNa9ihaBciRSC7XHjliYS9VwUGOIud4PB18="; pin-
sha256="RRM1dGqnDFsCJXBTHky16vilobOlCgFFn/yOhI/y+ho="; pin-
sha256="k2v657xBsOVe1PQRwOsHsw3bsGT2VzIqz5K+59sNQws="; pin-
sha256="K87oWBWM9UZfyddvDfoxL+81pNyoUB2ptGtn0fv6G2Q="; pin-
sha256="IQBnNBEiFuhj+8x6X8XLgh01V9Ic5/V3IRQLNFFc7v4="; pin-
sha256="iie1VXtL7HzAMF+/PVPR9xzT80kQxdZeJ+zduCB3uj0="; pin-
sha256="LvRiGEjRqfzurezaWuj8Wie2gyHMrW5Q06LspMnox7A="; includeSubDomains
X-Content-Type-Options: nosniff
X-Frame-Options: deny
X-XSS-Protection: 1; mode=block
X-Runtime-rack: 0.036536
Vary: Accept-Encoding
X-Served-By: 29885c8097c6d503a86029451b2e021c
X-GitHub-Request-Id: 9144:282AF:FE7E37:17F7695:594BD3AB
```

How it works...

This is a short recipe where we access the social code-sharing site, `https://www.github.com`, with a public proxy server found on Google search. The proxy address argument has been passed to the `urlopen()` method of `urllib`. We print the HTTP `header` of the response to show that the proxy settings work here.

Checking whether a web page exists with the HEAD request

You would like to check the existence of a web page without downloading the HTML content. This means that we need to send a get `HEAD` request with a browser client. According to Wikipedia, the `HEAD` request asks for the response identical to the one that would correspond to a `GET` request, but without the response body. This is useful for retrieving meta-information written in response headers, without having to transport the entire content.

How to do it...

We would like to send a HEAD request to http://www.python.org. This will not download the content of the home page, rather it checks whether the server returns one of the valid responses, for example, OK, FOUND, MOVED PERMANENTLY, and so on.

Listing 4.6 explains checking a web page with the HEAD request as follows:

```
#!/usr/bin/env python
# Python Network Programming Cookbook -- Chapter - 4
# This program requires Python 3.5.2 or any later version
# It may run on any other version with/without modifications.
#
# Follow the comments inline to make it run on Python 2.7.x.

import argparse

import http.client
# Comment out the above line and uncomment the below for Python 2.7.x.
#import httplib

import urllib.parse
# Comment out the above line and uncomment the below for Python 2.7.x.
#import urlparse

import re
import urllib.request, urllib.error
# Comment out the above line and uncomment the below for Python 2.7.x.
#import urllib

DEFAULT_URL = 'http://www.python.org'

HTTP_GOOD_CODES =  [http.client.OK, http.client.FOUND,
http.client.MOVED_PERMANENTLY]
# Comment out the above line and uncomment the below for Python 2.7.x.
#HTTP_GOOD_CODES =  [httplib.OK, httplib.FOUND, httplib.MOVED_PERMANENTLY]

def get_server_status_code(url):
    """
    Download just the header of a URL and
    return the server's status code.
    """
    host, path = urllib.parse.urlparse(url)[1:3]
    # Comment out the above line and uncomment the below for Python 2.7.x.
    #host, path = urlparse.urlparse(url)[1:3]
    try:
        conn = http.client.HTTPConnection(host)
```

```
        # Comment out the above line and uncomment the below for
            Python 2.7.x.
        #conn = httplib.HTTPConnection(host)

        conn.request('HEAD', path)
        return conn.getresponse().status

    except Exception as e:
        print ("Server: %s status is: %s " %(url, e))
        # Comment out the above line and uncomment the below for
            Python 2.7.x.
        #except StandardError:
        return None
if __name__ == '__main__':
    parser = argparse.ArgumentParser(description='Example HEAD Request')
    parser.add_argument('--url', action="store", dest="url",
                        default=DEFAULT_URL)
    given_args = parser.parse_args()
    url = given_args.url
    if get_server_status_code(url) in HTTP_GOOD_CODES:
        print ("Server: %s status is OK: %s "
                %(url, get_server_status_code(url)))
    else:
        print ("Server: %s status is NOT OK: %s"
                %(url, get_server_status_code(url)))
```

Executing this script shows the success or error if the page is found by the HEAD request as follows:

```
$ python 4_6_checking_webpage_with_HEAD_request.py
Server: http://www.python.org status is OK.
$ python 4_6_checking_webpage_with_HEAD_request.py --url=http://www.cnn.com
Server: http://www.cnn.com status is OK.
$ python3 4_6_checking_webpage_with_HEAD_request.py --
url=http://www.zytho.org
Server: http://www.zytho.org status is: [Errno -2] Name or service not
known
Server: http://www.zytho.org status is: [Errno -2] Name or service not
known
Server: http://www.zytho.org status is NOT OK: None
```

How it works...

We used the `HTTPConnection()` method of `httplib`, which can make a `HEAD` request to a server. We can specify the path if necessary. Here, the `HTTPConnection()` method checks the home page or path of `http://www.python.org`. However, if the URL is not correct, it can't find the return response inside the accepted list of return codes.

Spoofing Mozilla Firefox in your client code

From your Python code, you would like to pretend to the web server that you are browsing from Mozilla Firefox.

How to do it...

You can send the custom `user-agent` values in the HTTP request `header`.

Listing 4.7 explains spoofing Mozilla Firefox in your client code as follows:

```python
#!/usr/bin/env python
# Python Network Programming Cookbook -- Chapter - 4
# This program requires Python 3.5.2 or any later version
# It may run on any other version with/without modifications.
#
# Follow the comments inline to make it run on Python 2.7.x.

import urllib.request, urllib.error, urllib.parse
# Comment out the above line and uncomment the below for Python 2.7.x.
#import urllib2

BROWSER = 'Mozilla/5.0 (Windows NT 5.1; rv:20.0) Gecko/20100101
Firefox/20.0'
URL = 'http://www.python.org'

def spoof_firefox():

    opener = urllib.request.build_opener()
    # Comment out the above line and uncomment the below for Python 2.7.x.
    #opener = urllib2.build_opener()

    opener.addheaders = [('User-agent', BROWSER)]
    result = opener.open(URL)
    print ("Response headers:")
```

```
    for header in  result.headers:
    # Comment out the above line and uncomment the below for Python 2.7.x.
    #for header in  result.headers.headers:
        print ("%s: %s" %(header, result.headers.get(header)))
        # Comment out the above line and uncomment the below for
            Python 2.7.x.
        #print (header)
if __name__ == '__main__':
    spoof_firefox()
```

If you execute this script, you will see the following output:

```
$ python 4_7_spoof_mozilla_firefox_in_client_code.py
Response headers:
Server: nginx
Content-Type: text/html; charset=utf-8
X-Frame-Options: SAMEORIGIN
X-Clacks-Overhead: GNU Terry Pratchett
Content-Length: 47755
Accept-Ranges: bytes
Date: Thu, 22 Jun 2017 15:38:39 GMT
Via: 1.1 varnish
Age: 834
Connection: close
X-Served-By: cache-ams4150-AMS
X-Cache: HIT
X-Cache-Hits: 1
X-Timer: S1498145920.740508,VS0,VE2
Vary: Cookie
Strict-Transport-Security: max-age=63072000; includeSubDomains
```

How it works...

We used the `build_opener()` method of `urllib2` to create our custom browser whose user-agent string has been set up as `Mozilla/5.0 (Windows NT 5.1; rv:20.0) Gecko/20100101 Firefox/20.0)`.

Saving bandwidth in web requests with the HTTP compression

You would like to give your web server users better performance in downloading web pages. By compressing HTTP data, you can speed up the serving of web contents.

How to do it...

Let us create a web server that serves contents after compressing it to the `gzip` format.

Listing 4.8 explains the HTTP compression as follows:

```python
#!/usr/bin/env python
# Python Network Programming Cookbook -- Chapter - 4
# This program requires Python 3.5.2 or any later version
# It may run on any other version with/without modifications.
#
# Follow the comments inline to make it run on Python 2.7.x.

import argparse
import string
import os
import sys
import gzip

import io
# Comment out the above line and uncomment the below for Python 2.7.x.
#import cStringIO

from http.server import BaseHTTPRequestHandler, HTTPServer
# Comment out the above line and uncomment the below for Python 2.7.x.
#from BaseHTTPServer import BaseHTTPRequestHandler, HTTPServer

DEFAULT_HOST = '127.0.0.1'
DEFAULT_PORT = 8800

HTML_CONTENT = b"""<html><body><h1>Compressed Hello
World!</h1></body></html>"""
# Comment out the above line and uncomment the below for Python 2.7.x.
#HTML_CONTENT = b"""<html><body><h1>Compressed Hello
World!</h1></body></html>"""

class RequestHandler(BaseHTTPRequestHandler):
    """ Custom request handler"""
    def do_GET(self):
        """ Handler for the GET requests """
        self.send_response(200)
        self.send_header('Content-type','text/html')
        self.send_header('Content-Encoding','gzip')
        zbuf = self.compress_buffer(HTML_CONTENT)
        sys.stdout.write("Content-Encoding: gzip\r\n")
        self.send_header('Content-Length',len(zbuf))
        self.end_headers()
        # Send the message to browser
```

```
        zbuf = self.compress_buffer(HTML_CONTENT)
        sys.stdout.write("Content-Encoding: gzip\r\n")
        sys.stdout.write("Content-Length: %d\r\n" % (len(zbuf)))
        sys.stdout.write("\r\n")

        self.wfile.write(zbuf)

        return
    def compress_buffer(self, buf):

        zbuf = io.BytesIO()
        # Comment out the above line and uncomment the below for
            Python 2.7.x.
        #zbuf = cStringIO.StringIO()

        zfile = gzip.GzipFile(mode = 'wb',
        fileobj = zbuf, compresslevel = 6)
        zfile.write(buf)
        zfile.close()
        return zbuf.getvalue()

if __name__ == '__main__':
    parser = argparse.ArgumentParser(description='Simple HTTP
     Server Example')
    parser.add_argument('--port', action="store",
     dest="port", type=int, default=DEFAULT_PORT)
    given_args = parser.parse_args()
    port = given_args.port
    server_address =  (DEFAULT_HOST, port)
    server = HTTPServer(server_address, RequestHandler)
    server.serve_forever()
```

You can execute this script and see the **Compressed Hello World!** text (as a result of the HTTP compression) on your browser screen when accessing http://localhost:8800 as follows:

```
$ python 4_8_http_compression.py
localhost - - [22/Feb/2014 12:01:26] "GET / HTTP/1.1" 200 -
Content-Encoding: gzip
Content-Encoding: gzip
Content-Length: 71
localhost - - [22/Feb/2014 12:01:26] "GET /favicon.ico HTTP/1.1" 200 -
Content-Encoding: gzip
Content-Encoding: gzip
Content-Length: 71
```

The following screenshot illustrates serving compressed content by a web server:

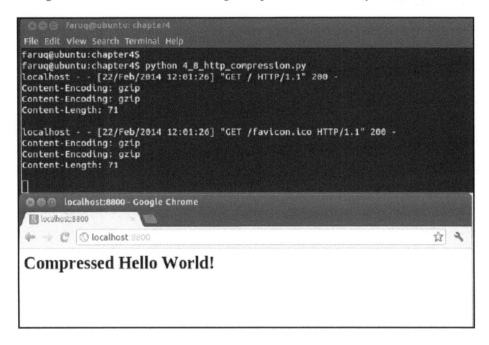

Compressed Content in a Web Server

How it works...

We created a web server by instantiating the HTTPServer class from the BaseHTTPServer module. We attached a custom request handler to this server instance, which compresses every client response using a compress_buffer() method. A predefined HTML content has been supplied to the clients.

Writing an HTTP fail-over client with resume and partial downloading

You would like to create a fail-over client that will resume downloading a file if it fails for any reason in the first instance.

How to do it...

Let us download the Python 2.7 code from `http://www.python.org`. A `resume_download()` file will resume any unfinished download of that file.

Listing 4.9 explains resume downloading as follows:

```python
#!/usr/bin/env python
# Python Network Programming Cookbook -- Chapter - 4
# This program requires Python 3.5.2 or any later version
# It may run on any other version with/without modifications.
#
# Follow the comments inline to make it run on Python 2.7.x.

import urllib.request, urllib.parse, urllib.error
# Comment out the above line and uncomment the below for Python 2.7.x.
#import urllib

import os

TARGET_URL = 'http://python.org/ftp/python/2.7.4/'
TARGET_FILE = 'Python-2.7.4.tgz'

class CustomURLOpener(urllib.request.FancyURLopener):
# Comment out the above line and uncomment the below for Python 2.7.x.
#class CustomURLOpener(urllib.FancyURLopener):
    """Override FancyURLopener to skip error 206 (when a
       partial file is being sent)
    """
    def http_error_206(self, url, fp, errcode, errmsg, headers, data=None):
        pass

def resume_download():
    file_exists = False
    CustomURLClass = CustomURLOpener()
    if os.path.exists(TARGET_FILE):
        out_file = open(TARGET_FILE,"ab")
        file_exists = os.path.getsize(TARGET_FILE)
        #If the file exists, then only download the unfinished part
        CustomURLClass.addheader("range","bytes=%s-" % (file_exists))
    else:
        out_file = open(TARGET_FILE,"wb")

    web_page = CustomURLClass.open(TARGET_URL + TARGET_FILE)

    #Check if last download was OK
    if int(web_page.headers['Content-Length']) == file_exists:
        loop = 0
```

```
            print ("File already downloaded!")

    byte_count = 0
    while True:
            data = web_page.read(8192)
            if not data:
                    break
            out_file.write(data)
            byte_count = byte_count + len(data)

    web_page.close()
    out_file.close()

    for k,v in list(web_page.headers.items()):
      # Comment out the above line and uncomment the below for Python 2.7.x.
    #for k,v in web_page.headers.items():
            print (k, "=",v)
    print ("File copied", byte_count, "bytes from", web_page.url)

if __name__ == '__main__':
    resume_download()
```

Executing this script will result in the following output:

```
$   python 4_9_http_fail_over_client.py
content-length = 14489063
content-encoding = x-gzip
accept-ranges = bytes
connection = close
server = Apache/2.2.16 (Debian)
last-modified = Sat, 06 Apr 2013 14:16:10 GMT
content-range = bytes 0-14489062/14489063
etag = "1748016-dd15e7-4d9b1d8685e80"
date = Tue, 07 May 2013 12:51:31 GMT
content-type = application/x-tar
File copied 14489063 bytes from
http://python.org/ftp/python/2.7.4/Python-2.7.4.tgz
```

How it works...

In this recipe, we created a CustomURLOpener class inheriting from the FancyURLopener method of urllib, but http_error_206() is overridden where partial content is downloaded. So, our method checks the existence of the target file and if it is not present, it tries to download with the custom URL opener class.

Writing a simple HTTPS server code with Python and OpenSSL

You need a secure web server code written in Python. You already have your SSL keys and certificate files ready with you.

Getting ready

You need to install the third-party Python module, pyOpenSSL. This can be grabbed from PyPI (https://pypi.python.org/pypi/pyOpenSSL). Both on Windows and Linux hosts, you may need to install some additional packages, which are documented at http://pytho nhosted.org//pyOpenSSL/.

How to do it...

After placing a certificate file on the current working folder, we can create a web server that makes use of this certificate to serve encrypted content to the clients.

Listing 4.10 explains the code for a secure HTTP server as follows:

```
#!/usr/bin/env python
# Python Network Programming Cookbook -- Chapter - 4
# This program requires Python 3.5.2 or any later version
# It may run on any other version with/without modifications.
#
# Follow the comments inline to make it run on Python 2.7.x.
# Requires pyOpenSSL and SSL packages installed

import socket, os
from OpenSSL import SSL

from socketserver import BaseServer
from http.server import HTTPServer
from http.server import SimpleHTTPRequestHandler
# Comment out the above 3 lines and uncomment the below 3 lines for Python
2.7.x.
#from SocketServer import BaseServer
#from BaseHTTPServer import HTTPServer
#from SimpleHTTPServer import SimpleHTTPRequestHandler


class SecureHTTPServer(HTTPServer):
```

```
    def __init__(self, server_address, HandlerClass):
        BaseServer.__init__(self, server_address, HandlerClass)
        ctx = SSL.Context(SSL.SSLv23_METHOD)
        fpem = 'server.pem' # location of the server private
            key and the server certificate
        ctx.use_privatekey_file (fpem)
        ctx.use_certificate_file(fpem)
        self.socket = SSL.Connection(ctx,
        socket.socket(self.address_family, self.socket_type))
        self.server_bind()
        self.server_activate()


class SecureHTTPRequestHandler(SimpleHTTPRequestHandler):
    def setup(self):
        self.connection = self.request
        self.rfile = socket._fileobject(self.request, "rb", self.rbufsize)
        self.wfile = socket._fileobject(self.request, "wb", self.wbufsize)


def run_server(HandlerClass = SecureHTTPRequestHandler,
        ServerClass = SecureHTTPServer):
    server_address = ('', 4443) # port needs to be accessible by user
    server = ServerClass(server_address, HandlerClass)
    running_address = server.socket.getsockname()
    print ("Serving HTTPS Server on %s:%s ..." % (running_address[0],
     running_address[1]))
    server.serve_forever()


if __name__ == '__main__':
    run_server()
```

If you execute this script, it will result in the following output:

```
$ python 4_10_https_server.py
Serving HTTPS Server on 0.0.0.0:4443 ...
```

How it works...

If you notice the previous recipes that create the web server, there is not much difference in terms of the basic procedure. The main difference is in applying the SSL Context() method with the SSLv23_METHOD argument. We have created the SSL socket with the pyOpenSSL third-party module's Connection() class. This class takes this context object along with the address family and socket type.

The server's certificate file is kept in the current directory, and this has been applied with the context object. Finally, the server has been activated with the `server_activate()` method.

Building asynchronous network applications with Twisted

Twisted is an event-driven network engine written in Python. Twisted can be used to develop asynchronous and publish/subscribe based Python applications.

Getting ready

You need to install the third-party Python module, `twisted`. This can be grabbed from PyPI (`https://pypi.org/project/Twisted/`). Both on Windows and Linux hosts, you may need to install some additional packages. The installation procedure is documented at `http s://twistedmatrix.com/trac/`.

Follow the following guidelines to install Twisted in your Debian/Ubuntu based Linux distributions.

Twisted suggests against installing anything into global site-package. It recommends using `virtualenv` to set up isolated publish/subscribe modules. `virtualenv` is a product aimed to create isolated execution environments for Python. While we can indeed make Twisted work by directly installing the bundles using `pip`, we respect the suggestion of Twisted, and follow their installation guidelines for this recipe. Read more on this at `https://hynek .me/articles/virtualenv-lives/`.

You may install `virtualenv` by the following, in Ubuntu:

```
$ sudo apt install virtualenv
```

Now you are ready to initialize the execution environment with Twisted, by following this command:

```
$ virtualenv try-twisted
```

The preceding command uses the current directory to set up the Python test environment under the subdirectory `try-twisted`. You may activate/initialize the environment as indicated here:

```
$ . try-twisted/bin/activate
$ sudo pip install twisted[tls]
```

Once you have installed Twisted (following the preceding instructions or otherwise), you will be able to build asynchronous network applications. To make sure you have installed Twisted successfully, you may execute the following:

```
$ twist --help
Usage: twist [options] plugin [plugin_options]
Options:
      --reactor=      The name of the reactor to use. (options: "asyncio",
"kqueue", "glib2", "win32", "iocp", "default", "cf", "epoll", "gtk2",
"poll", "gtk3", "gi", "wx", "select")
  ..
Commands:
    conch           A Conch SSH service.
    ftp             An FTP server.
    manhole         An interactive remote debugger service accessible via
telnet and ssh and providing syntax coloring and basic line editing
functionality.
    web             A general-purpose web server which can serve from a
filesystem or application resource.
```

How to do it...

We will build a publish-subscribe paradigm based server-client system in this recipe. In this simple application, all the clients are subscribed to all the messages sent by the other clients. This can be configured further to alter the client or server behavior.

Listing 4.11 explains the code for a publish/subscribe server as follows:

```python
#!/usr/bin/env python
# Python Network Programming Cookbook, Second Edition -- Chapter - 3
# This program is optimized for Python 2.7.12 and Python 3.5.2.
# It may run on any other version with/without modifications.

import argparse
from twisted.internet import reactor, protocol, endpoints
from twisted.protocols import basic

class PubProtocol(basic.LineReceiver):
    def __init__(self, factory):
```

```
            self.factory = factory

    def connectionMade(self):
        self.factory.clients.add(self)

    def connectionLost(self, reason):
        self.factory.clients.remove(self)

    def lineReceived(self, line):
        for c in self.factory.clients:
            source = u"<{}>
".format(self.transport.getHost()).encode("ascii")
            c.sendLine(source + line)

class PubFactory(protocol.Factory):
    def __init__(self):
        self.clients = set()

    def buildProtocol(self, addr):
        return PubProtocol(self)


if __name__ == '__main__':
    parser = argparse.ArgumentParser(description='Socket Server
    Example with Epoll')
    parser.add_argument('--port', action="store", dest="port",
    type=int, required=True)
    given_args = parser.parse_args()
    port = given_args.port
    endpoints.serverFromString(reactor,
      "tcp:%s" %port).listen(PubFactory())
    reactor.run()
```

Run the following script to start the server in the specified port:

```
$ python 4_11_twisted_async_server.py --port=9999
```

Now, start two or more telnet clients to the same port. Type something from one of those telnet instances, and you will be able to see the same message echoed from all the client (telnet) instances:

```
Sending telnet client:
$ telnet localhost 9999
Trying 127.0.0.1...
Connected to localhost.
Escape character is '^]'.
zszz
<IPv4Address(TCP, '127.0.0.1', 9999)> zszz
```

```
Receiving telnet client:
$ telnet localhost 9999
Trying 127.0.0.1...
Connected to localhost.
Escape character is '^]'.
<IPv4Address(TCP, '127.0.0.1', 9999)> zszz
```

The following screenshot indicates the outputs of the environment: publish/subscribe server along with four telnet clients subscribed to the messages sent to the server by other instances:

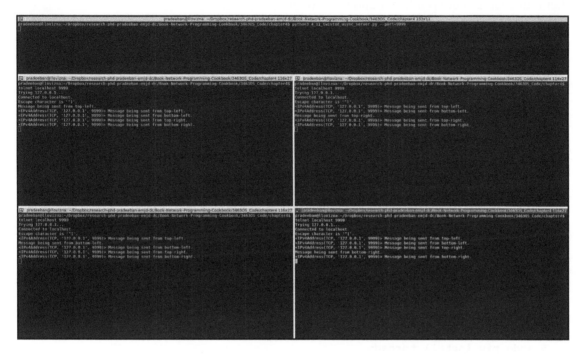

Pub/Sub Server and Telnet Clients

How it works...

Twisted is developed as an asynchronous service development bundle, developed for Python 2. Currently it has also been ported to Python 3.

The system has a server that listens to the messages published to it. The server functions as a broker in the publish/subscribe paradigm. Any of the clients that send messages to the server (in this example, a telnet client), functions as the publisher. All the other instances function as the subscriber. As all the instances in this example listen to each other, each of them function as both publisher and subscriber.

You may use various options and commands of the `twisted` module to achieve various tasks such as SSH and FTP servers effectively.

Building asynchronous network applications with Tornado

Developed in Python, Tornado is a highly-scalable framework to build asynchronous network applications. In this recipe, we will build a simple asynchronous application using Tornado.

Getting ready

Tornado is a web framework that can be considered an alternative to Twisted. In order to execute this recipe, first you need to install Tornado in your computer, which can be done by the following command in Linux environments:

```
$ sudo pip install tornado
```

How to do it...

We will build an asynchronous application to illustrate the functionality of Tornado. In this example, `AsyncHttpClient` of Tornado has been used.

Listing 4.12 explains the code for a simple network application using Tornado:

```python
#!/usr/bin/env python
# Python Network Programming Cookbook, Second Edition -- Chapter - 3
# This program is optimized for Python 2.7.12 and Python 3.5.2.
# It may run on any other version with/without modifications.

import argparse
import tornado.ioloop
import tornado.httpclient


class TornadoAsync():
    def handle_request(self, response):
        if response.error:
            print ("Error:", response.error)
        else:
            print (response.body)
        tornado.ioloop.IOLoop.instance().stop()

def run_server(url):
    tornadoAsync = TornadoAsync()
    http_client = tornado.httpclient.AsyncHTTPClient()
    http_client.fetch(url, tornadoAsync.handle_request)
    tornado.ioloop.IOLoop.instance().start()

if __name__ == '__main__':
    parser = argparse.ArgumentParser(description='Async Server Example')
    parser.add_argument('--url', action="store", dest="url",
     type=str, required=True)
    given_args = parser.parse_args()
    url = given_args.url
    run_server(url)
```

Execute the following script to start the asynchronous application to fetch any web page. We will use it to fetch `http://www.axn.com/` as follows:

```
$ python 4_12_tornado_async_server.py --url="http://www.axn.com/"
```

The following screenshot indicates the output of the execution:

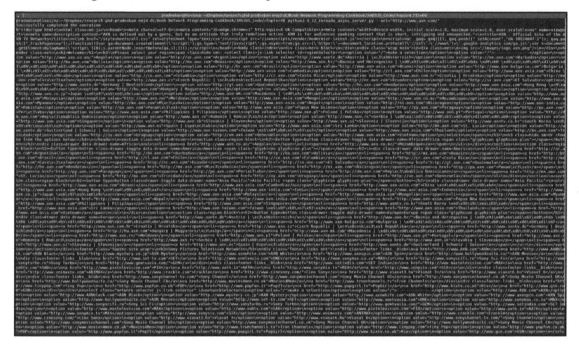

Fetching axn.com Asynchronously

How it works...

Tornado is a framework to build asynchronous network applications. It is developed for Python 2 and Python 3. In the preceding example, `http_client` is an object of the `AsyncHTTPClient` class of Tornado. As it is developed in a non-blocking manner, the execution does not wait until the application to finish fetching the website. It returns even before the method returns the output.

On the other hand, if it was developed as a synchronous blocking manner using the `HTTPClient` class of Tornado, the application will wait for the method to complete before proceeding further.

Building concurrent applications with Tornado Future

Tornado **Future** construct allows us to develop non-blocking and asynchronous calls in a more efficient way. In this recipe, we will develop a simple asynchronous application based on Tornado Future constructs.

 To learn more about the concurrent and asynchronous applications in Tornado with Future, please visit: `http://www.tornadoweb.org/en/stab le/concurrent.html`.

Getting ready

Tornado is a web framework. In order to execute this recipe, first you need to install Tornado in your computer, which can be done by using the following command in Linux environments:

```
$ sudo pip install tornado
```

How to do it...

We will build a concurrent application to illustrate the functionality of Tornado. In this example, the `tornado.concurrent` module of Tornado has been used.

Listing 4.13 explains the code for a simple concurrent application using Tornado:

```python
#!/usr/bin/env python
# Python Network Programming Cookbook, Second Edition -- Chapter - 3
# This program is optimized for Python 3.5.2.
# It may run on any other version with/without modifications.

import argparse
import time
import datetime

import tornado.httpserver
import tornado.ioloop
import tornado.options
import tornado.web

from tornado import gen
```

```
from tornado.concurrent import return_future

class AsyncUser(object):
    @return_future
    def req1(self, callback=None):
        time.sleep(0.1)
        result = datetime.datetime.utcnow()
        callback(result)

    @return_future
    def req2(self, callback=None):
        time.sleep(0.2)
        result = datetime.datetime.utcnow()
        callback(result)


class Application(tornado.web.Application):
    def __init__(self):
        handlers = [
            (r"/", UserHandler),
        ]
        tornado.web.Application.__init__(self, handlers)


class UserHandler(tornado.web.RequestHandler):
    @gen.coroutine
    def get(self):
        user = AsyncUser()
        response1 = yield (user.req1())
        response2 = yield (user.req2())
        print ("response1,2: %s %s" %(response1, response2))
        self.finish()

def main(port):
    http_server = tornado.httpserver.HTTPServer(Application())
    print("Server listening at Port: ", port)
    http_server.listen(port)
    tornado.ioloop.IOLoop.instance().start()


if __name__ == "__main__":
    parser = argparse.ArgumentParser(description='Async Server Example')
    parser.add_argument('--port', action="store",
     dest="port", type=int, required=True)
    given_args = parser.parse_args()
    port = given_args.port
    main(port)
```

Execute the following script to start the concurrent application:

```
$ python 4_13_tornado_conc_future.py --port=3333
```

The following screenshot indicates the output of the execution:

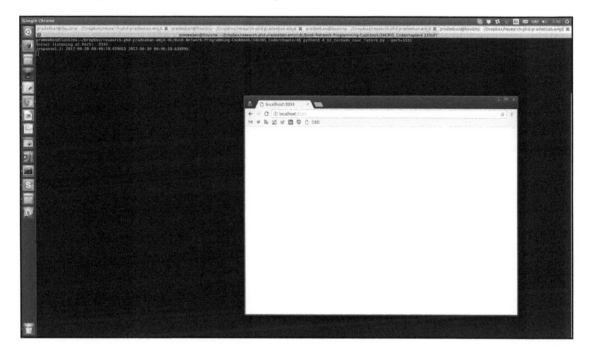

Execution of the Concurrent Application

How it works...

The concurrent.futures package is a concurrent programming pattern offered by Python. It consists of the future class, which is useful in building concurrent applications in a concise manner.

In the preceding example, req1 and req2 represent sample concurrent methods. In place of a workload, we have included small code fraction that waits for a time interval and returns the current time. Either a callback is given to retrieve the execution outcome in a non-blocking manner, or the Future will wait for the function to complete if yield is used (as illustrated by this recipe).

By leveraging the methods and constructs of concurrent.future efficiently, we can build concurrent and non-blocking applications.

5
Email Protocols, FTP, and CGI Programming

In this chapter, we will cover the following recipes:

- Listing the files in a remote FTP server
- Uploading a local file to a remote FTP server
- Emailing your current working directory as a compressed ZIP file
- Downloading your Google email with POP3
- Checking your remote email with IMAP
- Sending an email with an attachment via the Gmail SMTP server
- Writing a guest book for your (Python-based) web server with CGI
- Finding the mail server from an email address
- Writing a simple SMTP server
- Writing a secure SMTP client using TLS
- Writing a simple POP3 client

Introduction

This chapter explores the FTP, email, and CGI communications protocol with a Python recipe. Using Python, you can easily code simple FTP actions such as a file download and upload.

There are some interesting recipes in this chapter, such as manipulating your Google email, also known as the Gmail account, from your Python script. You can use these recipes to check, download, and send emails with IMAP, POP3, and SMTP protocols. In another recipe, a web server with CGI also demonstrates the basic CGI action, such as writing a guest comment form in your web application.

Listing the files in a remote FTP server

You would like to list the files available on the official Linux kernel's FTP site, `ftp.kernel.org`. You can select any other FTP site to try this recipe.

Getting ready

If you work on a production/enterprise FTP site with a user account, you need a username and password. However, in this instance, you don't need a username (and password) with the anonymous FTP server at the University of Edinburgh as you can log in anonymously.

How to do it...

We can use the `ftplib` library to fetch files from our selected FTP site. A detailed documentation of this library can be found at `https://docs.python.org/3/library/ftplib.html` for Python 3 and at `http://docs.python.org/2/library/ftplib.html` for Python 2.

`ftplib` is a built-in Python module, and you do not need to install it separately. Let us see how we can fetch some files with `ftplib`.

Listing 5.1 gives a simple FTP connection test as follows:

```
#!/usr/bin/env python
# Python Network Programming Cookbook, Second Edition -- Chapter - 5
# This program is optimized for Python 2.7.12 and Python 3.5.2.
# It may run on any other version with/without modifications.


FTP_SERVER_URL = 'ftp.ed.ac.uk'

import ftplib
from ftplib import FTP
```

```
def test_ftp_connection(path, username, email):
    #Open ftp connection
    ftp = ftplib.FTP(path, username, email)
    #List the files in the /pub directory
    ftp.cwd("/pub")
    print ("File list at %s:" %path)
    files = ftp.dir()
    print (files)

    ftp.quit()

if __name__ == '__main__':
    test_ftp_connection(path=FTP_SERVER_URL, username='anonymous',
                        email='nobody@nourl.com',
                        )
```

This recipe will list the files and folders present in the FTP path, ftp.kernel.org/pub. If you run this script, you can see the following output:

```
$ python 5_1_list_files_on_ftp_server.py
File list at ftp.ed.ac.uk:
drwxr-xr-x    4 1005      bin           4096 Oct 11  1999 EMWAC
drwxr-xr-x   13 31763     netserv       4096 May  5  2010 EdLAN
drwxrwxr-x    4 6267      6268          4096 Oct 11  1999 ITFMP
drwxr-xr-x    4 1407      bin           4096 Oct 11  1999 JIPS
drwxr-xr-x    2 root      bin           4096 Oct 11  1999 Mac
drwxr-xr-x    2 10420     7525          4096 Oct  7  2003 PaedTBI
drwxr-xr-x    2 jaw       bin           4096 Oct 11  1999 Printing
drwxr-xr-x    3 root      bin           4096 Oct 11  1999 Student_Societies
drwxr-xr-x    6 root      bin           4096 Feb 19  2014 Unix
drwxr-xr-x    2 root      bin           4096 Oct 11  2016 Unix1
drwxr-xr-x    2 1109      bin           4096 Oct 19  2016 Unix2
drwxr-xr-x    2 2022      bin           4096 Oct 11  1999 X.400
drwxr-xr-x    2 20076     bin           4096 Feb 17  2000 atoz
drwxr-xr-x    2 1403      bin           4096 Aug  9  2001 bill
drwxr-xr-x    2 4414      bin           4096 Oct 11  1999 cartonet
drwxr-xr-x    2 1115      bin           4096 Oct 11  1999 courses
drwxr-xr-x    2 10498     bin           4096 Oct 11  1999 esit04
drwxr-xr-x    2 6314      bin           4096 Oct 11  1999 flp
drwxr-xr-x    2 1400      bin           4096 Nov 19  1999 george
drwxr-xr-x    3 309643    root          4096 Sep 10  2008 geos
drwxr-xr-x    2 1663      root          4096 Apr 23  2013 hssweb
drwxr-xr-x    2 6251      bin           4096 Oct 11  1999 ierm
drwxr-xr-x    2 2126      bin           4096 Nov 12  2004 jbm
drwxr-xr-x    2 1115      bin           4096 Oct 11  1999 kusch
drwxr-xr-x    2 root      bin           4096 Oct 11  1999 lrtt
drwxr-xr-x    7 scott     bin           4096 Nov  9  2015 mail
drwxr-xr-x    3 1407      bin           4096 Oct 11  1999 maps
```

```
drwxr-xr-x   2 2009    bin      4096 Oct 11  1999 mmaccess
drwxr-xr-x   2 2009    bin      4096 Oct 11  1999 mmsurvey
drwx--x--x   3 1943    bin      4096 Dec  1  2000 mww
drwxr-xr-x   2 root    bin      4096 Oct 11  1999 pbowers
drwxr-xr-x   5 7324    bin      4096 Oct 11  1999 rip99
drwxr-xr-x  11 2223    bin      4096 Sep 30  2011 soroti
drwxr-xr-x   2 root    bin      4096 Oct  6  2000 steve
drwxr-xr-x   2 2000    bin      4096 Oct 11  1999 ucsg
drwxr-xr-x   7 20099   bin      4096 Jul 28  2003 unixhelp
drwxr-xr-x   2 root    bin      4096 Oct 11  1999 utopia
drwxr-xr-x   2 2022    bin      4096 Oct 11  1999 whiteosi
None
```

How it works...

This recipe uses `ftplib` to create an FTP client session with `ftp.kernel.org`. The `test_ftp_connection()` function takes the FTP `path`, `username`, and `email` address for connecting to the FTP server.

An FTP client session can be created by calling the `FTP()` function of `ftplib` with the preceding connection's credentials. This returns a client handle, which then can be used to run the usual FTP commands, such as the command to change the working directory or `cwd()`. The `dir()` method returns the directory listing.

It is a good idea to quit the FTP session by calling `ftp.quit()`.

Common error

If you encounter the following error when you run the program, check whether you still can access the `FTP_SERVER_URL`, by pinging to it:

```
Traceback (most recent call last):
  File "5_1_list_files_on_ftp_server.py", line 25, in <module>
    email='nobody@nourl.com',
  File "5_1_list_files_on_ftp_server.py", line 13, in test_ftp_connection
    ftp = ftplib.FTP(path, username, email)
  File "/usr/lib/python3.5/ftplib.py", line 118, in __init__
    self.connect(host)
  File "/usr/lib/python3.5/ftplib.py", line 153, in connect
    source_address=self.source_address)
  File "/usr/lib/python3.5/socket.py", line 693, in create_connection
    for res in getaddrinfo(host, port, 0, SOCK_STREAM):
  File "/usr/lib/python3.5/socket.py", line 732, in getaddrinfo
    for res in _socket.getaddrinfo(host, port, family, type, proto, flags):
```

```
socket.gaierror: [Errno -2] Name or service not known
```

Usually, the preceding error means the FTP does not exist anymore, or is not open any more with the anonymous access.

If so, replace the URL with another FTP address that allows anonymous access.

You may verify that the FTP address is valid by trying to open it through your FTP client:

```
$ ftp
ftp> open ftp.ed.ac.uk
Connected to luther.is.ed.ac.uk.
```

Give anonymous and your email address as the username and password when prompted. The outcome is depicted in the following screenshot:

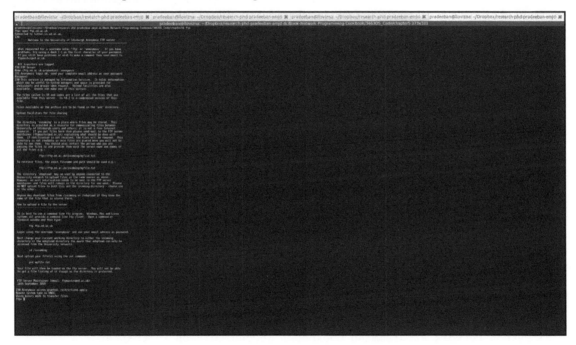

Accessing the FTP Server

Uploading a local file to a remote FTP server

You would like to upload a file to an FTP server.

Getting ready

Let us set up a local FTP server. In Unix/Linux, you can install **VSFTPD** (**Very Secure File Transfer Protocol Daemon**) FTP Server using the following command:

```
$ sudo apt-get install vsftpd
```

On a Windows machine, you can install the FileZilla FTP server, which can be downloaded from `https://filezilla-project.org/download.php?type=server`. FileZilla can also be installed in Linux. For example, in Debian-based Linux distributions such as Ubuntu:

```
$ sudo apt-get install filezilla
```

You should create an FTP user account following the FTP server package's user manual.

You would also like to upload a file to an FTP server. You can specify the server address, login credentials, and filename as the input argument of your script. You should create a local file called `readme.txt` with any text in it.

How to do it...

Using the following script, let's set up a local FTP server. Once you have installed the FTP Server such as VSFTPD or FileZilla, you can upload a file to the logged-in user's `home` directory. You can specify the server address, login credentials, and filename as the input argument of your script.

Listing 5.2 gives the FTP upload example as follows:

```python
#!/usr/bin/env python
# Python Network Programming Cookbook, Second Edition -- Chapter - 5
# This program is optimized for Python 2.7.12 and Python 3.5.2.
# It may run on any other version with/without modifications.

import os
import argparse
import ftplib
import getpass

LOCAL_FTP_SERVER = 'localhost'
```

```
LOCAL_FILE = 'readme.txt'

def ftp_upload(ftp_server, username, password, file_name):
    print ("Connecting to FTP server: %s" %ftp_server)
    ftp = ftplib.FTP(ftp_server)
    print ("Login to FTP server: user=%s" %username)
    ftp.login(username, password)
    ext = os.path.splitext(file_name)[1]
    if ext in (".txt", ".htm", ".html"):
        ftp.storlines("STOR " + file_name, open(file_name))
    else:
        ftp.storbinary("STOR " + file_name, open(file_name, "rb"), 1024)
    print ("Uploaded file: %s" %file_name)


if __name__ == '__main__':
    parser = argparse.ArgumentParser(description='FTP Server Upload
Example')
    parser.add_argument('--ftp-server', action="store",
    dest="ftp_server", default=LOCAL_FTP_SERVER)
    parser.add_argument('--file-name', action="store",
    dest="file_name", default=LOCAL_FILE)
    parser.add_argument('--username', action="store",
    dest="username", default=getpass.getuser())
    given_args = parser.parse_args()
    ftp_server, file_name, username = given_args.ftp_server,
     given_args.file_name, given_args.username
    password = getpass.getpass(prompt="Enter you FTP password: ")
    ftp_upload(ftp_server, username, password, file_name)
```

If you set up a local FTP server and run the following script, this script will log in to the FTP server and then will upload a file. If a filename argument is not supplied from the command line by default, it will upload the readme.txt file:

```
$ python 5_2_upload_file_to_ftp_server.py
Enter your FTP password:
Connecting to FTP server: localhost
Login to FTP server: user=faruq
Uploaded file: readme.txt
$ cat /home/faruq/readme.txt
This file describes what to do with the .bz2 files you see elsewhere on
this site (ftp.kernel.org).
```

How it works...

In this recipe, we assume that a local FTP server is running. Alternatively, you can connect to a remote FTP server. The `ftp_upload()` method uses the `FTP()` function of Python's `ftplib` to create an FTP connection object. With the `login()` method, it logs in to the server.

After a successful login, the `ftp` object sends the STOR command with either the `storlines()` or `storbinary()` method. The first method is used for sending ASCII text files such as HTML or text files. The latter method is used for binary data such as zipped archive.

It's a good idea to wrap these FTP methods with try-catch error-handling blocks, which is not shown here for the sake of brevity.

Emailing your current working directory as a compressed ZIP file

It might be interesting to send the current working directory contents as a compressed ZIP archive. You can use this recipe to quickly share your files with your friends.

Getting ready

If you don't have any mail server installed on your machine, you need to install a local mail server such as **Postfix**. On a Debian/Ubuntu system, this can be installed with default settings using `apt-get`, as shown in the following command:

```
$ sudo apt-get install postfix
```

How to do it...

Let us first compress the current directory and then create an email message. We can send the email message via an external SMTP host, or we can use a local email server to do this. Like other recipes, let us get the sender and recipient information from parsing the command-line inputs.

Listing 5.3 shows how to convert an `email` folder into a compressed ZIP file as follows:

```python
#!/usr/bin/env python
# Python Network Programming Cookbook, Second Edition -- Chapter - 5
# This program is optimized for Python 2.7.12 and Python 3.5.2.
# It may run on any other version with/without modifications.

import os
import argparse
import smtplib
import zipfile
import tempfile
from email import encoders
from email.mime.base import MIMEBase
from email.mime.multipart import MIMEMultipart

def email_dir_zipped(sender, recipient):
    zf = tempfile.TemporaryFile(prefix='mail', suffix='.zip')
    zip = zipfile.ZipFile(zf, 'w')
    print ("Zipping current dir: %s" %os.getcwd())
    for file_name in os.listdir(os.getcwd()):
        zip.write(file_name)
    zip.close()
    zf.seek(0)

    # Create the message
    print ("Creating email message...")
    email_msg = MIMEMultipart()
    email_msg['Subject'] = 'File from path %s' %os.getcwd()
    email_msg['To'] = ', '.join(recipient)
    email_msg['From'] = sender
    email_msg.preamble = 'Testing email from Python.\n'
    msg = MIMEBase('application', 'zip')
    msg.set_payload(zf.read())
    encoders.encode_base64(msg)
    msg.add_header('Content-Disposition', 'attachment',
                   filename=os.getcwd()[-1] + '.zip')
    email_msg.attach(msg)
    email_msg = email_msg.as_string()

    # send the message
    print ("Sending email message...")
    try:
        smtp = smtplib.SMTP('localhost')
        smtp.set_debuglevel(1)
        smtp.sendmail(sender, recipient, email_msg)
    except Exception as e:
        print ("Error: %s" %str(e))
```

```
        finally:
            smtp.close()

    if __name__ == '__main__':
        parser = argparse.ArgumentParser(description='Email Example')
        parser.add_argument('--sender', action="store",
        dest="sender", default='you@you.com')
        parser.add_argument('--recipient', action="store",
        dest="recipient")
        given_args = parser.parse_args()
        email_dir_zipped(given_args.sender, given_args.recipient)
```

Running this recipe shows the following output. The extra output is shown because we enabled the email debug level:

```
$ python 5_3_email_current_dir_zipped.py --recipient=faruq@localhost
Zipping current dir: /home/faruq/Dropbox/PacktPub/pynet-
cookbook/pynetcookbook_code/chapter5
Creating email message...
Sending email message...
send: 'ehlo [127.0.0.1]\r\n'
reply: '250-debian6.debian2013.com\r\n'
reply: '250-PIPELINING\r\n'
reply: '250-SIZE 10240000\r\n'
reply: '250-VRFY\r\n'
reply: '250-ETRN\r\n'
reply: '250-STARTTLS\r\n'
reply: '250-ENHANCEDSTATUSCODES\r\n'
reply: '250-8BITMIME\r\n'
reply: '250 DSN\r\n'
reply: retcode (250); Msg: debian6.debian2013.com
PIPELINING
SIZE 10240000
VRFY
ETRN
STARTTLS
ENHANCEDSTATUSCODES
8BITMIME
DSN
send: 'mail FROM:<you@you.com> size=9141\r\n'
reply: '250 2.1.0 Ok\r\n'
reply: retcode (250); Msg: 2.1.0 Ok
send: 'rcpt TO:<faruq@localhost>\r\n'
reply: '250 2.1.5 Ok\r\n'
reply: retcode (250); Msg: 2.1.5 Ok
send: 'data\r\n'
reply: '354 End data with <CR><LF>.<CR><LF>\r\n'
reply: retcode (354); Msg: End data with <CR><LF>.<CR><LF>
```

```
data: (354, 'End data with <CR><LF>.<CR><LF>')
send: 'Content-Type: multipart/mixed;
boundary="================0388489101==...[TRUNCATED]
reply: '250 2.0.0 Ok: queued as 42D2F34A996\r\n'
reply: retcode (250); Msg: 2.0.0 Ok: queued as 42D2F34A996
data: (250, '2.0.0 Ok: queued as 42D2F34A996')
```

How it works...

We have used Python's `zipfile`, `smtplib`, and an `email` module to achieve our objective of emailing a folder as a zipped archive. This is done using the `email_dir_zipped()` method. This method takes two arguments: the sender and recipient's email addresses to create the email message.

In order to create a ZIP archive, we create a temporary file with the `tempfile` module's `TemporaryFile()` class. We supply a `filename`, `prefix`, `mail`, and `suffix`, `.zip`. Then, we initialize the ZIP archive object with the `ZipFile()` class by passing the temporary file as its argument. Later, we add files of the current directory with the ZIP object's `write()` method call.

To send an email, we create a multipart MIME message with the `MIMEmultipart()` class from the `email.mime.multipart` module. Like our usual email message, the subject, recipient, and sender information is added in the `email` header.

We create the email attachment with the `MIMEBase()` method. Here, we first specify the application/ZIP header and call `set_payload()` on this message object. Then, in order to encode the message correctly, the `encode_base64()` method from encoder's module is used. It is also helpful to use the `add_header()` method to construct the attachment header. Now, our attachment is ready to be included in the main email message with an `attach()` method call.

Sending an email requires you to call the `SMTP()` class instance of `smtplib`. There is a `sendmail()` method that will utilize the routine provided by the OS to actually send the email message correctly. Its details are hidden under the hood. However, you can see a detailed interaction by enabling the debug option as shown in this recipe.

See also

Further information about the Python libraries can be found at:
`http://docs.python.org/3/library/smtplib.html` for Python 3 and
`http://docs.python.org/2/library/smtplib.html` for Python 2.

Downloading your Google email with POP3

You would like to download your Google (or virtually any other email provider's) email via the POP3 protocol.

Getting ready

To run this recipe, you should have an email account with Google or any other service provider.

How to do it...

Here, we attempt to download the first email message from a user's Google email account. The username is supplied from a command line, but the password is kept secret and not passed from the command line. This is rather entered while the script is running and kept hidden from display.

Listing 5.4 shows how to download our Google email via POP3 as follows:

```python
#!/usr/bin/env python
# Python Network Programming Cookbook, Second Edition -- Chapter - 5
# This program is optimized for Python 2.7.12 and Python 3.5.2.
# It may run on any other version with/without modifications.

import argparse
import getpass
import poplib

GOOGLE_POP3_SERVER = 'pop.googlemail.com'

def download_email(username):
    mailbox = poplib.POP3_SSL(GOOGLE_POP3_SERVER, '995')
    mailbox.user(username)
    password = getpass.getpass(prompt="Enter your Google password: ")
    mailbox.pass_(password)
```

```
num_messages = len(mailbox.list()[1])
print ("Total emails: %s" %num_messages)
print ("Getting last message")
for msg in mailbox.retr(num_messages)[1]:
    print (msg)
mailbox.quit()

if __name__ == '__main__':
    parser = argparse.ArgumentParser(description='Email Download Example')
    parser.add_argument('--username', action="store",
    dest="username", default=getpass.getuser())
    given_args = parser.parse_args()
    username = given_args.username
    download_email(username)
```

If you run this script, you will see an output similar to the following one. The message is truncated for the sake of privacy:

```
$ python 5_4_download_google_email_via_pop3.py --username=<USERNAME>
Enter your Google password:
Total emails: 333
Getting last message
...[TRUNCATED]
```

How it works...

This recipe downloads a user's first Google message via POP3. The `download_email()` method creates a mailbox object with Python, the `POP3_SSL()` class of `poplib`. We passed the Google POP3 server and port address to the class constructor. The mailbox object then sets up a user account with the `user()` method call. The password is collected from the user securely using the `getpass` module's `getpass()` method and then passed to the `mailbox` object. The mailbox's `list()` method gives us the email messages as a Python list.

This script first displays the number of email messages stored in the mailbox and retrieves the first message with the `retr()` method call. Finally, it's safe to call the `quit()` method on the mailbox to clean up the connection.

Checking your remote email with IMAP

Instead of using POP3, you can also use IMAP to retrieve the email message from your Google account. In this case, the message won't be deleted after retrieval.

Getting ready

To run this recipe, you should have an email account with Google or any other service provider.

How to do it...

Let us connect to your Google email account and read the first email message. If you don't delete it, the first email message would be the welcome message from Google.

Listing 5.5 shows us how to check Google email with IMAP as follows:

```
#!/usr/bin/env python
# Python Network Programming Cookbook, Second Edition -- Chapter - 5
# This program is optimized for Python 2.7.12 and Python 3.5.2.
# It may run on any other version with/without modifications.

import argparse
import getpass
import imaplib

GOOGLE_IMAP_SERVER = 'imap.googlemail.com'

def check_email(username):
    mailbox = imaplib.IMAP4_SSL(GOOGLE_IMAP_SERVER, '993')
    password = getpass.getpass(prompt="Enter your Google password: ")
    mailbox.login(username, password)
    mailbox.select('Inbox')
    typ, data = mailbox.search(None, 'ALL')
    for num in data[0].split():
        typ, data = mailbox.fetch(num, '(RFC822)')
        print ('Message %s\n%s\n' % (num, data[0][1]))
        break
    mailbox.close()
    mailbox.logout()

if __name__ == '__main__':
    parser = argparse.ArgumentParser(description='Email Download Example')
    parser.add_argument('--username', action="store",
    dest="username", default=getpass.getuser())
    given_args = parser.parse_args()
    username = given_args.username
    check_email(username)
```

If you run this script, this will show the following output. In order to remove the private part of the data, we truncated some user data:

```
$ python 5_5_check_remote_email_via_imap.py --username=<USER_NAME>
Enter your Google password:
Message 1
Received: by 10.140.142.16; Sat, 17 Nov 2007 09:26:31 -0800 (PST)
Message-ID: <...>@mail.gmail.com>
Date: Sat, 17 Nov 2007 09:26:31 -0800
From: "Gmail Team" <mail-noreply@google.com>
To: "<User Full Name>" <USER_NAME>@gmail.com>
Subject: Gmail is different. Here's what you need to know.
MIME-Version: 1.0
Content-Type: multipart/alternative;
    boundary="----=_Part_7453_30339499.1195320391988"
------=_Part_7453_30339499.1195320391988
Content-Type: text/plain; charset=ISO-8859-1
Content-Transfer-Encoding: 7bit
Content-Disposition: inline
Messages that are easy to find, an inbox that organizes itself, great
spam-fighting tools and built-in chat. Sound cool? Welcome to Gmail.
To get started, you may want to:
[TRUNCATED]
```

How it works...

The preceding script takes a Google username from the command line and calls the check_email() function. This function creates an IMAP mailbox with the IMAP4_SSL() class of imaplib, which is initialized with Google's IMAP server and default port.

Then, this function logs in to the mailbox with a password, which is captured by the getpass() method of the getpass module. The inbox folder is selected by calling the select() method on the mailbox object.

The mailbox object has many useful methods. Two of them are search() and fetch() that are used to get the first email message. Finally, it's safer to call the close() and logout() method on the mailbox object to end the IMAP connection.

Sending an email with an attachment via Gmail SMTP server

You would like to send an email message from your Google email account to another account. You also need to attach a file with this message.

Getting ready

To run this recipe, you should have an email account with Google or any other service provider.

How to do it...

We can create an email message and attach Python's `python-logo.gif` file with the email message. Then, this message is sent from a Google account to a different account.

Listing 4.6 shows us how to send an email from your Google account:

```python
#!/usr/bin/env python
# Python Network Programming Cookbook, Second Edition -- Chapter - 5
# This program is optimized for Python 2.7.12 and Python 3.5.2.
# It may run on any other version with/without modifications.

import argparse
import os
import getpass
import re
import sys
import smtplib
from email.mime.image import MIMEImage
from email.mime.multipart import MIMEMultipart
from email.mime.text import MIMEText
SMTP_SERVER = 'smtp.gmail.com'
SMTP_PORT = 587
def send_email(sender, recipient):
    """ Send email message """
    msg = MIMEMultipart()
    msg['Subject'] = 'Python Emaill Test'
    msg['To'] = recipient
    msg['From'] = sender
    subject = 'Python email Test'
    message = 'Images attached.'
```

```
    # attach imgae files
    files = os.listdir(os.getcwd())
    gifsearch = re.compile(".gif", re.IGNORECASE)
    files = filter(gifsearch.search, files)
    for filename in files:
        path = os.path.join(os.getcwd(), filename)
        if not os.path.isfile(path):
            continue
        img = MIMEImage(open(path, 'rb').read(), _subtype="gif")
        img.add_header('Content-Disposition', 'attachment',
        filename=filename)
        msg.attach(img)
    part = MIMEText('text', "plain")
    part.set_payload(message)
    msg.attach(part)
    # create smtp session
    session = smtplib.SMTP(SMTP_SERVER, SMTP_PORT)
    session.ehlo()
    session.starttls()
    session.ehlo
    password = getpass.getpass(prompt="Enter your Google password: ")
    session.login(sender, password)
    session.sendmail(sender, recipient, msg.as_string())
    print ("Email sent.")
    session.quit()
if __name__ == '__main__':
    parser = argparse.ArgumentParser(description='Email Sending Example')
    parser.add_argument('--sender', action="store", dest="sender")
    parser.add_argument('--recipient', action="store", dest="recipient")
    given_args = parser.parse_args()
    send_email(given_args.sender, given_args.recipient)
```

Running the following script outputs the success of sending an email to any email address if you provide your Google account details correctly. After running this script, you can check your recipient email account to verify that the email is actually sent:

```
$ python 5_6_send_email_from_gmail.py --sender=<USERNAME>@gmail.com -
recipient=<USER>@<ANOTHER_COMPANY.com>
Enter you Google password:
Email sent.
```

How it works...

In this recipe, an email message is created in the send_email() function. This function is supplied with a Google account from where the email message will be sent. The message header object, msg, is created by calling the MIMEMultipart() class and then subject, recipient, and sender information is added on it.

Python's regular expression-handling module is used to filter the .gif image on the current path. The image attachment object, img, is then created with the MIMEImage() method from the email.mime.image module. A correct image header is added to this object and finally, the image is attached with the msg object created earlier. We can attach multiple image files within a for loop as shown in this recipe. We can also attach a plain text attachment in a similar way.

To send the email message, we create an SMTP session. We call some testing method on this session object, such as ehlo() or starttls(). Then, log in to the Google SMTP server with a username and password and a sendmail() method is called to send the email.

Writing a guestbook for your (Python-based) web server with CGI

Common Gateway Interface (**CGI**) is a standard in web programming by which custom scripts can be used to produce web server output. You would like to catch the HTML form input from a user's browser, redirect it to another page, and acknowledge a user action.

Getting ready

To run this recipe, you first need to run a web server that supports CGI scripts.

How to do it...

We placed our Python CGI script inside a cgi-bin/ subdirectory and then visited the HTML page that contains the feedback form. Upon submitting this form, our web server will send the form data to the CGI script, and we'll see the output produced by this script.

Listing 5.7 shows us how the Python web server supports CGI:

```python
#!/usr/bin/env python
# Python Network Programming Cookbook -- Chapter - 5
# This program requires Python 3.5.2 or any later version
# It may run on any other version with/without modifications.
#
# Follow the comments inline to make it run on Python 2.7.x.

import os
import cgi
import argparse

import http.server
# Comment out the above line and uncomment the below for Python 2.7.x.
#import BaseHTTPServer

# Uncomment the below line for Python 2.7.x.
#import CGIHTTPServer

import cgitb
cgitb.enable()  ## enable CGI error reporting


def web_server(port):

    server = http.server.HTTPServer
    # Comment out the above line and uncomment the below for Python 2.7.x.
    #server = BaseHTTPServer.HTTPServer

    handler = http.server.CGIHTTPRequestHandler #RequestsHandler
    # Comment out the above line and uncomment the below for Python 2.7.x.
    #handler = CGIHTTPServer.CGIHTTPRequestHandler #RequestsHandler

    server_address = ("", port)
    handler.cgi_directories = ["/cgi-bin", ]
    httpd = server(server_address, handler)
    print ("Starting web server with CGI support on port: %s ..." %port)
    httpd.serve_forever()

if __name__ == '__main__':
    parser = argparse.ArgumentParser(description='CGI Server Example')
    parser.add_argument('--port', action="store",
    dest="port", type=int, required=True)
    given_args = parser.parse_args()
    web_server(given_args.port)
```

The following screenshot shows a CGI enabled web server serving contents:

CGI Enabled Web Server

If you run this recipe, you will see the following output:

```
$ python 5_7_cgi_server.py --port=8800
Starting web server with CGI support on port: 8800 ...
localhost - - [19/May/2013 18:40:22] "GET / HTTP/1.1" 200 -
```

Now, you need to visit http://localhost:8800/5_7_send_feedback.html from your browser.

You will see an input form. We assume that you provide the following input to this form:

```
Name:    User1
Comment: Comment1
```

The following screenshot shows the entering user comment in a web form:

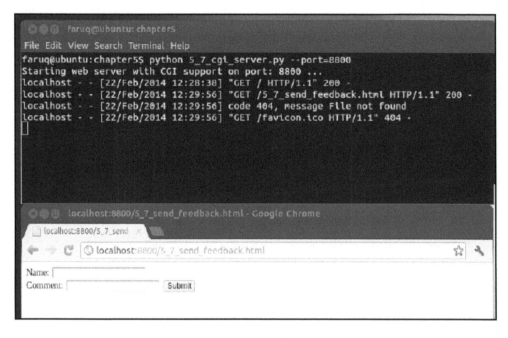

User Comment Input in the Form

Then, your browser will be redirected to
`http://localhost:8800/cgi-bin/5_7_get_feedback.py` where you can see the
following output:

Output from the Browser

How it works...

We have used a basic HTTP server setup that can handle CGI requests. Python 3 provides these interfaces in the `http.server` module. Python 2 had the modules `BaseHTTPServer` and `CGIHTTPserver` to offer the same, which were merged in Python into `http.server`.

The handler is configured to use the `/cgi-bin` path to launch the CGI scripts. No other path can be used to run the CGI scripts.

The HTML feedback form located on `5_7_send_feedback.html` shows a very basic HTML form containing the following code:

```html
<html>
   <body>
         <form action="/cgi-bin/5_7_get_feedback.py" method="post">
                Name: <input type="text" name="Name">   <br />
                Comment: <input type="text" name="Comment" />
                <input type="submit" value="Submit" />
         </form>
   </body>
</html>
```

Note that the form method is POST and action is set to the `/cgi-bin/5_7_get_feedback.py` file. The contents of this file are as follows:

```python
#!/usr/bin/env python
# Python Network Programming Cookbook, Second Edition -- Chapter - 5
# This program is optimized for Python 2.7.12 and Python 3.5.2.
# It may run on any other version with/without modifications.


#!/usr/bin/python

# Import modules for CGI handling
import cgi
import cgitb

# Create instance of FieldStorage
form = cgi.FieldStorage()

# Get data from fields
name = form.getvalue('Name')
comment  = form.getvalue('Comment')

print ("Content-type:text/html\r\n\r\n")
print ("<html>")
print ("<head>")
```

```
print ("<title>CGI Program Example </title>")
print ("</head>")
print ("<body>")
print ("<h2> %s sends a comment: %s</h2>" % (name, comment))
print ("</body>")
print ("</html>")
```

In this CGI script, the `FieldStorage()` method is called from `cgilib`. This returns a `form` object to process the HTML form inputs. Two inputs are parsed here (`name` and `comment`) using the `getvalue()` method. Finally, the script acknowledges the user input by echoing a line back saying that the user x has sent a comment.

If you encounter any errors as follows:

```
127.0.0.1 - - [22/Jun/2017 00:03:51] code 403, message CGI script is not
executable ('/cgi-bin/5_7_get_feedback.py')
```

Make it executable. It can be done by following the following command in Linux:

```
$ chmod a+x cgi-bin/5_7_get_feedback.py
```

Once it is made executable, you can rerun the program without any issue.

Finding the mail server from an email address

Websites often need to verify an email that is entered by a user for validity. We can verify an email in a few lines of code in Python. First step is to confirm that the email is of the accepted format, to ensure that no random input is accepted as an email. Next is to see whether the email address indeed exists. Due to restrictions in the major email service providers such as Gmail and Hotmail, this code may not work completely. Nevertheless, it gives an overall idea on a given email address.

Getting ready

To run this recipe, you first need to have a from email address that you will use to test the other email addresses (marked as `toaddress`).

How to do it...

Listing 5.8 shows us the code that finds the domain name from the given email address and verifies it:

```python
#!/usr/bin/env python
# Python Network Programming Cookbook, Second Edition -- Chapter - 5
# This program is optimized for Python 2.7.12 and Python 3.5.2.
# It may run on any other version with/without modifications.

import re
import smtplib
import dns.resolver
import argparse


def mail_checker(fromAddress, toAddress):

    regex = '^[a-z0-9][a-z0-9._%+-]{0,63}@[a-z0-9-]+
            (\.[a-z0-9-]+)*(\.[a-z]{2,})$'

    addressToVerify = str(toAddress)

    match = re.match(regex, addressToVerify)
    if match == None:
        print('Bad Syntax in the address to verify.
              Re-enter the correct value')
        raise ValueError('Bad Syntax')

    splitAddress = addressToVerify.split('@')
    domain = str(splitAddress[1])

    records = dns.resolver.query(domain, 'MX')
    mxRecord = records[0].exchange
    mxRecord = str(mxRecord)


    server = smtplib.SMTP()
    server.set_debuglevel(1)

    try:
        server.connect(mxRecord)
    except Exception as e:
        print ("Mail Check Failed Due to Error: %s" %str(e))
        return
    server.helo(server.local_hostname)
    server.mail(fromAddress)
    code, message = server.rcpt(str(addressToVerify))
```

```
    server.quit()

    if code == 250:
        print('Successfully verified the email: %s', fromAddress)
    else:
        print('Failed to verify the email: %s', fromAddress)



if __name__ == '__main__':
    parser = argparse.ArgumentParser(description='Mail Server Example')
    parser.add_argument('--fromAddress', action="store",
    dest="fromAddress", type=str, required=True)
    parser.add_argument('--toAddress', action="store",
    dest="toAddress", type=str, required=True)
    given_args = parser.parse_args()
    mail_checker(given_args.fromAddress, given_args.toAddress)
```

If you run this recipe, you will see the following output:

```
$ python 5_8_verify_email.py --fromAddress=tester@webname.com
--toAddress=test+234@gmail.com
connect: ('alt2.gmail-smtp-in.1.google.com.', 25)
connect: ('alt2.gmail-smtp-in.1.google.com.', 25)
Successfully verified the email: test+234@gmail.com
```

The preceding output is printed when 250 is returned from the mail server. The program may also produce the following output, since mail servers such as Gmail block outside access to port 25, which is the port of Simple Mail Transfer Protocol (SMTP) that we are checking:

```
$ python 5_8_verify_email.py --fromAddress=tester@webname.com --
toAddress=test+234@gmail.com
connect: ('alt2.gmail-smtp-in.1.google.com.', 25)
connect: ('alt2.gmail-smtp-in.1.google.com.', 25)
Mail Check Failed Due to Error: [Errno 101] Network is unreachable
```

If you use an invalid domain name as follows, there will be an error message:

```
$ python 5_8_verify_email.py --fromAddress=tester@webname.com --
toAddress=pradeeban@slt.lxx
Traceback (most recent call last):
  File "5_8_verify_email.py", line 57, in <module>
    mail_checker(given_args.fromAddress, given_args.toAddress)
  File "5_8_verify_email.py", line 26, in mail_checker
    records = dns.resolver.query(domain, 'MX')
  File "/usr/local/lib/python2.7/dist-packages/dns/resolver.py", line 1132,
in query
```

```
    raise_on_no_answer, source_port)
  File "/usr/local/lib/python2.7/dist-packages/dns/resolver.py", line 1051,
in query
    raise NXDOMAIN(qnames=qnames_to_try, responses=nxdomain_responses)
dns.resolver.NXDOMAIN: None of DNS query names exist: slt.lxx., slt.lxx.
```

How it works...

We have used a few Python libraries in getting this work. **Regular Expressions** (**RegEx**) in confirming that the emails belong to the correct format are done by using the `re` library. The library `smtplib` is an SMTP protocol client for Python programs, to execute methods such as sending a message to an SMTP server. You may read more about SMTP at `https://docs.python.org/3/library/smtplib.html`.

Writing a simple SMTP server

In this recipe, we will learn how to build an SMTP server and a client, as a simple mail server and a client. We will use Python's `smtpd` library for this recipe. You may read more about smtpd at `https://docs.python.org/3/library/smtpd.html`.

Getting ready

First, we will write an SMTP server that listens on a particular host and a particular port. Then we will write an SMTP client that connects to the same host and port, with the `fromaddress`, `toaddress`, `subject`, and message passed as the other arguments.

How to do it...

The server receives the messages from the clients and logs them to the console.

Listing 5.9a gives the code for the SMTP server as follows:

```
#!/usr/bin/env python
# Python Network Programming Cookbook, Second Edition -- Chapter - 5
# This program is optimized for Python 2.7.12 and Python 3.5.2.
# It may run on any other version with/without modifications.

import smtplib
import email.utils
```

```
import argparse
from email.mime.text import MIMEText

def mail_client(host, port, fromAddress, toAddress, subject, body):
    msg = MIMEText(body)
    msg['To'] = email.utils.formataddr(('Recipient', toAddress))
    msg['From'] = email.utils.formataddr(('Author', fromAddress))
    msg['Subject'] = subject

    server = smtplib.SMTP(host, port)
    server.set_debuglevel(True)
    try:
        server.sendmail(fromAddress, toAddress, msg.as_string())
    finally:
        server.quit()


if __name__ == '__main__':
    parser = argparse.ArgumentParser(description='Mail Server Example')
    parser.add_argument('--host', action="store",
    dest="host", type=str, required=True)
    parser.add_argument('--port', action="store",
    dest="port", type=int, required=True)
    parser.add_argument('--fromAddress', action="store",
    dest="fromAddress", type=str, required=True)
    parser.add_argument('--toAddress', action="store",
    dest="toAddress", type=str, required=True)
    parser.add_argument('--subject', action="store",
    dest="subject", type=str, required=True)
    parser.add_argument('--body', action="store",
    dest="body", type=str, required=True)
    given_args = parser.parse_args()
    mail_client(given_args.host, given_args.port,
    given_args.fromAddress, given_args.toAddress,
    given_args.subject, given_args.body)
```

Listing 5.9b gives the code for the SMTP client as follows:

```
#!/usr/bin/env python
# Python Network Programming Cookbook, Second Edition -- Chapter - 5
# This program is optimized for Python 2.7.12 and Python 3.5.2.
# It may run on any other version with/without modifications.

import smtpd
import asyncore
import argparse

class CustomSMTPServer(smtpd.SMTPServer):
```

```
    def process_message(self, peer, mailfrom, rcpttos, data):
        print ('Message Received from:', peer)
        print ('From:', mailfrom)
        print ('To  :', rcpttos)
        print ('Message :', data)
        return

if __name__ == '__main__':
    parser = argparse.ArgumentParser(description='Mail Server Example')
    parser.add_argument('--host', action="store",
    dest="host", type=str, required=True)
    parser.add_argument('--port', action="store",
    dest="port", type=int, required=True)
    given_args = parser.parse_args()
    server = CustomSMTPServer((given_args.host, given_args.port), None)
    asyncore.loop()
```

You may run the server and client code. The server handles the emails from the clients, as follows:

```
$ python 5_9a_mail_server.py --host='127.0.0.1' --port=1025
Message Received from the peer: ('127.0.0.1', 47916)
Addressed from: tester@webname.com
Addressed to  : ['test@gmail.com']
Message : Content-Type: text/plain; charset="us-ascii"
MIME-Version: 1.0
Content-Transfer-Encoding: 7bit
To: Recipient <test@gmail.com>
From: Author <tester@webname.com>
Subject: Hi, Hello
$ python 5_9b_mail_client.py --host='127.0.0.1' --port=1025 --
fromAddress=tester@webname.com --toAddress=test@gmail.com --subject="Hi,
Hello" --body="Good to see you all. Keep in touch. Take Care"
send: 'ehlo [127.0.1.1]\r\n'
reply: b'250-llovizna\r\n'
reply: b'250-SIZE 33554432\r\n'
reply: b'250 HELP\r\n'
reply: retcode (250); Msg: b'llovizna\nSIZE 33554432\nHELP'
send: 'mail FROM:<tester@webname.com> size=232\r\n'
reply: b'250 OK\r\n'
reply: retcode (250); Msg: b'OK'
send: 'rcpt TO:<test@gmail.com>\r\n'
reply: b'250 OK\r\n'
reply: retcode (250); Msg: b'OK'
send: 'data\r\n'
reply: b'354 End data with <CR><LF>.<CR><LF>\r\n'
reply: retcode (354); Msg: b'End data with <CR><LF>.<CR><LF>'
data: (354, b'End data with <CR><LF>.<CR><LF>')
```

```
send: b'Content-Type: text/plain; charset="us-ascii"\r\nMIME-Version:
1.0\r\nContent-Transfer-Encoding: 7bit\r\nTo: Recipient
<test@gmail.com>\r\nFrom: Author <tester@webname.com>\r\nSubject: Hi,
Hello\r\n\r\nGood to see you all. Keep in touch. Take Care\r\n.\r\n'
reply: b'250 OK\r\n'
reply: retcode (250); Msg: b'OK'
data: (250, b'OK')
send: 'quit\r\n'
reply: b'221 Bye\r\n'
reply: retcode (221); Msg: b'Bye'
```

The output is depicted by the following screenshot:

SMTP Server and Client

How it works...

The `email.utils` module offers the utility methods for the email server, such as
formatting the to and from addresses. The `smtplib` module lets us create a mail server,
while `smtpd` lets us create an email client daemon. The `asyncore` module offers a basic
infrastructure to write asynchronous clients and servers.

Writing a secure SMTP client using TLS

Now we will look into how to connect to the mail servers such as Gmail and Yahoo through a simple SMTP client secured with TLS.

Getting ready

This program requires accessing a mail account in a less secured way. Many modern email servers may block your login account. For example, you may have to make sure that *access for less secure apps has been turned on*.

How to do it...

You need to offer a valid email address and password to send an email through this recipe. We pass the email server, SMTP port, fromaddress, toaddress, email subject, and email body as the arguments, and receive the password to your email (from) address using the getpass library (so that your email password is not displayed in plain text).

Listing 5.10 gives the simple email client as follows:

```python
#!/usr/bin/env python
# Python Network Programming Cookbook, Second Edition -- Chapter - 5
# This program is optimized for Python 2.7.12 and Python 3.5.2.
# It may run on any other version with/without modifications.

import smtplib
from email.mime.multipart import MIMEMultipart
from email.mime.text import MIMEText
import argparse
import getpass

def mail_client(host, port, fromAddress, password, toAddress, subject,
body):
    msg = MIMEMultipart()

    msg['From'] = fromAddress
    msg['To'] = toAddress
    msg['Subject'] = subject
    message = body
    msg.attach(MIMEText(message))

    mailserver = smtplib.SMTP(host,port)
```

```
# Identify to the SMTP Gmail Client
mailserver.ehlo()

# Secure with TLS Encryption
mailserver.starttls()

# Reidentifying as an encrypted connection
mailserver.ehlo()
mailserver.login(fromAddress, password)

mailserver.sendmail(fromAddress,toAddress,msg.as_string())
print ("Email sent from:", fromAddress)

mailserver.quit()


if __name__ == '__main__':
    parser = argparse.ArgumentParser(description='Mail Server Example')
    parser.add_argument('--host', action="store",
    dest="host", type=str, required=True)
    parser.add_argument('--port', action="store",
    dest="port", type=int, required=True)
    parser.add_argument('--fromAddress', action="store",
    dest="fromAddress", type=str, required=True)
    parser.add_argument('--toAddress', action="store",
    dest="toAddress", type=str, required=True)
    parser.add_argument('--subject', action="store",
    dest="subject", type=str, required=True)
    parser.add_argument('--body', action="store",
    dest="body", type=str, required=True)
    password = getpass.getpass("Enter your Password:")
    given_args = parser.parse_args()
    mail_client(given_args.host, given_args.port,
    given_args.fromAddress, password, given_args.toAddress,
    given_args.subject, given_args.body)
```

This recipe logs in as a simple Python-based email client for your email account, and sends a plain-text email to the `toaddress` that you have specified. Running this program gives the following output:

```
$ python 5_10_secure_mail_client.py --host='smtp.gmail.com' --port=587 --
fromAddress=kathiravell@gmail.com --toAddress=kk.pradeeban@gmail.com -
subject="Hi, Hello.." --body="Good to see you all. Keep in touch. Take
Care"
python3 5_10_secure_mail_client.py --host='smtp.gmail.com' --port=587 --
fromAddress=kathiravell@gmail.com --toAddress=kk.pradeeban@gmail.com -
subject="Hi, Hello.." --body="Good to see you all. Keep in touch. Take
```

```
Care"
Enter your Password:
Email sent from: kathiravell@gmail.com
```

The output is indicated by the following screenshot of the console, as well as the email received:

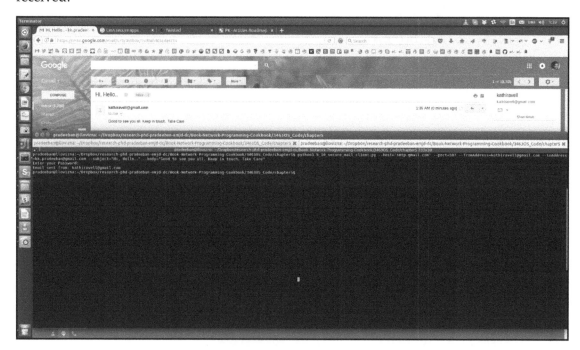

Sending Email from your Email Address

How it works...

If you have not enabled less secure apps to access your email account, it may produce an error message similar to the following:

```
$ python 5_10_secure_mail_client.py
Enter your Password:
Traceback (most recent call last):
  File "5_10_secure_mail_client.py", line 50, in <module>
    mail_client(given_args.host, given_args.port, given_args.fromAddress,
password, given_args.toAddress, given_args.subject, given_args.body)
  File "5_10_secure_mail_client.py", line 31, in mail_client
    mailserver.login(fromAddress, password)
  File "/usr/lib/python3.5/smtplib.py", line 729, in login
```

```
        raise last_exception
   File "/usr/lib/python3.5/smtplib.py", line 720, in login
      initial_response_ok=initial_response_ok)
   File "/usr/lib/python3.5/smtplib.py", line 641, in auth
      raise SMTPAuthenticationError(code, resp)
smtplib.SMTPAuthenticationError: (534, b'5.7.14
<https://accounts.google.com/signin/continue?sarp=1&scc=1&plt=AKgnsbv9\n5.7
.14 d-4CxD9A0qK3z36XteHYO1FaK2-
idda9-3CG5ckc1xi_E1OgaK2aftyHvZvti9jX6fC1kd\n5.7.14
fbTWvC5gKXK_A94zOBm8YQ_myr0uzInTP-
Tf2pTdAZcz3owptTesXl1HyXD2SCRHEXRJtk\n5.7.14 nr-
x8QQneko1ZBJCvsbtEmo5EXgETNbESSXmbX7acCZQGukSJJ-5akizNPUrxb6NVMsJwh\n5.7.14
L-f5XsY11BjmI1X9GVyQEZQSB-Iis> Please log in via your web browser
and\n5.7.14 then try again.\n5.7.14  Learn more at\n5.7.14
https://support.google.com/mail/answer/78754 o36sm9782398edc.39 - gsmtp')
```

In addition, your email program would have sent you a warning on this login attempt, advising you on potential compromise of your account, or if the login attempt was indeed you, suggesting you to enable less secure apps.

If the credentials are not correct, it will return a different error:

```
smtplib.SMTPAuthenticationError: (535, b'5.7.8 Username and Password not
accepted. Learn more at\n5.7.8
https://support.google.com/mail/?p=BadCredentials b4sm9037328eda.34 -
gsmtp')
```

Writing an email client with POP3

Now we will look into how to connect to the mail servers with POP3 to fetch an email from the email account.

Getting ready

This program requires accessing a mail account in a less secured way. Many modern email servers may block your login account. For example, you may have to make sure that *access for less secure apps has been turned on.*

How to do it...

You need to offer a valid email address and password to send an email through this recipe. We pass the email server, POP3 `port`, `user` and `password` as the arguments, and receive the password to your email account using the `getpass` library (so that your email password is not displayed in plain text).

Listing 5.11 gives the simple POP3 email client as follows:

```python
#!/usr/bin/env python
# Python Network Programming Cookbook, Second Edition -- Chapter - 5
# This program is optimized for Python 2.7.12 and Python 3.5.2.
# It may run on any other version with/without modifications.

import getpass
import poplib
import argparse

def mail_client(host, port, user, password):
    Mailbox = poplib.POP3_SSL(host, port)
    Mailbox.user(user)
    Mailbox.pass_(password)
    numMessages = len(Mailbox.list()[1])
    print (Mailbox.retr(1)[1])
    Mailbox.quit()


if __name__ == '__main__':
    parser = argparse.ArgumentParser(description='Mail Server Example')
    parser.add_argument('--host', action="store",
    dest="host", type=str, required=True)
    parser.add_argument('--port', action="store",
    dest="port", type=int, required=True)
    parser.add_argument('--user', action="store",
    dest="user", type=str, required=True)
    password = getpass.getpass("Enter your Password:")
    given_args = parser.parse_args()
    mail_client(given_args.host, given_args.port,
    given_args.user, password)
```

This recipe logs in as a simple Python-based POP3 email client for your email account, and retrieves an email from your email account. Running this program gives the following output:

```
$ python 5_11_pop3_mail_client.py --host='pop.googlemail.com' --port=995 --
user=kathiravell@gmail.com
Enter your Password:
[b'Received: by 10.70.31.12 with HTTP; Mon, 24 Dec 2007 11:48:08 -0800
(PST)', b'Message-ID:
<a80d78ee0712241148v78b4e964u80876a1d6bfdae32@mail.gmail.com>', b'Date:
Tue, 25 Dec 2007 01:18:08 +0530', b'From: "KANAPATHIPILLAI KATHIRAVELU
....
[Retrieved Email Truncated Here..]
```

How it works...

If you have not enabled less secure apps to access your email account, it may produce an error message.

Once you have enabled access through less secure apps, this recipe can log in as a POP3 client to your email account, retrieve an email from the account, and post it in the console.

6
Programming Across Machine Boundaries

In this chapter, we will cover the following recipes:

- Executing a remote shell command using telnet
- Copying a file to a remote machine by SFTP
- Printing a remote machine's CPU information
- Installing a Python package remotely
- Running a MySQL command remotely
- Transferring files to a remote machine over SSH
- Configuring Apache remotely to host a website

Introduction

This chapter promotes some interesting Python libraries. The recipes are presented aiming at the system administrators and advanced Python programmers who like to write code that connects to remote systems and executes commands. The chapter begins with lightweight recipes with a built-in Python library, `telnetlib`. It then brings `Paramiko`, a well-known remote access library. Finally, the powerful remote system administration library, `fabric`, is presented. The `fabric` library is loved by developers who regularly script for automatic deployments, for example, deploying web applications or building custom application binaries.

Executing a remote shell command using telnet

If you need to connect an old network switch or router via telnet, you can do so from a Python script instead of using a bash script or an interactive shell. This recipe will create a simple telnet session. It will show you how to execute shell commands to the remote host.

Getting ready

You need to install the telnet server on your machine and ensure that it's up and running. You can use a package manager that is specific to your operating system to install the telnet server package. For example, on Debian/Ubuntu, you can use `apt-get` or `aptitude` to install the `telnetd` package, as shown in the following command:

```
$ sudo apt-get install telnetd
$ telnet localhost
```

How to do it...

Let us define a function that will take a user's login credentials from the Command Prompt and connect to a telnet server.

Upon successful connection, it will send the Unix `'ls'` command. Then, it will display the output of the command, for example, listing the contents of a directory.

Listing 6.1 shows the code for a telnet session that executes a Unix command remotely as follows:

```python
#!/usr/bin/env python
# Python Network Programming Cookbook, Second Edition -- Chapter - 6
# This program is optimized for Python 3.5.2.
# It may run on any other version with/without modifications.
# To make it run on Python 2.7.x, needs some changes due to API
differences.
# Follow the comments inline to make the program work with Python 2.


import getpass
import sys
import telnetlib

HOST = "localhost"
```

```
def run_telnet_session():

    user = input("Enter your remote account: ")
    # Comment out the above line and uncomment
      the below line for Python 2.7.
    # user = raw_input("Enter your remote account: ")

    password = getpass.getpass()
    session = telnetlib.Telnet(HOST)
    session.read_until(b"login: ")
    session.write(user.encode('ascii') + b"\n")
    if password:
        session.read_until(b"Password: ")
        session.write(password.encode('ascii') + b"\n")
    session.write(b"ls\n")
    session.write(b"exit\n")
    print (session.read_all())

if __name__ == '__main__':
    run_telnet_session()
```

If you run a telnet server on your local machine and run this code, it will ask you for your remote user account and password. The following output shows a telnet session executed on an Ubuntu machine:

```
$ python 6_1_execute_remote_telnet_cmd.py
Enter your remote account: pradeeban
Password:
ls
exit
Last login: Tue Jun  6 22:39:44 CEST 2017 from localhost on pts/20
Welcome to Ubuntu 16.04.2 LTS (GNU/Linux 4.8.0-53-generic x86_64)
* Documentation:  https://help.ubuntu.com
* Management:     https://landscape.canonical.com
* Support:        https://ubuntu.com/advantage
89 packages can be updated.
3 updates are security updates.
pradeeban@llovizna:~$ ls
INESC-ID GSD     openflow
Desktop                      MEOCloud          software
Documents                    Downloads       Dropbox
Obidos           floodlight                  OpenDaylight
pradeeban@llovizna:~$ exit
logout
```

How it works...

This recipe relies on Python's built-in `telnetlib` networking library to create a telnet session. The `run_telnet_session()` function takes the username and password from the Command Prompt. The `getpass` module's `getpass()` function is used to get the password as this function won't let you see what is typed on the screen.

In order to create a telnet session, you need to instantiate a `Telnet()` class, which takes a hostname parameter to initialize. In this case, `localhost` is used as the hostname. You can use the `argparse` module to pass a hostname to this script.

The telnet session's remote output can be captured with the `read_until()` method. In the first case, the login prompt is detected using this method. Then, the username with a new line feed is sent to the remote machine by the `write()` method (in this case, the same machine accessed as if it's remote). Similarly, the password was supplied to the remote host.

Then, the `ls` command is sent to be executed. Finally, to disconnect from the remote host, the `exit` command is sent, and all session data received from the remote host is printed on screen using the `read_all()` method.

Copying a file to a remote machine by SFTP

If you want to upload or copy a file from your local machine to a remote machine securely, you can do so via **Secure File Transfer Protocol (SFTP)**.

Getting ready

This recipe uses a powerful third-party networking library, `Paramiko`, to show you an example of file copying by SFTP, as shown in the following command. You can grab the latest code of `Paramiko` from GitHub (`https://github.com/paramiko/paramiko`) or PyPI:

```
$ pip install paramiko
Make sure to have the SSH server and client installed on the target host
and local host accordingly. In this example, since we are having localhost
also as the target, install SSH locally:
$ sudo apt-get install ssh
```

How to do it...

This recipe takes a few command-line inputs: the remote hostname, server port, source filename, and destination filename. For the sake of simplicity, we can use default or hard-coded values for these input parameters.

In order to connect to the remote host, we need the username and password, which can be obtained from the user from the command line.

Listing 6.2 explains how to copy a file remotely by SFTP, as shown in the following code:

```python
#!/usr/bin/env python
# Python Network Programming Cookbook, Second Edition -- Chapter - 6
# This program is optimized for Python 3.5.2.
# It may run on any other version with/without modifications.
# To make it run on Python 2.7.x, needs some changes due to API
differences.
# Follow the comments inline to make the program work with Python 2.


import argparse
import paramiko
import getpass


SOURCE = '6_2_copy_remote_file_over_sftp.py'
DESTINATION ='/tmp/6_2_copy_remote_file_over_sftp.py '


def copy_file(hostname, port, username, password, src, dst):
    client = paramiko.SSHClient()
    client.load_system_host_keys()
    print (" Connecting to %s \n with username=%s...
             \n" % (hostname,username))
    t = paramiko.Transport(hostname, port)
    t.connect(username=username,password=password)
    sftp = paramiko.SFTPClient.from_transport(t)
    print ("Copying file: %s to path: %s" % (src, dst))
    sftp.put(src, dst)
    sftp.close()
    t.close()


if __name__ == '__main__':
    parser = argparse.ArgumentParser(description='Remote file copy')
    parser.add_argument('--host', action="store",
                        dest="host", default='localhost')
```

```
parser.add_argument('--port', action="store",
                     dest="port", default=22, type=int)
parser.add_argument('--src', action="store",
                     dest="src", default=SOURCE)
parser.add_argument('--dst', action="store",
                     dest="dst", default=DESTINATION)
given_args = parser.parse_args()
hostname, port = given_args.host, given_args.port
src, dst = given_args.src, given_args.dst
user = input("Enter your remote account: ")
# Comment out the above line and uncomment the
  below line for Python 2.7.
# user = raw_input("Enter your remote account: ")

password = getpass.getpass("Enter password for %s: " %user)
copy_file(hostname, port, user, password, src, dst)
```

If you run this script, you will see an output similar to the following:

```
$ python3 6_2_copy_remote_file_over_sftp.py
Enter your remote account: pradeeban
Enter password for pradeeban:
 Connecting to localhost
 with username=pradeeban...
Copying file: 6_2_copy_remote_file_over_sftp.py to path:
/tmp/6_2_copy_remote_file_over_sftp.py
```

How it works...

This recipe can take the various inputs for connecting to a remote machine and copying a file over SFTP.

This recipe passes the command-line input to the `copy_file()` function. It then creates an SSH client calling the `SSHClient` class of `paramiko`. The client needs to load the system host keys. It then connects to the remote system, thus creating an instance of the `transport` class. The actual SFTP connection object, `sftp`, is created by calling the `SFTPClient.from_transport()` function of `paramiko`. This takes the `transport` instance as an input.

After the SFTP connection is ready, the local file is copied over this connection to the remote host using the `put()` method.

Finally, it is a good idea to clean up the SFTP connection and underlying objects by calling the `close()` method separately on each object.

Printing a remote machine's CPU information

Sometimes, we need to run a simple command on a remote machine over SSH. For example, we need to query the remote machine's CPU or RAM information. This can be done from a Python script as shown in this recipe.

Getting ready

You need to install the third-party package, `Paramiko`, as shown in the following command, from the source available from GitHub's repository at `https://github.com/paramiko/paramiko`:

```
$ pip install paramiko
```

How to do it...

We can use the `paramiko` module to create a remote session to a Unix machine. Then, from this session, we can read the remote machine's `/proc/cpuinfo` file to extract the CPU information.

Listing 6.3 gives the code for printing a remote machine's CPU information, as follows:

```python
#!/usr/bin/env python
# Python Network Programming Cookbook, Second Edition -- Chapter - 6
# This program is optimized for Python 3.5.2.
# It may run on any other version with/without modifications.
# To make it run on Python 2.7.x, needs some changes due to API
differences.
# Follow the comments inline to make the program work with Python 2.


import argparse
import getpass
import paramiko

RECV_BYTES = 4096
COMMAND = 'cat /proc/cpuinfo'

def print_remote_cpu_info(hostname, port, username, password):
    client = paramiko.Transport((hostname, port))
    client.connect(username=username, password=password)
```

```
        stdout_data = []
        stderr_data = []
        session = client.open_channel(kind='session')
        session.exec_command(COMMAND)
        while True:
            if session.recv_ready():
                stdout_data.append(session.recv(RECV_BYTES))
            if session.recv_stderr_ready():
                stderr_data.append(session.recv_stderr(RECV_BYTES))
            if session.exit_status_ready():
                break
        print ('exit status: ', session.recv_exit_status())
        print (b''.join(stdout_data))
        print (b''.join(stderr_data))
        session.close()
        client.close()


if __name__ == '__main__':
    parser = argparse.ArgumentParser(description='Remote file copy')
    parser.add_argument('--host', action="store",
                        dest="host", default='localhost')
    parser.add_argument('--port', action="store",
                        dest="port", default=22, type=int)
    given_args = parser.parse_args()
    hostname, port =  given_args.host, given_args.port
    user = input("Enter your remote account: ")
    # Comment out the above line and uncomment the
      below line for Python 2.7.
    # user = raw_input("Enter your remote account: ")

    password = getpass.getpass("Enter password for %s: " %user)
    print_remote_cpu_info(hostname, port, user, password)
```

Running this script will show the CPU information of a given host, in this case, the local machine. Since my computer is 8 core, it shows the information of all the eight processors as follows (some of the processors are omitted in the following output for brevity):

```
$ python2 6_3_print_remote_cpu_info.py
Enter your remote account: pradeeban
Enter password for pradeeban:
('exit status: ', 0)
processor   : 0
vendor_id   : GenuineIntel
cpu family  : 6
model       : 60
model name  : Intel(R) Core(TM) i7-4700MQ CPU @ 2.40GHz
stepping    : 3
microcode   : 0x17
```

```
cpu MHz          : 2401.171
cache size  : 6144 KB
physical id : 0
siblings    : 8
core id          : 0
cpu cores   : 4
apicid           : 0
initial apicid   : 0
fpu         : yes
fpu_exception    : yes
cpuid level : 13
wp          : yes
flags       : fpu vme de pse tsc msr pae mce cx8 apic sep mtrr pge mca cmov
pat pse36 clflush dts acpi mmx fxsr sse sse2 ss ht tm pbe syscall nx
pdpe1gb rdtscp lm constant_tsc arch_perfmon pebs bts rep_good nopl
xtopology nonstop_tsc aperfmperf eagerfpu pni pclmulqdq dtes64 monitor
ds_cpl vmx est tm2 ssse3 sdbg fma cx16 xtpr pdcm pcid sse4_1 sse4_2 movbe
popcnt tsc_deadline_timer aes xsave avx f16c rdrand lahf_lm abm epb
tpr_shadow vnmi flexpriority ept vpid fsgsbase tsc_adjust bmi1 avx2 smep
bmi2 erms invpcid xsaveopt dtherm ida arat pln pts
bugs        :
bogomips    : 4789.08
clflush size     : 64
cache_alignment  : 64
address sizes    : 39 bits physical, 48 bits virtual
power management:
processor   : 1
vendor_id   : GenuineIntel
cpu family  : 6
model       : 60
model name  : Intel(R) Core(TM) i7-4700MQ CPU @ 2.40GHz
stepping    : 3
microcode   : 0x17
cpu MHz          : 2384.033
cache size  : 6144 KB
physical id : 0
siblings    : 8
core id          : 0
cpu cores   : 4
apicid           : 1
initial apicid   : 1
fpu         : yes
fpu_exception    : yes
cpuid level : 13
wp          : yes
flags       : fpu vme de pse tsc msr pae mce cx8 apic sep mtrr pge mca cmov
pat pse36 clflush dts acpi mmx fxsr sse sse2 ss ht tm pbe syscall nx
pdpe1gb rdtscp lm constant_tsc arch_perfmon pebs bts rep_good nopl
```

```
xtopology nonstop_tsc aperfmperf eagerfpu pni pclmulqdq dtes64 monitor
ds_cpl vmx est tm2 ssse3 sdbg fma cx16 xtpr pdcm pcid sse4_1 sse4_2 movbe
popcnt tsc_deadline_timer aes xsave avx f16c rdrand lahf_lm abm epb
tpr_shadow vnmi flexpriority ept vpid fsgsbase tsc_adjust bmi1 avx2 smep
bmi2 erms invpcid xsaveopt dtherm ida arat pln pts
bugs         :
bogomips     : 4789.08
clflush size     : 64
cache_alignment  : 64
address sizes    : 39 bits physical, 48 bits virtual
power management:
. . . .
. . .
. . .
. . .
. . .
processor    : 7
vendor_id    : GenuineIntel
cpu family   : 6
model        : 60
model name   : Intel(R) Core(TM) i7-4700MQ CPU @ 2.40GHz
stepping     : 3
microcode    : 0x17
cpu MHz          : 2439.843
cache size   : 6144 KB
physical id  : 0
siblings     : 8
core id          : 3
cpu cores    : 4
apicid           : 7
initial apicid   : 7
fpu          : yes
fpu_exception    : yes
cpuid level  : 13
wp           : yes
flags        : fpu vme de pse tsc msr pae mce cx8 apic sep mtrr pge mca cmov
pat pse36 clflush dts acpi mmx fxsr sse sse2 ss ht tm pbe syscall nx
pdpe1gb rdtscp lm constant_tsc arch_perfmon pebs bts rep_good nopl
xtopology nonstop_tsc aperfmperf eagerfpu pni pclmulqdq dtes64 monitor
ds_cpl vmx est tm2 ssse3 sdbg fma cx16 xtpr pdcm pcid sse4_1 sse4_2 movbe
popcnt tsc_deadline_timer aes xsave avx f16c rdrand lahf_lm abm epb
tpr_shadow vnmi flexpriority ept vpid fsgsbase tsc_adjust bmi1 avx2 smep
bmi2 erms invpcid xsaveopt dtherm ida arat pln pts
bugs         :
bogomips     : 4789.08
clflush size     : 64
cache_alignment  : 64
address sizes    : 39 bits physical, 48 bits virtual
```

```
power management:
```

How it works...

First, we collect the connection parameters such as `hostname`, `port`, `username`, and `password`. These parameters are then passed to the `print_remote_cpu_info()` function.

This function creates an SSH client session by calling the `transport` class of `paramiko`. The connection is made thereafter using the supplied username and password. We can create a raw communication session using `open_channel()` on the SSH client. In order to execute a command on the remote host, `exec_command()` can be used.

After sending the command to the remote host, the response from the remote host can be caught by blocking the `recv_ready()` event of the session object. We can create two lists, `stdout_data` and `stderr_data`, and use them to store the remote output and error messages.

When the command exits in the remote machine, it can be detected using the `exit_status_ready()` method, and the remote session data can be concatenated using the `join()` string method.

Finally, the session and client connection can be closed using the `close()` method on each object.

Installing a Python package remotely

While dealing with the remote host in the previous recipes, you may have noticed that we need to do a lot of stuff related to the connection setup. For efficient execution, it is desirable that they become abstract and only the relevant high-level part is exposed to the programmers. It is cumbersome and slow to always explicitly set up connections to execute commands remotely.

Fabric (http://fabfile.org/), a third-party Python module, solves this problem. It only exposes as many APIs as can be used to efficiently interact with remote machines.

In this recipe, a simple example of using Fabric will be shown.

Getting ready

We need Fabric to be installed first. You can install Fabric using the Python packing tools, `pip` or `easy_install`, as shown in the following command. Fabric relies on the `paramiko` module, which will be installed automatically:

```
$ pip install fabric
```

Currently the default Fabric does not seem to support Python 3. You may install `fabric3` to fix this:

```
$ sudo pip install fabric3
```

Here, we will connect the remote host using the SSH protocol. So, it's necessary to run the SSH server on the remote end. If you like to test with your local machine (pretending to access as a remote machine), you may install the `openssh` server package locally. On a Debian/Ubuntu machine, this can be done with the package manager, `apt-get`, as shown in the following command:

```
$ sudo apt-get install openssh-server
```

How to do it...

Here's the code for installing a Python package using Fabric.

Listing 6.4 gives the code for installing a Python package remotely as follows:

```python
#!/usr/bin/env python
# Python Network Programming Cookbook, Second Edition -- Chapter - 6
# This program is optimized for Python 2.7.12 and Python 3.5.2.
# It may run on any other version with/without modifications.

from getpass import getpass
from fabric.api import settings, run, env, prompt


def remote_server():
    env.hosts = ['127.0.0.1']
    env.user = prompt('Enter user name: ')
    env.password = getpass('Enter password: ')
def install_package():
    run("pip install yolk")
```

Fabric scripts are run in a different way as compared to the normal Python scripts. All functions using the `fabric` library must be referred to a Python script called `fabfile.py`. There's no traditional __main__ directive in this script. Instead, you can define your method using the Fabric APIs and execute these methods using the command-line tool, `fab`. So, instead of calling `python <script>.py`, you can run a Fabric script, which is defined in a `fabfile.py` script and located under the current directory, by calling `fab one_function_name another_function_name`.

So, let's create a `fabfile.py` script as shown in the following command. For the sake of simplicity, you can create a file shortcut or link from any file to a `fabfile.py` script. First, delete any previously created `fabfile.py` file and create a shortcut to `fabfile`:

```
$ rm -rf fabfile.py
$ ln -s 6_4_install_python_package_remotely.py fabfile.py
```

If you call the `fabfile` now, it will produce the following output after installing the Python package, `yolk`, remotely as follows:

```
$ ln -sfn 6_4_install_python_package_remotely.py fabfile.py
$ fab remote_server install_package
Enter user name: faruq
Enter password:
[127.0.0.1] Executing task 'install_package'
[127.0.0.1] run: pip install yolk
[127.0.0.1] out: Downloading/unpacking yolk
[127.0.0.1] out:    Downloading yolk-0.4.3.tar.gz (86kB):
[127.0.0.1] out:    Downloading yolk-0.4.3.tar.gz (86kB): 100%   86kB
[127.0.0.1] out:    Downloading yolk-0.4.3.tar.gz (86kB):
[127.0.0.1] out:    Downloading yolk-0.4.3.tar.gz (86kB): 86kB
downloaded
[127.0.0.1] out:    Running setup.py egg_info for package yolk
[127.0.0.1] out:      Installing yolk script to /home/faruq/env/bin
[127.0.0.1] out: Successfully installed yolk
[127.0.0.1] out: Cleaning up...
[127.0.0.1] out:
Done.
Disconnecting from 127.0.0.1... done.
```

How it works...

This recipe demonstrates how a system administration task can be done remotely using a Python script. There are two functions present in this script. The `remote_server()` function sets up the Fabric `env` environment variables, for example, the hostname, user, password, and so on.

The other function, `install_package()`, calls the `run()` function. This takes the commands that you usually type in the command line. In this case, the command is `pip install yolk`. This installs the Python package, `yolk`, with `pip`. As compared to the previously described recipes, this method of running a remote command using Fabric is easier and more efficient.

Running a MySQL command remotely

If you ever need to administer a MySQL server remotely, this recipe is for you. It will show you how to send database commands to a remote MySQL server from a Python script. If you need to set up a web application that relies on a backend database, this recipe can be used as a part of your web application setup process.

Getting ready

This recipe also needs Fabric to be installed first. You can install Fabric using the Python packing tools, `pip` or `easy_install`, as shown in the following command. Fabric relies on the `paramiko` module, which will be installed automatically:

```
$ pip install fabric
```

Here, we will connect the remote host using the SSH protocol. So, it's necessary to run the SSH server on the remote end. You also need to run a MySQL server on the remote host. On a Debian/Ubuntu machine, this can be done with the package manager, `apt-get`, as shown in the following command:

```
$ sudo apt-get install openssh-server mysql-server
```

How to do it...

We defined the Fabric environment settings and a few functions for administering MySQL remotely. In these functions, instead of calling the mysql executable directly, we send the SQL commands to mysql via echo. This ensures that arguments are passed properly to the mysql executable.

Listing 6.5 gives the code for running MySQL commands remotely, as follows:

```python
#!/usr/bin/env python
# Python Network Programming Cookbook, Second Edition -- Chapter - 6
# This program is optimized for Python 2.7.12 and Python 3.5.2.
# It may run on any other version with/without modifications.

from getpass import getpass
from fabric.api import run, env, prompt, cd
def remote_server():
    env.hosts = ['127.0.0.1']
    env.user = prompt('Enter your system username: ')
    env.password = getpass('Enter your system user password: ')
    env.mysqlhost = 'localhost'
    env.mysqluser = prompt('Enter your db username: ')
    env.mysqlpassword = getpass('Enter your db user password: ')
    env.db_name = ''

def show_dbs():
    """ Wraps mysql show databases cmd"""
    q = "show databases"
    run("echo '%s' | mysql -u%s -p%s" %(q, env.mysqluser,
        env.mysqlpassword))


def run_sql(db_name, query):
    """ Generic function to run sql"""
    with cd('/tmp'):
        run("echo '%s' | mysql -u%s -p%s -D %s" %(query,
            env.mysqluser, env.mysqlpassword, db_name))

def create_db():
    """Create a MySQL DB for App version"""
    if not env.db_name:
        db_name = prompt("Enter the DB name:")
    else:
        db_name = env.db_name
    run('echo "CREATE DATABASE %s default character set
        utf8 collate utf8_unicode_ci;"|mysql
        --batch --user=%s --password=%s --host=%s'\
```

```
            % (db_name, env.mysqluser, env.mysqlpassword,
             env.mysqlhost), pty=True)

def ls_db():
    """ List a dbs with size in MB """
    if not env.db_name:
        db_name = prompt("Which DB to ls?")
    else:
        db_name = env.db_name
    query = """SELECT table_schema
                            "DB Name",
        Round(Sum(data_length + index_length) / 1024 / 1024, 1)
         "DB Size in MB"
         FROM   information_schema.tables
         WHERE table_schema = \"%s\"
         GROUP  BY table_schema """ %db_name
    run_sql(db_name, query)


def empty_db():
    """ Empty all tables of a given DB """
    db_name = prompt("Enter DB name to empty:")
    cmd = """
    (echo 'SET foreign_key_checks = 0;';
    (mysqldump -u%s -p%s --add-drop-table --no-data %s |
     grep ^DROP);
     echo 'SET foreign_key_checks = 1;') | \
     mysql -u%s -p%s -b %s
    """ %(env.mysqluser, env.mysqlpassword, db_name,
          env.mysqluser, env.mysqlpassword, db_name)
    run(cmd)
```

In order to run this script, you should create a shortcut, fabfile.py. From the command line, you can do this by typing the following command:

```
$ ln -sfn 6_5_run_mysql_command_remotely.py fabfile.py
```

Then, you can call the fab executable in various forms.

The following command will show a list of databases (using the SQL query, show databases):

```
$ fab remote_server show_dbs
```

The following command will create a new MySQL database. If you haven't defined the Fabric environment variable, db_name, a prompt will be shown to enter the target database name. This database will be created using the SQL command, CREATE DATABASE <database_name> default character set utf8 collate utf8_unicode_ci;:

```
$ fab remote_server create_db
```

This Fabric command will show the size of a database:

```
$ fab remote_server ls_db()
```

The following Fabric command will use the mysqldump and mysql executables to empty a database. This behavior of this function is similar to the truncating of a database, except it removes all the tables. The result is as if you created a fresh database without any tables:

```
$ fab remote_server empty_db()
```

The following will be the output:

```
$ fab remote_server show_dbs
[127.0.0.1] Executing task 'show_dbs'
[127.0.0.1] run: echo 'show databases' | mysql -uroot -p<DELETED>
[127.0.0.1] out: Database
[127.0.0.1] out: information_schema
[127.0.0.1] out: mysql
[127.0.0.1] out: phpmyadmin
[127.0.0.1] out:
Done.
Disconnecting from 127.0.0.1... done.
$ fab remote_server create_db
[127.0.0.1] Executing task 'create_db'
Enter the DB name: test123
[127.0.0.1] run: echo "CREATE DATABASE test123 default character set utf8
collate utf8_unicode_ci;"|mysql --batch --user=root --password=<DELETED> --
host=localhost
Done.
Disconnecting from 127.0.0.1... done.
$ fab remote_server show_dbs
[127.0.0.1] Executing task 'show_dbs'
[127.0.0.1] run: echo 'show databases' | mysql -uroot -p<DELETED>
[127.0.0.1] out: Database
[127.0.0.1] out: information_schema
```

```
[127.0.0.1] out: collabtive
[127.0.0.1] out: test123
[127.0.0.1] out: testdb
[127.0.0.1] out:
Done.
Disconnecting from 127.0.0.1... done.
```

How it works...

This script defines a few functions that are used with Fabric. The first function, `remote_server()`, sets the environment variables. The local loopback IP (`127.0.0.1`) is put to the list of hosts. The local system user and MySQL login credentials are set and collected via `getpass()`.

The other function utilizes the Fabric `run()` function to send MySQL commands to the remote MySQL server by echoing the command to the `mysql` executable.

The `run_sql()` function is a generic function that can be used as a wrapper in other functions. For example, the `empty_db()` function calls it to execute the SQL commands. This can keep your code a bit more organized and cleaner.

Transferring files to a remote machine over SSH

While automating a remote system administration task using Fabric, if you want to transfer files between your local machine and the remote machine with SSH, you can use the Fabric's built-in `get()` and `put()` functions. This recipe shows you how we can create custom functions to transfer files smartly by checking the disk space before and after the transfer.

Getting ready

This recipe also needs Fabric to be installed first. You can install Fabric using Python packing tools, `pip` or `easy_install`, as shown in the following command:

```
$ pip install fabric
```

Here, we will connect the remote host using the SSH protocol. So, it's necessary to install and run the SSH server on the remote host.

How to do it...

Let us first set up the Fabric environment variables and then create two functions, one for downloading files and the other for uploading files.

Listing 6.6 gives the code for transferring files to a remote machine over SSH as follows:

```python
#!/usr/bin/env python
# Python Network Programming Cookbook, Second Edition -- Chapter - 6
# This program is optimized for Python 2.7.12 and Python 3.5.2.
# It may run on any other version with/without modifications.


from getpass import getpass
from fabric.api import local, run, env, get, put, prompt, open_shell

def remote_server():
    env.hosts = ['127.0.0.1']
    env.password = getpass('Enter your system password: ')
    env.home_folder = '/tmp'

def login():
    open_shell(command="cd %s" %env.home_folder)


def download_file():
    print ("Checking local disk space...")
    local("df -h")
    remote_path = prompt("Enter the remote file path:")
    local_path = prompt("Enter the local file path:")
    get(remote_path=remote_path, local_path=local_path)
    local("ls %s" %local_path)


def upload_file():
    print ("Checking remote disk space...")
    run("df -h")
    local_path = prompt("Enter the local file path:")
    remote_path = prompt("Enter the remote file path:")
    put(remote_path=remote_path, local_path=local_path)
    run("ls %s" %remote_path)
```

In order to run this script, you should create a shortcut, `fabfile.py`. From the command line, you can do this by typing the following command:

```
$ ln -sfn 6_6_transfer_file_over_ssh.py fabfile.py
```

Then, you can call the `fab` executable in various forms.

First, to log on to a remote server using your script, you can run the following Fabric function:

```
$ fab remote_server login
```

This will give you a minimum shell-like environment. Then, you can download a file from a remote server to your local machine using the following command:

```
$ fab remote_server download_file
```

Similarly, to upload a file, you can use the following command:

```
$ fab remote_server upload_file
```

In this example, the local machine is used via SSH. So, you have to install the SSH server locally to run these scripts. Otherwise, you can modify the `remote_server()` function and point it to a remote server, as follows:

```
$ fab remote_server login
[127.0.0.1] Executing task 'login'
Linux debian6 2.6.32-5-686 #1 SMP Mon Feb 25 01:04:36 UTC 2013 i686
The programs included with the Debian GNU/Linux system are free software;
the exact distribution terms for each program are described in the
individual files in /usr/share/doc/*/copyright.
Debian GNU/Linux comes with ABSOLUTELY NO WARRANTY, to the extent permitted
by applicable law.
You have new mail.
Last login: Wed Aug 21 15:08:45 2013 from localhost
cd /tmp
faruq@debian6:~$ cd /tmp
faruq@debian6:/tmp$
<CTRL+D>
faruq@debian6:/tmp$ logout
Done.
Disconnecting from 127.0.0.1... done.
$ fab remote_server download_file
[127.0.0.1] Executing task 'download_file'
Checking local disk space...
[localhost] local: df -h
Filesystem            Size  Used Avail Use% Mounted on
/dev/sda1              62G   47G   12G  81% /
```

```
tmpfs                   506M     0   506M    0% /lib/init/rw
udev                    501M  160K   501M    1% /dev
tmpfs                   506M  408K   505M    1% /dev/shm
Z_DRIVE                1012G  944G    69G   94% /media/z
C_DRIVE                 466G  248G   218G   54% /media/c
Enter the remote file path: /tmp/op.txt
Enter the local file path: .
[127.0.0.1] download: chapter7/op.txt <- /tmp/op.txt
[localhost] local: ls .
6_1_execute_remote_telnet_cmd.py    6_3_print_remote_cpu_info.py
6_5_run_mysql_command_remotely.py
6_7_configure_Apache_for_hosting_website_remotely.py   fabfile.pyc
__init__.py   test.txt
6_2_copy_remote_file_over_sftp.py   6_4_install_python_package_remotely.py
6_6_transfer_file_over_ssh.py fabfile.py                      index.html
op.txt         vhost.conf
Done.
Disconnecting from 127.0.0.1... done.
```

How it works...

In this recipe, we used a few of Fabric's built-in functions to transfer files between local and remote machines. The `local()` function does an action on the local machine, whereas the remote actions are carried out by the `run()` function.

This is useful to check the available disk space on the target machine before uploading a file and vice versa.

This is achieved by using the Unix command, `df`. The source and destination file paths can be specified via the Command Prompt or can be hard coded in the source file in case of an unattended automatic execution.

Configuring Apache remotely to host a website

Fabric functions can be run as both regular and super users. If you need to host a website in a remote Apache web server, you need the administrative user privileges to create configuration files and restart the web server. This recipe introduces the Fabric `sudo()` function that runs commands in the remote machine as a superuser. Here, we would like to configure the Apache virtual host for running a website.

Getting ready

This recipe needs Fabric to be installed first on your local machine. You can install Fabric using the Python packing tools, `pip` or `easy_install`, as shown in the following command:

```
$ pip install fabric
```

Here, we will connect the remote host using the SSH protocol. So, it's necessary to install and run the SSH server on the remote host. It is also assumed that the Apache web server is installed and running on the remote server. On a Debian/Ubuntu machine, this can be done with the package manager, `apt-get`, as shown in the following command:

```
$ sudo apt-get install openssh-server apache2
```

How to do it...

First, we collect our Apache installation paths and some configuration parameters, such as web server user, group, virtual host configuration path, and initialization scripts. These parameters can be defined as constants.

Then, we set up two functions, `remote_server()` and `setup_vhost()`, to execute the Apache configuration task using Fabric.

Listing 6.7 gives the code for configuring Apache remotely to host a website as follows:

```python
#!/usr/bin/env python
# Python Network Programming Cookbook, Second Edition -- Chapter - 6
# This program is optimized for Python 2.7.12 and Python 3.5.2.
# It may run on any other version with/without modifications.

from getpass import getpass
from fabric.api import env, put, sudo, prompt
from fabric.contrib.files import exists

WWW_DOC_ROOT = "/data/apache/test/"
WWW_USER = "www-data"
WWW_GROUP = "www-data"
APACHE_SITES_PATH = "/etc/apache2/sites-enabled/"
APACHE_INIT_SCRIPT = "/etc/init.d/apache2 "


def remote_server():
    env.hosts = ['127.0.0.1']
    env.user = prompt('Enter user name: ')
```

```
    env.password = getpass('Enter your system password: ')


def setup_vhost():
    """ Setup a test website """
    print ("Preparing the Apache vhost setup...")
    print ("Setting up the document root...")
    if exists(WWW_DOC_ROOT):
        sudo("rm -rf %s" %WWW_DOC_ROOT)
    sudo("mkdir -p %s" %WWW_DOC_ROOT)
    sudo("chown -R %s.%s %s" %(env.user, env.user, WWW_DOC_ROOT))
    put(local_path="index.html", remote_path=WWW_DOC_ROOT)
    sudo("chown -R %s.%s %s" %(WWW_USER, WWW_GROUP, WWW_DOC_ROOT))
    print ("Setting up the vhost...")
    sudo("chown -R %s.%s %s" %(env.user, env.user, APACHE_SITES_PATH))
    put(local_path="vhost.conf", remote_path=APACHE_SITES_PATH)
    sudo("chown -R %s.%s %s" %('root', 'root', APACHE_SITES_PATH))
    sudo("%s restart" %APACHE_INIT_SCRIPT)
    print ("Setup complete. Now open the server path
http://abc.remote-server.org/ in your web browser.")
```

In order to run this script, the following line should be appended on your host file, for example, /etc/hosts:

```
127.0.0.1 abc.remote-server.org abc
```

You should also create a shortcut, fabfile.py. From the command line, you can do this by typing the following command:

$ ln -sfn 6_7_configure_Apache_for_hosting_website_remotely.py fabfile.py

Then, you can call the fab executable in various forms.

First, to log on to a remote server using your script, you can run the following Fabric function. This will result in the following output:

```
$ fab remote_server setup_vhost
[127.0.0.1] Executing task 'setup_vhost'
Preparing the Apache vhost setup...
Setting up the document root...
[127.0.0.1] sudo: rm -rf /data/apache/test/
[127.0.0.1] sudo: mkdir -p /data/apache/test/
[127.0.0.1] sudo: chown -R faruq.faruq /data/apache/test/
[127.0.0.1] put: index.html -> /data/apache/test/index.html
[127.0.0.1] sudo: chown -R www-data.www-data /data/apache/test/
Setting up the vhost...
[127.0.0.1] sudo: chown -R faruq.faruq /etc/apache2/sites-enabled/
[127.0.0.1] put: vhost.conf -> /etc/apache2/sites-enabled/vhost.conf
```

```
[127.0.0.1] sudo: chown -R root.root /etc/apache2/sites-enabled/
[127.0.0.1] sudo: /etc/init.d/apache2 restart
[127.0.0.1] out: Restarting web server: apache2apache2: Could not reliably
determine the server's fully qualified domain name, using 127.0.0.1 for
ServerName
[127.0.0.1] out:  ... waiting apache2: Could not reliably determine the
server's fully qualified domain name, using 127.0.0.1 for ServerName
[127.0.0.1] out: .
[127.0.0.1] out:
Setup complete. Now open the server path http://abc.remote-server.org/ in
your web browser.
Done.
Disconnecting from 127.0.0.1... done.
```

After you execute this recipe, you can open your browser and try to access the path you set up on the host file (for example, /etc/hosts). It should show the following output on your browser:

It works!

This is the default web page for this server.

The web server software is running but no content has been added, yet.

How it works...

This recipe sets up the initial Apache configuration parameters as constants and then defines two functions. In the remote_server() function, the usual Fabric environment parameters, for example, hosts, user, password, and so on, are placed.

The setup_vhost() function executes a series of privileged commands. First, it checks whether the website's document root path is already created using the exists() function. If it exists, it removes that path and creates it in the next step. Using chown, it ensures that the path is owned by the current user.

In the next step, it uploads a bare bone HTML file, `index.html`, to the document root path. After uploading the file, it reverts the permission of the files to the web server user.

After setting up the document root, the `setup_vhost()` function uploads the supplied `vhost.conf` file to the Apache site configuration path. Then, it sets its owner as the root user.

Finally, the script restarts the Apache service so that the configuration is activated. If the configuration is successful, you should see the sample output shown earlier when you open the URL, `http://abc.remote-server.org/`, in your browser.

7

Working with Web Services – XML-RPC, SOAP, and REST

In this chapter, we will cover the following recipes:

- Querying a local XML-RPC server
- Writing a multithreaded, multicall XML-RPC server
- Running an XML-RPC server with a basic HTTP authentication
- Collecting some photo information from Flickr using REST
- Searching for SOAP methods from an Amazon S3 web service
- Searching Amazon for books through the product search API
- Creating RESTful web applications with Flask

Introduction

This chapter presents some interesting Python recipes on web services using three different approaches, namely, **XML Remote Procedure Call** (**XML-RPC**), **Simple Object Access Protocol** (**SOAP**), and **Representational State Transfer** (**REST**). The idea behind the web services is to enable an interaction between two software components over the web through a carefully designed protocol. The interface is machine readable. Various protocols are used to facilitate the web services.

Here, we bring examples from three commonly used protocols. XML-RPC uses HTTP as the transport medium, and communication is done using XML contents. A server that implements XML-RPC waits for a call from a suitable client. The client calls that server to execute remote procedures with different parameters. XML-RPC is simpler and comes with a minimum security in mind. On the other hand, SOAP has a rich set of protocols for enhanced remote procedure calls. REST is an architectural style to facilitate web services. It operates with HTTP request methods, namely, GET(), POST(), PUT(), and DELETE(). This chapter presents the practical use of these web services protocols and styles to achieve some common tasks.

Querying a local XML-RPC server

If you do a lot of web programming, it's most likely that you will come across this task: to get some information from a website that runs an XML-RPC service. Before we go into the depth of an XML-RPC service, let's launch an XML-RPC server and talk to it first.

Getting ready

In this recipe, we will use the Python Supervisor program that is widely used to launch and manage a bunch of executable programs. Supervisor can be run as a background daemon and can monitor child processes and restart if they die suddenly. We can install Supervisor by simply running the following command:

```
$pip install supervisor
```

Supervisor works on Python 2.x version - 2.4 and later. However, it does not work under Python 3 at the time of writing. So in order to run this example, you need to have Python 2 installed on your computer.

How to do it...

We need to create a configuration file for Supervisor. A sample configuration is given in this recipe. In this example, we define the Unix HTTP server socket and a few other parameters. Note the rpcinterface:supervisor section where rpcinterface_factory is defined to communicate with clients.

Using Supervisor, we configure a simple server program in the program: `7_2_multithreaded_multicall_xmlrpc_server.py` section by specifying the command and some other parameters.

Listing 7.1a gives the code for a minimal Supervisor configuration, as shown:

```
[unix_http_server]
file=/tmp/supervisor.sock    ; (the path to the socket file)
chmod=0700                   ; socket file mode (default 0700)

[supervisord]
logfile=/tmp/supervisord.log
loglevel=info
pidfile=/tmp/supervisord.pid
nodaemon=true

[rpcinterface:supervisor]
supervisor.rpcinterface_factory =
supervisor.rpcinterface:make_main_rpcinterface

[program:7_2_multithreaded_multicall_xmlrpc_server.py]
command=python 7_2_multithreaded_multicall_xmlrpc_server.py ; the
program (relative uses PATH, can take args)
process_name=%(program_name)s ; process_name expr (default
%(program_name)s)
```

If you create the preceding Supervisor configuration file in your favorite editor, you can run Supervisor by simply calling it.

Now, we can code an XML-RPC client that can act as a Supervisor proxy and give us the information about the running processes.

Listing 7.1b gives the code for querying a local XML-RPC server, as shown:

```
#!/usr/bin/env python
# Python Network Programming Cookbook, Second Edition -- Chapter - 7
# This program is optimized for Python 2.7.12.
# Supervisor requires Python 2.x, and does not run on Python 3.x.


import supervisor.xmlrpc
import xmlrpclib

def query_supervisr(sock):
    transport = supervisor.xmlrpc.SupervisorTransport(None, None,
                'unix://%s' %sock)
    proxy = xmlrpclib.ServerProxy('http://127.0.0.1',
```

```
                    transport=transport)
        print ("Getting info about all running processes
                    via Supervisord...")
        print (proxy.supervisor.getAllProcessInfo())

if __name__ == '__main__':
    query_supervisr(sock='/tmp/supervisor.sock')
```

If you run the `Supervisor` daemon, it will show output similar to the following:

```
$ supervisord
2013-09-27 16:40:56,861 INFO RPC interface 'supervisor' initialized
2013-09-27 16:40:56,861 CRIT Server 'unix_http_server' running
without any HTTP authentication checking
2013-09-27 16:40:56,861 INFO supervisord started with pid 27436
2013-09-27 16:40:57,864 INFO spawned:
'7_2_multithreaded_multicall_xmlrpc_server.py' with pid 27439
2013-09-27 16:40:58,940 INFO success:
7_2_multithreaded_multicall_xmlrpc_server.py entered RUNNING state,
process has stayed up for > than 1 seconds (startsecs)
```

Note that our child process, `7_2_multithreaded_multicall_xmlrpc_server.py`, has been launched.

Now, if you run the client code, it will query the XML-RPC server interface of Supervisor and list the running processes, as shown:

```
$ python 7_1_query_xmlrpc_server.py
Getting info about all running processes via Supervisord...
[{'now': 1380296807, 'group':
'7_2_multithreaded_multicall_xmlrpc_server.py', 'description': 'pid
27439, uptime 0:05:50', 'pid': 27439, 'stderr_logfile':
'/tmp/7_2_multithreaded_multicall_xmlrpc_server.py-stderr---
supervisor-i_VmKz.log', 'stop': 0, 'statename': 'RUNNING', 'start':
1380296457, 'state': 20, 'stdout_logfile':
'/tmp/7_2_multithreaded_multicall_xmlrpc_server.py-stdout---
supervisor-eMuJqk.log', 'logfile':
'/tmp/7_2_multithreaded_multicall_xmlrpc_server.py-stdout---
supervisor-eMuJqk.log', 'exitstatus': 0, 'spawnerr': '', 'name':
'7_2_multithreaded_multicall_xmlrpc_server.py'}]
```

How it works...

This recipe relies on running the `Supervisor` daemon (configured with `rpcinterface`) in the background. Supervisor launches another XML-RPC server, as follows:
`7_2_multithreaded_multicall_xmlrpc_server.py`.

The client code has a `query_supervisr()` method, which takes an argument for the Supervisor socket. In this method, an instance of `SupervisorTransport` is created with the Unix socket path. Then, an XML-RPC server proxy is created by instantiating the `ServerProxy()` class of `xmlrpclib` by passing the server address and previously created transport.

The XML-RPC server proxy then calls the Supervisor's `getAllProcessInfo()` method, which prints the process information of the child process. This process includes `pid`, `statename`, `description`, and so on.

Writing a multithreaded, multicall XML-RPC server

You can make your XML-RPC server accept multiple calls simultaneously. This means that multiple function calls can return a single result. In addition to this, if your server is multithreaded, then you can execute more code after the server is launched in a single thread. The program's main thread will not be blocked in this manner.

How to do it...

We can create a `ServerThread` class inheriting from the threading. Thread class and wrap a `SimpleXMLRPCServer` instance in an attribute of this class. This can be set up to accept multiple calls.

Then, we can create two functions: one launches the multithreaded, multicall XML-RPC server, and the other creates a client to that server.

Listing 7.2 gives the code for writing a multithreaded, multicall XML-RPC server, as shown:

```
#!/usr/bin/env python
# Python Network Programming Cookbook, Second Edition -- Chapter - 7
# This program is optimized for Python 3.5.2.
# To make it work with Python 2.7.12:
#      Follow through the code inline for some changes.
# It may run on any other version with/without modifications.

import argparse
import xmlrpc
# Comment out the above line and uncomment the below line for Python 2.x.
#import xmlrpclib
```

```
import threading

from xmlrpc.server import SimpleXMLRPCServer
# Comment out the above line and uncomment the below line for Python 2.x.
#from SimpleXMLRPCServer import SimpleXMLRPCServer

# some trivial functions
def add(x,y):
    return x+y

def subtract(x, y):
    return x-y

def multiply(x, y):
    return x*y

def divide(x, y):
    return x/y


class ServerThread(threading.Thread):
    def __init__(self, server_addr):
        threading.Thread.__init__(self)
        self.server = SimpleXMLRPCServer(server_addr)
        self.server.register_multicall_functions()
        self.server.register_function(add, 'add')
        self.server.register_function(subtract, 'subtract')
        self.server.register_function(multiply, 'multiply')
        self.server.register_function(divide, 'divide')

    def run(self):
        self.server.serve_forever()
def run_server(host, port):
    # server code
    server_addr = (host, port)
    server = ServerThread(server_addr)
    server.start() # The server is now running
    print ("Server thread started. Testing the server...")

def run_client(host, port):

    # client code
    proxy = xmlrpc.client.ServerProxy("http://%s:%s/" %(host, port))
    # Comment out the above line and uncomment the
      below line for Python 2.x.
    #proxy = xmlrpclib.ServerProxy("http://%s:%s/" %(host, port))

    multicall = xmlrpc.client.MultiCall(proxy)
```

```
# Comment out the above line and uncomment the
   below line for Python 2.x.
#multicall = xmlrpclib.MultiCall(proxy)

multicall.add(7,3)
multicall.subtract(7,3)
multicall.multiply(7,3)
multicall.divide(7,3)
result = multicall()
print ("7+3=%d, 7-3=%d, 7*3=%d, 7/3=%d" % tuple(result))

if __name__ == '__main__':
    parser = argparse.ArgumentParser(description='Multithreaded
            multicall XMLRPC Server/Proxy')
    parser.add_argument('--host', action="store", dest="host",
                        default='localhost')
    parser.add_argument('--port', action="store", dest="port",
                        default=8000, type=int)
    # parse arguments
    given_args = parser.parse_args()
    host, port =  given_args.host, given_args.port
    run_server(host, port)
    run_client(host, port)
```

If you run this script, you will see output similar to the following:

```
$ python 7_2_multithreaded_multicall_xmlrpc_server.py --port=8000
Server thread started. Testing the server...
127.0.0.1 - - [13/Jun/2017 23:00:27] "POST / HTTP/1.1" 200 -
7+3=10, 7-3=4, 7*3=21, 7/3=2
```

How it works...

In this recipe, we have created a `ServerThread` subclass inheriting from the Python threading library's `thread` class. This subclass initializes a server attribute that creates an instance of the `SimpleXMLRPC` server. The XML-RPC server address can be given through the command-line input. In order to enable the multicall function, we called the `register_multicall_functions()` method on the server instance.

Then, four trivial functions are registered with this XML-RPC server: `add()`, `subtract()`, `multiply()`, and `divide()`. These functions do exactly the same operation as their names suggest.

In order to launch the server, we pass a host and port to the `run_server()` function. A server instance is created using the `ServerThread` class discussed earlier. The start() method of this server instance launches the XML-RPC server.

On the client side, the `run_client()` function accepts the same host and port arguments from the command line. It then creates a proxy instance of the XML-RPC server discussed earlier by calling the `ServerProxy()` class from `xmlrpclib`. This proxy instance is then passed onto the `multicall` class instance, multicall. Now, the preceding four trivial RPC methods can be run, for example, add, subtract, multiply, and divide. Finally, we can get the result through a single call, for example, `multicall()`. The result tuple is then printed in a single line.

Running an XML-RPC server with a basic HTTP authentication

Sometimes, you may need to implement authentication with an XML-RPC server. This recipe presents an example of a basic HTTP authentication with an XML-RPC server.

How to do it...

We can create a subclass of `SimpleXMLRPCServer` and override its request handler so that when a request comes, it is verified against given login credentials.

Listing 7.3a gives the code for running an XML-RPC server with a basic HTTP authentication, as shown:

```
#!/usr/bin/env python
# Python Network Programming Cookbook, Second Edition -- Chapter - 7
# This program is optimized for Python 3.5.2.
# To make it work with Python 2.7.12:
#       Follow through the code inline for some changes.
# It may run on any other version with/without modifications.


import argparse
import xmlrpc
# Comment out the above line and uncomment the below line for Python 2.x.
#import xmlrpclib
from base64 import b64decode

from xmlrpc.server import SimpleXMLRPCServer, SimpleXMLRPCRequestHandler
```

```
# Comment out the above line and uncomment the below line for Python 2.x.
#from SimpleXMLRPCServer  import SimpleXMLRPCServer,
SimpleXMLRPCRequestHandler


class SecureXMLRPCServer(SimpleXMLRPCServer):

    def __init__(self, host, port, username, password, *args, **kargs):
        self.username = username
        self.password = password
        # authenticate method is called from inner class
        class VerifyingRequestHandler(SimpleXMLRPCRequestHandler):
            # method to override
            def parse_request(request):
                if SimpleXMLRPCRequestHandler.
                   parse_request(request):
                    # authenticate
                    if self.authenticate(request.headers):
                        return True
                    else:
                        # if authentication fails return 401
                        request.send_error(401, 'Authentication
                        failed, Try agin.')
                return False
        # initialize
        SimpleXMLRPCServer.__init__(self, (host, port),
        requestHandler=VerifyingRequestHandler, *args, **kargs)

    def authenticate(self, headers):
        headers = headers.get('Authorization').split()
        basic, encoded = headers[0], headers[1]
        if basic != 'Basic':
            print ('Only basic authentication supported')
            return False
        secret = b64decode(encoded).split(b':')
        username, password = secret[0].decode("utf-8"),
                        secret[1].decode("utf-8")
        return True if (username == self.username and
                  password == self.password) else False

def run_server(host, port, username, password):
    server = SecureXMLRPCServer(host, port, username, password)
    # simple test function
    def echo(msg):
        """Reply client in  uppser case """
        reply = msg.upper()
        print ("Client said: %s. So we echo that in uppercase: %s"
             %(msg, reply))
```

```
        return reply
    server.register_function(echo, 'echo')
    print ("Running a HTTP auth enabled XMLRPC server
            on %s:%s..." %(host, port))
    server.serve_forever()


if __name__ == '__main__':
    parser = argparse.ArgumentParser(description='Multithreaded
            multicall XMLRPC Server/Proxy')
    parser.add_argument('--host', action="store", dest="host",
                        default='localhost')
    parser.add_argument('--port', action="store", dest="port",
                         default=8000, type=int)
    parser.add_argument('--username', action="store",
                        dest="username", default='user')
    parser.add_argument('--password', action="store",
                        dest="password", default='pass')
    # parse arguments
    given_args = parser.parse_args()
    host, port =  given_args.host, given_args.port
    username, password = given_args.username, given_args.password
    run_server(host, port, username, password)
```

If this server is run, then the following output can be seen by default:

```
$ python 7_3a_xmlrpc_server_with_http_auth.py --port=8000
Running a HTTP auth enabled XMLRPC server on localhost:8000...
Client said: hello server.... So we echo that in uppercase: HELLO SERVER...
127.0.0.1 - - [13/Jun/2017 23:32:14] "POST /RPC2 HTTP/1.1" 200 -
```

Now, let us create a simple client proxy and use the same login credentials as used with the server.

Listing 7.3b gives the code for the XML-RPC client, as shown:

```
#!/usr/bin/env python
# Python Network Programming Cookbook, Second Edition -- Chapter - 7
# This program is optimized for Python 3.5.2.
# To make it work with Python 2.7.12:
#       Follow through the code inline for some changes.
# It may run on any other version with/without modifications.


import argparse
import xmlrpc
# Comment out the above line and uncomment the below line for Python 2.x.
#import xmlrpclib
```

```
from xmlrpc.server import SimpleXMLRPCServer
# Comment out the above line for Python 2.x.

def run_client(host, port, username, password):
    server = xmlrpc.client.ServerProxy('http://%s:%s@%s:%s'
             %(username, password, host, port, ))
    # Comment out the above line and uncomment the
      below line for Python 2.x.
    #server = xmlrpclib.ServerProxy('http://%s:%s@%s:%s'
              %(username, password, host, port, ))
    msg = "hello server..."
    print ("Sending message to server: %s  " %msg)
    print ("Got reply: %s" %server.echo(msg))

if __name__ == '__main__':
    parser = argparse.ArgumentParser(description='Multithreaded
             multicall XMLRPC Server/Proxy')
    parser.add_argument('--host', action="store", dest="host",
                        default='localhost')
    parser.add_argument('--port', action="store", dest="port",
                        default=8000, type=int)
    parser.add_argument('--username', action="store",
                        dest="username", default='user')
    parser.add_argument('--password', action="store",
                        dest="password", default='pass')
    # parse arguments
    given_args = parser.parse_args()
    host, port =  given_args.host, given_args.port
    username, password = given_args.username, given_args.password
    run_client(host, port, username, password)
```

If you run the client, then it shows the following output:

```
$ python 7_3b_xmprpc_client.py --port=8000
Sending message to server: hello server...
Got reply: HELLO SERVER...
```

The following screenshot shows the server and client:

How it works...

In the server script, the SecureXMLRPCServer subclass is created by inheriting from SimpleXMLRPCServer. In this subclass initialization code, we created the VerifyingRequestHandler class that actually intercepts the request and does the basic authentication using the authenticate() method.

In the authenticate() method, the HTTP request is passed as an argument. This method checks the presence of the value of authorization. If its value is set to basic, it then decodes the encoded password with the b64decode() function from the base64 standard module. After extracting the username and password, it then checks that with the server's given credentials set up initially.

In the run_server() function, a simple echo() sub function is defined and registered with the SecureXMLRPCServer instance.

In the client script, `run_client()` simply takes the server address and login credentials and passes them to the `ServerProxy()` instance. It then sends a single line message through the `echo()` method.

Collecting some photo information from Flickr using REST

Many Internet websites provide a web services interface through their REST APIs. Flickr, a famous photo sharing website, has a REST interface. Let's try to gather some photo information to build a specialized database or other photo-related applications.

To run this recipe, you need to install `requests` using pip:

```
$ sudo pip install requests
```

How to do it...

We need the REST URLs for making the HTTP requests. For simplicity's sake, the URLs are hard coded in this recipe. We can use the third-party requests module to make the REST requests. It has the convenient `GET()`, `POST()`, `PUT()`, and `DELETE()` methods.

In order to talk to Flickr web services, you need to register yourself and get a secret API key. This API key can be placed in a `local_settings.py` file or supplied through the command line.

Listing 7.4 gives the code for collecting some photo information from Flickr using REST, as shown:

```python
#!/usr/bin/env python
# Python Network Programming Cookbook, Second Edition -- Chapter - 7
# This program is optimized for Python 2.7.12 and Python 3.5.2.
# It may run on any other version with/without modifications.
# Supply Flickr API key via local_settings.py

import argparse
import json
import requests

try:
    from local_settings import flickr_apikey
except ImportError:
```

```
        pass


def collect_photo_info(api_key, tag, max_count):
    """Collects some interesting info about some photos from Flickr.com for
a given tag """
    photo_collection = []
    url =
"http://api.flickr.com/services/rest/?method=flickr.photos.search&tags=%s&f
ormat=json&
        nojsoncallback=1&api_key=%s" %(tag, api_key)
    resp = requests.get(url)
    results = resp.json()
    count  = 0
    for p in results['photos']['photo']:
        if count >= max_count:
            return photo_collection
        print ('Processing photo: "%s"' % p['title'])
        photo = {}
        url = "http://api.flickr.com/services/rest/?
        method=flickr.photos.getInfo&photo_id=" + p['id'] +
        "&format=json&nojsoncallback=1&api_key=" + api_key
        info = requests.get(url).json()
        photo["flickrid"] = p['id']
        photo["title"] = info['photo']['title']['_content']
        photo["description"] = info['photo']['description']
                            ['_content']
        photo["page_url"] = info['photo']['urls']['url'][0]
                            ['_content']
        photo["farm"] = info['photo']['farm']
        photo["server"] = info['photo']['server']
        photo["secret"] = info['photo']['secret']
        # comments
        numcomments = int(info['photo']['comments']['_content'])
        if numcomments:
            #print "    Now reading comments (%d)..." % numcomments
            url = "http://api.flickr.com/services/rest/?
                method=flickr.photos.comments.
                getList&photo_id=" + p['id'] +
                "&format=json&nojsoncallback=1&
                api_key=" + api_key
            comments = requests.get(url).json()
            photo["comment"] = []
            for c in comments['comments']['comment']:
                comment = {}
                comment["body"] = c['_content']
                comment["authorid"] = c['author']
                comment["authorname"] = c['authorname']
```

```
                photo["comment"].append(comment)
            photo_collection.append(photo)
            count = count + 1
        return photo_collection


if __name__ == '__main__':
    parser = argparse.ArgumentParser(description='Get photo
            info from Flickr')
    parser.add_argument('--api-key', action="store",
            dest="api_key", default=flickr_apikey)
    parser.add_argument('--tag', action="store",
            dest="tag", default='Python')
    parser.add_argument('--max-count', action="store",
            dest="max_count", default=3, type=int)
    # parse arguments
    given_args = parser.parse_args()
    api_key, tag, max_count =  given_args.api_key,
     given_args.tag, given_args.max_count
    photo_info = collect_photo_info(api_key, tag, max_count)
    for photo in photo_info:
        for k,v in photo.iteritems():
            if k == "title":
                print ("Showiing photo info....")
            elif k == "comment":
                "\tPhoto got %s comments." %len(v)
            else:
                print ("\t%s => %s" %(k,v))
```

You can run this recipe with your Flickr API key either by placing it in a
`local_settings.py` file or supplying it from the command line (through the `--api-key`
argument). In addition to the API key, a search tag and maximum count of the result
arguments can be supplied. By default, this recipe will search for the Python tag and restrict
the result to three entries, as shown in the following output:

```
$ python 7_4_get_flickr_photo_info.py
Processing photo: "legolas"
Processing photo: ""The Dance of the Hunger of Kaa""
Processing photo: "Rocky"
    description => Stimson Python
Showiing photo info....
    farm => 8
    server => 7402
    secret => 6cbae671b5
    flickrid => 10054626824
    page_url => http://www.flickr.com/photos/102763809@N03/10054626824/
    description => &quot; 'Good. Begins now the dance--the Dance of the
```

Hunger of Kaa. Sit still and watch.'

He turned twice or thrice in a big circle, weaving his head from right to left.

Then he began making loops and figures of eight with his body, and soft, oozy triangles that melted into squares and five-sided figures, and coiled mounds, never resting, never hurrying, and never stopping his low humming song. It grew darker and darker, till at last the dragging, shifting coils disappeared, but they could hear the rustle of the scales."

(From "Kaa's Hunting" in "The Jungle Book" (1893) by Rudyard Kipling)

These old abandoned temples built around the 12th century belong to the abandoned city which inspired Kipling's Jungle Book.

They are rising at the top of a mountain which dominates the jungle at 811 meters above sea level in the centre of the jungle of Bandhavgarh located in the Indian state Madhya Pradesh.

Baghel King Vikramaditya Singh abandoned Bandhavgarh fort in 1617 when Rewa, at a distance of 130 km was established as a capital.

Abandonment allowed wildlife development in this region.

When Baghel Kings became aware of it, he declared Bandhavgarh as their hunting preserve and strictly prohibited tree cutting and wildlife hunting...

Join the photographer at <a href="http://www.facebook.com/laurent.goldstein.photography" rel="nofollow">www.facebook.com/laurent.goldstein.photography</a>

© All photographs are copyrighted and all rights reserved.

Please do not use any photographs without permission (even for private use).

The use of any work without consent of the artist is PROHIBITED and will lead automatically to consequences.

Showiing photo info....
```
    farm => 6
    server => 5462
    secret => 6f9c0e7f83
    flickrid => 10051136944
    page_url => http://www.flickr.com/photos/design1dg/10051136944/
    description => Ball Python
```
Showiing photo info....
```
    farm => 4
    server => 3744
    secret => 529840767f
    flickrid => 10046353675
    page_url =>
```
http://www.flickr.com/photos/megzzdollphotos/10046353675/

How it works...

This recipe demonstrates how to interact with Flickr using its REST APIs. In this example, the `collect_photo_info()` tag takes three parameters: Flickr API key, a search tag, and the desired number of search results.

We construct the first URL to search for photos. Note that in this URL, the value of the method parameter is `flickr.photos.search` and the desired result format is JSON.

The results of the first `GET()` call are stored in the resp variable and then converted to the JSON format by calling the `json()` method on resp. Now, the JSON data is read in a loop looking into the `['photos']['photo']` iterator. A `photo_collection` list is created to return the result after organizing the information. In this list, each photo's information is represented by a dictionary. The keys of this dictionary are populated by extracting information from the earlier JSON response and another GET request to get the information regarding the specific photo.

Note that to get the comments about a photo, we need to make another `GET()` request and gather comment information from the `['comments']['comment']` elements of the returned JSON. Finally, these comments are appended to a list and attached to the photo dictionary entry.

In the main function, we extract the `photo_collection` dictionary and print some useful information about each photo.

Searching for SOAP methods from an Amazon S3 web service

If you need to interact with a server that implements web services in SOAP, then this recipe can help to get a starting point.

Getting ready

We can use the third-party `SOAPpy` library for this task. This can be installed by running the following command:

```
$ sudo pip install SOAPpy
```

How to do it...

We create a proxy instance and introspect the server methods before we can call them.

In this recipe, let's interact with an Amazon S3 storage service. We have got a test URL for the web services API. An API key is necessary to do this simple task.

Listing 7.5 gives the code for searching for SOAP methods from an Amazon S3 web service, as shown:

```python
#!/usr/bin/env python
# Python Network Programming Cookbook -- Chapter - 7
# This program requires Python 2.7 or any later version
# SOAPpy has discontinued its support for Python 3.
# You may find more information and other potential libraries at
https://stackoverflow.com/questions/7817303/what-soap-libraries-exist-for-p
ython-3-x

import SOAPpy

TEST_URL = 'http://s3.amazonaws.com/ec2-downloads/2009-04-04.ec2.wsdl'


def list_soap_methods(url):
    proxy = SOAPpy.WSDL.Proxy(url)
    print ('%d methods in WSDL:' % len(proxy.methods) + '\n')
    for key in proxy.methods.keys():
        print ("Key Name: %s" %key)
        print ("Key Details:")
        for k,v in proxy.methods[key].__dict__.iteritems():
            print ("%s ==> %s" %(k,v))
        break

if __name__ == '__main__':
    list_soap_methods(TEST_URL)
```

If you run this script, it will print the total number of available methods that support **web services definition language** (**WSDL**) and the details of one arbitrary method, as shown:

```
$ python 7_5_search_amazonaws_with_SOAP.py
/home/faruq/env/lib/python2.7/site-packages/wstools/XMLSchema.py:1280:
UserWarning: annotation is
ignored
  warnings.warn('annotation is ignored')
43 methods in WSDL:
Key Name: ReleaseAddress
Key Details:
```

```
    encodingStyle ==> None
    style ==> document
    methodName ==> ReleaseAddress
    retval ==> None
    soapAction ==> ReleaseAddress
    namespace ==> None
    use ==> literal
    location ==> https://ec2.amazonaws.com/
    inparams ==> [<wstools.WSDLTools.ParameterInfo instance at
0x8fb9d0c>]
    outheaders ==> []
    inheaders ==> []
    transport ==> http://schemas.xmlsoap.org/soap/http
    outparams ==> [<wstools.WSDLTools.ParameterInfo instance at
0x8fb9d2c>]
```

How it works...

This script defines a method called `list_soap_methods()` that takes a URL and constructs a SOAP proxy object by calling the `WSDL.Proxy()` method of `SOAPpy`. The available SOAP methods are available under this proxy's method attribute.

An iteration over the proxy's method keys are done to introspect the method keys. A for loop just prints the details of a single SOAP method, that is, the name of the key and details about it.

Searching Amazon for books through the product search API

If you like to search for products on Amazon and include some of them in your website or application, this recipe can help you to do that. We can see how to search Amazon for books.

Getting ready

This recipe depends on the third-party Python `bottlenose` library. You can install this library using pip, as shown in the following command:

```
$ pip install  bottlenose
```

First, you need to place your Amazon account's access key, secret key, and affiliate ID into `local_settings.py`. A sample settings file is provided with the book code. You can also edit this script and place it here as well.

How to do it...

We can use the `bottlenose` library that implements the Amazon's product search APIs.

Listing 7.6 gives the code for searching Amazon for books through product search APIs, as shown:

```python
#!/usr/bin/env python
# Python Network Programming Cookbook, Second Edition -- Chapter - 7
# This program is optimized for Python 2.7.12 and Python 3.5.2.
# It may run on any other version with/without modifications.
# Supply the Amazon Access and Secret Keys via local_settings.py

import argparse
import bottlenose
from xml.dom import minidom as xml

try:
    from local_settings import amazon_account
except ImportError:
    pass

ACCESS_KEY = amazon_account['access_key']
SECRET_KEY = amazon_account['secret_key']
AFFILIATE_ID = amazon_account['affiliate_id']


def search_for_books(tag, index):
    """Search Amazon for Books """
    amazon = bottlenose.Amazon(ACCESS_KEY,  SECRET_KEY,  AFFILIATE_ID)
    results = amazon.ItemSearch(
                SearchIndex = index,
                Sort = "relevancerank",
                Keywords = tag
```

```
                )
        parsed_result = xml.parseString(results)

        all_items = []
        attrs = ['Title','Author', 'URL']

        for item in parsed_result.getElementsByTagName('Item'):
            parse_item = {}

            for attr in attrs:
                parse_item[attr] = ""
                try:
                    parse_item[attr] = item.getElementsByTagName(attr)
                                        [0].childNodes[0].data
                except:
                    pass
            all_items.append(parse_item)
        return all_items

if __name__ == '__main__':
    parser = argparse.ArgumentParser(description='Search
            info from Amazon')
    parser.add_argument('--tag', action="store",
     dest="tag", default='Python')
    parser.add_argument('--index', action="store",
     dest="index", default='Books')
    # parse arguments
    given_args = parser.parse_args()
    books = search_for_books(given_args.tag, given_args.index)
    for book in books:
        for k,v in book.iteritems():
            print ("%s: %s" %(k,v))
        print ("-" * 80)
```

If you run this recipe with a search tag and index, you can see some results similar to the following output:

```
$ python 7_6_search_amazon_for_books.py --tag=Python --index=Books
URL:
http://www.amazon.com/Python-In-Day-Basics-Coding/dp/tech-data/1490475575%3
FSubscriptionId%3DAKIAIPPW3IK76PBRLWBA%26tag%3D7052-6929-7878%261inkCode%3D
xm2%26camp%3D2025%26creative%3D386001%26creativeASIN%3D1490475575
Author: Richard Wagstaff
Title: Python In A Day: Learn The Basics, Learn It Quick, Start Coding Fast
(In A Day Books) (Volume 1)
------------------------------------------------------------------
URL:
http://www.amazon.com/Learning-Python-Mark-Lutz/dp/tech-data/1449355730%3FS
```

```
ubscriptionId%3DAKIAIPPW3IK76PBRLWBA%26tag%3D7052-6929-7878%26linkCode%3Dxm
2%26camp%3D2025%26creative%3D386001%26creativeASIN%3D1449355730
Author: Mark Lutz
Title: Learning Python
-----------------------------------------------------------------------
URL:
http://www.amazon.com/Python-Programming-Introduction-Computer-Science/dp/t
ech-
data/1590282418%3FSubscriptionId%3DAKIAIPPW3IK76PBRLWBA%26tag%3D7052-6929-7
878%26linkCode%3Dxm2%26camp%3D2025%26creative%3D386001%26creativeASIN%3D159
0282418
Author: John Zelle
Title: Python Programming: An Introduction to Computer Science 2nd Edition
-----------------------------------------------------------------------
```

How it works...

This recipe uses the third-party `bottlenose` library's `Amazon()` class to create an object for searching Amazon through the product search API. This is done by the top-level `search_for_books()` function. The `ItemSearch()` method of this object is invoked with passing values to the `SearchIndex` and `Keywords` keys. It uses the `relevancerank` method to sort the search results.

The search results are processed using the XMLmodule's `minidom` interface, which has a useful `parseString()` method. It returns the parsed XML tree-like data structure. The `getElementsByTagName()` method on this data structure helps to find the item's information. The item attributes are then looked up and placed in a dictionary of parsed items. Finally, all the parsed items are appended in a `all_items()` list and returned to the user.

Creating RESTful web applications with Flask

Creating a simple RESTful web service or a web application with a set of RESTful applications with Python has never been easier. Now you can create a simple web service and make it run in a matter of minutes in Python.

Getting ready

This recipe depends on the third-party Python `Flask` library. If it is not already available in your local Python installation, you can install this library using pip as follows:

```
$ pip install  Flask
```

How to do it...

We can use the `Flask` library to create simple RESTful web services and web applications without having to install any complex web service engines or web application containers.

Listing 7.7 gives the code for a simple web service that gets a number as an input to the RESTful service, and outputs the Fibonacci number and Square of the number:

```python
#!/usr/bin/env python
# Python Network Programming Cookbook, Second Edition -- Chapter - 7
# This program is optimized for Python 2.7.12 and Python 3.5.2.
# It may run on any other version with/without modifications.

from flask import Flask
app = Flask(__name__)

@app.route('/<int:num>')
def index(num=1):
    return "Your Python Web Service <hr>Fibonacci("+ str(num) + "):
     "+ str(fibonacci(num))+ "<hr>Square("+ str(num) + "):
     "+ str(square(num))

def fibonacci(n):
    if n == 0:
        return 0
    elif n == 1:
        return 1
    else:
        return fibonacci(n-1) + fibonacci(n-2)


def square(n):
    print ("Calculating for the number %s" %n)
    return n*n

if __name__ == '__main__':
    app.run(debug=True)
```

If you run this recipe with a search tag and index, you can see some results similar to the following output:

```
$ python 7_7_create_restful_webservice.py
* Running on http://127.0.0.1:5000/ (Press CTRL+C to quit)
* Restarting with stat
* Debugger is active!
* Debugger PIN: 145-461-290
Calculating for the number 25
127.0.0.1 - - [15/Jun/2017 22:16:12] "GET /25 HTTP/1.1" 200 -
127.0.0.1 - - [15/Jun/2017 22:16:12] "GET /favicon.ico HTTP/1.1" 404 -
```

The output is shown in the following screenshot:

Instead of accessing the web service by the browser, you may also access it through curl.

Curl is very useful for testing RESTful web services. If it is not installed in your computer, you may install it using the following command:

```
$ sudo apt-get install curl
```

Once installed, you may access the RESTful interface of your application using curl:

```
$ curl -i http://127.0.0.1:5000/23
HTTP/1.0 200 OK
Content-Type: text/html; charset=utf-8
Content-Length: 67
Server: Werkzeug/0.12.2 Python/3.5.2
Date: Thu, 15 Jun 2017 21:16:07 GMT
Your Python Web Service <hr>Fibonacci(23): 28657<hr>Square(23): 529
```

The output is displayed in the following screenshot:

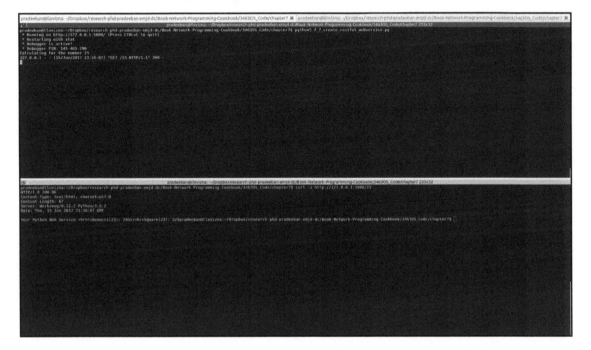

How it works...

This recipe uses the third-party `Flask` library to create a simple RESTful application with the services that we design.

As we designed, the web service accepts the inputs in the formal:

```
http://127.0.0.1:5000/<int>
```

The integer value is taken as the input to both our Fibonacci and Square functions. The computation is done in the Python backend and the output is printed back in the browser—as the output of the web service.

The program can be run with debug mode turned off as well, though in our example we have left it in the debug mode to get more verbose logs.

To learn more about Flask, visit their website at: `http://flask.pocoo.org/`. There are other alternatives to Flask such as Django (`https://docs.djangoproject.com/en/1.11/`) and other frameworks that are built on top of Flask such as Eve (`http://python-eve.org/`) that you may also find useful to build RESTful web services and web applications using Python.

8
Network Monitoring and Security

In this chapter, we will cover the following recipes:

- Sniffing packets on your network
- Saving packets in the pcap format using the pcap dumper
- Adding an extra header in HTTP packets
- Scanning the ports of a remote host
- Customizing the IP address of a packet
- Replaying traffic by reading from a saved pcap file
- Scanning the broadcast of packets

Introduction

This chapter presents some interesting Python recipes for network security monitoring and vulnerability scanning. We begin by sniffing packets on a network using the pcap library. Then, we start using Scapy, which is a **Swiss knife** type of library that can do many similar tasks. Some common tasks in packet analysis are presented using Scapy, such as saving a packet in the pcap format, adding an extra header, and modifying the IP address of a packet.

Some other advanced tasks on network intrusion detection are also included in this chapter, for example, replaying traffic from a saved pcap file and broadcast scanning.

Sniffing packets on your network

If you are interested in sniffing packets on your local network, this recipe can be used as the starting point. Remember that you may not be able to sniff packets other than what is destined to your machine, as decent network switches will only forward traffic that is designated for your machine.

Getting ready

You need to install the `pylibpcap` library (Version 0.6.4 or greater) for this recipe to work. In Debian-based Linux systems, you may install it using the following command:

```
$ sudo apt-get install python-libpcap
```

It is also available at SourceForge (`http://sourceforge.net/projects/pylibpcap/`).

Python 3 may require you to install `pypcap` using `pip` instead:

```
$ sudo pip install pypcap
```

You also need to install the `construct` library, which can be installed from PyPI via `pip` or `easy_install`, as shown in the following command:

```
$ easy_install construct
```

 You may also install `construct` directly from `https://github.com/construct/construct/releases`.

How to do it...

We can supply command-line arguments, for example, the network interface name and TCP port number, for sniffing.

Listing 8.1 gives the code for sniffing packets on your network, as follows:

```
#!/usr/bin/env python
# Python Network Programming Cookbook, Second Edition -- Chapter - 8
# This program is optimized for Python 2.7.12.
# It may run on any other version with/without modifications.

import argparse
```

```
import pcap
from construct.protocols.ipstack import ip_stack


def print_packet(pktlen, data, timestamp):
    """ Callback for priniting the packet payload"""
    if not data:
        return
    stack = ip_stack.parse(data)
    payload = stack.next.next.next
    print (payload)

def main():
    # setup commandline arguments
    parser = argparse.ArgumentParser(description='Packet Sniffer')
    parser.add_argument('--iface', action="store",
     dest="iface", default='eth0')
    parser.add_argument('--port', action="store",
     dest="port", default=80, type=int)
    # parse arguments
    given_args = parser.parse_args()
    iface, port =  given_args.iface, given_args.port
    # start sniffing
    pc = pcap.pcapObject()
    pc.open_live(iface, 1600, 0, 100)
    pc.setfilter('dst port %d' %port, 0, 0)
    print ('Press CTRL+C to end capture')
    try:
        while True:
            pc.dispatch(1, print_packet)
    except KeyboardInterrupt:
        print ('Packet statistics: %d packets received,
                %d packets dropped, %d packets
                dropped by the interface' % pc.stats())

if __name__ == '__main__':
    main()
```

If you run this script by passing the command-line arguments, --iface=eth0 and --port=80, this script will sniff all the HTTP packets from your web browser. So, after running this script, if you access http://www.google.com on your browser, you can then see a raw packet output like the following:

```
python 8_1_packet_sniffer.py --iface=eth0 --port=80
Press CTRL+C to end capture
''
0000    47 45 54 20 2f 20 48 54 54 50 2f 31 2e 31 0d 0a    GET / HTTP/1.1..
0010    48 6f 73 74 3a 20 77 77 77 2e 67 6f 6f 67 6c 65    Host: www.google
```

```
0020   2e 63 6f 6d 0d 0a 43 6f 6e 6e 65 63 74 69 6f 6e   .com..Connection
0030   3a 20 6b 65 65 70 2d 61 6c 69 76 65 0d 0a 41 63   : keep-alive..Ac
0040   63 65 70 74 3a 20 74 65 78 74 2f 68 74 6d 6c 2c   cept: text/html,
0050   61 70 70 6c 69 63 61 74 69 6f 6e 2f 78 68 74 6d   application/xhtm
0060   6c 2b 78 6d 6c 2c 61 70 70 6c 69 63 61 74 69 6f   l+xml,applicatio
0070   6e 2f 78 6d 6c 3b 71 3d 30 2e 39 2c 2a 2f 2a 3b   n/xml;q=0.9,*/*;
0080   71 3d 30 2e 38 0d 0a 55 73 65 72 2d 41 67 65 6e   q=0.8..User-Agen
0090   74 3a 20 4d 6f 7a 69 6c 6c 61 2f 35 2e 30 20 28   t: Mozilla/5.0 (
00A0   58 31 31 3b 20 4c 69 6e 75 78 20 69 36 38 36 29   X11; Linux i686)
00B0   20 41 70 70 6c 65 57 65 62 4b 69 74 2f 35 33 37    AppleWebKit/537
00C0   2e 33 31 20 28 4b 48 54 4d 4c 2c 20 6c 69 6b 65   .31 (KHTML, like
00D0   20 47 65 63 6b 6f 29 20 43 68 72 6f 6d 65 2f 32    Gecko) Chrome/2
00E0   36 2e 30 2e 31 34 31 30 2e 34 33 20 53 61 66 61   6.0.1410.43 Safa
00F0   72 69 2f 35 33 37 2e 33 31 0d 0a 58 2d 43 68 72   ri/537.31..X-Chr
0100   6f 6d 65 2d 56 61 72 69 61 74 69 6f 6e 73 3a 20   ome-Variations:
0110   43 50 71 31 79 51 45 49 6b 62 62 4a 41 51 69 59   CPq1yQEIkbbJAQiY
0120   74 73 6b 42 43 4b 4f 32 79 51 45 49 70 37 62 4a   tskBCKO2yQEIp7bJ
0130   41 51 69 70 74 73 6b 42 43 4c 65 32 79 51 45 49   AQiptskBCLe2yQEI
0140   2b 6f 50 4b 41 51 3d 3d 0d 0a 44 4e 54 3a 20 31   +oPKAQ==..DNT: 1
0150   0d 0a 41 63 63 65 70 74 2d 45 6e 63 6f 64 69 6e   ..Accept-Encodin
0160   67 3a 20 67 7a 69 70 2c 64 65 66 6c 61 74 65 2c   g: gzip,deflate,
0170   73 64 63 68 0d 0a 41 63 63 65 70 74 2d 4c 61 6e   sdch..Accept-Lan
0180   67 75 61 67 65 3a 20 65 6e 2d 47 42 2c 65 6e 2d   guage: en-GB,en-
0190   55 53 3b 71 3d 30 2e 38 2c 65 6e 3b 71 3d 30 2e   US;q=0.8,en;q=0.
01A0   36 0d 0a 41 63 63 65 70 74 2d 43 68 61 72 73 65   6..Accept-Charse
01B0   74 3a 20 49 53 4f 2d 38 38 35 39 2d 31 2c 75 74   t: ISO-8859-1,ut
01C0   66 2d 38 3b 71 3d 30 2e 37 2c 2a 3b 71 3d 30 2e   f-8;q=0.7,*;q=0.
01D0   33 0d 0a 43 6f 6f 6b 69 65 3a 20 50 52 45 46 3d   3..Cookie: PREF=
....
^CPacket statistics: 17 packets received, 0 packets dropped, 0
packets dropped by the interface
```

How it works...

This recipe relies on the `pcapObject()` class from the `pcap` library to create an instance of sniffer. In the `main()` method, an instance of this class is created, and a filter is set using the `setfilter()` method so that only the HTTP packets are captured. Finally, the `dispatch()` method starts sniffing and sends the sniffed packet to the `print_packet()` function for postprocessing.

In the `print_packet()` function, if a packet has data, the payload is extracted using the `ip_stack.parse()` method from the `construct` library. This library is useful for low-level data processing.

Saving packets in the pcap format using the pcap dumper

The `pcap` format, abbreviated from **packet capture**, is a common file format for saving network data. More details on the `pcap` format can be found at `http://wiki.wireshark.org/Development/LibpcapFileFormat`.

If you want to save your captured network packets to a file and later reuse them for further processing, this recipe can be a working example for you.

How to do it...

In this recipe, we use the `Scapy` library to sniff packets and write to a file. All utility functions and definitions of `Scapy` can be imported using the wild card import, as shown in the following command:

```
from scapy.all import *
```

This is only for demonstration purposes and is not recommended for production code.

The `sniff()` function of `Scapy` takes the name of a `callback` function. Let's write a `callback` function that will write the packets onto a file.

Listing 8.2 gives the code for saving packets in the `pcap` format using the `pcap` dumper, as follows:

```python
#!/usr/bin/env python
# Python Network Programming Cookbook, Second Edition -- Chapter - 8
# This program is optimized for Python 2.7.12 and Python 3.5.2.
# It may run on any other version with/without modifications.


import os
from scapy.all import *

pkts = []
count = 0
pcapnum = 0

def write_cap(x):
    global pkts
    global count
    global pcapnum
```

```
        pkts.append(x)
        count += 1
        if count == 3:
            pcapnum += 1
            pname = "pcap%d.pcap" % pcapnum
            wrpcap(pname, pkts)
            pkts = []
            count = 0

def test_dump_file():
    print ("Testing the dump file...")
    dump_file = "./pcap1.pcap"
    if os.path.exists(dump_file):
        print ("dump fie %s found." %dump_file)
        pkts = sniff(offline=dump_file)
        count = 0
        while (count <=2):
            print ("----Dumping pkt:%s----" %count)
            print (hexdump(pkts[count]))
            count += 1
    else:
        print ("dump fie %s not found." %dump_file)

if __name__ == '__main__':
    print ("Started packet capturing and dumping... Press
            CTRL+C to exit")
    sniff(prn=write_cap)
    test_dump_file()
```

If you run this script, you will see an output similar to the following:

```
# python 8_2_save_packets_in_pcap_format.py
^CStarted packet capturing and dumping... Press CTRL+C to exit
Testing the dump file...
dump fie ./pcap1.pcap found.
----Dumping pkt:0----
0000   08 00 27 95 0D 1A 52 54   00 12 35 02 08 00 45 00   ..'...RT..5...E.
0010   00 DB E2 6D 00 00 40 06   7C 9E 6C A0 A2 62 0A 00   ...m..@.|.1..b..
0020   02 0F 00 50 99 55 97 98   2C 84 CE 45 9B 6C 50 18   ...P.U..,..E.1P.
0030   FF FF 53 E0 00 00 48 54   54 50 2F 31 2E 31 20 32   ..S...HTTP/1.1 2
0040   30 30 20 4F 4B 0D 0A 58   2D 44 42 2D 54 69 6D 65   00 OK..X-DB-Time
0050   6F 75 74 3A 20 31 32 30   0D 0A 50 72 61 67 6D 61   out: 120..Pragma
0060   3A 20 6E 6F 2D 63 61 63   68 65 0D 0A 43 61 63 68   : no-cache..Cach
0070   65 2D 43 6F 6E 74 72 6F   6C 3A 20 6E 6F 2D 63 61   e-Control: no-ca
0080   63 68 65 0D 0A 43 6F 6E   74 65 6E 74 2D 54 79 70   che..Content-Typ
0090   65 3A 20 74 65 78 74 2F   70 6C 61 69 6E 0D 0A 44   e: text/plain..D
00a0   61 74 65 3A 20 53 75 6E   2C 20 31 35 20 53 65 70   ate: Sun, 15 Sep
00b0   20 32 30 31 33 20 31 35   3A 32 32 3A 33 36 20 47    2013 15:22:36 G
```

```
00c0    4D 54 0D 0A 43 6F 6E 74    65 6E 74 2D 4C 65 6E 67    MT..Content-Leng
00d0    74 68 3A 20 31 35 0D 0A    0D 0A 7B 22 72 65 74 22    th: 15....{"ret"
00e0    3A 20 22 70 75 6E 74 22    7D                         : "punt"}
None
----Dumping pkt:1----
0000    52 54 00 12 35 02 08 00    27 95 0D 1A 08 00 45 00    RT..5...'.....E.
0010    01 D2 1F 25 40 00 40 06    FE EF 0A 00 02 0F 6C A0    ...%@.@.......l.
0020    A2 62 99 55 00 50 CE 45    9B 6C 97 98 2D 37 50 18    .b.U.P.E.l..-7P.
0030    F9 28 1C D6 00 00 47 45    54 20 2F 73 75 62 73 63    .(....GET /subsc
0040    72 69 62 65 3F 68 6F 73    74 5F 69 6E 74 3D 35 31    ribe?host_int=51
0050    30 35 36 34 37 34 36 26    6E 73 5F 6D 61 70 3D 31    0564746&ns_map=1
0060    36 30 36 39 36 39 39 34    5F 33 30 30 38 30 38 34    60696994_3008084
0070    30 37 37 31 34 2C 31 30    31 39 34 36 31 31 5F 31    07714,10194611_1
0080    31 30 35 33 30 39 38 34    33 38 32 30 32 31 31 2C    105309843820211,
0090    31 34 36 34 32 38 30 35    32 5F 33 32 39 34 33 38    146428052_329438
00a0    36 33 34 34 30 38 34 2C    31 31 36 30 31 35 33 31    6344084,11601531
00b0    5F 32 37 39 31 38 34 34    37 35 37 37 31 2C 31 30    _279184475771,10
00c0    31 39 34 38 32 38 5F 33    30 30 37 34 39 36 35 39    194828_300749659
00d0    30 30 2C 33 33 30 39 39    31 39 38 32 5F 38 31 39    00,330991982_819
00e0    33 35 33 37 30 36 30 36    2C 31 36 33 32 37 38 35    35370606,1632785
00f0    35 5F 31 32 39 30 31 32    32 39 37 34 33 26 75 73    5_12901229743&us
0100    65 72 5F 69 64 3D 36 35    32 30 33 37 32 26 6E 69    er_id=6520372&ni
0110    64 3D 32 26 74 73 3D 31    33 37 39 32 35 38 35 36    d=2&ts=137925856
0120    31 20 48 54 54 50 2F 31    2E 31 0D 0A 48 6F 73 74    1 HTTP/1.1..Host
0130    3A 20 6E 6F 74 69 66 79    33 2E 64 72 6F 70 62 6F    : notify3.dropbo
0140    78 2E 63 6F 6D 0D 0A 41    63 63 65 70 74 2D 45 6E    x.com..Accept-En
0150    63 6F 64 69 6E 67 3A 20    69 64 65 6E 74 69 74 79    coding: identity
0160    0D 0A 43 6F 6E 6E 65 63    74 69 6F 6E 3A 20 6B 65    ..Connection: ke
0170    65 70 2D 61 6C 69 76 65    0D 0A 58 2D 44 72 6F 70    ep-alive..X-Drop
0180    62 6F 78 2D 4C 6F 63 61    6C 65 3A 20 65 6E 5F 55    box-Locale: en_U
0190    53 0D 0A 55 73 65 72 2D    41 67 65 6E 74 3A 20 44    S..User-Agent: D
01a0    72 6F 70 62 6F 78 44 65    73 6B 74 6F 70 43 6C 69    ropboxDesktopCli
01b0    65 6E 74 2F 32 2E 30 2E    32 32 20 28 4C 69 6E 75    ent/2.0.22 (Linu
01c0    78 3B 20 32 2E 36 2E 33    32 2D 35 2D 36 38 36 3B    x; 2.6.32-5-686;
01d0    20 69 33 32 3B 20 65 6E    5F 55 53 29 0D 0A 0D 0A     i32; en_US)....
None
----Dumping pkt:2----
0000    08 00 27 95 0D 1A 52 54    00 12 35 02 08 00 45 00    ..'...RT..5...E.
0010    00 28 E2 6E 00 00 40 06    7D 50 6C A0 A2 62 0A 00    .(.n..@.}Pl..b..
0020    02 0F 00 50 99 55 97 98    2D 37 CE 45 9D 16 50 10    ...P.U..-7.E..P.
0030    FF FF CA F1 00 00 00 00    00 00 00 00                ............
None
```

You may have to run this program using admin privileges, as otherwise it may produce the Operation not permitted error, as follows:

```
$ python 8_2_save_packets_in_pcap_format.py
WARNING: No route found for IPv6 destination :: (no default route?)
Started packet capturing and dumping... Press CTRL+C to exit
Traceback (most recent call last):
  File "8_2_save_packets_in_pcap_format.py", line 43, in <module>
    sniff(prn=write_cap)
  File "/usr/local/lib/python2.7/dist-packages/scapy/sendrecv.py", line
561, in sniff
    s = L2socket(type=ETH_P_ALL, *arg, **karg)
  File "/usr/local/lib/python2.7/dist-packages/scapy/arch/linux.py", line
451, in __init__
    self.ins = socket.socket(socket.AF_PACKET, socket.SOCK_RAW,
socket.htons(type))
  File "/usr/lib/python2.7/socket.py", line 191, in __init__
    _sock = _realsocket(family, type, proto)
socket.error: [Errno 1] Operation not permitted
```

How it works...

This recipe uses the sniff() and wrpacp() utility functions of the Scapy library to capture all the network packets and dump them onto a file. After capturing a packet via sniff(), the write_cap() function is called on that packet. Some global variables are used to work on packets one after another. For example, packets are stored in a pkts[] list and packet and variable counts are used. When the value of the count is 3, the pkts list is dumped onto a file named pcap1.pcap, the count variable is reset so that we can continue capturing another three packets and dumped onto pcap2.pcap, and so on.

In the test_dump_file() function, assume the presence of the first dump file, pcap1.dump, in the working directory. Now, sniff() is used with an offline parameter, which captured packets from the file instead of network. Here, the packets are decoded one after another using the hexdump() function. The contents of the packets are then printed on the screen.

Adding an extra header in HTTP packets

Sometimes, you would like to manipulate an application by supplying a custom HTTP header that contains custom information. For example, adding an authorization header can be useful to implement the HTTP basic authentication in your packet capture code. As with the previous recipe, this recipe requires admin privileges to run too.

How to do it...

Let us sniff the packets using the `sniff()` function of `Scapy` and define a callback function, `modify_packet_header()`, which adds an extra header of certain packets.

Listing 8.3 gives the code for adding an extra header in HTTP packets, as follows:

```python
#!/usr/bin/env python
# Python Network Programming Cookbook, Second Edition -- Chapter - 8
# This program is optimized for Python 2.7.12 and Python 3.5.2.
# It may run on any other version with/without modifications.


from scapy.all import *

def modify_packet_header(pkt):
    """ Parse the header and add an extra header"""
    if pkt.haslayer(TCP) and pkt.getlayer(TCP).dport == 80
     and pkt.haslayer(Raw):
        hdr = pkt[TCP].payload.__dict__
        extra_item = {'Extra Header' : ' extra value'}
        hdr.update(extra_item)
        send_hdr = '\r\n'.join(hdr)
        pkt[TCP].payload = send_hdr
        pkt.show()
        del pkt[IP].chksum
        send(pkt)

if __name__ == '__main__':
    # start sniffing
    sniff(filter="tcp and ( port 80 )", prn=modify_packet_header)
```

If you run this script, it will show a captured packet; print the modified version of it and send it to the network, as shown in the following output. This can be verified by other packet capturing tools such as tcpdump or wireshark:

```
$ python 8_3_add_extra_http_header_in_sniffed_packet.py
###[ Ethernet ]###
   dst        = 52:54:00:12:35:02
   src        = 08:00:27:95:0d:1a
   type       = 0x800
###[ IP ]###
     version    = 4L
     ihl        = 5L
     tos        = 0x0
     len        = 525
     id         = 13419
     flags      = DF
     frag       = 0L
     ttl        = 64
     proto      = tcp
     chksum     = 0x171
     src        = 10.0.2.15
     dst        = 82.94.164.162
     \options   \
###[ TCP ]###
        sport      = 49273
        dport      = www
        seq        = 107715690
        ack        = 216121024
        dataofs    = 5L
        reserved   = 0L
        flags      = PA
        window     = 6432
        chksum     = 0x50f
        urgptr     = 0
        options    = []
###[ Raw ]###
           load       = 'Extra
Header\r\nsent_time\r\nfields\r\naliastypes\r\npost_transforms\r\nunderlaye
r\r\nfieldtype\r\ntime\r\ninitialized\r\noverloaded_fields\r\npacketfields\
r\r\npayload\r\ndefault_fields'
.

Sent 1 packets.
```

How it works...

First, we set up the packet sniffing using the `sniff()` function of `Scapy`, specifying `modify_packet_header()` as the `callback` function for each packet. All TCP packets having TCP and a raw layer that are destined to port `80` (HTTP) are considered for modification. So, the current packet header is extracted from the packet's payload data.

The extra header is then appended to the existing header dictionary. The packet is then printed on screen using the `show()` method, and for avoiding the correctness checking failure, the packet checksum data is removed from the packet. Finally, the packet is sent over the network.

Scanning the ports of a remote host

If you are trying to connect to a remote host using a particular port, sometimes you get a message saying that `Connection is refused`. The reason for this is that, most likely, the server is down on the remote host. In such a situation, you can try to see whether the port is open or in the listening state. You can scan multiple ports to identify the available services in a machine.

How to do it...

Using Python's standard `socket` library, we can accomplish this port-scanning task. We can take three command-line arguments: target `host`, and `start_port` and `end_port` numbers.

Listing 8.4 gives the code for scanning the ports of a remote host, as follows:

```
#!/usr/bin/env python
# Python Network Programming Cookbook, Second Edition -- Chapter - 8
# This program is optimized for Python 2.7.12 and Python 3.5.2.
# It may run on any other version with/without modifications.

import argparse
import socket
import sys
def scan_ports(host, start_port, end_port):
    """ Scan remote hosts """
    #Create socket
    try:
        sock = socket.socket(socket.AF_INET, socket.SOCK_STREAM)
```

```
        except socket.error as err_msg:
            print ('Socket creation failed. Error code:
                '+ str(err_msg[0]) + ' Error mesage: ' + err_msg[1])
            sys.exit()
        #Get IP of remote host
        try:
            remote_ip = socket.gethostbyname(host)
        except socket.error as error_msg:
            print (error_msg)
            sys.exit()
        #Scan ports
        end_port += 1
        for port in range(start_port,end_port):
            try:
                sock.connect((remote_ip,port))
                print ('Port ' + str(port) + ' is open')
                sock.close()
                sock = socket.socket(socket.AF_INET,socket.SOCK_STREAM)
            except socket.error:
                pass # skip various socket errors

if __name__ == '__main__':
    # setup commandline arguments
    parser = argparse.ArgumentParser(description='Remote
                                        Port Scanner')
    parser.add_argument('--host', action="store",
                        dest="host", default='localhost')
    parser.add_argument('--start-port', action="store",
                        dest="start_port", default=1, type=int)
    parser.add_argument('--end-port', action="store",
                        dest="end_port", default=100, type=int)
    # parse arguments
    given_args = parser.parse_args()
    host, start_port, end_port =  given_args.host,
    given_args.start_port, given_args.end_port
    scan_ports(host, start_port, end_port)
```

If you execute this recipe to scan your local machine's port 1 to 100 to detect open ports, you will get an output similar to the following:

```
# python 8_4_scan_port_of_a_remote_host.py --host=localhost --start-port=1
--end-port=100
Port 21 is open
Port 22 is open
Port 23 is open
Port 25 is open
Port 80 is open
```

How it works...

This recipe demonstrates how to scan open ports of a machine using Python's standard `socket` library. The `scan_port()` function takes three arguments: `host`, `start_port`, and `end_port`. Then, it scans the entire port range in three steps:

1. Create a TCP socket using the `socket()` function.
2. If the socket is created successfully, then resolve the IP address of the remote host using the `gethostbyname()` function.
3. If the target host's IP address is found, try to connect to the IP using the `connect()` function. If that's successful, then it implies that the port is open. Now, close the port with the `close()` function and repeat the first step for the next port.

Customizing the IP address of a packet

If you ever need to create a network packet and customize the source and destination IP or ports, this recipe can serve as the starting point.

How to do it...

We can take all the useful command-line arguments such as network interface name, protocol name, source IP, source port, destination IP, destination port, and optional TCP flags.

We can use the `Scapy` library to create a custom TCP or UDP packet and send it over the network. As with the previous recipes, this recipe requires admin privilege to run.

Listing 8.5 gives the code for customizing the IP address of a packet, as follows:

```
#!/usr/bin/env python
# Python Network Programming Cookbook, Second Edition -- Chapter - 8
# This program is optimized for Python 2.7.12 and Python 3.5.2.
# It may run on any other version with/without modifications.


import argparse
import sys
import re
from random import randint
```

```
from scapy.all import IP,TCP,UDP,conf,send


def send_packet(protocol=None, src_ip=None, src_port=None, flags=None,
dst_ip=None, dst_port=None, iface=None):
    """Modify and send an IP packet."""
    if protocol == 'tcp':
        packet = IP(src=src_ip, dst=dst_ip)/TCP(flags=flags,
                    sport=src_port, dport=dst_port)
    elif protocol == 'udp':
        if flags: raise Exception(" Flags are not supported for udp")
        packet = IP(src=src_ip, dst=dst_ip)/UDP(sport=src_port,
                    dport=dst_port)
    else:
        raise Exception("Unknown protocol %s" % protocol)

    send(packet, iface=iface)

if __name__ == '__main__':
    # setup commandline arguments
    parser = argparse.ArgumentParser(description='Packet Modifier')
    parser.add_argument('--iface', action="store",
                        dest="iface", default='eth0')
    parser.add_argument('--protocol', action="store",
                        dest="protocol", default='tcp')
    parser.add_argument('--src-ip', action="store",
                        dest="src_ip", default='1.1.1.1')
    parser.add_argument('--src-port', action="store",
                        dest="src_port", default=randint(0, 65535))
    parser.add_argument('--dst-ip', action="store",
                        dest="dst_ip", default='192.168.1.51')
    parser.add_argument('--dst-port', action="store",
                        dest="dst_port", default=randint(0, 65535))
    parser.add_argument('--flags', action="store",
                        dest="flags", default=None)
    # parse arguments
    given_args = parser.parse_args()
    iface, protocol, src_ip,  src_port, dst_ip, dst_port,
    flags =  given_args.iface, given_args.protocol,
    given_args.src_ip,\
      given_args.src_port, given_args.dst_ip,
      given_args.dst_port, given_args.flags
    send_packet(protocol, src_ip, src_port, flags,
      dst_ip, dst_port, iface)
```

In order to run this script, enter the following commands:

```
$ sudo tcpdump src 192.168.1.66
tcpdump: verbose output suppressed, use -v or -vv for full protocol decode
listening on eth0, link-type EN10MB (Ethernet), capture size 65535 bytes
^C18:37:34.309992 IP 192.168.1.66.60698 > 192.168.1.51.666: Flags [S], seq
0, win 8192, length 0
1 packets captured
1 packets received by filter
0 packets dropped by kernel
$ python 8_5_modify_ip_in_a_packet.py
WARNING: No route found for IPv6 destination :: (no default route?)
.
Sent 1 packets.
```

How it works...

This script defines a `send_packet()` function to construct the IP packet using `Scapy`. The source and destination addresses and ports are supplied to it. Depending on the protocol, for example, TCP or UDP, it constructs the correct type of packet. If the packet is TCP, the `flags` argument is used; if not, an exception is raised.

In order to construct a TCP packet, `Sacpy` supplies the `IP()`/`TCP()` function. Similarly, in order to create a UDP packet, the `IP()`/`UDP()` function is used.

Finally, the modified packet is sent using the `send()` function.

Replaying traffic by reading from a saved pcap file

While playing with network packets, you may need to replay traffic by reading from a previously saved `pcap` file. In that case, you'd like to read the `pcap` file and modify the source or destination IP addresses before sending them.

How to do it...

Let us use `Scapy` to read a previously saved `pcap` file. If you don't have a `pcap` file, you can use the *Saving packets in the pcap format using pcap dumper* recipe of this chapter to do that.

Then, parse the arguments from the command line and pass them to a `send_packet()` function along with the parsed raw packets. As with the previous recipes, this recipe requires admin privileges to run.

Listing 8.6 gives the code for replaying traffic by reading from a saved `pcap` file, as follows:

```python
#!/usr/bin/env python
# Python Network Programming Cookbook, Second Edition -- Chapter - 8
# This program is optimized for Python 2.7.12 and Python 3.5.2.
# It may run on any other version with/without modifications.


import argparse
from scapy.all import *


def send_packet(recvd_pkt, src_ip, dst_ip, count):
    """ Send modified packets"""
    pkt_cnt = 0
    p_out = []

    for p in recvd_pkt:
        pkt_cnt += 1
        new_pkt = p.payload
        new_pkt[IP].dst = dst_ip
        new_pkt[IP].src = src_ip
        del new_pkt[IP].chksum
        p_out.append(new_pkt)
        if pkt_cnt % count == 0:
            send(PacketList(p_out))
            p_out = []

    # Send rest of packet
    send(PacketList(p_out))
    print ("Total packets sent: %d" %pkt_cnt)

if __name__ == '__main__':
    # setup commandline arguments
    parser = argparse.ArgumentParser(description='Packet Sniffer')
    parser.add_argument('--infile', action="store", dest="infile",
      default='pcap1.pcap')
    parser.add_argument('--src-ip', action="store", dest="src_ip",
      default='1.1.1.1')
    parser.add_argument('--dst-ip', action="store", dest="dst_ip",
      default='2.2.2.2')
    parser.add_argument('--count', action="store", dest="count",
      default=100, type=int)
    # parse arguments
```

```
given_args = ga = parser.parse_args()
global src_ip, dst_ip
infile, src_ip, dst_ip, count =  ga.infile, ga.src_ip,
 ga.dst_ip, ga.count
try:
    pkt_reader = PcapReader(infile)
    send_packet(pkt_reader, src_ip, dst_ip, count)
except IOError:
    print ("Failed reading file %s contents" % infile)
    sys.exit(1)
```

If you run this script, it will read the saved pcap file, pcap1.pcap, by default and send the packet after modifying the source and destination IP addresses to 1.1.1.1 and 2.2.2.2 respectively, as shown in the following output. If you use the tcpdump utility, you can see these packet transmissions:

```
# python 8_6_replay_traffic.py
. . .
Sent 3 packets.
Total packets sent 3
----
# tcpdump src 1.1.1.1
tcpdump: verbose output suppressed, use -v or -vv for full protocol
decode
listening on eth0, link-type EN10MB (Ethernet), capture size 65535
bytes
^C18:44:13.186302 IP 1.1.1.1.www > ARennes-651-1-107-2.w2-
2.abo.wanadoo.fr.39253: Flags [P.], seq 2543332484:2543332663, ack
3460668268, win 65535, length 179
1 packets captured
3 packets received by filter
0 packets dropped by kernel
```

How it works...

This recipe reads a saved pcap file, pcap1.pcap, from the disk using the PcapReader() function of Scapy that returns an iterator of packets. The command-line arguments are parsed if they are supplied. Otherwise, the default value is used as shown in the preceding output.

The command-line arguments and the packet list are passed to the `send_packet()` function. This function places the new packets in the `p_out` list and keeps track of the processed packets. In each packet, the payload is modified, thus changing the source and destination IPs. In addition to this, the `checksum` packet is deleted as it was based on the original IP address.

After processing one of the packets, it is sent over the network immediately. After that, the remaining packets are sent in one go.

As with the previous recipes, this recipe requires admin privileges to run.

Scanning the broadcast of packets

If you encounter the issue of detecting a network broadcast, this recipe is for you. We can learn how to find the information from the broadcast packets.

How to do it...

We can use `Scapy` to sniff the packets arriving to a network interface. After each packet is captured, they can be processed by a callback function to get the useful information from it.

Listing 8.7 gives the code for scanning the broadcast of packets, as follows:

```python
#!/usr/bin/env python
# Python Network Programming Cookbook, Second Edition -- Chapter - 8
# This program is optimized for Python 2.7.12 and Python 3.5.2.
# It may run on any other version with/without modifications.


from scapy.all import *
import os
captured_data = dict()

END_PORT = 1000
def monitor_packet(pkt):
    if IP in pkt:
        if pkt[IP].src not in captured_data:
            captured_data[pkt[IP].src] = []
    if TCP in pkt:
        if pkt[TCP].sport <=  END_PORT:
            if not str(pkt[TCP].sport) in captured_data[pkt[IP].src]:
                captured_data[pkt[IP].src].append(str(pkt[TCP].sport))
    os.system('clear')
```

```
    ip_list = sorted(captured_data.keys())
    for key in ip_list:
        ports=', '.join(captured_data[key])
        if len (captured_data[key]) == 0:
            print ('%s' % key)
        else:
            print ('%s (%s)' % (key, ports))

if __name__ == '__main__':
    sniff(prn=monitor_packet, store=0)
```

If you run this script, you can list the broadcast traffic's source IP and ports. The following is a sample output from which the first octet of the IP is replaced:

```
# python 8_7_broadcast_scanning.py
127.0.0.1
127.0.1.1
13.81.252.207 (443)
162.125.17.5 (443)
162.125.18.133 (443)
162.125.65.3 (443)
172.217.17.69 (443)
173.194.69.189 (443)
192.168.137.1
192.168.137.95
216.58.212.174 (443)
34.253.167.3 (443)
40.115.1.44 (443)
40.77.226.194 (443)
52.208.1.170 (443)
52.215.50.173 (443)
54.86.79.27 (443)
68.232.34.200 (443)
```

The following screenshot shows the execution output:

How it works...

This recipe sniffs packets in a network using the `sniff()` function of `Scapy`. It has a `monitor_packet()` callback function that does the postprocessing of packets. Depending on the protocol, for example, IP or TCP, it sorts the packets in a dictionary called `captured_data`.

If an individual IP is not already present in the dictionary, it creates a new entry; otherwise, it updates the dictionary with the port number for that specific IP. Finally, it prints the IP addresses and ports in each line.

9
Network Modeling

In this chapter, we will cover the following recipes:

- Simulating networks with ns-3
- Emulating networks with Mininet
- Distributed network emulation with MaxiNet
- Emulating wireless networks with Mininet-WiFi
- Extending Mininet to emulate containers

Introduction

This chapter explores an early and important aspect of network systems development—network modeling. Specifically, it addresses the simulations and emulations of networks with Python-based projects.

First we will look into network simulations that can model very large systems within a single computer. We will discuss ns-3, a network simulator originally written in C++ with Python bindings, making it easy to simulate networks in Python.

The chapter goes on to network emulation that indeed models resources one-to-one. It discusses Mininet, the most popular network emulator developed in Python. We will further discuss the extensions to Mininet, such as MaxiNet and Mininet-WiFi. The chapter concludes with how to extend existing simulators and emulators and to build a cloud network leveraging these platforms.

Simulating networks with ns-3

Data centers and cloud networks span across a large number of nodes. Network topologies and applications of that scale often can be tested first in simulations to ensure that early results are verified quick before an extensive deployment and testing in a more realistic emulation or a physical test bench. In this recipe, we will learn to simulate network systems with ns-3.

Getting ready

First download ns-3 from `https://www.nsnam.org/ns-3-26/download/`. We are using ns-3.26 in this recipe. Extract the downloaded archive and run from the root directory `ns-allinone-3.26`:

```
$ ./build.py.
```

Since the `allinone` folder contains all the bundles, this build will consume a few minutes.

It shows the following upon the completion of the build:

```
'build' finished successfully (14m22.645s)
Modules built:
antenna                aodv                  applications
bridge                 buildings             config-store
core                   csma                  csma-layout
dsdv                   dsr                   energy
fd-net-device          flow-monitor          internet
internet-apps          lr-wpan               lte
mesh                   mobility              mpi
netanim (no Python)    network               nix-vector-routing
olsr                   point-to-point        point-to-point-layout
propagation            sixlowpan             spectrum
stats                  tap-bridge            test (no Python)
topology-read          traffic-control       uan
virtual-net-device     wave                  wifi           wimax
Modules not built (see ns-3 tutorial for explanation):
brite                  click                 openflow
visualizer
Leaving directory `./ns-3.26'
```

In the preceding snippet, you may notice that a few modules including `openflow` are not built when built from the `root` directory. This is the expected behavior.

You may test ns-3 for one of the existing simulations. First go to the `ns-3.26 directory`:

```
$ cd ns-3.26
```

Now, let's test the bench-simulator included in ns-3. We will use `waf`, a Python-based build tool for this:

```
$ ./waf --run bench-simulator
Waf: Entering directory `/home/pradeeban/programs/ns-
allinone-3.26/ns-3.26/build'
Waf: Leaving directory `/home/pradeeban/programs/ns-
allinone-3.26/ns-3.26/build'
Build commands will be stored in build/compile_commands.json
'build' finished successfully (1.473s)
ns3.26-bench-simulator-debug:
ns3.26-bench-simulator-debug: scheduler: ns3::MapScheduler
ns3.26-bench-simulator-debug: population: 100000
ns3.26-bench-simulator-debug: total events: 1000000
ns3.26-bench-simulator-debug: runs: 1
ns3.26-bench-simulator-debug: using default exponential distribution
Run #        Inititialization:        Simulation:
Time (s)     Rate (ev/s) Per (s/ev)   Time (s)    Rate (ev/s) Per (s/ev)
-----------  ----------- -----------  ----------- ----------- -----------
(prime)      0.72        138889       7.2e-06     2.84        352113
2.84e-06
0            0.23        434783       2.3e-06     2.94        340136
2.94e-06
```

The screenshot of this simple bench simulation is as follows:

```
pradeeban@llovizna: ~/programs/ns-allinone-3.26/ns-3.26 165x48
pradeeban@llovizna:~/programs/ns-allinone-3.26/ns-3.26$ ./waf --run bench-simulator
Waf: Entering directory '/home/pradeeban/programs/ns-allinone-3.26/ns-3.26/build'
Waf: Leaving directory '/home/pradeeban/programs/ns-allinone-3.26/ns-3.26/build'
Build commands will be stored in build/compile_commands.json
'build' finished successfully (1.567s)
ns3.26-bench-simulator-debug:
ns3.26-bench-simulator-debug: scheduler: ns3::MapScheduler
ns3.26-bench-simulator-debug: population: 100000
ns3.26-bench-simulator-debug: total events: 1000000
ns3.26-bench-simulator-debug: runs: 1
ns3.26-bench-simulator-debug: using default exponential distribution

Run #    Inititialization:                     Simulation:
         Time (s)   Rate (ev/s) Per (s/ev)   Time (s)   Rate (ev/s) Per (s/ev)
------------------------------------------------------------------------------
(prime)  1.54       64935.1     1.54e-05     4.27       234192      4.27e-06
0        0.32       312500      3.2e-06      4.08       245098      4.08e-06

pradeeban@llovizna:~/programs/ns-allinone-3.26/ns-3.26$
```

Bench Simulation with ns-3

How to do it...

ns-3 can be used to quickly prototype network protocol implementations and applications. Once you have configured ns-3 correctly, you may start running the Python examples from the folder `ns-allinone-3.26/ns-3.26/examples/tutorial`. More information on this can be found from `https://www.nsnam.org/docs/manual/html/python.html`.

Listing 9.1 simulates a network with two nodes with UDP messages between them:

```
#!/usr/bin/env python
# Python Network Programming Cookbook, Second Edition -- Chapter - 9
# This program is optimized for Python 2.7.12 and Python 3.5.2.
# It may run on any other version with/without modifications.

import ns.applications
import ns.core
import ns.internet
import ns.network
```

```
import ns.point_to_point
import argparse


def simulate(ipv4add, ipv4mask):
    # Enabling logs at INFO level for both the server and the client.
    ns.core.LogComponentEnable("UdpEchoClientApplication",
     ns.core.LOG_LEVEL_INFO)
    ns.core.LogComponentEnable("UdpEchoServerApplication",
     ns.core.LOG_LEVEL_INFO)
    # Create the 2 nodes.
    nodes = ns.network.NodeContainer()
    nodes.Create(2)

    pointToPoint = ns.point_to_point.PointToPointHelper()

    devices = pointToPoint.Install(nodes)

    stack = ns.internet.InternetStackHelper()
    stack.Install(nodes)

    # Set addresses based on the input args.
    address = ns.internet.Ipv4AddressHelper()
    address.SetBase(ns.network.Ipv4Address(ipv4add),
     ns.network.Ipv4Mask(ipv4mask))

    interfaces = address.Assign(devices)

    # Running the echo server
    echoServer = ns.applications.UdpEchoServerHelper(9)
    serverApps = echoServer.Install(nodes.Get(1))

    # Running the echo client
    echoClient = ns.applications.
    UdpEchoClientHelper(interfaces.GetAddress(1), 3)
    clientApps = echoClient.Install(nodes.Get(0))

    # Running the simulator
    ns.core.Simulator.Run()
    ns.core.Simulator.Destroy()


if __name__ == '__main__':
    parser = argparse.ArgumentParser(description='NS-3 Simple Simulation')
    parser.add_argument('--ipv4add', action="store",
     dest="ipv4add", type=str, required=True)
    parser.add_argument('--ipv4mask', action="store",
     dest="ipv4mask", type=str, required=True)
```

```
            given_args = parser.parse_args()
            simulate(given_args.ipv4add, given_args.ipv4mask)
```

First run the `waf` shell to get the dependencies for the ns-3 simulation before executing the actual simulation:

```
    ns-allinone-3.26/ns-3.26$ ./waf shell
```

Next, run the simulation:

```
    python 9_1_ns3_simulation.py --ipv4add=100.10.100.0 --
    ipv4mask=255.255.255.0
    At time 0s client sent 100 bytes to 100.10.100.2 port 3
    At time 1s client sent 100 bytes to 100.10.100.2 port 3
    At time 2s client sent 100 bytes to 100.10.100.2 port 3
    ...
    At time 97s client sent 100 bytes to 100.10.100.2 port 3
    At time 98s client sent 100 bytes to 100.10.100.2 port 3
    At time 99s client sent 100 bytes to 100.10.100.2 port 3
```

How it works...

ns-3 simulates the networks including the nodes and the flows. As there is no real emulation of network, complex algorithms and large network systems can be simulated by ns-3. In this recipe, we simulated a simple UDP client-server architecture to pass messages between them, as an echo client. More complex systems can be simulated by following the ns-3 user manuals further.

Emulating networks with Mininet

Emulating networks offer more accurate and realistic results. Therefore, despite the high requirements for resources, emulations are often preferred over simulations in networking systems. Mininet is an enterprise-grade open source network emulator that is widely used in industries and academia. Mininet API and orchestration modules are written in Python, with core emulation performed by compiled C code. You may easily write Python code to emulate networks with Mininet, or to extend it with more capabilities. Mininet is capable of emulating an entire network one-to-one in your laptop. Each node in the network can be represented by a process in Mininet.

Due to its precision, Mininet is extended further for various use cases, including Mininet-WiFi (`https://github.com/intrig-unicamp/mininet-wifi`) to emulate wireless networks, MaxiNet (`https://maxinet.github.io/`) to emulate networks in a cluster, and Containernet (`https://github.com/containernet/containernet`) to have container support to network emulations. In this recipe, we will look into emulating networks with Mininet.

Getting ready

First, install Mininet on your computer. In Debian/Ubuntu based systems, you just need to issue the following command to install Mininet:

```
$ sudo apt-get install mininet
```

Mininet must run as a root, as it should be able to access the programs installed in the host as the processes of the emulated nodes. Thus, this recipe needs to be run as root too, as it has a Mininet emulation.

While it is possible to make Mininet work in Python 3.x, by default it works on Python 2.7.x. Thus, you may need to install Python 2.7.x or later versions of Python 2, if you are using Python 3.x.

How to do it...

Mininet consists of a few network topologies that are predefined. You may define your own topology. In this recipe, we are using tree topology, which is probably the most common and the most basic network topology. We ping one emulated host from another emulated host.

Listing 9.2 emulates a simple network with a tree topology:

```python
#!/usr/bin/env python
# Python Network Programming Cookbook, Second Edition -- Chapter - 9
# This program is optimized for Python 2.7.12.
# It may run on any other version with/without modifications.

import argparse
from mininet.net import Mininet
from mininet.topolib import TreeTopo

# Emulate a network with depth of depth_ and fanout of fanout_
def emulate(depth_, fanout_):
```

```
# Create a network with tree topology
tree_ = TreeTopo(depth=depth_, fanout=fanout_)
# Initiating the Mininet instance
net = Mininet(topo=tree_)
# Start Execution of the Emulated System.
net.start()

# Name two of the instances as h1 and h2.
h1, h2  = net.hosts[0], net.hosts[depth_]

# Ping from an instance to another, and print the output.
print (h1.cmd('ping -c1 %s' % h2.IP()))

# Stop the Mininet Emulation.
net.stop()

if __name__ == '__main__':
    parser = argparse.ArgumentParser(description='Mininet
      Simple Emulation')
    parser.add_argument('--depth', action="store",
      dest="depth", type=int, required=True)
    parser.add_argument('--fanout', action="store",
      dest="fanout", type=int, required=True)
    given_args = parser.parse_args()
    emulate(given_args.depth, given_args.fanout)
```

Tree topology is defined by its `depth` and `fanout`. A network configured to be a complete tree can have (`fanout`) to the power of `depth` number of leaves. As the hosts make the leaves, this leads us to (`fanout`) to the power of `depth` number of hosts in the network. The following figure illustrates a network of tree topology with **Fanout = 2** and **Depth = 3**:

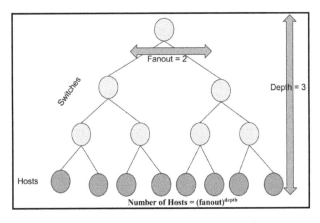

Tree Representation

The following output is printed when the program is executed with the depth of 2 and fanout of 3 as the arguments:

```
$ sudo python 9_2_mininet_emulation.py --depth=2 --fanout=3
PING 10.0.0.3 (10.0.0.3) 56(84) bytes of data.
64 bytes from 10.0.0.3: icmp_seq=1 ttl=64 time=2.86 ms
--- 10.0.0.3 ping statistics ---
1 packets transmitted, 1 received, 0% packet loss, time 0ms
rtt min/avg/max/mdev = 2.864/2.864/2.864/0.000 ms
```

How it works...

In this recipe, we pinged (depth)th host from the 0th host. As (depth < the number of hosts), this works well. Note that subsequent executions will give different outcomes as the ping statistics. This is because the network is actually emulated with real processes, and hence the ping actually occurs between the emulated processes.

You may re-execute the program to see different outcomes to the previous:

```
$ sudo python 9_2_mininet_emulation.py --depth=2 --fanout=3
PING 10.0.0.3 (10.0.0.3) 56(84) bytes of data.
64 bytes from 10.0.0.3: icmp_seq=1 ttl=64 time=3.33 ms
--- 10.0.0.3 ping statistics ---
1 packets transmitted, 1 received, 0% packet loss, time 0ms
rtt min/avg/max/mdev = 3.332/3.332/3.332/0.000 ms
```

Distributed network emulation with MaxiNet

Mininet requires a large amount of resources to emulate large networks. Hence, it is not always feasible to emulate a complex system using Mininet in a single computer or server within a given time. MaxiNet attempts to address this by extending Mininet, and thus enabling an efficient distributed execution on a cluster. In this recipe, we will look into configuring MaxiNet in a cluster and emulating a network in the cluster using MaxiNet.

Getting ready

First, get the MaxiNet installer to all the servers that you would like to install it:

```
$ wget https://github.com/MaxiNet/MaxiNet/raw/v1.0/installer.sh
```

Make sure you can sudo without entering a password for the user. In Ubuntu, this can be done by adding the following line to the /etc/sudoers file:

```
myusername ALL=(ALL) NOPASSWD: ALL
```

Here, replace myusername with your username.

Now if you type:

```
$ sudo su
```

It should not ask for the password.

You will have to install python-setuptools, or upgrade it with pip, to make the MaxiNet installation work:

```
$ sudo apt-get install python-setuptools
$ pip install --upgrade --user setuptools pip
```

Run the script from all the servers as the user that would run MaxiNet later:

```
$ sh installer.sh
```

Once installed, copy the MaxiNet.cfg to /etc/:

```
$ sudo cp ~/MaxiNet/share/MaxiNet-cfg-sample /etc/MaxiNet.cfg
```

Modify it to include the two lines:

```
sshuser = yourusername
usesudo = True
```

For example:

```
[all]
...
sshuser = ubuntu
usesudo = True
```

Once you have followed through in all your servers, you have MaxiNet ready in all of them! Alternatively, you may just download the MaxiNet VMs and host them in your servers:

```
$ wget http://groups.uni-paderborn.de/fg-karl/maxinet/MaxiNet-1.0-rc1.ova
```

Now, from the server that you would like to use as the master instance to run the emulations, run the following:

```
$ screen -d -m -S MaxiNetFrontend MaxiNetFrontendServer
$ screen -d -m -S MaxiNetWorker sudo MaxiNetWorker
```

All your emulations should be executed from this instance. It will communicate and coordinate with the other worker instances on its own.

From the other servers, run the following to make them as worker instances:

```
$ sudo screen -d -m -S MaxiNetWorker MaxiNetWorker
```

 For more information on MaxiNet, follow through https://maxinet.gith ub.io/#quickstart.

How to do it...

In this recipe, we will rewrite the same recipe of 9.2 for MaxiNet. As you can notice, with minor changes, the code and the API remains compatible with that of Mininet's.

Listing 9.2 adopts the listing 9.1 for MaxiNet, as follows:

```python
#!/usr/bin/env python
# Python Network Programming Cookbook, Second Edition -- Chapter - 9
# This program is optimized for Python 2.7.12.
# It may run on any other version with/without modifications.

import sys
import maxinet
from mininet.topolib import TreeTopo

# Emulate a network with depth of depth_ and fanout of fanout_
def emulate(depth_, fanout_):
    # Start the MaxiNet as a Mininet cluster.
    cluster = maxinet.MininetCluster("pc1","pc2","pc3")
    cluster.start()

    # Emulate the network topology.
```

```
    emu = maxinet.Emulation(cluster, TreeTopo(depth_,fanout_))

    # Start Execution of the Emulated System.
    emu.setup()

    # Name two of the instances as h1 and h2.
    h1, h2 = net.hosts[0], net.hosts[depth_]

    # Ping from an instance to another, and print the output.
    print (h1.cmd('ping -c1 %s' % h2.IP()))

    # Stop the MaxiNet Emulation.
    emu.stop()
    cluster.stop()

if __name__ == '__main__':
    parser = argparse.ArgumentParser(description='Maxinet
            Simple Emulation')
    parser.add_argument('--depth', action="store",
      dest="depth", type=int, required=True)
    parser.add_argument('--fanout', action="store",
      dest="fanout", type=int, required=True)
    given_args = parser.parse_args()
    emulate(given_args.depth, given_args.fanout)
```

Now you may run this from the master instance, as you would have run this on a Mininet emulation. The master instance communicates with the other worker instance to distribute the workload:

```
$ sudo python 9_3_maxinet_emulation.py --depth=2 --fanout=3
PING 10.0.0.3 (10.0.0.3) 56(84) bytes of data.
64 bytes from 10.0.0.3: icmp_seq=1 ttl=64 time=1.82 ms
--- 10.0.0.3 ping statistics ---
1 packets transmitted, 1 received, 0% packet loss, time 0ms
rtt min/avg/max/mdev = 1.827/1.827/1.827/0.000 ms
```

How it works...

MaxiNet is Mininet executing in a cluster. It aims to keep the API changes minimal (if any), to be able to offer a quick adoption to the existing Mininet users. Make sure that all the worker instances in MaxiNet can indeed communicate. As you may have noticed, this emulation workload is too little to actually offer any benefits for us to distribute it across a cluster. However, when you start emulating larger networks and complex systems, the advantages become apparent.

Emulating wireless networks with Mininet-WiFi

You may emulate wireless networks and mobile networks through Mininet-WiFi, which was developed as an extension to Mininet. While Mininet enables emulation of Software-Defined Networks, Mininet-WiFi supports emulation of Software-Defined Wireless Networks. Mininet-WiFi emulates mobile terminals efficiently, while also providing a visual graphical user interface of emulated wireless networks.

Getting ready

First install Mininet-WiFi on your computer:

```
$ git clone https://github.com/intrig-unicamp/mininet-wifi
$ cd mininet-wifi
$ sudo util/install.sh -Wnfvl
```

How to do it...

You may emulate **mobile ad hoc network** (**MANET**) and **vehicular ad hoc network** (**VANET**) using Mininet-WiFi, and visualize them in a graphical interface. VANET is a subset of MANET, which can be emulated by sub-classing the generic interfaces of Mininet-WiFi. In this recipe, we will adopt and extend an example from the Mininet-WiFi.

> More examples can be found at `https://github.com/intrig-unicamp/mininet-wifi/tree/master/examples`.

Listing 9.4 shows the code to emulate a mobile network:

```python
#!/usr/bin/env python
# Python Network Programming Cookbook, Second Edition -- Chapter - 9
# This program is optimized for Python 2.7.12.
# It may run on any other version with/without modifications.

from mininet.net import Mininet
from mininet.node import Controller, OVSKernelAP
from mininet.link import TCLink
from mininet.cli import CLI
from mininet.log import setLogLevel
```

```
def emulate():
    # Setting the position of nodes and providing mobility

    # Create a network.
    net = Mininet(controller=Controller, link=TCLink,
            accessPoint=OVSKernelAP)

    print ("*** Creating nodes")
    # Add the host
    h1 = net.addHost('h1', mac='00:00:00:00:00:01', ip='10.0.0.1/8')

    # Add 3 mobile stations, sta1, sta2, sta3.
    sta1 = net.addStation('sta1', mac='00:00:00:00:00:02', ip='10.0.0.2/8')
    sta2 = net.addStation('sta2', mac='00:00:00:00:00:03', ip='10.0.0.3/8')
    sta3 = net.addStation('sta3', mac='00:00:00:00:00:04', ip='10.0.0.4/8')

    # Add an access point
    ap1 = net.addAccessPoint('ap1', ssid='new-ssid',
            mode='g', channel='1', position='45,40,30')

    # Add a controller
    c1 = net.addController('c1', controller=Controller)

    print ("*** Configuring wifi nodes")
    net.configureWifiNodes()

    print ("*** Associating and Creating links")
    net.addLink(ap1, h1)
    net.addLink(ap1, sta1)
    net.addLink(ap1, sta2)
    net.addLink(ap1, sta3)

    print ("*** Starting network")
    net.build()
    c1.start()
    ap1.start([c1])

    # Plot a 3-dimensional graph.
    net.plotGraph(max_x=100, max_y=100, max_z=200)

    # Start the mobility at the start of the emulation.
    net.startMobility(time=0)

    # Start the mobile stations from their initial positions.
    net.mobility(sta1, 'start', time=1, position='40.0,30.0,20.0')
    net.mobility(sta2, 'start', time=2, position='40.0,40.0,90.0')
    net.mobility(sta3, 'start', time=3, position='50.0,50.0,160.0')
```

```
    # Indicate the final destination of the mobile stations during
        the emulation.
    net.mobility(sta1, 'stop', time=12, position='31.0,10.0,50.0')
    net.mobility(sta2, 'stop', time=22, position='55.0,31.0,30.0')
    net.mobility(sta3, 'stop', time=32, position='75.0,99.0,120.0')

    # Stop the mobility at certain time.
    net.stopMobility(time=33)

    print ("*** Running CLI")
    CLI(net)

    print ("*** Stopping network")
    net.stop()

if __name__ == '__main__':
    setLogLevel('info')
    emulate()
```

In this recipe, we emulate a mobile network with a host, an access point, a controller, and three mobile stations. We start the mobile stations with their initial positions, and let them move to their final positions during the emulation. Once the emulation is done, we stop the mobility and the emulation:

```
$ sudo python 9_4_mininet_wifi_emulation.py
*** Creating nodes
*** Configuring wifi nodes
*** Associating and Creating links
Associating sta1-wlan0 to ap1
Associating sta2-wlan0 to ap1
Associating sta3-wlan0 to ap1
*** Starting network
*** Configuring hosts
Mobility started at 0 second(s)
*** Running CLI
*** Starting CLI:
mininet-wifi> exit
*** Stopping network
*** Stopping 1 controllers
c1
*** Stopping 1 links
.
*** Stopping switches and/or access points
ap1
*** Stopping hosts and/or stations
h1 sta1 sta2 sta3
*** Done
```

The following screenshots indicate the graph at the start and end of the emulation. The following screenshot shows the positions of the mobile stations at the start of the emulation:

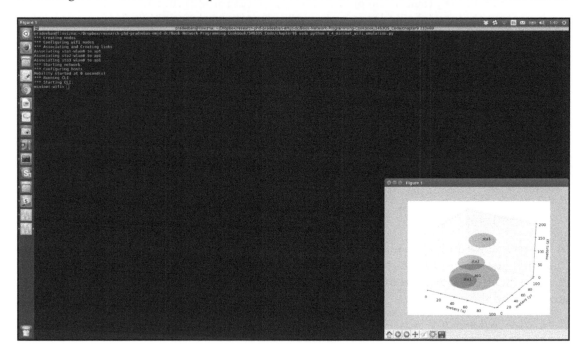

Starting State of the Emulation

The following screenshot shows the position at the end of the emulation:

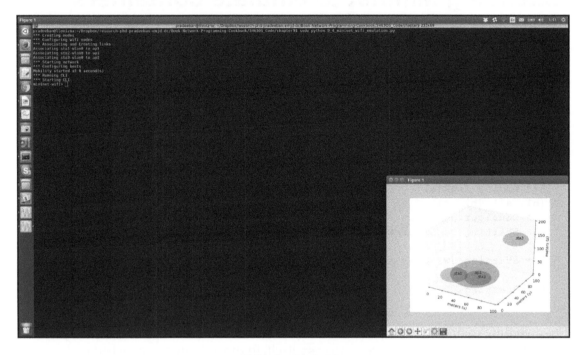

Finishing State of the Emulation

During the course, you may monitor how the mobile stations move between their initial and final positions.

How it works...

Mininet-WiFi extends Mininet for networks that are mobile in nature. In this recipe, we emulated wireless network stations. Following our previous recipe on pinging the hosts, you may easily extend this recipe to let the mobile stations communicate between themselves. You may further model more complex and larger vehicular networks using Mininet-WiFi.

Extending Mininet to emulate containers

Mininet can leverage the applications installed in the server to attach them as processes to the hosts that it emulates. For example, see the following, a `vim` started from a host in Mininet:

```
$ sudo mn
*** Creating network
*** Adding controller
*** Adding hosts and stations:
h1 h2
*** Adding switches and access point(s):
s1
*** Adding link(s):
(h1, s1) (h2, s1)
*** Configuring hosts
*** Starting controller(s)
c0
*** Starting switches and/or access points
s1 ...
*** Starting CLI:
mininet-wifi> h1 vim
```

The preceding command will open a `vim` instance in the Terminal! You may even try other applications such as `gedit`, or even `mininet` itself, to run as a process attached to the emulated host. However, note that these are real processes from the applications that are installed on the server. Not an emulation.

Containernet extends Mininet to use Docker containers as hosts in Mininet emulations, by extending the `host` class of Mininet. Hence, container enables emulation of more interesting and complex functionalities, attaching Docker containers directly as hosts. This allows the programs installed in a container available to the host.

Getting ready

In this recipe, we use Containernet as an example to show how to extend Mininet for more use cases, while using Containernet to show a simple emulation with Docker containers as hosts in Mininet. More complex Mininet algorithms can be run on Containernet, along with its capabilities to run containers as hosts.

First, install Containernet in your computer. Since Containernet uses Ansible for this, you need to install it before:

```
$ sudo apt-get install ansible git aptitude
$ sudo vim /etc/ansible/hosts
```

Add: `localhost ansible_connection=local`

Now, to actually install Containernet:

```
$ git clone https://github.com/containernet/containernet.git
$ cd containernet/ansible
$ sudo ansible-playbook install.yml
```

Alternatively, you may use Vagrant to get Containernet up and running faster, without actually installing it manually. First make sure to have a hypervisor such as Virtualbox installed:

```
$ sudo apt-get install virtualbox
```

Now, you may execute the following to get Vagrant for Containernet:

```
$ cd containernet
$ vagrant up
$ vagrant ssh
```

You may confirm that you have installed Vagrant correctly by running the following from the `containernet` directory:

```
$ sudo py.test -v mininet/test/test_containernet.py
```

The following screenshot indicates the output to the preceding execution in Vagrant:

Emulating Containers

How to do it...

In this recipe, we will attach existing containers to our simple network emulation. To avoid creating Docker images on our own, as it is out of scope for this book, we will use the example included in the Containernet Vagrant image.

Docker containers can be initialized in place of hosts and switches as nodes in constructing the links. Various parameters and the volumes that define the container can be specified.

Listing 9.5 gives a simple emulation of a network with containers as follows:

```
#!/usr/bin/env python
# Python Network Programming Cookbook, Second Edition -- Chapter - 9
# This program is optimized for Python 2.7.12.
# It may run on any other version with/without modifications.

# Adopted from
https://github.com/containernet/containernet/blob/master/examples/dockerhos
ts.py
```

```
"""
This example shows how to create a simple network and
how to create docker containers (based on existing images)
to it.
"""

from mininet.net import Containernet
from mininet.node import Controller, Docker, OVSSwitch
from mininet.cli import CLI
from mininet.log import setLogLevel, info
from mininet.link import TCLink, Link


def emulate():

    "Create a network with some docker containers acting as hosts."

    net = Containernet(controller=Controller)

    info('*** Adding controller\n')
    net.addController('c0')

    info('*** Adding hosts\n')
    h1 = net.addHost('h1')
    h2 = net.addHost('h2')

    info('*** Adding docker containers\n')
    d1 = net.addDocker('d1', ip='10.0.0.251', dimage="ubuntu:trusty")
    # A container with more specific params: cpu period and cpu quota
    d2 = net.addDocker('d2', ip='10.0.0.252', dimage="ubuntu:trusty",
            cpu_period=50000, cpu_quota=25000)

    # Add a container as a host, using Docker class option.
    d3 = net.addHost('d3', ip='11.0.0.253', cls=Docker,
            dimage="ubuntu:trusty", cpu_shares=20)

    # Add a container with a specific volume.
    d5 = net.addDocker('d5', dimage="ubuntu:trusty",
            volumes=["/:/mnt/vol1:rw"])

    info('*** Adding switch\n')
    s1 = net.addSwitch('s1')
    s2 = net.addSwitch('s2', cls=OVSSwitch)
    s3 = net.addSwitch('s3')

    info('*** Creating links\n')
    net.addLink(h1, s1)
    net.addLink(s1, d1)
```

```
    net.addLink(h2, s2)
    net.addLink(d2, s2)
    net.addLink(s1, s2)

    # try to add a second interface to a docker container
    net.addLink(d2, s3, params1={"ip": "11.0.0.254/8"})
    net.addLink(d3, s3)

    info('*** Starting network\n')
    net.start()

    # The typical ping example, with two docker instances
        in place of hosts.
    net.ping([d1, d2])

    # our extended ping functionality
    net.ping([d1], manualdestip="10.0.0.252")
    net.ping([d2, d3], manualdestip="11.0.0.254")

    info('*** Dynamically add a container at runtime\n')
    d4 = net.addDocker('d4', dimage="ubuntu:trusty")

    # we have to specify a manual ip when we add a link at runtime
    net.addLink(d4, s1, params1={"ip": "10.0.0.254/8"})

    # Ping docker instance d1.
    net.ping([d1], manualdestip="10.0.0.254")

    info('*** Running CLI\n')
    CLI(net)

    info('*** Stopping network')
    net.stop()

if __name__ == '__main__':
    setLogLevel('info')
    emulate()
```

This is the simple `ping` example that we have been testing in previous recipes, this time with container support. You may extend this to have more container-specific workloads and tasks. You may leverage more processes from the container itself, than from the hosting server (as opposed to the previous situation where we were able to execute applications such as `vim` and `gedit` installed in the server from the hosts emulated in Mininet):

```
$ python 9_5_containernet_emulation.py
*** Adding controller
*** Adding hosts
*** Adding docker containers
d1: update resources {'cpu_quota': -1}
d2: update resources {'cpu_period': 50000, 'cpu_quota': 25000}
d3: update resources {'cpu_quota': -1, 'cpu_shares': 20}
d5: update resources {'cpu_quota': -1}
*** Adding switch
*** Creating links
*** Starting network
*** Configuring hosts
h1 h2 d1 d2 d3 d5 *** defaultIntf: warning: d5 has no interfaces
*** Starting controller
c0
*** Starting 3 switches
s1 s2 s3 ...
d1 -> d2
d2 -> d1
*** Results: 0% dropped (2/2 received)
d1 -> 10.0.0.252
*** Results: 0% dropped (1/1 received)
d2 -> 11.0.0.254
d3 -> 11.0.0.254
*** Results: 0% dropped (2/2 received)
*** Dynamically add a container at runtime
d4: update resources {'cpu_quota': -1}
d1 -> 10.0.0.254
*** Results: 0% dropped (1/1 received)
*** Running CLI
*** Starting CLI:
containernet>
```

How it works...

Containernet extends Mininet with the container support specifically for Docker. It can be installed locally as your Mininet installation, or installed as a Vagrant image.

While MaxiNet aims to increase the scalability and throughput of Mininet, Mininet-WiFi and Containernet aim to offer more features to Mininet. As Mininet offers a Python-based API, it can be extended with Python modules. In the core, you may extend its kernel with C code.

Similar to Mininet-WiFi, Containernet too thrives to maintain backward-compatibility with Mininet. Thus emulations written in Mininet should work in these projects that are started as a fork of Mininet. Moreover, the APIs are maintained to resemble that of Mininet with minimal changes, it is easy to adopt to these emulation platforms.

While these recipes presented the ability to simulate containers in the networks and wireless sensor networks, they also serve the purpose to illustrate the potential to extend Mininet with more capabilities.

10
Getting Started with SDN

In this chapter, we will cover the following recipes:

- SDN emulation with Mininet
- Developing Software-Defined Networks with OpenDaylight controller
- Developing Software-Defined Networks with ONOS controller
- Developing Software-Defined Networks with Floodlight controller
- Developing Software-Defined Networks with Ryu controller
- Developing Software-Defined Networks with POX controller
- Developing Software-Defined Networks visually with MiniEdit

Introduction

Software-Defined Networking (SDN) is an important innovation in networking. OpenFlow is a core SDN protocol that enables a centralized control to the data planes, standardizing the way the switches are controlled from a logical software controller. In this chapter, we will look into building Software-Defined Networks with various open source SDN controllers such as Ryu, OpenDaylight, Floodlight, ONOS, and POX.

SDN controllers are written in high-level languages such as Java and Python, and hence can easily be programmed by software developers. They can be used in conjunction with the physical networks as well as network emulators to control physical and emulated/virtual network data planes. We will use Mininet to emulate the network data plane in this chapter. We will further look into extending POX and Ryu, two of the controllers that are written in Python.

SDN emulation with Mininet

Mininet is the standard emulator used to emulate and prototype SDN systems quickly. As we do not assume that our readers have access to complex networks with SDN switches, we will use Mininet to build Software-Defined Networks throughout this chapter.

Getting ready

If your emulation stalled for some reason, before running your next emulation make sure to clean up the environment:

```
$ sudo mn -c
```

How to do it...

OpenFlow, an SDN protocol, is commonly used to control data plane consisting of switches in a centralized manner. This steers up network softwarization where networks can easily be reprogrammed from the controller. This essentially takes away the control of the network from the individual switches, and unifies and consolidates the control to a centralized controller. Thus, the controller is aware of the global network status and can modify the routing tables in the switches in an efficient manner.

In this recipe, we will emulate a large network along with a single `RemoteController` of Mininet.

The port number 6653 is assigned for OpenFlow (http://www.iana.org/assignments/service-names-port-numbers/service-names-port-numbers.xhtml?search=openflow) and most network emulators (including Mininet) and all the SDN controllers adhere to this standard.

It is possible that a previous execution of an emulator or a controller makes the port 6653 busy, and hence preventing the controller to start execution. If a message pops up mentioning port 6653 to be busy, kill it using the following command:

```
$ sudo fuser -k 6653/tcp
```

Listing 10.1 gives an emulation of a large-scale SDN-based data center:

```python
#!/usr/bin/env python
# Python Network Programming Cookbook, Second Edition -- Chapter - 10
# This program is optimized for Python 2.7.12.
# It may run on any other version with/without modifications.

from mininet.net import Mininet
from mininet.node import OVSSwitch, Controller, RemoteController
from mininet.cli import CLI
from mininet.log import setLogLevel

def execute():
    net = Mininet()
    # Creating nodes in the network.
    c1 = net.addController(name='c1', controller=RemoteController,
        ip='127.0.0.1')

    GSD1=net.addSwitch('GSD1')
    GSD2=net.addSwitch('GSD2')
    GSD3=net.addSwitch('GSD3')
    GSD4=net.addSwitch('GSD4')
    GSD5=net.addSwitch('GSD5')
    GSD6=net.addSwitch('GSD6')
    GSD7=net.addSwitch('GSD7')
    GSD8=net.addSwitch('GSD8')
    GSD9=net.addSwitch('GSD9')
    GSD10=net.addSwitch('GSD10')
    GSD11=net.addSwitch('GSD11')
[Truncated due to excess length. Check the source code of
10_1_sdn_mininet_emulation.py from the accompanying zip]

    GZSA17=net.addSwitch('GZSA17')
    GZSA18=net.addSwitch('GZSA18')
    GZSA19=net.addSwitch('GZSA19')
    GZSA20=net.addSwitch('GZSA20')

    # Creating links between nodes in network
    net.addLink(GSD1, GSD2)
    net.addLink(GSD1, GSD5)
    net.addLink(GSD1, GSD20)
    net.addLink(GSD1, GSD30)
    net.addLink(GSD1, GSD40)
    net.addLink(GSD2, GSD1)
    net.addLink(GSD2, GSD3)
    net.addLink(GSD2, GSD4)
    net.addLink(GSD3, GSD2)
    net.addLink(GSD3, GSD5)
```

```
net.addLink(GSD3, GSD6)
net.addLink(GSD4, GSD2)
net.addLink(GSD4, GSD7)
net.addLink(GSD4, GSD8)

[Truncated due to excess length. Check the source code of
10_1_sdn_mininet_emulation.py from the accompanying zip]

net.addLink(GZSA19, GZSA16)
net.addLink(GZSA19, GZSA20)
net.addLink(GZSA20, GZSA19)
net.addLink(GZSA20, GZSA1)


net.start()
CLI( net )
net.stop()

if __name__ == '__main__':
    setLogLevel( 'info' )  # for CLI output
    execute()
```

This code emulates a number of switches, followed by a number of links between them, before emulating the network consisting of them:

```
$ sudo python 10_1_sdn_mininet_emulation.py  [sudo] password for pradeeban:
Connecting to remote controller at 127.0.0.1:6653*** Configuring hosts***
Starting controller(s)c1 *** Starting switches and/or access pointsGSD1
GSD2 GSD3 GSD4 GSD5 GSD6 GSD7 GSD8 GSD9 GSD10 GSD11 GSD12 GSD13 GSD14 GSD15
GSD16 GSD17 GSD18 GSD19 GSD20 GSD21 GSD22 GSD23 GSD24 GSD25 GSD26 GSD27
GSD28 GSD29 GSD30 GSD31 GSD32 GSD33 GSD34 GSD35 ...GZSA15 GZSA16 GZSA17
GZSA18 GZSA19 GZSA20 ...*** Starting CLI:mininet-wifi> exit*** Stopping 1
controllersc1 *** Stopping 1184
links.........................................................................
.............................................................................
.............................................................................
.............................................................................
.............................................................................
..........................................*** Stopping switches and/or
access pointsGSD1 GSD2 GSD3 GSD4 GSD5 GSD6 GSD7 GSD8 GSD9 GSD10 GSD11 GSD12
GSD13 GSD14 GSD15 GSD16 GSD17 GSD18 GSD19 GSD20 GSD21 GSD22 GSD23 GSD24
GSD25 GSD26 GSD27 GSD28 GSD29 GSD30 GSD31 GSD32 GSD33 GSD34 GSD35
....GZSA15 GZSA16 GZSA17 GZSA18 GZSA19 GZSA20 *** Stopping hosts and/or
stations*** Done
```

The preceding output is truncated due to its length. The entire output is captured in the following screenshot:

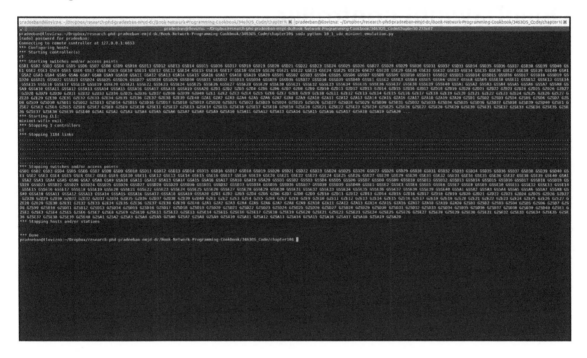

SDN Emulation with Mininet

How it works...

This recipe emulates a data center with a single SDN controller managing 400 switches. The Python code recreates the network by manually producing the 1184 links across the 400 switches, controlled by the SDN controller c1 of type, RemoteController in 127.0.0.1. RemoteController is the default controller option of Mininet, which can be replaced by enterprise-grade controllers such as OpenDaylight or Floodlight. By adding each of the switches and links, the recipe creates the complex topology manually using Python.

Common topologies such as tree and linear topologies can be built without adding switches and links one-by-one. More topologies such as leaf-spine topologies too can be custom-built using Python for Mininet to emulate the large networks. However, even this large manual addition of switches and links can be automated; hence making this easier than it appears to be. Adding hosts to the topology is omitted in this recipe due to space.

Developing Software-Defined Networks with OpenDaylight controller

OpenDaylight is an enterprise controller commonly used in production. We will look into configuring OpenDaylight as the controller to use with Mininet.

Getting ready

In this recipe, we will first install OpenDaylight locally. We will use its *Beryllium* version, as the latter versions removed OpenDaylight DLUX (the graphical user interface module) from bundling by default in the released binary ZIP:

```
wget
https://nexus.opendaylight.org/content/repositories/opendaylight.release/or
g/opendaylight/integration/distribution-karaf/0.4.4-Beryllium-
SR4/distribution-karaf-0.4.4-Beryllium-SR4.zip
```

You may also download other versions (such as Boron, Carbon, or latter versions in the future) from `https://www.opendaylight.org/downloads`. However, you will have to download and install the bundles such as DLUX on your own.

Unzip the distribution ZIP archive:

```
$ unzip distribution-karaf-0.4.4-Beryllium-SR4.zip
```

Then go to the `bin` folder:

```
$ cd distribution-karaf-0.4.4-Beryllium-SR4/bin
```

Now run the OpenDaylight controller by executing the `karaf` file:

```
$ ./karaf
karaf: Ignoring predefined value for KARAF_HOME
Java HotSpot(TM) 64-Bit Server VM warning: ignoring option
MaxPermSize=512m; support was removed in 8.0
```

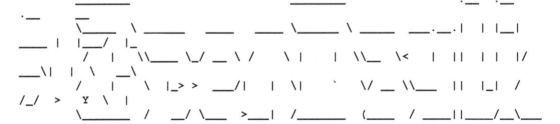

```
/|__|  /__|
              \/|__|        \/     \/      \/     \/\/
/____/         \/
Hit '<tab>' for a list of available commands
and '[cmd] --help' for help on a specific command.
Hit '<ctrl-d>' or type 'system:shutdown' or 'logout' to shutdown
OpenDaylight.
```

OpenDaylight is a component-based software developed following the OSGi model. It uses Apache Karaf OSGi engine as its core. So you may notice that we run `karaf` to start OpenDaylight, opening an OSGi console as seen previously.

Install the DLUX and prerequisites:

```
opendaylight-user@root>feature:install odl-restconf odl-l2switch-switch
odl-mdsal-apidocs odl-dlux-core
```

Now you should be able to access the DLUX web interface of OpenDaylight.

Navigate to `http://localhost:8181/index.html` in your browser. The default username and password are both `admin`.

Now, run Mininet from another window:

```
$  sudo mn --controller=remote,ip=127.0.0.1 --topo tree,depth=3,fanout=2
$ sudo mn --controller=remote,ip=127.0.0.1 --topo tree,depth=3,fanout=2
*** Creating network
*** Adding controller
Connecting to remote controller at 127.0.0.1:6653
*** Adding hosts and stations:
h1 h2 h3 h4 h5 h6 h7 h8
*** Adding switches and access point(s):
s1 s2 s3 s4 s5 s6 s7
*** Adding link(s):
(s1, s2) (s1, s5) (s2, s3) (s2, s4) (s3, h1) (s3, h2) (s4, h3) (s4, h4)
(s5, s6) (s5, s7) (s6, h5) (s6, h6) (s7, h7) (s7, h8)
*** Configuring hosts
*** Starting controller(s)
c0
*** Starting switches and/or access points
s1 s2 s3 s4 s5 s6 s7 ...
*** Starting CLI:
mininet-wifi>
```

Here, `controller=remote`, points to the OpenDaylight controller in `127.0.0.1`. Make sure to run the controller first before running Mininet, as otherwise Mininet would have started its own internal controller as the remote controller in the same port.

The following screenshot indicates the admin console of OpenDaylight, indicating the network topology emulated by Mininet:

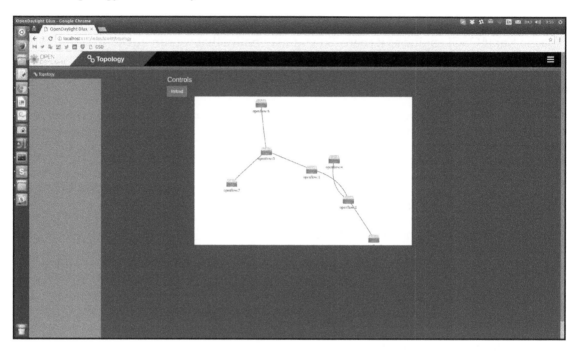

Network Topology in OpenDaylight DLUX

Next, we will run a simple Python program that emulates a network with switches and hosts with Mininet, and a remote controller. We will start OpenDaylight first as the remote controller.

How to do it...

The following line adds a `controller` as `RemoteController` to the network emulated:

```
c1 = net.addController(name='c1',
controller=RemoteController, ip='127.0.0.1')
```

If a `RemoteController` does not exist in the given IP (since the port is not mentioned, default OpenFlow controller port `6653` is assumed), it will start Mininet's controller. Thus, make sure to start OpenDaylight (or any other SDN controller of your choice) first.

Listing 10.2 gives an execution of a Software-Defined Network with a controller, a few nodes (switches and hosts), and links as follows:

```python
#!/usr/bin/env python
# Python Network Programming Cookbook, Second Edition -- Chapter - 10
# This program is optimized for Python 2.7.12.
# It may run on any other version with/without modifications.

from mininet.net import Mininet
from mininet.node import OVSSwitch, Controller, RemoteController
from mininet.cli import CLI
from mininet.log import setLogLevel

def execute():

    # Create Mininet instance.
    net = Mininet()

    # Add the SDN controller to the network.
    c1 = net.addController(name='c1',
        controller=RemoteController, ip='127.0.0.1')

    # Add hosts to the network.
    h0=net.addHost('h0')
    h1=net.addHost('h1')

    # Add switches to the network.
    s0=net.addSwitch('s0')
    s1=net.addSwitch('s1')
    s2=net.addSwitch('s2')

    # Creating links between the switches in the network
    net.addLink(s0, s1)
    net.addLink(s1, s2)
    net.addLink(s0, s2)

    # Connect hosts to the relevant switches in the network.
    net.addLink(h0, s0)
    net.addLink(h1, s1)

    # Start execution.
    net.start()
```

```
    CLI( net )

if __name__ == '__main__':
    setLogLevel( 'info' )  # for CLI output
    execute()
```

This is a simple Python program that uses Open vSwitch for virtual emulated switches, and remote SDN `Controller` module of Mininet to connect to an executing controller (or if none exists, start its own).

First, we start the OpenDaylight controller from the `bin` directory:

```
$ ./karaf
karaf: Ignoring predefined value for KARAF_HOME
Java HotSpot(TM) 64-Bit Server VM warning: ignoring option
MaxPermSize=512m; support was removed in 8.0

    _____       _____      ___     _____     _____      _____    ___ .___. ._  ._  ._  __  _
    \____   \ ____  ___   _____  \ ____    __:_.| | |_| ___|
   |___/  |_
        /  |    \\____ \_/ __ \ /    \ |    | \\__  \<   |  ||   ||  |/ __\|
   |  \   _\
       /   |    \  |_> >   __/|   | \|       `  \/ __ \\___  ||  |_|  / /_/ >
  Y  \  |
       _____ /  __/ \___  >__| /_____    (____  / ___||___/__\___
  /|___| /_|
            \/|__|          \/      \/         \/     \/\/              /____/
  \/
Hit '<tab>' for a list of available commands
and '[cmd] --help' for help on a specific command.
Hit '<ctrl-d>' or type 'system:shutdown' or 'logout' to shutdown
OpenDaylight.
```

Then we execute our program:

```
$ sudo python 10_2_sdn_opendaylight.py
[sudo] password for pradeeban:
Connecting to remote controller at 127.0.0.1:6653
*** Configuring hosts
*** Starting controller(s)
c1
*** Starting switches and/or access points
s0 s1 s2 ...
*** Starting CLI:
mininet-wifi>
```

We can also access the controller GUI (DLUX) through a browser, at `http://localhost:8181/index.html#` as we did before. The following screenshot indicates the output from the console and the browser:

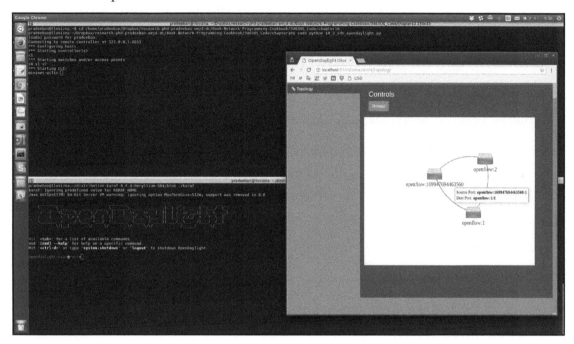

SDN with OpenDaylight

How it works...

OpenDaylight DLUX shows the switches and links. While it is a nice extension to OpenDaylight, the controller can be programmed entirely through the console or its extensions.

Developing Software-Defined Networks with ONOS controller

ONOS and OpenDaylight are two SDN controllers developed by many enterprises as a collaboration under the Linux Foundation. Developed in Java, both are modular, developed with Apache Karaf OSGi controller.

Getting ready

First, you need to download ONOS to your computer:

```
$ wget https://downloads.onosproject.org/release/onos-1.10.2.zip
```

You may also download other versions from https://wiki.onosproject.org/display/ONOS/Downloads.

Extract the ZIP into the /opt directory:

```
$ unzip https://downloads.onosproject.org/release/onos-1.10.2.zip
```

Rename the extracted folder to onos and go to the onos/bin directory:

```
$ mv onos-1.10.2 onos
$ cd onos/bin
```

Now, start ONOS:

```
./onos-service start
```

```
    Apache Karaf (3.0.3)

Hit '<tab>' for a list of available commands
and '[cmd] --help' for help on a specific command.
Hit '<ctrl-d>' or type 'system:shutdown' or 'logout' to shutdown Karaf.
karaf@root()>
```

Despite the misleading name, please note that this just starts ONOS Apache Karaf console. It does not start ONOS as a Linux service.

 For further information on installing ONOS in your server as a single stand-alone installation, you may refer to https://wiki.onosproject.org/display/ONOS/Installing+on+a+single+machine.

Now your ONOS controller is ready in your laptop. You may test it by running a Mininet emulation to connect to ONOS:

```
$ sudo mn --controller=remote,ip=127.0.0.1 --topo tree,depth=3,fanout=2
[sudo] password for pradeeban:
*** Creating network
*** Adding controller
```

```
Connecting to remote controller at 127.0.0.1:6653
*** Adding hosts and stations:
h1 h2 h3 h4 h5 h6 h7 h8
*** Adding switches and access point(s):
s1 s2 s3 s4 s5 s6 s7
*** Adding link(s):
(s1, s2) (s1, s5) (s2, s3) (s2, s4) (s3, h1) (s3, h2) (s4, h3) (s4, h4)
(s5, s6) (s5, s7) (s6, h5) (s6, h6) (s7, h7) (s7, h8)
*** Configuring hosts
*** Starting controller(s)
c0
*** Starting switches and/or access points
s1 s2 s3 s4 s5 s6 s7 ...
*** Starting CLI:
mininet-wifi>
```

This creates a network of tree topology with ONOS as the SDN controller. The following screenshot shows ONOS and Mininet execution:

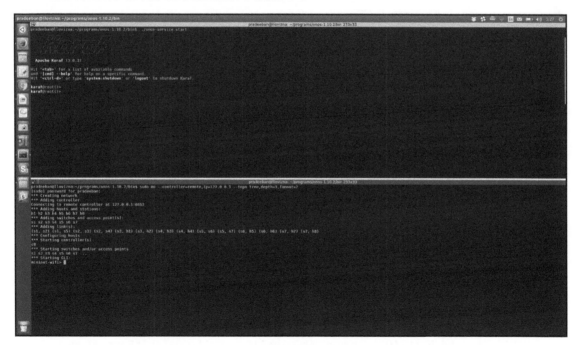

SDN with ONOS

How to do it...

We first need to start the ONOS controller, and then initiate the Python program consisting of Mininet emulation of the network.

Listing 10.3 gives a Software-Defined Network with ONOS controller:

```python
#!/usr/bin/env python
# Python Network Programming Cookbook, Second Edition -- Chapter - 10
# This program is optimized for Python 2.7.12.
# It may run on any other version with/without modifications.

from mininet.net import Mininet
from mininet.node import Controller, RemoteController, OVSController
from mininet.node import CPULimitedHost, Host, Node
from mininet.node import OVSKernelSwitch, UserSwitch
from mininet.cli import CLI
from mininet.log import setLogLevel, info
from mininet.link import TCLink, Intf
from subprocess import call

def myNetwork():

    net = Mininet( topo=None,
                   build=False,
                   ipBase='10.0.0.0/8')

    info( '*** Adding controller\n' )
    c0=net.addController(name='c0',
                      controller=RemoteController,
                      ip='127.0.0.1',
                      protocol='tcp',
                      port=6653)

    info( '*** Add switches\n')
    s2 = net.addSwitch('s2', cls=OVSKernelSwitch)
    s1 = net.addSwitch('s1', cls=OVSKernelSwitch)
    s5 = net.addSwitch('s5', cls=OVSKernelSwitch, failMode='standalone')

    info( '*** Add hosts\n')
    h2 = net.addHost('h2', cls=Host, ip='10.0.0.2', defaultRoute=None)
    h1 = net.addHost('h1', cls=Host, ip='10.0.0.1', defaultRoute=None)
    h4 = net.addHost('h4', cls=Host, ip='10.0.0.4', defaultRoute=None)
    h3 = net.addHost('h3', cls=Host, ip='10.0.0.3', defaultRoute=None)

    info( '*** Add links\n')
    s1s2 = {'bw':400,'loss':0}
    net.addLink(s1, s2, cls=TCLink , **s1s2)
```

```
    s2h1 = {'bw':1000,'loss':10,'max_queue_size':10,'speedup':40}
    net.addLink(s2, h1, cls=TCLink , **s2h1)
    s2h2 = {'bw':120,'loss':0}
    net.addLink(s2, h2, cls=TCLink , **s2h2)
    s2h3 = {'bw':400,'loss':20}
    net.addLink(s2, h3, cls=TCLink , **s2h3)
    s1s5 = {'bw':200,'delay':'12','loss':10}
    net.addLink(s1, s5, cls=TCLink , **s1s5)
    s5h4 = {'bw':100,'loss':50}
    net.addLink(s5, h4, cls=TCLink , **s5h4)

    info( '*** Starting network\n')
    net.build()
    info( '*** Starting controllers\n')
    for controller in net.controllers:
        controller.start()

    info( '*** Starting switches\n')
    net.get('s2').start([c0])
    net.get('s1').start([c0])
    net.get('s5').start([])

    info( '*** Post configure switches and hosts\n')

    CLI(net)
    net.stop()

if __name__ == '__main__':
    setLogLevel( 'info' )
    myNetwork()
```

Start the ONOS controller first, and then execute this recipe as follows:

```
$ sudo python 10_3_sdn_onos.py
*** Adding controller
*** Add switches
*** Add hosts
*** Add links
(400.00Mbit 0.00000% loss) (400.00Mbit 0.00000% loss) (1000.00Mbit
10.00000% loss) (1000.00Mbit 10.00000% loss) (120.00Mbit 0.00000% loss)
(120.00Mbit 0.00000% loss) (400.00Mbit 20.00000% loss) (400.00Mbit
20.00000% loss) (200.00Mbit 12 delay 10.00000% loss) (200.00Mbit 12 delay
10.00000% loss) (100.00Mbit 50.00000% loss) (100.00Mbit 50.00000% loss) ***
Starting network
*** Configuring hosts
*** Starting controllers
*** Starting switches
(400.00Mbit 0.00000% loss) (1000.00Mbit 10.00000% loss) (120.00Mbit
```

```
0.00000% loss) (400.00Mbit 20.00000% loss) (400.00Mbit 0.00000% loss)
(200.00Mbit 12 delay 10.00000% loss) (200.00Mbit 12 delay 10.00000% loss)
(100.00Mbit 50.00000% loss) *** Post configure switches and hosts
*** Starting CLI:
```

How it works...

In this recipe, we first add a remote SDN controller pointing to the ONOS controller and the switches—two SDN switches (s1 and s2) and on legacy switch (s5, marked by failMode='standalone'). We then add hosts and links with various properties. The link properties including bandwidth, loss rate, maximum queue size, delay, and speed up are modeled.

Once the network is built, the controller is started. The SDN switches s1 and s2 are started from the controller:

```
net.get('s2').start([c0])
net.get('s1').start([c0])
```
However, the legacy switch s5 does not support OpenFlow or any SDN
protocols. Hence it is started on its own.
```
net.get('s5').start([])
```

However, s5 is still connected to another SDN switch s1, which acts as the core switch of the network. ONOS controls this network as it is emulated.

Developing Software-Defined Networks with Floodlight controller

Floodlight is another SDN controller developed in Java. Floodlight is more compact and easier to start with.

Getting ready

First download Floodlight controller. You may simply download a Floodlight **virtual machine** (**VM**) from http://www.projectfloodlight.org/download/.

Alternatively, you may download the source code archive from Floodlight and build it:

```
$ wget https://github.com/floodlight/floodlight/archive/v1.2.zip
```

Many open source Java projects such as OpenDaylight and ONOS are built using Apache Maven. You may install Maven in Ubuntu/Debian based systems using the following command:

```
$ sudo apt-get install maven
```

Floodlight requires Apache Ant in addition to Apache Maven for its build. You may install Ant using the following command:

```
$ sudo apt-get install ant
```

Maven requires Java for its execution. The preceding command will install Java as well. However, if you choose to install Maven by other means, make sure that Java is also correctly installed in your computer prior to installing Maven. Floodlight requires Java 8 for its execution.

Extract the Floodlight ZIP and go to the floodlight-1.2 directory:

```
$ unzip https://github.com/floodlight/floodlight/archive/v1.2.zip
$ cd floodlight-1.2
```

Now proceed to build Floodlight using Ant:

```
$ ant
Buildfile: /home/pradeeban/programs/floodlight-1.2/build.xml
init:
    [mkdir] Created dir: /home/pradeeban/programs/floodlight-1.2/
    target/bin
    [mkdir] Created dir: /home/pradeeban/programs/floodlight-1.2/
    target/bin-test
    [mkdir] Created dir: /home/pradeeban/programs/floodlight-1.2/
    target/lib
    [mkdir] Created dir: /home/pradeeban/programs/floodlight-1.2/
    target/test
compile:
    [javac] Compiling 527 source files to /home/pradeeban/programs/
    floodlight-1.2/target/bin
    [javac] warning: [options] bootstrap class path not set in
```

```
         conjunction with -source 1.7
         [javac] Note: Some input files use or override a deprecated API.
         [javac] Note: Recompile with -Xlint:deprecation for details.
         [javac] Note: Some input files use unchecked or unsafe operations.
         [javac] Note: Recompile with -Xlint:unchecked for details.
         [javac] 1 warning
         [copy] Copying 54 files to /home/pradeeban/programs/
         floodlight-1.2/target/bin
compile-test:
         [javac] Compiling 90 source files to /home/pradeeban/programs/
         floodlight-1.2/target/bin-test
         [javac] warning: [options] bootstrap class path not set in
         conjunction with -source 1.7
         [javac] 1 warning
dist:
         [jar] Building jar: /home/pradeeban/programs/floodlight-1.2/
         target/floodlight.jar
         [jar] Building jar: /home/pradeeban/programs/floodlight-1.2/
         target/floodlight-test.jar
BUILD SUCCESSFUL
Total time: 12 seconds
```

After the successful build, you will find the built `floodlight.jar` in the `floodlight-1.2/target` directory. You may run it using the following command:

```
$ java -jar target/floodlight.jar
```

Floodlight is quite verbose with its info logs. You will see a lot of logs when it runs. You may run Mininet to connect to it:

```
$ sudo mn --controller=remote,ip=127.0.0.1 --topo tree,depth=3,fanout=2
```

The following screenshot shows Floodlight and Mininet in execution. The logs are informative on OpenFlow switches connected and LLDP packets sent to the enabled ports.

SDN with Floodlight

You may run Wireshark to listen to the OpenFlow packets:

```
$ wireshark
```

You may need to issue the following command to execute Wireshark as a non-root user before running Wireshark:

```
$ sudo setcap 'CAP_NET_RAW+eip CAP_NET_ADMIN+eip' /usr/bin/dumpcap
```

The following screenshot shows the Wireshark, highlighting an OpenFlow capture:

OpenFlow Capture with Wireshark

How to do it...

In this recipe, we will run a simple network emulation with two switches - one `OVSKernelSwitch` and the other, Indigo Virtual Switch (`IVSSwitch`). First let's install `IVSSwitch` (`https://github.com/floodlight/ivs`), which is Floodlight's own implementation of a virtual switch. We start with installing the dependencies:

```
$ sudo apt-get install libnl-3-dev libnl-genl-3-dev libnl-route-3-dev pkg-
config python-tz libpcap-dev libcap2-dev
```

Clone the IVS repository:

```
$ git clone --recurse-submodules https://github.com/floodlight/ivs.git
```

Compile it:

```
$ cd ivs
$ make
$ sudo make install
```

Make sure to execute Floodlight before running this recipe. Now, IVS is ready to run:

```
$ sudo ivs -c 127.0.0.1
```

Now you may run the listing 10.4, which constructs the network with the `switches`, `hosts`, and `links`:

```python
#!/usr/bin/env python
# Python Network Programming Cookbook, Second Edition -- Chapter - 10
# This program is optimized for Python 2.7.12.
# It may run on any other version with/without modifications.

from mininet.net import Mininet
from mininet.node import Controller, RemoteController, OVSController
from mininet.node import CPULimitedHost, Host, Node
from mininet.node import OVSKernelSwitch, UserSwitch
from mininet.node import IVSSwitch
from mininet.cli import CLI
from mininet.log import setLogLevel, info
from mininet.link import TCLink, Intf
from subprocess import call

def myNetwork():

    net = Mininet( topo=None,
                   build=False,
                   ipBase='10.0.0.0/8')

    info( '*** Adding controller\n' )
    c0=net.addController(name='c0',
                      controller=RemoteController,
                      ip='127.0.0.1',
                      protocol='tcp',
                      port=6653)

    info( '*** Add switches\n')
    s2 = net.addSwitch('s2', cls=OVSKernelSwitch)
    s1 = net.addSwitch('s1', cls=IVSSwitch)
```

```
        info( '*** Add hosts\n')
        h2 = net.addHost('h2', cls=Host, ip='10.0.0.2', defaultRoute=None)
        h1 = net.addHost('h1', cls=Host, ip='10.0.0.1', defaultRoute=None)
        h3 = net.addHost('h3', cls=Host, ip='10.0.0.3', defaultRoute=None)

        info( '*** Add links\n')
        s1s2 = {'bw':400,'loss':0}
        net.addLink(s1, s2, cls=TCLink , **s1s2)
        s2h1 = {'bw':1000,'loss':10,'max_queue_size':10,'speedup':40}
        net.addLink(s2, h1, cls=TCLink , **s2h1)
        s2h2 = {'bw':120,'loss':0}
        net.addLink(s2, h2, cls=TCLink , **s2h2)
        s2h3 = {'bw':400,'loss':20}
        net.addLink(s2, h3, cls=TCLink , **s2h3)

        info( '*** Starting network\n')
        net.build()
        info( '*** Starting controllers\n')
        for controller in net.controllers:
            controller.start()

        info( '*** Starting switches\n')
        net.get('s2').start([c0])
        net.get('s1').start([c0])

        info( '*** Post configure switches and hosts\n')

        CLI(net)
        net.stop()

if __name__ == '__main__':
    setLogLevel( 'info' )
    myNetwork()
```

The virtual switches communicate with the controller. The network is managed by Floodlight controller centrally. Here you may see the output of the execution of this recipe:

```
$ sudo python 10_4_sdn_floodlight.py
*** Adding controller
*** Add switches
*** Add hosts
*** Add links
(400.00Mbit 0.00000% loss) (400.00Mbit 0.00000% loss) (1000.00Mbit
10.00000% loss) (1000.00Mbit 10.00000% loss) (120.00Mbit 0.00000% loss)
(120.00Mbit 0.00000% loss) (400.00Mbit 20.00000% loss) (400.00Mbit
20.00000% loss) *** Starting network
*** Configuring hosts
*** Starting controllers
```

```
*** Starting switches
(400.00Mbit 0.00000% loss) (1000.00Mbit 10.00000% loss) (120.00Mbit
0.00000% loss) (400.00Mbit 20.00000% loss) *** Post configure switches and
hosts
*** Starting CLI:
```

How it works...

Floodlight controller and IVS are open source SDN projects of Floodlight. We leverage both of them to control our network emulated by the Mininet-based Python program.

Developing Software-Defined Networks with Ryu controller

Ryu is an SDN controller written in Python. As a component-based application, Ryu is easy to extend for network management and control. It supports various SDN protocols, including OpenFlow, Netconf, and OF-CONFIG.

Getting ready

First we need to install Ryu:

```
$ sudo pip install ryu
```

It is very simple as it can be installed with `pip`.

Confirm Ryu has been installed correctly by using the following command:

```
$ sudo mn --controller=ryu,ip=127.0.0.1 --topo linear,2
*** Creating network
*** Adding controller
warning: no Ryu modules specified; running simple_switch only
*** Adding hosts and stations:
h1 h2
*** Adding switches and access point(s):
s1 s2
*** Adding link(s):
(h1, s1) (h2, s2) (s2, s1)
*** Configuring hosts
*** Starting controller(s)
c0
```

```
*** Starting switches and/or access points
s1 s2 ...
*** Starting CLI:
mininet-wifi>
```

The preceding command uses `ryu` as the controller in the network emulated by Mininet. It uses a simple switch in this process.

Now we will write a simple SDN application to get notified when a topology changes. We will use `wscat` for this recipe. You may install it using:

```
$ sudo apt install node-ws
```

How to do it...

In this recipe, we will monitor and notify when new links are added to the network. Listing 10.5 gives a simple monitoring for link changes:

```python
#!/usr/bin/env python
# Python Network Programming Cookbook, Second Edition -- Chapter - 10
# This program is optimized for Python 2.7.12.
# It may run on any other version with/without modifications.
# Adopted from
https://github.com/osrg/ryu/blob/master/ryu/app/ws_topology.py

from socket import error as SocketError
from tinyrpc.exc import InvalidReplyError
from ryu.app.wsgi import (
    ControllerBase,
    WSGIApplication,
    websocket,
    WebSocketRPCClient
)
from ryu.base import app_manager
from ryu.topology import event, switches
from ryu.controller.handler import set_ev_cls


class WebSocketTopology(app_manager.RyuApp):
    _CONTEXTS = {
        'wsgi': WSGIApplication,
        'switches': switches.Switches,
    }

    def __init__(self, *args, **kwargs):
        super(WebSocketTopology, self).__init__(*args, **kwargs)
```

```
        self.rpc_clients = []

        wsgi = kwargs['wsgi']
        wsgi.register(WebSocketTopologyController, {'app': self})

    # Monitor the events / topology changes
    # EventSwitchEnter and EventSwitchLeave for switches
      entering and leaving.
    # EventLinkAdd and EventLinkDelete for links addition and deletion.
    # EventHostAdd for hosts addition.

    # Event - Link added
    @set_ev_cls(event.EventLinkAdd)
    def _event_link_add_handler(self, ev):
        msg = ev.link.to_dict()
        self._rpc_broadcall('event_link_add', msg)
    # Event - Link deleted
    @set_ev_cls(event.EventLinkDelete)
    def _event_link_delete_handler(self, ev):
        msg = ev.link.to_dict()
        self._rpc_broadcall('event_link_delete', msg)


    def _rpc_broadcall(self, func_name, msg):
        disconnected_clients = []
        for rpc_client in self.rpc_clients:
            rpc_server = rpc_client.get_proxy()
            try:
                getattr(rpc_server, func_name)(msg)
            except SocketError:
                self.logger.debug('WebSocket disconnected: %s',
                 rpc_client.ws)
                disconnected_clients.append(rpc_client)
            except InvalidReplyError as e:
                self.logger.error(e)

        for client in disconnected_clients:
            self.rpc_clients.remove(client)


class WebSocketTopologyController(ControllerBase):

    def __init__(self, req, link, data, **config):
        super(WebSocketTopologyController, self).__init__(
            req, link, data, **config)
        self.app = data['app']

    @websocket('topology', '/v1.0/topology/ws')
```

```
    def _websocket_handler(self, ws):
        rpc_client = WebSocketRPCClient(ws)
        self.app.rpc_clients.append(rpc_client)
        rpc_client.serve_forever()
```

Run this recipe using `ryu-manager`:

```
$ ryu-manager --verbose --observe-links 10_5_sdn_ryu.py
Registered VCS backend: git
Registered VCS backend: hg
Registered VCS backend: svn
Registered VCS backend: bzr
loading app 10_5_sdn_ryu.py
loading app ryu.controller.ofp_handler
instantiating app None of Switches
creating context switches
creating context wsgi
instantiating app ryu.controller.ofp_handler of OFPHandler
instantiating app 10_5_sdn_ryu.py of WebSocketTopology
BRICK switches
  PROVIDES EventLinkDelete TO {'WebSocketTopology': set()}
  PROVIDES EventLinkAdd TO {'WebSocketTopology': set()}
  CONSUMES EventOFPPortStatus
  CONSUMES EventLinkRequest
  CONSUMES EventHostRequest
  CONSUMES EventOFPPacketIn
  CONSUMES EventOFPStateChange
  CONSUMES EventSwitchRequest
BRICK ofp_event
  PROVIDES EventOFPPortStatus TO {'switches': {'main'}}
  PROVIDES EventOFPPacketIn TO {'switches': {'main'}}
  PROVIDES EventOFPStateChange TO {'switches': {'main',
  'dead'}}
  CONSUMES EventOFPEchoReply
  CONSUMES EventOFPSwitchFeatures
  CONSUMES EventOFPHello
  CONSUMES EventOFPPortStatus
  CONSUMES EventOFPEchoRequest
  CONSUMES EventOFPErrorMsg
  CONSUMES EventOFPPortDescStatsReply
BRICK WebSocketTopology
  CONSUMES EventLinkDelete
  CONSUMES EventLinkAdd
(32456) wsgi starting up on http://0.0.0.0:8080
Next, run wscat:
$ wscat -c ws://localhost:8080/v1.0/topology/ws
connected (press CTRL+C to quit)
This will print the below line to the ryu-manager in the previous window:
```

```
(32456) accepted ('127.0.0.1', 60740).
Now, start the network emulation with Mininet:
$ sudo mn --controller=remote,ip=127.0.0.1 --topo tree,depth=3,fanout=2
[sudo] password for pradeeban:
*** Creating network
*** Adding controller
Connecting to remote controller at 127.0.0.1:6653
*** Adding hosts and stations:
h1 h2 h3 h4 h5 h6 h7 h8
*** Adding switches and access point(s):
s1 s2 s3 s4 s5 s6 s7
*** Adding link(s):
(s1, s2) (s1, s5) (s2, s3) (s2, s4) (s3, h1) (s3, h2) (s4, h3) (s4, h4)
(s5, s6) (s5, s7) (s6, h5) (s6, h6) (s7, h7) (s7, h8)
*** Configuring hosts
*** Starting controller(s)
c0
*** Starting switches and/or access points
s1 s2 s3 s4 s5 s6 s7 ...
*** Starting CLI:
This will make the following event to be printed to the wscat:
< {"id": 1, "method": "event_link_add", "jsonrpc": "2.0", "params":
[{"dst": {"name": "s5-eth1", "dpid": "0000000000000005", "hw_addr":
"ba:91:f4:f2:5f:0c", "port_no": "00000001"}, "src": {"name": "s6-eth3",
"dpid": "0000000000000006", "hw_addr": "7a:95:e0:95:fb:34", "port_no":
"00000003"}}]}
```

At the same time, `ryu-manager` will print lines of messages indicating the changes.

The following screenshot captures `ryu-manager`, `wscat`, and Mininet in action for this recipe:

SDN with Ryu

How it works...

`ryu-manager` runs the Python programs written for Ryu. The `--verbose` flag prints more detailed logs to the console. The `--observe-links` flag observes link discovery events.

By running,

```
$ ryu-manager --help
```

you may find brief information about all the flags of `ryu-manager`.

`wscat` (`node-ws`) is a web socket listener based on Node.js. When Mininet joins, it triggers an event of change in links, as an `EventLinkAdd` event. This is reported and logged in the `wscat`. Similarly, we can also listen to the other changes in the topology, including addition and deletion of switches and addition of hosts to the topology.

Developing Software-Defined Networks with POX controller

POX is another controller written in Python. It can also function as an SDN switch, or a network operating system. POX is very easy to install and test from the source.

POX requires Python 2.7 to run, and currently it does not support Python 3. This is documented in the POX wiki: `https://openflow.stanford.edu/display/ONL/POX+Wiki #POXWiki-DoesPOXsupportPython3%3F`. Python 2 is still the commonest version even in SDN emulators such as Mininet, and hence it is advisable to have it installed for these recipes.

Getting ready

You may check out the source code of POX using:

```
$ git clone http://github.com/noxrepo/pox
```

In order to clone the source repository, make sure you have `git` installed in your computer. In Ubuntu, you may install `git` using,

```
$ sudo apt install git
```

Once you have cloned the source code locally into your computer, running POX is similar to running any other Python program. You may run it using the following command:

```
$ python pox.py
POX 0.2.0 (carp) / Copyright 2011-2013 James McCauley, et al.
INFO:core:POX 0.2.0 (carp) is up.
Now the POX controller is up and waiting to manage the SDN switches. It is
time to emulate the switches with Mininet. Run the below from Mininet:
$ sudo mn --controller=remote,ip=127.0.0.1 --topo tree,depth=3,fanout=2
[sudo] password for pradeeban:
*** Creating network
*** Adding controller
Unable to contact the remote controller at 127.0.0.1:6653
Connecting to remote controller at 127.0.0.1:6633
*** Adding hosts and stations:
h1 h2 h3 h4 h5 h6 h7 h8
*** Adding switches and access point(s):
s1 s2 s3 s4 s5 s6 s7
*** Adding link(s):
(s1, s2) (s1, s5) (s2, s3) (s2, s4) (s3, h1) (s3, h2) (s4, h3) (s4, h4)
(s5, s6) (s5, s7) (s6, h5) (s6, h6) (s7, h7) (s7, h8)
```

```
*** Configuring hosts
*** Starting controller(s)
c0
*** Starting switches and/or access points
s1 s2 s3 s4 s5 s6 s7 ...
*** Starting CLI:
mininet-wifi>
Now, you will see the below logs from POX:
INFO:openflow.of_01:[None 1] closed
INFO:openflow.of_01:[00-00-00-00-00-06 3] connected
INFO:openflow.of_01:[00-00-00-00-00-07 2] connected
INFO:openflow.of_01:[00-00-00-00-00-05 7] connected
INFO:openflow.of_01:[00-00-00-00-00-04 4] connected
INFO:openflow.of_01:[00-00-00-00-00-03 6] connected
INFO:openflow.of_01:[00-00-00-00-00-01 5] connected
INFO:openflow.of_01:[00-00-00-00-00-02 8] connected
Now terminate the Mininet instance by calling exit():
mininet-wifi> exit
*** Stopping 1 controllers
c0
*** Stopping 14 links
.............
*** Stopping switches and/or access points
s1 s2 s3 s4 s5 s6 s7
*** Stopping hosts and/or stations
h1 h2 h3 h4 h5 h6 h7 h8
*** Done
completed in 53.020 seconds
You will see the below logs printed in the POX terminal:
INFO:openflow.of_01:[00-00-00-00-00-07 2] closed
INFO:openflow.of_01:[00-00-00-00-00-04 3] closed
INFO:openflow.of_01:[00-00-00-00-00-06 4] closed
INFO:openflow.of_01:[00-00-00-00-00-01 5] closed
INFO:openflow.of_01:[00-00-00-00-00-03 6] closed
INFO:openflow.of_01:[00-00-00-00-00-02 7] closed
INFO:openflow.of_01:[00-00-00-00-00-05 8] closed
```

The following screenshot depicts the preceding execution of both POX and Mininet:

SDN with POX

In this simple recipe, we will make the OpenFlow switches run as simple hubs. You may follow this execution to make more complex realistic applications for OpenFlow. First place `10_6_sdn_pox.py` in your POX parent directory. Now you may run it with POX as a POX application.

How to do it...

We define a listener method that makes the OpenFlow switches act as a simple hub. Then we call from the `launch()`, which is invoked at the start of the application.

Listing 10.6 gives a simple FTP connection test as follows:

```
#!/usr/bin/env python
# Python Network Programming Cookbook, Second Edition -- Chapter - 10
# This program is optimized for Python 2.7.12.
# It may run on any other version with/without modifications.
# Adopted from
https://github.com/noxrepo/pox/blob/carp/pox/forwarding/hub.py
```

```
# For more examples and tutorials:
#    https://github.com/noxrepo/pox/tree/carp/pox

from pox.core import core
import pox.openflow.libopenflow_01 as of
from pox.lib.util import dpidToStr

log = core.getLogger()

# The listener definition: A simple and stupid hub.
def _handle_ConnectionUp (event):
    msg = of.ofp_flow_mod()
    msg.actions.append(of.ofp_action_output(port = of.OFPP_FLOOD))
    event.connection.send(msg)
    # log the action.
    log.info("Hubifying %s", dpidToStr(event.dpid))


# When the application is launched with POX.
def launch ():
    #Add a listener (defined above) to the pox.core openflow.
    core.openflow.addListenerByName("ConnectionUp",
     _handle_ConnectionUp)
    log.info("Hub is running.")
```

The execution of this recipe prints the following output:

```
$ ./pox.py log.level --DEBUG 10_6_sdn_pox
POX 0.2.0 (carp) / Copyright 2011-2013 James McCauley, et al.
INFO:10_6_sdn_pox:Hub is running.
DEBUG:core:POX 0.2.0 (carp) going up...
DEBUG:core:Running on CPython (2.7.12/Nov 19 2016 06:48:10)
DEBUG:core:Platform is Linux-4.8.0-58-generic-x86_64-with-Ubuntu-16.04-
xenial
INFO:core:POX 0.2.0 (carp) is up.
DEBUG:openflow.of_01:Listening on 0.0.0.0:6633
```

How it works...

The program 10_6_sdn_pox.py is invoked at the start of NOX, printing the logs:
INFO:10_6_sdn_pox:Hub is running. We have enabled DEBUG logs for the execution, to make the logs verbose. This application is not useful, as it merely transforms an OpenFlow switch into a plain hub. However, you may extend this to implement your own application logic for the OpenFlow switches.

Developing Software-Defined Networks visually with MiniEdit

MiniEdit is a Mininet application in Python that lets you develop Software-Defined Networks in a visual manner. You can create networks visually for a Mininet emulation using MiniEdit, or load an existing Mininet topology (saved as an .mn file) into MiniEdit to edit it. You may also emulate the networks directly through the MiniEdit's GUI, which invokes Mininet as its backend for the emulations.

In this recipe, we will load an existing .mn file to recreate a Python program and emulate the network represented by it.

Getting ready

Download MiniEdit:

```
$ wget
https://raw.githubusercontent.com/mininet/mininet/master/examples/miniedit.
py
```

Now, MiniEdit is ready to run as any other Python program:

```
$ sudo python miniedit.py
```

How to do it...

Run MiniEdit, find and open 10_7_sdn_miniedit.mn, which will create a visual representation of the Python program of listing 10.7 listed as follows:

```
#!/usr/bin/env python
# Python Network Programming Cookbook, Second Edition -- Chapter - 10
# This program is optimized for Python 2.7.12.
# It may run on any other version with/without modifications.

from mininet.net import Mininet
from mininet.node import Controller, RemoteController, OVSController
from mininet.node import CPULimitedHost, Host, Node
from mininet.node import OVSKernelSwitch, UserSwitch
from mininet.node import IVSSwitch
from mininet.cli import CLI
from mininet.log import setLogLevel, info
from mininet.link import TCLink, Intf
```

```
from subprocess import call

def myNetwork():

    net = Mininet( topo=None,
                   build=False,
                   ipBase='10.0.0.0/8')

    info( '*** Adding controller\n' )
    c0=net.addController(name='c0',
                         controller=Controller,
                         protocol='tcp',
                         port=6633)

    info( '*** Add switches\n')
    s9 = net.addSwitch('s9', cls=OVSKernelSwitch)
    s8 = net.addSwitch('s8', cls=OVSKernelSwitch)
    s4 = net.addSwitch('s4', cls=OVSKernelSwitch)
    s5 = net.addSwitch('s5', cls=OVSKernelSwitch)
    s7 = net.addSwitch('s7', cls=OVSKernelSwitch)
    s6 = net.addSwitch('s6', cls=OVSKernelSwitch)
    s10 = net.addSwitch('s10', cls=OVSKernelSwitch)
    s1 = net.addSwitch('s1', cls=OVSKernelSwitch)
    s3 = net.addSwitch('s3', cls=OVSKernelSwitch)
    s2 = net.addSwitch('s2', cls=OVSKernelSwitch)

    info( '*** Add hosts\n')
    h3 = net.addHost('h3', cls=Host, ip='10.0.0.3', defaultRoute=None)
    h9 = net.addHost('h9', cls=Host, ip='10.0.0.9', defaultRoute=None)
    h1 = net.addHost('h1', cls=Host, ip='10.0.0.1', defaultRoute=None)
    h7 = net.addHost('h7', cls=Host, ip='10.0.0.7', defaultRoute=None)
    h10 = net.addHost('h10', cls=Host, ip='10.0.0.10', defaultRoute=None)
    h2 = net.addHost('h2', cls=Host, ip='10.0.0.2', defaultRoute=None)
    h6 = net.addHost('h6', cls=Host, ip='10.0.0.6', defaultRoute=None)
    h4 = net.addHost('h4', cls=Host, ip='10.0.0.4', defaultRoute=None)
    h11 = net.addHost('h11', cls=Host, ip='10.0.0.11', defaultRoute=None)
    h8 = net.addHost('h8', cls=Host, ip='10.0.0.8', defaultRoute=None)
    h5 = net.addHost('h5', cls=Host, ip='10.0.0.5', defaultRoute=None)

    info( '*** Add links\n')
    s7s1 = {'bw':250,'loss':0}
    net.addLink(s7, s1, cls=TCLink , **s7s1)
    s7s8 = {'bw':250,'loss':0}
    net.addLink(s7, s8, cls=TCLink , **s7s8)
    s8s2 = {'bw':250,'loss':0}
    net.addLink(s8, s2, cls=TCLink , **s8s2)
    net.addLink(s1, s3)
    net.addLink(s1, s4)
```

```
    net.addLink(s1, s9)
    net.addLink(s1, s10)
    net.addLink(s1, s5)
    net.addLink(s1, s6)
    net.addLink(s2, s3)
    net.addLink(s2, s4)
    net.addLink(s2, s9)
    net.addLink(s2, s10)
    net.addLink(s2, s5)
    net.addLink(s2, s6)
    net.addLink(s3, h1)
    net.addLink(s3, h2)
    net.addLink(s4, h3)
    net.addLink(s4, h4)
    net.addLink(s9, h5)
    net.addLink(s9, h6)
    net.addLink(s10, h7)
    net.addLink(s10, h8)
    net.addLink(s5, h9)
    net.addLink(s6, h10)
    net.addLink(s6, h11)

    info( '*** Starting network\n')
    net.build()
    info( '*** Starting controllers\n')
    for controller in net.controllers:
        controller.start()

    info( '*** Starting switches\n')
    net.get('s9').start([])
    net.get('s8').start([c0])
    net.get('s4').start([])
    net.get('s5').start([])
    net.get('s7').start([c0])
    net.get('s6').start([])
    net.get('s10').start([])
    net.get('s1').start([])
    net.get('s3').start([])
    net.get('s2').start([])

    info( '*** Post configure switches and hosts\n')

    CLI(net)
    net.stop()

if __name__ == '__main__':
    setLogLevel( 'info' )
    myNetwork()
```

Running this recipe will produce the following output:

```
$ sudo python 10_7_sdn_miniedit.py
*** Adding controller
*** Add switches
*** Add hosts
*** Add links
(250.00Mbit 0.00000% loss) (250.00Mbit 0.00000% loss) (250.00Mbit 0.00000%
loss) (250.00Mbit 0.00000% loss) (250.00Mbit 0.00000% loss) (250.00Mbit
0.00000% loss) *** Starting network
*** Configuring hosts
*** Starting controllers
*** Starting switches
(250.00Mbit 0.00000% loss) (250.00Mbit 0.00000% loss) (250.00Mbit 0.00000%
loss) (250.00Mbit 0.00000% loss) (250.00Mbit 0.00000% loss) (250.00Mbit
0.00000% loss) *** Post configure switches and hosts
*** Starting CLI:
```

Opening and running `10_7_sdn_miniedit.mn` will produce the same output as the preceding recipe, since both the `.mn` and `.py` files of this recipe were originally exported from the same network designed using MiniEdit. The following screenshot indicates the network topology emulated by the preceding recipe as opened from the `.mn` file, along with its execution output:

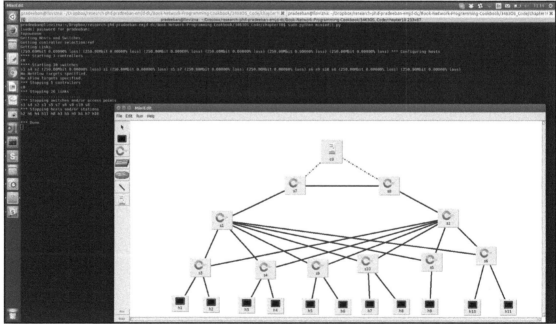

Emulate SDN Visually with MiniEdit

How it works...

MiniEdit is a graphical environment to create Software-Defined Networks. Once you have designed a network visually, you may export the level 2 script as an *.mn file, which can later be opened and modified, or executed by MiniEdit. The designed network can also be saved as a Python script that can be run as any other Mininet emulation (that is, a Python program emulating networks with Mininet). Thus, MiniEdit lets you design reproducible network designs that can be executed in Python as a Mininet emulation, or emulated directly through MiniEdit (which in turn invokes Mininet for the backend emulation in a console).

In this recipe, we created a variant of leaf-spine topology for this recipe with the help of MiniEdit and saved it as .py and .mn, which we later executed. As you may notice, properties of hosts, switches, links, and controllers may be specified through the GUI of MiniEdit.

11
Authentication, Authorization, and Accounting (AAA)

In this chapter, we will cover the following recipes:

- Finding DNS names of a network
- Finding DNS host information
- Finding DNS resource records
- Making DNS zone transfer
- Querying NTP servers
- Connecting to an LDAP server
- Making LDAP bind
- Reading and writing LDAP
- Authenticating REST APIs with Eve
- Throttling requests with RequestsThrottler

Introduction

Authentication, authorization, and accounting (**AAA**) are the three major pillars of access control. Authentication identifies the user, authorization identifies the roles of the user, and accounting ensures that the user actions are performed within the usage limits (such as throttling). AAA, as they are collectively known, are crucial for networks for proper functioning and security. Hence network projects consider AAA as a crucial factor in their network architecture—remarkably the OpenDaylight's AAA project is considered to be a core project in the SDN controller ecosystem. In this chapter, we will look into the AAA options for networking, and how to configure AAA with Python for the networks. We start the chapter with simpler recipes before going into more complex ones.

Finding DNS names of a network

There are a few libraries in Python for managing the **Domain Name Servers** (**DNS**) of the internet. Each network administrator needs to effectively manage the DNS mappings of their network. In this recipe, we will start by introducing dnspython, a simple DNS toolkit developed in Python to manage DNS.

Getting ready

First, install dnspython (https://github.com/rthalley/dnspython) using the pip:

```
$ sudo pip install dnspython
```

How to do it...

We import dns.name of dnspython to do a simple exercise to find the DNS names from the user inputs of two web URLs, and how these web URLs are related.

Listing 11.1 evaluates the user input of two web URLs for the DNS names as follows:

```
#!/usr/bin/env python
# Python Network Programming Cookbook, Second Edition
  -- Chapter - 11
# This program is optimized for Python 2.7.12 and
  Python 3.5.2.
# It may run on any other version with/without
  modifications.
```

```
import argparse
import dns.name

def main(site1, site2):
    _site1 = dns.name.from_text(site1)
    _site2 = dns.name.from_text(site2)
    print("site1 is subdomain of site2: ",
    _site1.is_subdomain(_site2))
    print("site1 is superdomain of site2: ",
    _site1.is_superdomain(_site2))
    print("site1 labels: ", _site1.labels)
    print("site2 labels: ", _site2.labels)

if __name__ == '__main__':
    parser = argparse.ArgumentParser(description=
                                     'DNS Python')
    parser.add_argument('--site1', action="store",
    dest="site1",  default='www.dnspython.org')
    parser.add_argument('--site2', action="store",
    dest="site2",  default='dnspython.org')
    given_args = parser.parse_args()
    site1 = given_args.site1
    site2 = given_args.site2
    main (site1, site2)
```

The code performs a check to see whether the site1 is either a subdomain or a superdomain of site2, and it finally prints the labels of the sites.

Executing this with two arguments produces the following output:

```
$ python 11_1_dns_names_with_dnspython.py --site1="edition.cnn.com" --
site2="cnn.com"
('site1 is subdomain of site2: ', True)
('site1 is superdomain of site2: ', False)
('site1 labels: ', ('edition', 'cnn', 'com', ''))
('site2 labels: ', ('cnn', 'com', ''))
$ python 11_1_dns_names_with_dnspython.py --site1="edition.cnn.com" --
site2="www.cnn.com"
('site1 is subdomain of site2: ', False)
('site1 is superdomain of site2: ', False)
('site1 labels: ', ('edition', 'cnn', 'com', ''))
('site2 labels: ', ('www', 'cnn', 'com', ''))
$ python 11_1_dns_names_with_dnspython.py --site1="edition.cnn.com" --
site2="edition.cnn.com"
('site1 is subdomain of site2: ', True)
('site1 is superdomain of site2: ', True)
('site1 labels: ', ('edition', 'cnn', 'com', ''))
('site2 labels: ', ('edition', 'cnn', 'com', ''))
```

How it works...

The `dns.name.from_text()` retrieves the DNS name from the Terminal user input. Then it compares the inputs to check whether they are each other's subdomain or superdomain. With `labels` property, we may also retrieve the labels associated with each of the site. These simple methods can be useful in tracing the relationship of two URLs and automating the detection of subdomains and superdomains from the list of URLs.

Finding DNS host information

It may be useful for us to know the domain name of a given IP address. First given an address, we need to know whether it even resolves to a valid address identifiable in the internet. We may use the `dnspython` library for these tasks.

Getting ready

First install `dnspython` (`https://github.com/rthalley/dnspython`) using the `pip`:

```
$ sudo pip install dnspython
```

How to do it...

We import `dns.reversename` of `dnspython` to do a simple exercise of finding the reverse name of an address from the given address. We use `dns.resolver` to find the address that an IP address resolves to be.

Listing 11.2 gives the domain information for a given IP address as follows:

```
#!/usr/bin/env python
# Python Network Programming Cookbook, Second Edition
    -- Chapter - 11
# This program is optimized for Python 2.7.12 and
    Python 3.5.2.
# It may run on any other version with/without
    modifications.


import argparse
import dns.reversename
import dns.resolver
```

```
def main(address):
    n = dns.reversename.from_address(address)
    print(n)
    print(dns.reversename.to_address(n))

    try:
        # Pointer records (PTR) maps a network
          interface (IP) to the host name.
        domain = str(dns.resolver.query(n,"PTR")[0])
        print(domain)
    except Exception as e:
        print ("Error while resolving %s: %s" %(address, e))


if __name__ == '__main__':
    parser = argparse.ArgumentParser(description='DNS Python')
    parser.add_argument('--address', action="store",
    dest="address",  default='127.0.0.1')
    given_args = parser.parse_args()
    address = given_args.address
    main (address)
```

We run this recipe with various inputs for addresses. First with localhost, followed by two valid addresses in the internet, and then an invalid address.

```
$ python 11_2_dns_host_with_dnspython.py --address="127.0.0.1"
1.0.0.127.in-addr.arpa.
b'127.0.0.1'
localhost.
$ python 11_2_dns_host_with_dnspython.py --address="216.58.199.78"
78.199.58.216.in-addr.arpa.
b'216.58.199.78'
syd15s01-in-f78.1e100.net.
$ python 11_2_dns_host_with_dnspython.py --address="172.217.19.193"
193.19.217.172.in-addr.arpa.
b'172.217.19.193'
ams16s31-in-f1.1e100.net.
$ python 11_2_dns_host_with_dnspython.py --address="52.95.3.61"
61.3.95.52.in-addr.arpa.
b'52.95.3.61'
Error while resolving 52.95.3.61: The DNS query name does not exist:
61.3.95.52.in-addr.arpa.
```

How it works...

When we input an invalid IP address, the resolving fails with the message, `The DNS query name does not exist`. It reports the reverse domain name (`{reverse-IP}.in-addr.arpa`) in the message as it could not resolve it to a valid address. If a valid address is found by `dns.resolver.query()`, it is returned. **Pointer records** (**PTR**) is used in resolving the IP address to its domain, as it maps a network interface (IP) to the host name.

Finding DNS resource records

You may secure your DNS information with **transaction signature** (**TSIG**). This ensures a secured authorized update to DNS record. You may receive the **Start of Authority** (**SOA**) information of a host with the DNS lookup utilities `host` and `dig`. We first look at `host` utility followed by `dig` before looking into the Python code for our current recipe to retrieve the same information:

```
$ host cnn.com
cnn.com has address 151.101.129.67
cnn.com has address 151.101.193.67
cnn.com has address 151.101.1.67
cnn.com has address 151.101.65.67
cnn.com has IPv6 address 2a04:4e42:600::323
cnn.com has IPv6 address 2a04:4e42:400::323
cnn.com has IPv6 address 2a04:4e42:200::323
cnn.com has IPv6 address 2a04:4e42::323
cnn.com mail is handled by 10 mxb-000c6b02.gslb.pphosted.com.
cnn.com mail is handled by 10 mxa-000c6b02.gslb.pphosted.com.
$ host axn.com
axn.com has address 198.212.50.74
axn.com mail is handled by 0 mxa-001d1702.gslb.pphosted.com.
axn.com mail is handled by 0 mxb-001d1702.gslb.pphosted.com.
```

The output indicates that no IPv6 addresses were found for `https://www.axn.com/`.

```
$ host -t soa cnn.com
cnn.com has SOA record ns-47.awsdns-05.com. awsdns-hostmaster.amazon.com. 1
7200 900 1209600 86400
```

The -t flag above indicates the type of the query. The type can also be cname, ns, sig, key, or axfr. We will look into the name servers of http://edition.cnn.com/ here:

```
$ host -t ns cnn.com
cnn.com name server ns-47.awsdns-05.com.
cnn.com name server ns-576.awsdns-08.net.
cnn.com name server ns-1086.awsdns-07.org.
cnn.com name server ns-1630.awsdns-11.co.uk.
```

We may receive the CNAME, SIG, or KEY resource records (RR) of the site by using the cname, sig, and key types (-t) respectively.

```
$  host -t sig cnn.com
cnn.com has no SIG record
$  host -t key cnn.com
cnn.com has no KEY record
$  host -t cname cnn.com
cnn.com has no CNAME record
```

Outputs of the preceding three operations indicate that no SIG, KEY, or CNAME records were found for http://cnn.com. You may also use the dig command for further information of the site:

```
$ dig SOA cnn.com
; <<>> DiG 9.10.3-P4-Ubuntu <<>> SOA cnn.com
;; global options: +cmd
;; Got answer:
;; ->>HEADER<<- opcode: QUERY, status: NOERROR, id: 34225
;; flags: qr rd ra; QUERY: 1, ANSWER: 1, AUTHORITY: 4, ADDITIONAL: 1
;; OPT PSEUDOSECTION:
; EDNS: version: 0, flags:; udp: 4096
;; QUESTION SECTION:
;cnn.com.                   IN    SOA
;; ANSWER SECTION:
cnn.com.            285    IN    SOA    ns-47.awsdns-05.com. awsdns-
hostmaster.amazon.com. 1 7200 900 1209600 86400
;; AUTHORITY SECTION:
cnn.com.            1771   IN    NS     ns-1086.awsdns-07.org.
cnn.com.            1771   IN    NS     ns-1630.awsdns-11.co.uk.
cnn.com.            1771   IN    NS     ns-47.awsdns-05.com.
cnn.com.            1771   IN    NS     ns-576.awsdns-08.net.
;; Query time: 9 msec
;; SERVER: 127.0.1.1#53(127.0.1.1)
;; WHEN: Sun Jul 23 18:08:28 CEST 2017
;; MSG SIZE  rcvd: 233
```

Notice that the ANSWER SECTION of the output for `dig SOA <domain-name>` matches the output for the `host -t soa <domain-name>` command.

Getting ready

First install the `dnspython` (`https://github.com/rthalley/dnspython`) using the following `pip`:

```
$ sudo pip install dnspython
```

How to do it...

Now we will use `dnspython` to find the same details of a web URL that we earlier found using `dig` and `host` commands.

Listing 11.3 gives a simple, yet verbose code to offer the details of resource records of a given URL:

```python
#!/usr/bin/env python
# Python Network Programming Cookbook, Second Edition
  -- Chapter - 11
# This program is optimized for Python 2.7.12 and
  Python 3.5.2.
# It may run on any other version with/without
  modifications.

import argparse
import dns.zone
import dns.resolver
import socket

def main(address):
    # IPv4 DNS Records
    answer = dns.resolver.query(address, 'A')
    for i in xrange(0, len(answer)):
        print("Default: ", answer[i])

    # IPv6 DNS Records
    try:
        answer6 = dns.resolver.query(address, 'AAAA')
        for i in xrange(0, len(answer6)):
            print("Default: ", answer6[i])
    except dns.resolver.NoAnswer as e:
        print("Exception in resolving the IPv6
```

```
                Resource Record:", e)

    # MX (Mail Exchanger) Records
    try:
        mx = dns.resolver.query(address, 'MX')
        for i in xrange(0, len(mx)):
            print("Default: ", mx[i])
    except dns.resolver.NoAnswer as e:
        print("Exception in resolving the MX
                Resource Record:", e)

    try:
        cname_answer = dns.resolver.query(address, 'CNAME')
        print("CNAME: ", cname_answer)
    except dns.resolver.NoAnswer as e:
        print('Exception retrieving CNAME', e)

    try:
        ns_answer = dns.resolver.query(address, 'NS')
        print(ns_answer)
    except dns.resolver.NoAnswer as e:
        print("Exception in resolving the NS Resource Record:", e)

    try:
        sig_answer = dns.resolver.query(address, 'SIG')
        print("SIG: ", sig_answer)
    except dns.resolver.NoAnswer as e:
        print('Exception retrieving SIG', e)

    try:
        key_answer = dns.resolver.query(address, 'KEY')
        print("KEY: ", key_answer)
    except dns.resolver.NoAnswer as e:
        print('Exception retrieving KEY', e)

    soa_answer = dns.resolver.query(address, 'SOA')
    print("SOA Answer: ", soa_answer[0].mname)
    master_answer = dns.resolver.query(soa_answer[0].mname, 'A')
    print("Master Answer: ", master_answer[0].address)


if __name__ == '__main__':
    parser = argparse.ArgumentParser(description='DNS Python')
    parser.add_argument('--address', action="store",
    dest="address",  default='dnspython.org')
    given_args = parser.parse_args()
    address = given_args.address
    main (address)
```

We test the program with a few addresses now.

```
$ python 11_3_find_dns_rr_details.py  --address="cnn.com"
('Default: ', <DNS IN A rdata: 151.101.193.67>)
('Default: ', <DNS IN A rdata: 151.101.1.67>)
('Default: ', <DNS IN A rdata: 151.101.65.67>)
('Default: ', <DNS IN A rdata: 151.101.129.67>)
('Default: ', <DNS IN AAAA rdata: 2a04:4e42::323>)
('Default: ', <DNS IN AAAA rdata: 2a04:4e42:200::323>)
('Default: ', <DNS IN AAAA rdata: 2a04:4e42:600::323>)
('Default: ', <DNS IN AAAA rdata: 2a04:4e42:400::323>)
('Default: ', <DNS IN MX rdata: 10 mxa-000c6b02.gslb.pphosted.com.>)
('Default: ', <DNS IN MX rdata: 10 mxb-000c6b02.gslb.pphosted.com.>)
('Exception retrieving CNAME', NoAnswer('The DNS response does not contain
an answer to the question: cnn.com. IN CNAME',))
<dns.resolver.Answer object at 0x7fb88ef23f90>
('Exception retrieving SIG', NoAnswer('The DNS response does not contain an
answer to the question: cnn.com. IN SIG',))
('Exception retrieving KEY', NoAnswer('The DNS response does not contain an
answer to the question: cnn.com. IN KEY',))
('SOA Answer: ', <DNS name ns-47.awsdns-05.com.>)
('Master Answer: ', u'205.251.192.47')
$ python 11_3_find_dns_rr_details.py  --address="google.com"
('Default: ', <DNS IN A rdata: 216.58.212.174>)
('Default: ', <DNS IN AAAA rdata: 2a00:1450:400e:801::200e>)
('Default: ', <DNS IN MX rdata: 50 alt4.aspmx.l.google.com.>)
('Default: ', <DNS IN MX rdata: 30 alt2.aspmx.l.google.com.>)
('Default: ', <DNS IN MX rdata: 10 aspmx.l.google.com.>)
('Default: ', <DNS IN MX rdata: 40 alt3.aspmx.l.google.com.>)
('Default: ', <DNS IN MX rdata: 20 alt1.aspmx.l.google.com.>)
('Exception retrieving CNAME', NoAnswer('The DNS response does not contain
an answer to the question: google.com. IN CNAME',))
<dns.resolver.Answer object at 0x7f30308b6f50>
('Exception retrieving SIG', NoAnswer('The DNS response does not contain an
answer to the question: google.com. IN SIG',))
('Exception retrieving KEY', NoAnswer('The DNS response does not contain an
answer to the question: google.com. IN KEY',))
('SOA Answer: ', <DNS name ns3.google.com.>)
('Master Answer: ', u'216.239.36.10')
$ python 11_3_find_dns_rr_details.py  --address="axn.com"
('Default: ', <DNS IN A rdata: 198.212.50.74>)
('Exception in resolving the IPv6 DNS Record:', NoAnswer('The DNS response
does not contain an answer to the question: axn.com. IN AAAA',))
('Default: ', <DNS IN MX rdata: 0 mxb-001d1702.gslb.pphosted.com.>)
('Default: ', <DNS IN MX rdata: 0 mxa-001d1702.gslb.pphosted.com.>)
('Exception retrieving CNAME', NoAnswer('The DNS response does not contain
an answer to the question: axn.com. IN CNAME',))
<dns.resolver.Answer object at 0x7fb085878f50>
```

```
('Exception retrieving SIG', NoAnswer('The DNS response does not contain an
answer to the question: axn.com. IN SIG',))
('Exception retrieving KEY', NoAnswer('The DNS response does not contain an
answer to the question: axn.com. IN KEY',))
('SOA Answer: ', <DNS name udns1.ultradns.net.>)
('Master Answer: ', u'204.69.234.1')
$ python 11_3_find_dns_rr_details.py --address="zonetransfer.me"
('Default: ', <DNS IN A rdata: 217.147.177.157>)
('Exception in resolving the IPv6 Resource Record:', NoAnswer('The DNS
response does not contain an answer to the question: zonetransfer.me. IN
AAAA',))
('Default: ', <DNS IN MX rdata: 0 ASPMX.L.GOOGLE.COM.>)
('Default: ', <DNS IN MX rdata: 20 ASPMX3.GOOGLEMAIL.COM.>)
('Default: ', <DNS IN MX rdata: 20 ASPMX4.GOOGLEMAIL.COM.>)
('Default: ', <DNS IN MX rdata: 20 ASPMX5.GOOGLEMAIL.COM.>)
('Default: ', <DNS IN MX rdata: 10 ALT2.ASPMX.L.GOOGLE.COM.>)
('Default: ', <DNS IN MX rdata: 20 ASPMX2.GOOGLEMAIL.COM.>)
('Default: ', <DNS IN MX rdata: 10 ALT1.ASPMX.L.GOOGLE.COM.>)
('Exception retrieving CNAME', NoAnswer('The DNS response does not contain
an answer to the question: zonetransfer.me. IN CNAME',))
<dns.resolver.Answer object at 0x7f3184ba2cd0>
('Exception retrieving SIG', NoAnswer('The DNS response does not contain an
answer to the question: zonetransfer.me. IN SIG',))
('Exception retrieving KEY', NoAnswer('The DNS response does not contain an
answer to the question: zonetransfer.me. IN KEY',))
('SOA Answer: ', <DNS name nsztm1.digi.ninja.>)
('Master Answer: ', u'81.4.108.41')
```

How it works...

The `dns.resolver.query(address, <type>)` resolves the address for the query type. The command `host` looks for A (IPv4 address), AAAA (IPv6 address), and MX resource records when the type is not specified. We specify A, AAAA, MX, SOA, CNAME, NS, SIG, and KEY as the resource record types to resolve the addresses in our recipe. The output indicates that some of these records are not set for the sites that we tested.

The websites that we tested do not contain a SIG, KEY, or CNAME record as we found before with the `host -t` command. Since we do not have the authorization or the key to actually perform the zone transfer for these sites, this will fail with the message `Failed to perform zone transfer`. Also note that http://axn.com notes that, there was no answer for the AAAA, thus pointing that no IPv6 DNS record found for the website.

Making DNS zone transfer

We may transfer the DNS zone with the `dnspython` bundle. SOA record consists of crucial information for a zone transfer. Our recipe attempts the DNS zone transfer and compares the output with that from the `dig` utility. While zone transfer is not something that is performed by website users, we used `zonetransfer.me` test website to test our recipe and show the zone transfer output. Thanks to `https://digi.ninja/projects/zonetransferme.php` for setting this site up and running for educational purposes. You may read more on zone transfer and the test website `zonetransfer.me` from the site.

Getting ready

First install `dnspython` (`https://github.com/rthalley/dnspython`) using the following pip:

```
$ sudo pip install dnspython
```

How to do it...

We will use `dnspython` for the DNS zone transfer.

Listing 11.4 gives a simple code for a zone transfer as follows:

```python
#!/usr/bin/env python
# Python Network Programming Cookbook, Second Edition
  -- Chapter - 11
# This program is optimized for Python 2.7.12 and
  Python 3.5.2.
# It may run on any other version with/without
  modifications.

import argparse
import dns.zone
import dns.resolver
import socket

def main(address):
    soa_answer = dns.resolver.query(address, 'SOA')
    master_answer = dns.resolver.query(soa_answer[0].mname, 'A')
    try:
        z = dns.zone.from_xfr(dns.query.
            xfr(master_answer[0].address, address))
        names = z.nodes.keys()
```

```
            names.sort()
            for n in names:
                print(z[n].to_text(n))
        except socket.error as e:
            print('Failed to perform zone transfer:', e)
        except dns.exception.FormError as e:
            print('Failed to perform zone transfer:', e)


    if __name__ == '__main__':
        parser = argparse.ArgumentParser(description='DNS Python')
        parser.add_argument('--address', action="store",
        dest="address", default='dnspython.org')
        given_args = parser.parse_args()
        address = given_args.address
        main(address)
```

We test the program with a few addresses now:

```
$ python 11_4_dns_zone_transfer.py --address="cnn.com"
('Failed to perform zone transfer:', error(104, 'Connection reset by
peer'))
$ python 11_4_dns_zone_transfer.py --address="google.com"
('Failed to perform zone transfer:', FormError('No answer or RRset not for
qname',))
$ python 11_4_dns_zone_transfer.py --address="axn.com"
('Failed to perform zone transfer:', FormError('No answer or RRset not for
qname',))
```

DNS zone transfer is a transaction where a copy of the database of the DNS server known as the **zone file**, is passed to another DNS server. As the zone file consists of server information that is sensitive and may open up avenues for attacks, zone servers are often restricted to the site administrators. Luckily for us, zonetransfer.me is a website set up solely for the purpose of testing zone transfers. Let's test our recipe again with this.

```
$ python 11_4_dns_zone_transfer.py --address="zonetransfer.me"
@ 7200 IN SOA nsztm1.digi.ninja. robin.digi.ninja. 2014101603 172800 900
1209600 3600
@ 7200 IN RRSIG SOA 8 2 7200 20160330133700 20160229123700 44244 @
GzQojkYAP8zuTOB9UAx66mTDiEGJ26hV IIP2ifk2DpbQLrEAPg4M77i4M0yFWHpN
fMJIuuJ8nMxQgFVCU3yTOeT/EMbN98FY C81VYwEZeWHtbMmS88jV1F+cOz2WarjC
dyV0+UJCTdGtBJriIczC52EXKkw2RCkv 3gtdKKVafBE=
@ 7200 IN NS nsztm1.digi.ninja.
@ 7200 IN NS nsztm2.digi.ninja.
@ 7200 IN RRSIG NS 8 2 7200 20160330133700 20160229123700 44244 @
TyFngBk2PMWxgJc6RtgCE/RhE0kqeWfw hYSBxFxezupFLeiDjHeVXo+SWZxP54Xv
wfk7j1FC1NZ91RNkL5qHyxRE1h1H1JJI 1hjvod0fycqLqCnxXIqkOzUCkm2Mxr8O
cGf2jVNDUcLPDO5XjHgOXCK9tRbVVKIp B92f4Qalulw=
```

```
@ 7200 IN A 217.147.177.157
@ 7200 IN RRSIG A 8 2 7200 20160330133700 20160229123700 44244 @
unoMaEPiyoAr0yAWg/coPbAFNznaAlUJ W3/QrvJleer50VvGLW/cK+VEDcZLfCu6
paQhgJHVddG4p145vVQe3QRvp7EJpUh+ SU7dX0I3gngmOa4Hk190S4utcXY5FhaN
7xBKHVWBlavQaSHTg61g/iuLSB01S1gp /DAMUpC+WzE=
@ 300 IN HINFO "Casio fx-700G" "Windows XP"
@ 300 IN RRSIG HINFO 8 2 300 20160330133700 20160229123700 44244 @
Xebvrpv8nCGn/+iHqok1rcItTPqcskV6 jpJ1pCo4WYbnqByLultzygWxJlyVzz+w
JHEqRQYDjqGbl0dyUgKn2FFnqb1O92kK ghcHHvoMEh+Jf5i70trtucpRs3AtlneL
j2vauOCIEdbjma4IxgdwPahKIhgtgWcU InVFh3RrSwM=
@ 7200 IN MX 0 ASPMX.L.GOOGLE.COM.
@ 7200 IN MX 10 ALT1.ASPMX.L.GOOGLE.COM.
@ 7200 IN MX 10 ALT2.ASPMX.L.GOOGLE.COM.
. . . . . . . . .
. . . . . . . . .
www 3600 IN RRSIG NSEC 8 3 3600 20160330133700 20160229123700 44244 @
0xCqc6tWcT11ACD24Ap68hc7HRyAcCf7 MrkDqe2HyYMGuGS9YSwosiF3QzffhuY5
qagIFbpI3f7xVGxykngThTk37/JO2Srf I7Z5kvqLHdEd6GD9sogsLqTfHE9UToOY
YfuasO+IsJLyPALh89yk3bY+NipvpEPn gSnxN6ehIkc=
xss 300 IN TXT "'><script>alert('Boo')</script>"
xss 300 IN RRSIG TXT 8 3 300 20160330133700 20160229123700 44244 @
yvLf2kmOIKO22VT7Ml7/zuz7GbO2Ugvs O/VxLwXrGx+ewE12g2VCwsElYg/eMtsp
jJ38g7CbU1tYLc5YydsdtFV3jzDAYbaw zFvugx0zmtN6kwpDa5LHs4BBSsjBBMM0
69IeD15ko5DLi+FWmPKoy5/CBNLlvwv8 a1S58MlHpU0=
xss 3600 IN NSEC @ TXT RRSIG NSEC
xss 3600 IN RRSIG NSEC 8 3 3600 20160330133700 20160229123700 44244 @
a7tFtY1bsTwztv/khjV/NEgaOQyiI8t2 R0xgQUp9ANKmAPqu83119rpIrwKpBF88
atlvQYTv9bRTjA/Y58WxsBYw+SOe3j3C UmH1QVbj8CJQpfJKcW1w7DoX8O1PYbWu
CAhciUyh1CV4Y5a8pcPBiZBM6225h4eA dE6Ahx3SXGY=
```

The following screenshot shows the verbose outcome of the zone transfer of
`zonetransfer.me` site with our Python program. You may use `zonetransfer.me` for
further testing:

DNS Zone Transfer

You may confirm the output of the preceding DNS zone transfer by using the `dig` utility to perform the zone transfer as well, it is as shown following:

```
$ dig axfr @nsztm1.digi.ninja zonetransfer.me
; <<>> DiG 9.10.3-P4-Ubuntu <<>> axfr @nsztm1.digi.ninja zonetransfer.me
; (1 server found)
;; global options: +cmd
zonetransfer.me.    7200  IN    SOA    nsztm1.digi.ninja. robin.digi.ninja.
2014101603 172800 900 1209600 3600
......
xss.zonetransfer.me.    3600  IN    NSEC  zonetransfer.me. TXT RRSIG NSEC
xss.zonetransfer.me.    3600  IN    RRSIG NSEC 8 3 3600 20160330133700
20160229123700 44244 zonetransfer.me.
a7tFtY1bsTwztv/khjV/NEgaOQyiI8t2R0xgQUp9ANKmAPqu83119rpI
rwKpBF88atlvQYTv9bRTjA/Y58WxsBYw+SOe3j3CUmHlQVbj8CJQpfJK
cW1w7DoX8O1PYbWuCAhciUyh1CV4Y5a8pcPBiZBM6225h4eAdE6Ahx3S XGY=
zonetransfer.me.    7200  IN    SOA    nsztm1.digi.ninja. robin.digi.ninja.
2014101603 172800 900 1209600 3600
;; Query time: 55 msec
;; SERVER: 81.4.108.41#53(81.4.108.41)
;; WHEN: Sun Jul 23 22:06:38 CEST 2017
;; XFR size: 153 records (messages 1, bytes 16183)
```

How it works...

The `dns.query.xfr()` takes two inputs similar to the `dig` utility (`dig axfr @nsztm1.digi.ninja zonetransfer.me`). It gets the first input parameter (in the case of `zonetransfer.me`, it is `nsztm1.digi.ninja`), by processing `master_answer[0].address`, which is essentially retrieved from the single command-line argument (and also the second input parameter), address. We print the sorted names after the zone transfer.

Querying NTP servers

Network Time Protocol (**NTP**): `http://www.ntp.org/ntpfaq/NTP-s-def.htm` is a protocol that is used to query and synchronize the clocks of the computers connected to the internet. In this recipe, we will be using `ntplib` (`https://pypi.python.org/pypi/ntplib/`), a Python module that offers an interface to query the NTP servers, to learn about the NTP servers, you may use `http://www.pool.ntp.org/en/use.html` which finds the closest NTP server for you to synchronize your server clock. It also gives guidelines on contributing your computing resources as an NTP server.

Getting ready

First install `ntplib` in your computer.

```
$ sudo apt-get install python-ntplib
```

`ntplib` works on Python 2. You may install `python3-ntplib` that works for Python 3 from `https://launchpad.net/ubuntu/yakkety/amd64/python3-ntplib/0.3.3-1`, or by following the succeeding commands:

```
$ wget
http://launchpadlibrarian.net/260811286/python3-ntplib_0.3.3-1_all.deb
$ sudo dpkg -i python3-ntplib_0.3.3-1_all.deb
```

How to do it...

Synchronizing your time is crucial accounting task. While it is not ideal to depend on the time from the internet for mission-critical systems, the NTP time is sufficiently accurate for most of the computing requirements.

Listing 11.5 gives a simple NTP server connection test as follows:

```
#!/usr/bin/env python
# Python Network Programming Cookbook, Second Edition
    -- Chapter - 11
# This program is optimized for Python 2.7.12 and
    Python 3.5.2.
# It may run on any other version with/without
    modifications.

import argparse
import ntplib
from time import ctime


def main(address, v):
    c = ntplib.NTPClient()
    response = c.request(address, version=v)
    print("Response Offset: ", response.offset)
    print("Version: ", response.version)
    print("Response (Time): ", ctime(response.tx_time))
    print("Leap: ", ntplib.leap_to_text(response.leap))
    print("Root Delay: ", response.root_delay)
    print(ntplib.ref_id_to_text(response.ref_id))


if __name__ == '__main__':
    parser = argparse.ArgumentParser(description='Query NTP Server')
    parser.add_argument('--address', action="store",
    dest="address",  default='pool.ntp.org')
    parser.add_argument('--version', action="store",
    dest="version",  type=int, default=3)
    given_args = parser.parse_args()
    address = given_args.address
    version = given_args.version
    main (address, version)
```

In this recipe, we provide an NTP server to query the time. Running this program provides
the following outcome:

```
$  python 11_5_query_ntp_server.py --address=europe.pool.ntp.org --
version=3
('Response Offset: ', -0.002687215805053711)
('Version: ', 3)
('Response (Time): ', 'Mon Jul 24 23:06:10 2017')
('Leap: ', 'no warning')
('Root Delay: ', 0.00372314453125)
10.176.63.115
```

```
This recipe is similar to the  standard NTP query program ntpq.
$ ntpq -pn
remote             refid       st t when poll reach   delay   offset  jitter
==============================================================
 0.ubuntu.pool.n .POOL.          16 p   -   64    0   0.000   0.000
 0.000
 1.ubuntu.pool.n .POOL.          16 p   -   64    0   0.000   0.000
 0.000
 2.ubuntu.pool.n .POOL.          16 p   -   64    0   0.000   0.000
 0.000
 3.ubuntu.pool.n .POOL.          16 p   -   64    0   0.000   0.000
 0.000
 ntp.ubuntu.com  .POOL.          16 p   -   64    0   0.000   0.000
 0.000
-91.189.91.157   132.246.11.231   2 u 257  512  377  94.363  -3.998
13.016
+193.190.147.153 193.190.230.65   2 u 184  512  377  10.327  -2.246
1.235
+91.189.89.198   17.253.52.125    2 u 169  512  377  14.206  -2.744
1.414
*94.143.184.140  .GPS.            1 u 279  512  377  14.208  -2.743
2.453
+213.189.188.3   193.190.230.65   2 u   1  512  377  11.015  -2.192
1.569
```

How it works...

We query and print the time from a remote NTP server using ctime(response.tx_time).
We can pass the address of an NTP server and version (1-7) as the arguments to the
program. When a generic address such as pool.ntp.org is used, the closest server is
picked based on the requesting server's location. Hence, you receive a response with
minimal latency.

Connecting to an LDAP server

Lightweight Directory Access Protocol (LDAP) is an identity management protocol
organizing individuals, organizations, resources, and the roles and access of those entities,
organized locally, in the intranet or in the internet. Many LDAP servers are available for
download and install and are free and open source, including the OpenLDAP and Apache
Directory.

Getting ready

For those who like to try an LDAP instance without actually going through the hassle of installing the server, there are a few open and public LDAP servers available online. Some of them offer write access, for example, FreeIPA (`https://www.freeipa.org/page/Main_P age`). FreeIPA is an integrated security information management solution that offers an online demo installation for testing purposes at `https://ipa.demo1.freeipa.org/ipa/ui /`. We will use it for our recipes. As with any public server with write access, FreeIPA server needs to be cleaned up daily. During these hours, it goes offline. The FreeIPA web interface is shown as follows:

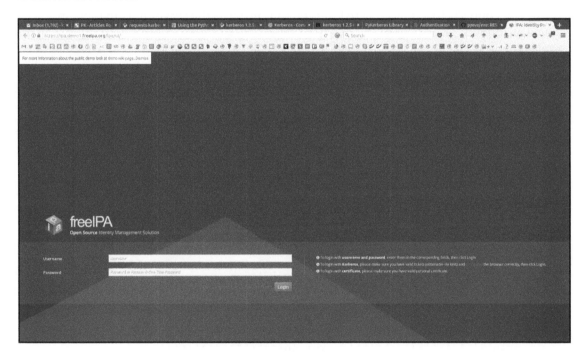

FreeIPA Log in Screen

You may also use `ldap.forumsys.com`, another public LDAP server with read-only access to test our recipes. You may find more LDAP servers accessible online with read-only and write accesses, or you may even configure your own LDAP server to have full control. In this recipe, we will connect to the LDAP server and receive information from it through our Python program.

First, install the `python-ldap3` (`http://ldap3.readthedocs.io/tutorial_intro.html`) package as a prerequisite for this recipe using the following command:

```
$ sudo pip install ldap3
```

How to do it...

We will use the `ldap3` library and import `Server`, `Connection`, and `ALL` modules from it. `ldap3` offers an object-oriented access to the directory servers of LDAP.

Listing 11.6 connects to a remote LDAP server and retrieves the server information and schema as follows:

```
#!/usr/bin/env python
# Python Network Programming Cookbook, Second Edition
  -- Chapter - 11
# This program is optimized for Python 2.7.12 and
  Python 3.5.2.
# It may run on any other version with/without
  modifications.

import argparse
from ldap3 import Server, Connection, ALL


def main(address):
    # Create the Server object with the given address.
    # Get ALL information.
    server = Server(address, get_info=ALL)
    #Create a connection object, and bind with auto
     bind set to true.
    conn = Connection(server, auto_bind=True)
    # Print the LDAP Server Information.
    print('*****************Server Info*************')
    print(server.info)

    # Print the LDAP Server Detailed Schema.
    print('*****************Server Schema************')
    print(server.schema)

if __name__ == '__main__':
    parser = argparse.ArgumentParser(description=
                              'Query LDAP Server')
    parser.add_argument('--address', action="store",
    dest="address",  default='ipa.demo1.freeipa.org')
    given_args = parser.parse_args()
```

```
        address = given_args.address
        main (address)
```

Here we pass the address to the LDAP server as a command-line argument to print a detailed information of it shown as following:

```
$ python 11_6_connect_ldap_server.py --address=ldap.forumsys.com
*******************Server Info**************
DSA info (from DSE):
Supported LDAP versions: 3
Naming contexts:
dc=example,dc=com
Supported controls:
1.2.826.0.1.3344810.2.3 - Matched Values - Control - RFC3876
1.2.840.113556.1.4.319 - LDAP Simple Paged Results - Control - RFC2696
1.3.6.1.1.12 - Assertion - Control - RFC4528
1.3.6.1.1.13.1 - LDAP Pre-read - Control - RFC4527
1.3.6.1.1.13.2 - LDAP Post-read - Control - RFC4527
1.3.6.1.4.1.4203.1.10.1 - Subentries - Control - RFC3672
2.16.840.1.113730.3.4.18 - Proxy Authorization Control - Control - RFC6171
2.16.840.1.113730.3.4.2 - ManageDsaIT - Control - RFC3296
Supported extensions:
1.3.6.1.1.8 - Cancel Operation - Extension - RFC3909
1.3.6.1.4.1.1466.20037 - StartTLS - Extension - RFC4511-RFC4513
1.3.6.1.4.1.4203.1.11.1 - Modify Password - Extension - RFC3062
1.3.6.1.4.1.4203.1.11.3 - Who am I - Extension - RFC4532
Supported features:
1.3.6.1.1.14 - Modify-Increment - Feature - RFC4525
1.3.6.1.4.1.4203.1.5.1 - All Op Attrs - Feature - RFC3673
1.3.6.1.4.1.4203.1.5.2 - OC AD Lists - Feature - RFC4529
1.3.6.1.4.1.4203.1.5.3 - True/False filters - Feature - RFC4526
1.3.6.1.4.1.4203.1.5.4 - Language Tag Options - Feature - RFC3866
1.3.6.1.4.1.4203.1.5.5 - language Range Options - Feature - RFC3866
Schema entry:
cn=Subschema
Vendor name: []
Vendor version: []
Other:
objectClass:
top
OpenLDAProotDSE
structuralObjectClass:
OpenLDAProotDSE
entryDN:
configContext:
cn=config
*****************Server Schema**************
DSA Schema from: cn=Subschema
```

```
Attribute types:{'olcAuthIDRewrite': Attribute type:
1.3.6.1.4.1.4203.1.12.2.3.0.6
Short name: olcAuthIDRewrite
Single value: False
Equality rule: caseIgnoreMatch
Syntax: 1.3.6.1.4.1.1466.115.121.1.15 [('1.3.6.1.4.1.1466.115.121.1.15',
'LDAP_SYNTAX', 'Directory String', 'RFC4517')]
Optional in: olcGlobal
Extensions:
X-ORDERED: VALUES
, 'olcUpdateDN': Attribute type: 1.3.6.1.4.1.4203.1.12.2.3.2.0.12
Short name: olcUpdateDN
Single value: True
Syntax: 1.3.6.1.4.1.1466.115.121.1.12 [('1.3.6.1.4.1.1466.115.121.1.12',
'LDAP_SYNTAX', 'DN', 'RFC4517')]
Optional in: olcDatabaseConfig
, 'namingContexts': Attribute type: 1.3.6.1.4.1.1466.101.120.5
Short name: namingContexts
Description: RFC4512: naming contexts
Single value: False
Usage: unknown
Syntax: 1.3.6.1.4.1.1466.115.121.1.12 [('1.3.6.1.4.1.1466.115.121.1.12',
'LDAP_SYNTAX', 'DN', 'RFC4517')]
OidInfo: ('1.3.6.1.4.1.1466.101.120.5', 'ATTRIBUTE_TYPE', 'namingContexts',
'RFC4512')
, 'olcAccess': Attribute type: 1.3.6.1.4.1.4203.1.12.2.3.0.1
Short name: olcAccess
Description: Access Control List
Single value: False
Equality rule: caseIgnoreMatch
Syntax: 1.3.6.1.4.1.1466.115.121.1.15 [('1.3.6.1.4.1.1466.115.121.1.15',
'LDAP_SYNTAX', 'Directory String', 'RFC4517')]
Optional in: olcDatabaseConfig
Extensions:
X-ORDERED: VALUES
, 'businessCategory': Attribute type: 2.5.4.15
Short name: businessCategory
........
......
```

The complete output of the execution for the address `https://ipa.demo1.freeipa.org/ip a/ui/` and `ldap.forumsys.com` are stored in the files `11_6_output_with_ipa.demo1.freeipa.org.txt` and `11_6_output_with_ldap.forumsys.com.txt` respectively.

Following is a screenshot of the execution, indicating the detailed output of the execution:

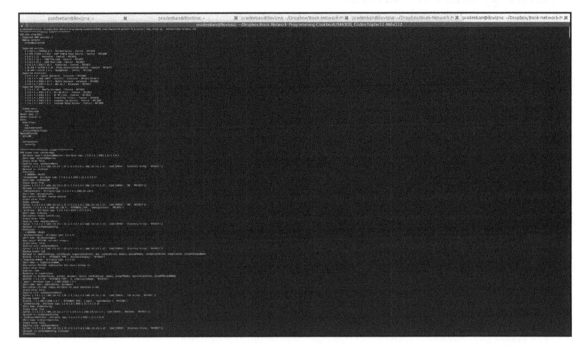

Connect to the LDAP Server

How it works...

In the server information, we receive details such as supported controls, extensions, and features. Moreover, we also get the schema entry and configuration context. In the LDAP server schema, we retrieve information on the various attributes as shown as follows:

```
'memberUid': Attribute type: 1.3.6.1.1.1.1.12
   Short name: memberUid
   Single value: False
   Equality rule: caseExactIA5Match
   Syntax: 1.3.6.1.4.1.1466.115.121.1.26 [('1.3.6.1.4.1.1466.115.121.1.26',
'LDAP_SYNTAX', 'IA5 String', 'RFC4517')]
   Optional in: posixGroup
```

Making LDAP bind

We need to authenticate an LDAP user with their password for accessing more information relevant for their role. In this recipe, we will attempt to make an LDAP bind with the correct password and an invalid one.

Getting ready

Install ldap3 Python client, the prerequisite for this recipe:

```
$ sudo pip install ldap3
```

How to do it...

We will provide the bind dn and password in addition to the address of the LDAP server address, as the input arguments.

Listing 11.7 elaborates how to make an LDAP bind:

```python
#!/usr/bin/env python
# Python Network Programming Cookbook, Second Edition
    -- Chapter - 11
# This program is optimized for Python 2.7.12 and
    Python 3.5.2.
# It may run on any other version with/without
    modifications.

import argparse
from ldap3 import Server, Connection, ALL, core


def main(address, dn, password):
    # Create the Server object with the given address.
    server = Server(address, get_info=ALL)
    #Create a connection object, and bind with the
     given DN and password.
    try:
        conn = Connection(server, dn, password, auto_bind=True)
        print('LDAP Bind Successful.')
        print(conn)
    except core.exceptions.LDAPBindError as e:
        # If the LDAP bind failed for reasons such
            as authentication failure.
        print('LDAP Bind Failed: ', e)
```

```
if __name__ == '__main__':
    parser = argparse.ArgumentParser(description='Query LDAP Server')
    parser.add_argument('--address', action="store",
    dest="address",  default='ldap.forumsys.com')
    parser.add_argument('--dn', action="store",
    dest="dn",  default='cn=read-only-admin,dc=example,dc=com')
    parser.add_argument('--password', action="store",
    dest="password",  default='password')
    given_args = parser.parse_args()
    address = given_args.address
    dn = given_args.dn
    password = given_args.password
    main (address, dn, password)
```

We will first test the recipe with a correct dn and password:

```
$ python 11_7_query_ldap_server.py --address=ldap.forumsys.com --
dn=cn=read-only-admin,dc=example,dc=com --password=password
LDAP Bind Successful.
ldap://ldap.forumsys.com:389 - cleartext - user: cn=read-only-
admin,dc=example,dc=com - not lazy - bound - open - <local:
109.141.39.196:60340 - remote: 54.196.176.103:389> - tls not started -
listening - SyncStrategy - internal decoder
```

Now again with a wrong combination of dn and password:

```
$ python 11_7_query_ldap_server.py --address=ldap.forumsys.com --
dn=ou=mathematicians,dc=example,dc=com --password=password1
LDAP Bind Failed:  automatic bind not successful - invalidCredentials
```

The LDAP bind will fail with the invalidCredentials error if the dn does not exist, or if the password is incorrect. The authentication error message does not differentiate these two cases, as a security best practice, thus not letting an attacker narrow down on their attacks.

To actually query the entries, we need to perform a search. We slightly modify our recipe as listed in 11_7_query_ldap_server_b.py for this. The following segment elaborates the changes in Listing 11.7:

```
try:
    conn = Connection(server, dn, password, auto_bind=True)
    print('LDAP Bind Successful.')
    # Perform a search for a pre-defined criteria.
    # Mention the search filter / filter type and attributes.
    conn.search('dc=example,dc=com', '(&(uid=euler))' ,
    attributes=['sn'])
    # Print the resulting entries.
```

```
        print(conn.entries[0])
    except core.exceptions.LDAPBindError as e:
        # If the LDAP bind failed for reasons such
          as authentication failure.
        print('LDAP Bind Failed: ', e)
```

We run the modified recipe to produce the following output:

```
$ python3 11_7_query_ldap_server_b.py --address=ldap.forumsys.com --
dn=cn=read-only-admin,dc=example,dc=com --password=password
LDAP Bind Successful.
DN: uid=euler,dc=example,dc=com - STATUS: Read - READ TIME:
2017-07-26T22:57:48.011791
    sn: Euler
```

Here we elaborated how the LDAP can be queried by providing the filter type and the attributes. Providing an invalid attribute type will result in an error. For example, seeking invalid attribute type of `krbLastPwdChange` in place of `sn` in the preceding code produces the following error message:

```
ldap3.core.exceptions.LDAPAttributeError: invalid attribute type
krbLastPwdChange
```

Similarly, an invalid filter throws the following error:

```
ldap3.core.exceptions.LDAPInvalidFilterError: invalid filter
```

How it works...

The LDAP bind succeeds with the correct credentials. Then you may define your search criteria with a relevant filter type and attributes. Once you have performed the search, you may iterate and print the resultant entries.

Reading and writing LDAP

In this recipe, we will read and write from the FreeIPA LDAP demo server.

Getting ready

Install `ldap3` Python client, the prerequisite for this recipe:

```
$ sudo pip install ldap3
```

How to do it...

First we will read LDAP with a `Reader` object as shown by Listing 11.8 as follows:

```python
#!/usr/bin/env python
# Python Network Programming Cookbook, Second Edition
  -- Chapter - 11
# This program is optimized for Python 2.7.12 and
  Python 3.5.2.
# It may run on any other version with/without
  modifications.
# Adopted from http://ldap3.readthedocs.io/tutorial_abstraction_basic.html

from ldap3 import Server, Connection, ObjectDef, AttrDef, Reader, Writer,
ALL


def main():
    server = Server('ipa.demo1.freeipa.org', get_info=ALL)
    conn = Connection(server,
'uid=admin,cn=users,cn=accounts,dc=demo1,dc=freeipa,dc=org', 'Secret123',
auto_bind=True)
    person = ObjectDef('person', conn)
    r = Reader(conn, person, 'ou=ldap3-
            tutorial,dc=demo1,dc=freeipa,dc=org')
    print(r)
    print('************')
    person+='uid'
    print(r)

if __name__ == '__main__':
    main ()
```

This recipe performs an implicit creation of a new attribute definition by the following line:

```python
        person+='uid'
```

By running this recipe, you may observe the following output:

```
$ python 11_8_read_ldap_server.py
CURSOR : Reader
CONN   : ldap://ipa.demo1.freeipa.org:389 - cleartext - user:
uid=admin,cn=users,cn=accounts,dc=demo1,dc=freeipa,dc=org - not lazy -
bound - open - <local: 192.168.137.95:44860 - remote: 52.57.162.88:389> -
tls not started - listening - SyncStrategy - internal decoder
DEFS   : [u'person'] [cn, description, objectClass, seeAlso, sn,
telephoneNumber, userPassword]
ATTRS  : [u'cn', u'description', u'objectClass', u'seeAlso', u'sn',
```

```
u'telephoneNumber', u'userPassword']
BASE    : 'ou=ldap3-tutorial,dc=demo1,dc=freeipa,dc=org' [SUB]
FILTER : u'(objectClass=person)'
*************
CURSOR : Reader
CONN    : ldap://ipa.demo1.freeipa.org:389 - cleartext - user:
uid=admin,cn=users,cn=accounts,dc=demo1,dc=freeipa,dc=org - not lazy -
bound - open - <local: 192.168.137.95:44860 - remote: 52.57.162.88:389> -
tls not started - listening - SyncStrategy - internal decoder
DEFS    : [u'person'] [cn, description, objectClass, seeAlso, sn,
telephoneNumber, uid, userPassword]
ATTRS   : [u'cn', u'description', u'objectClass', u'seeAlso', u'sn',
u'telephoneNumber', u'userPassword']
BASE    : 'ou=ldap3-tutorial,dc=demo1,dc=freeipa,dc=org' [SUB]
FILTER : u'(objectClass=person)'
```

As highlighted in the preceding recipe, after the attribute definition uid is added to the person object, it is reflected in the DEFS after the line: person+='uid'. However, if you re-execute the recipe, you will notice that the previous changes to the person object are not present. This is because the changes are not written with the Reader cursor. For that, you will need a Writer. You may initiate a Writer from the Reader cursor as shown here:

```
w = Writer.from_cursor(r)
w[0].sn += 'Smyth'
w.commit()
```

Make sure you have the write access to the LDAP server with the correct dn and password for the commit to succeed. It is recommended to try this in a private LDAP server that gives you complete admin access.

How it works...

We define the object in the line:

```
person = ObjectDef('person', conn)
```

Then we define a Reader cursor and read it by:

```
r = Reader(conn, person, 'ou=ldap3-
tutorial,dc=demo1,dc=freeipa,dc=org')
```

Authenticating REST APIs with Eve

Eve is a REST API server built in Python. We will test how to use Eve REST API framework with `BasicAuth`, global authentication. Eve can also be started without any authentication at all, as a simple REST API server. This recipe is a simple demonstration of serving the entire web server. However, Eve provides more sophisticated and more role-based access control that protects certain APIs with roles for the users.

The server is started with a username and password, and the client passes on the `base64` encode of the format `username:password` to the server to get authenticated.

Getting ready

First install Eve using Python:

```
$ sudo pip install eve
```

This will install Eve, along with its dependencies, `cerberus-0.9.2`, `eve-0.7.4`, `events-0.2.2`, `flask-0.12`, `flask-pymongo-0.5.1`, `pymongo-3.4.0`, `simplejson-3.11.1`, `werkzeug-0.11.15`.

In this recipe, we will start a simple server with a username and password as the basic authentication.

How to do it...

First make sure that you have the domain configurations saved as a Python file named `settings.py` in the same folder as your program. In this recipe, we have included a simple `settings.py` with the following content as a sample:

```
DOMAIN = {'people': {}}
```

If `settings.py` is not found, the program will halt with the following error:

```
eve.exceptions.ConfigException: DOMAIN dictionary missing or wrong.
```

Listing 11.9 gives a REST server with `BasicAuth` as follows:

```
#!/usr/bin/env python
# Python Network Programming Cookbook, Second Edition
  -- Chapter - 11
# This program is optimized for Python 2.7.12 and
  Python 3.5.2.
# It may run on any other version with/without
  modifications.

from eve import Eve
from eve.auth import BasicAuth

class MyBasicAuth(BasicAuth):
    def check_auth(self, username, password, allowed_roles,
    resource,
                   method):
        return username == 'admin' and password == 'secret'

def run_server():
    app = Eve(auth=MyBasicAuth)
    app.run()
if __name__ == '__main__':
    run_server()
```

We run the server with the username `admin` and password `secret`.

```
$ python 11_9_eve_basic_auth.py
  * Running on http://127.0.0.1:5000/ (Press CTRL+C to quit)
```

Assuming username `admin` and password `secret`, to retrieve the `base64` encoded string of this credentials, you may use the following command:

```
$ echo -n admin:secret | base64
YWRtaW46c2VjcmV0
```

Now we run the client with the correct `base64` encoded `secret`:

```
$ curl -H "Authorization: Basic YWRtaW46c2VjcmV0" -i http://127.0.0.1:5000
$ curl -H "Authorization: Basic YWRtaW46c2VjcmV0" -i http://127.0.0.1:5000
HTTP/1.0 200 OK
Content-Type: application/json
Content-Length: 62
Server: Eve/0.7.4 Werkzeug/0.11.15 Python/2.7.12
Date: Sat, 29 Jul 2017 12:10:04 GMT
{"_links": {"child": [{"href": "people", "title": "people"}]}}
```

If you run `curl` with no credentials, the following output will be produced:

```
$ curl -i http://127.0.0.1:5000
HTTP/1.0 401 UNAUTHORIZED
Content-Type: application/json
Content-Length: 91
WWW-Authenticate: Basic realm="eve"
Server: Eve/0.7.4 Werkzeug/0.11.15 Python/2.7.12
Date: Sat, 29 Jul 2017 12:09:02 GMT
{"_status": "ERR", "_error": {"message": "Please provide proper
credentials", "code": 401}}
```

The server will bring the following log to indicate the failed attempt:

```
127.0.0.1 - - [29/Jul/2017 14:09:02] "GET / HTTP/1.1" 401 -
```

The output for an attempt with wrong credentials would be similar to the preceding ones with no credentials:

```
curl -H "Authorization: Basic YV1" -i http://127.0.0.1:5000
```

How it works...

Eve can be initialized with custom authentication. We created our class as a simple basic authentication, with a given username and password (which can easily be extended to receive the credentials as command-line arguments). The check_auth() returns true if both the client provided username and password (as a base64 encoded string) matches the ones that the server is started with.

Throttling requests with RequestsThrottler

Networks need to have accounting in addition to authorization and authentication. Accounting ensures proper use of the resources, this means that everyone gets to use the services in a fair manner. Network throttling enables accounting in the web services. This is a simple recipe that offers a throttling service to the web requests.

Getting ready

We use `requests_throttler` Python module to throttle the web requests. First, install the module and configure our recipe using the following script:

```
$ sh 11_10_requests_throttling.sh
#!/bin/bash
##################################################
# Python Network Programming Cookbook, Second Edition --
Chapter - 11
##################################################
# Download and extract RequestsThrottler
wget
https://pypi.python.org/packages/d5/db/fc7558a14efa163cd2d3e4515cdfbbfc2dac
c1d2c4285b095104c58065c7/RequestsThrottler-0.1.0.tar.gz
tar -xvf RequestsThrottler-0.1.0.tar.gz
cd RequestsThrottler-0.1.0
# Copy our recipe into the folder
cp ../11_10_requests_throttling.py requests_throttler
# Configure and Install RequestsThrottling
python setup.py build
sudo python setup.py install
```

How to do it...

Now, you may execute your recipe by going to the folder, `RequestsThrottler-0.1.0/requests_throttler`.

```
$ cd RequestsThrottler-0.1.0/requests_throttler
```

Make sure to give the full addresses as the command-line argument. For example, provide `http://cnn.com`. Not `cnn.com`. Otherwise, you will receive an error message similar to the one shown following:

```
requests.exceptions.MissingSchema: Invalid URL 'cnn.com': No schema
supplied. Perhaps you meant http://cnn.com?
```

Run the recipe using the following command:

```
$ python 11_10_requests_throttling.py --address="http://cnn.com"
^[[1~[Thread=MainThread - 2017-07-29 19:34:08,897 - INFO]: Starting base
throttler 'base-throttler'...
[Thread=MainThread - 2017-07-29 19:34:08,897 - INFO]: Submitting request to
base throttler (url: http://cnn.com)...
[Thread=Thread-1 - 2017-07-29 19:34:08,897 - INFO]: Starting main loop...
[Thread=MainThread - 2017-07-29 19:34:08,900 - INFO]: Submitting request to
base throttler (url: http://cnn.com)...
[Thread=Thread-1 - 2017-07-29 19:34:08,900 - INFO]: Sending request (url:
http://cnn.com/)...
[Thread=MainThread - 2017-07-29 19:34:08,900 - INFO]: Submitting request to
base throttler (url: http://cnn.com)...
[Thread=MainThread - 2017-07-29 19:34:08,901 - INFO]: Submitting request to
base throttler (url: http://cnn.com)...
[Thread=MainThread - 2017-07-29 19:34:08,901 - INFO]: Submitting request to
base throttler (url: http://cnn.com)...
............
[Thread=Thread-1 - 2017-07-29 19:34:09,184 - INFO]: Request sent! (url:
http://cnn.com/)
[Thread=Thread-1 - 2017-07-29 19:34:09,184 - INFO]: Sending request (url:
http://cnn.com/)...
<Response [200]>
[Thread=Thread-1 - 2017-07-29 19:34:09,343 - INFO]: Request sent! (url:
http://www.cnn.com/)
<Response [200]>
[Thread=Thread-1 - 2017-07-29 19:34:10,401 - INFO]: Sending request (url:
http://cnn.com/)...
[Thread=Thread-1 - 2017-07-29 19:34:10,545 - INFO]: Request sent! (url:
http://www.cnn.com/)
<Response [200]>
.......
Success: 10, Failures: 0
[Thread=Thread-1 - 2017-07-29 19:34:22,412 - INFO]: Exited from main loop.
```

The following screenshot shows the output of our recipe:

Throttled Requests to a Web Server

Listing 11.10 shows our recipe, that sends requests to the website provided as the command-line input, in a throttled manner:

```python
#!/usr/bin/env python
# Python Network Programming Cookbook, Second Edition
   -- Chapter - 11
# This program is optimized for Python 2.7.12.
# It may run on any other version with/without
   modifications.

import argparse
import requests
from throttler.base_throttler import BaseThrottler


def main(address):

    # Throttle the requests with the BaseThrottler, delaying 1.5s.
    bt = BaseThrottler(name='base-throttler', delay=1.5)
```

```
# Visit the address provided by the user. Complete URL only.
r = requests.Request(method='GET', url=address)

# 10 requests.
reqs = [r for i in range(0, 10)]

# Submit the requests with the required throttling.
with bt:
    throttled_requests = bt.submit(reqs)

# Print the response for each of the requests.
for r in throttled_requests:
    print (r.response)

# Final status of the requests.
print ("Success: {s}, Failures: {f}".format(s=bt.successes,
        f=bt.failures))


if __name__ == '__main__':
    parser = argparse.ArgumentParser(description=
                            'Requests Throttling')
    parser.add_argument('--address', action="store",
    dest="address",  default='http://www.google.com')
    given_args = parser.parse_args()
    address = given_args.address
    main (address)
```

This recipe performs the accounting action, by making sure each request are sent only after a certain delay. Here we use `BaseThrottler`, this ensures that each request is started with a 1.5 second delay in between.

How it works...

The `requests_throttler` Python module supports throttling requests to the web servers. There are more throttling implementations based in Python, for example, throttle (`https://pypi.python.org/pypi/throttle`) is an implementation based on token bucket algorithm.

Throttling can ensure that only a given number of requests are satisfied for a given user in a given time interval. Thus, it protects the server from attackers who try to flood the server with the requests, as in **denial-of-service (DoS)** attacks.

12
Open and Proprietary Networking Solutions

In this chapter, we will cover the following recipes:

- Configuring Red PNDA
- Configuring VMware NSX for vSphere 6.3.2
- Configuring Juniper Contrail Server Manager
- Configuring OpenContrail controller
- Configuring OpenContrail cluster
- Interacting with devices running Cisco IOS XR
- Collaborating with Cisco Spark API

Introduction

We discussed Open SDN projects such as OpenDaylight and ONOS from the Linux Foundation and other open source efforts such as Floodlight in the previous chapters. In this chapter, we will look more into advanced open and vendor-specific SDN programming, and configure various networking projects. Cisco **Application Centric Infrastructure** (**ACI**) is an SDN solution from Cisco. Its building blocks include the hardware switches of Cisco Nexus 7000 and 9000 Series and Cisco **Application Policy Infrastructure Controller** (**APIC**). Juniper Contrail, which was later open sourced as **OpenContrail** is another example for a vendor-specific SDN. VMware NSX a proprietary SDN solution, also has its open source versions available for public download. This chapter will serve as an introduction to a wide range of enterprise options available for SDN and networking architecture. While we introduce many solutions, we will restrict our detailed discussions to the solutions that are available for free.

Configuring Red PNDA

PNDA is an open source platform for network data analytics. It is horizontally scalable and complex to deploy on a single computer. To be able to test smaller scale applications in the developer computers, a smaller downsized version of PNDA known as Red PNDA (https://github.com/pndaproject/red-pnda) is also available. In this recipe, we will configure Red PNDA, the minimal version of PNDA in a laptop.

Getting ready

You need to have a minimum of 4GB memory, 2 VCPUs, and 8GB hard disk to install Red PNDA. It requires up to an hour to configure and install, this also depends on how fast your internet connection is.

How to do it...

You may configure Red PNDA by following the succeeding commands. First clone the project code base:

```
$ git clone https://github.com/pndaproject/red-pnda.git
$ cd red-pnda
```

Build it as a super user.

```
$ sudo su
$ bash scripts/install-dependencies.sh wlo1
```

In the preceding command, replace `wlo1` with one of your active network interfaces. You may find it by using the `ifconfig` command in Linux and `ipcofig` in Windows.

The build requires an internet connection as it downloads the required dependencies. You may monitor the status of the build from the logs, as the build logs are verbose. Sample configuration logs (as observed in my laptop during the build) are provided in the `file 12_1_configure_red_pnda_output` for your reference. After an hour or so, the following message will be printed upon a successful installation:

```
....
Adding platformlibs 0.6.8 to easy-install.pth file
Installed /usr/local/lib/python3.5/dist-packages/platformlibs-0.6.8-
py2.7.egg
Processing dependencies for platformlibs==0.6.8
Searching for platformlibs==0.6.8
```

```
Reading https://pypi.python.org/simple/platformlibs/
Couldn't find index page for 'platformlibs' (maybe misspelled?)
Scanning index of all packages (this may take a while)
Reading https://pypi.python.org/simple/
No local packages or working download links found for platformlibs==0.6.8
error: Could not find suitable distribution for
Requirement.parse('platformlibs==0.6.8')
Failed to restart data-manager.service: Unit data-manager.service not
found.
#######################################################
Your Red-PNDA is successfully installed. Go to http://109.141.41.113 on
your browser to view the console!
```

In the log you may find some error messages. Some of them are due to the fact that PNDA is written for Python 2 and hence producing error or warning messages when built with Python 3 environment. If a few libraries failed to download or configure properly, you may manually resume and fix them accordingly. The last logs indicate the admin console URL of Red PNDA. Open the URL in your browser to access it. Red PNDA can be accessed from `http://localhost` or `http://<your-ip-address>` as shown here in the following screenshot:

RED PNDA Admin Console

Grafana (`https://grafana.com/`) is a platform for data analytics and monitoring that is used in PNDA and Red PNDA. You may access Grafana from the Red PNDA web console. You may register yourself as a PNDA user with an email address and password using the Grafana's **Log In** page or sign up if you haven't already registered.

Grafana can be accessed from `http://localhost:3000` or
`http://<your-ip-address>:3000` as shown in the following screenshot:

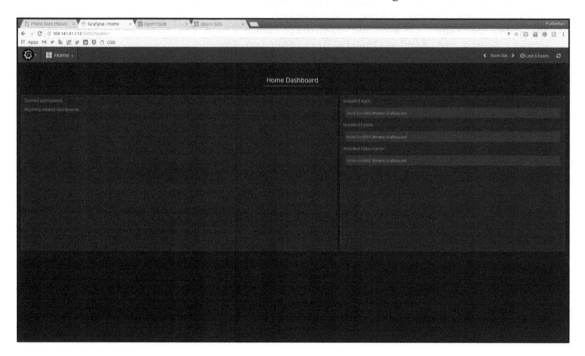

Grafana Admin Console

OpenTSDB (`http://opentsdb.net/`) is a scalable time series database used by PNDA. It
stores and serves time series data and its admin interface can be accessed from the Red
PNDA web console as well. OpenTSTB can be accessed from `http://localhost:4242/`
or `http://<your-ip-address>:4242/` as shown here in the following screenshot:

OpenTSTB Admin Console

Red PNDA consists of a few scripts that are important to configure the networking data analytics platform. Your Python knowledge comes in handy when extending and executing these Python programs.

You may find four Python programs in the folder, `red-pnda/scripts/files`. `producer.py` and `consumer.py` function which is a Kafka producer and a consumer. You need a Kafka broker running to make these producer and consumer communicate to each other. `hbase_spark_metric.py` connects to the HBase and Spark to store the status of the network. Finally, `create_or_update_ds.py` creates a data source in OpenTSTB, or updates an existing data source.

You may use the Python script with the username and password that you have created using Grafana before. The addresses indicate the URLs of the Grafana console and the OpenTSTB console.

```
$ python create_or_update_ds.py kk.pradeeban@gmail.com password
http://localhost:3000 '{ "name": "PNDA OpenTSDB", "type": "opentsdb",
"url": "http://localhost:4243", "access": "proxy", "basicAuth": false,
"isDefault": true }'
```

If the credentials are not correct, you will receive this error message:

```
requests.exceptions.HTTPError: 401 Client Error: Unauthorized for url:
http://localhost:3000/api/datasources
```

If the credentials are correct but the data source or OpenTSTB is not configured properly during the Red PNDA configuration, you will receive the following error message:

```
requests.exceptions.HTTPError: 403 Client Error: Forbidden for url:
http://localhost:3000/api/datasources
```

How it works...

Red PNDA is a minimalist version of PNDA networking data analytics platform. Unlike PNDA, Red PNDA is configured to be run in a single computer and should not be used as a production solution due to its limited horizontal scalability.

In addition to the software bundles that we discussed before in this recipe (such as Spark, Hbase, Kafka, OpenTSTB, and Grafana), Red PNDA also depends on the below additional software: PNDA console frontend (`https://github.com/pndaproject/platform-console-frontend`), PNDA console backend (`https://github.com/pndaproject/platform-console-backend`), PNDA platform testing (`https://github.com/pndaproject/platform-testing`), PNDA platform libraries (`https://github.com/pndaproject/platform-libraries`), Jupyter Notebook (`http://jupyter.org`), Kafka Manager (`https://github.com/yahoo/kafka-manager`), PNDA's example Kafka clients (`https://github.com/pndaproject/example-kafka-clients`), and JMXProxy 3.2.0 (`https://github.com/mk23/jmxproxy`).

Configuring VMware NSX for vSphere 6.3.2

NSX is a network virtualization and security platform offered by VMware in its effort towards creating a Software-Defined Data Center. You may download tarballs of NSX controller and NSX for vSphere 6.3.2 hypervisor at `https://my.vmware.com/group/vmware/details?downloadGroup=NSXV_632_OSS&productId=417`. With the server virtualization offered by vSphere and the network virtualization offered by NSX, VMware virtualizes an entire data center. The NSX controller functions as a control point for the logical switches and overlay transport tunnels. In this recipe, we will learn to use `pynsxv` (`https://github.com/vmware/pynsxv`), a Python-based library and CLI tool, to control NSX for vSphere.

Getting ready

First install `pynsxv` using `pip`:

```
$ sudo pip install pynsxv
```

You may confirm that the installation was successful by executing the following commands:

```
$ pynsxv -h
usage: pynsxv [-h] [-i INI] [-v] [-d] {lswitch,dlr,esg,dhcp,lb,dfw,usage}
...
PyNSXv Command Line Client for NSX for vSphere
positional arguments:
{lswitch,dlr,esg,dhcp,lb,dfw,usage}
lswitch          Functions for logical switches
dlr              Functions for distributed logical routers
esg              Functions for edge services gateways
dhcp             Functions for Edge DHCP
lb               Functions for Edge Load Balancer
dfw              Functions for distributed firewall
```

```
usage                   Functions to retrieve NSX-v usage statistics
optional arguments:
-h, --help              show this help message and exit
-i INI, --ini INI       nsx configuration file
-v, --verbose           increase output verbosity
-d, --debug             print low level debug of http transactions
```

You may encounter the following error due to some version mismatching:

```
pkg_resources.DistributionNotFound: The 'urllib3<1.22,>=1.21.1'
distribution was not found and is required by requests
```

By repeating with the version explicitly specified for pip, this issue can be fixed:

```
$ sudo pip2 install pynsxv
$ pynsxv lswitch -h
usage: pynsxv lswitch [-h] [-t TRANSPORT_ZONE] [-n NAME] command
Functions for logical switches
positional arguments:
command
                             create: create a new logical switch
                             read:   return the virtual wire id of a
logical switch
                             delete: delete a logical switch"
                             list:   return a list of all logical
switches
optional arguments:
-h, --help              show this help message and exit
-t TRANSPORT_ZONE, --transport_zone TRANSPORT_ZONE
                             nsx transport zone
-n NAME, --name NAME    logical switch name, needed for create, read and
delete
```

A Python code to use the RESTful API of NSX Manager can be downloaded from https
://code.vmware.com/samples/1988/python-code-to-use-the-nsx-manager-rest-api-
interface, and can be executed using the following command:

```
$ python snippet.py
```

Optionally, you may also install the Python nsx library for OpenStack using the following
command:

```
$ sudo pip install vmware-nsx
```

How to do it...

PyNSXv is a Python project to configure and control NSX based Software-Defined Data Centers. First configure `nsx.ini` to point to the correct values for the parameters:

```
[nsxv]
nsx_manager = <nsx_manager_IP>
nsx_username = admin
nsx_password = <nsx_manager_password>
[vcenter]
vcenter = <VC_IP_or_Hostname>
vcenter_user = administrator@domain.local
vcenter_passwd = <vc_password>
[defaults]
transport_zone = <transport_zone_name>
datacenter_name = <vcenter datacenter name>
edge_datastore = <datastore name to deploy edges in>
edge_cluster = <vcenter cluster for edge gateways>
```

Then `pynsxv` can offer a global view of the data center network to configure and control it as shown by the following output:

```
$ pynsxv lswitch list
+---------------------+-----------------+
| LS name             | LS ID           |
|---------------------+-----------------|
| edge_ls             | virtualwire-63  |
| dlr_ls              | virtualwire-64  |
+---------------------+-----------------+
```

How it works...

PyNSXv offers a Python-based API and interface to control NSX. You just need to offer the NSX Manager and the vCenter IP and credentials as well as names for the vCenter data center, edge data store, and edge cluster for the gateways. A complete *NSX API Guide* can be found at `https://pubs.vmware.com/NSX-6/topic/com.vmware.ICbase/PDF/nsx_604_api.pdf` and *NSX for vSphere API Guide* can be found at `https://docs.vmware.com/en/Vmware-NSX-for-vSphere/6.3/nsx_63_api.pdf`.

Configuring Juniper Contrail Server Manager

Juniper Networks (`http://www.juniper.net/us/en/`) offer a set of products aimed at network performance and security. It also provides Python-based open source projects (`https://github.com/Juniper`) to manage its platform. Contrail offers an SDN-enabled management solution and service delivery for wide area networks, thus supporting **Software-Defined Wide Area Networks** (**SD-WANs**).

Contrail Server Manager is a platform to manage the servers in a Contrail cluster. In this recipe, first we will set up Juniper Contrail Server Manager (`https://github.com/Juniper/contrail-server-manager`). You may learn more about configuring Contrail Server Manager and other Contrail bundles from `http://www.juniper.net/documentation/en_US/contrail4.0/information-products/pathway-pages/getting-started-pwp.pdf`.

Juniper is open sourcing many of its networking solutions under OpenContrail project. We will look into the open source scripts available to manage and configure Contrail. Written in Python 2, these scripts do not support Python 3.

Getting ready

You may download the relevant software bundle of Juniper Contrail Server Manager from `http://www.juniper.net/support/downloads/?p=contrail#sw` and install the Contrail Server Manager or Server Manager Lite directly from the command (after replacing with the relevant file number):

```
$ sudo dpkg -i contrail-server-manager-installer_2.22~juno_all.deb
```

More installation instructions can be found at `https://www.juniper.net/documentation/en_US/contrail4.0/topics/concept/install-containers-smlite.html`.

You may also seek a slot to test Juniper Contrail cloud automation platform and AppFormix cloud operations optimization tool in a sandbox environment from `http://www.juniper.net/us/en/cloud-software/trial/` for free as shown here in the following screenshot:

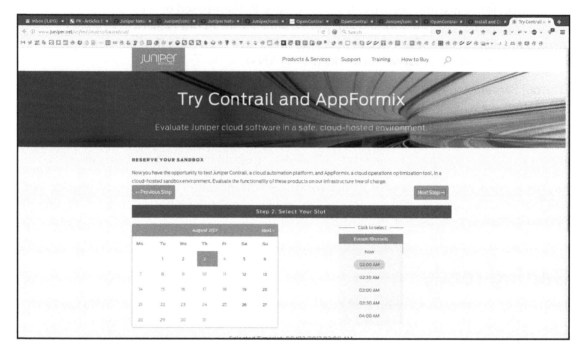

Reserve Your Slot at Juniper!

A sandbox user guide can be found at `http://www.juniper.net/documentation/cloud-software/ContrailSandbox-UserGuide.pdf`.

In this recipe, we will look deep into the Python source code repository of the server manager. You may configure the Contrail Server Manager through the following commands.

First checkout the source code from the code repository:

```
$ git clone https://github.com/Juniper/contrail-server-manager.git
```

Now build and install it through the setup script:

```
$ cd contrail-server-manager/
$ python setup.py build
$ sudo python setup.py install
```

You may receive help by using the following command:

```
$ sudo python setup.py -help
```

You may receive instruction specific help using the `--help` flag following a command. For example, to receive installation specific commands, use the following command:

```
$ python setup.py install --help
/usr/local/lib/python2.7/dist-packages/setuptools/dist.py:333: UserWarning:
Normalizing '0.1dev' to '0.1.dev0'
normalized_version,
Common commands: (see '--help-commands' for more)
setup.py build      will build the package underneath 'build/'
setup.py install    will install the package
Global options:
--verbose (-v)   run verbosely (default)
--quiet (-q)     run quietly (turns verbosity off)
--dry-run (-n)   don't actually do anything
--help (-h)      show detailed help message
--no-user-cfg    ignore pydistutils.cfg in your home directory
Options for 'install' command:
--prefix                    installation prefix
--exec-prefix               (Unix only) prefix for
                            platform-specific files
--home                      (Unix only) home directory
                            to install under
--user                      install in user site-package

'/home/pradeeban/.local/lib/python2.7/site-packages'
--install-base                  base installation directory (instead
of --prefix or --home)
--install-platbase              base installation directory for
platform-specific files (instead of --exec-prefix or --home)
--root                          install everything relative to this
alternate root directory
--install-purelib               installation directory for pure Python
module distributions
--install-platlib               installation directory for non-pure
module distributions
--install-lib                   installation directory for all module
distributions (overrides --install-purelib and --install-platlib)
--install-headers               installation directory for C/C++
```

```
headers
  --install-scripts                      installation directory for Python
scripts
  --install-data                         installation directory for data files
  --compile (-c)                         compile .py to .pyc [default]
  --no-compile                           don't compile .py files
  --optimize (-O)                        also compile with optimization: -O1
for "python -O", -O2 for "python -OO", and
  -O0 to disable [default: -O0]
  --force (-f)                           force installation (overwrite any
existing files)
  --skip-build                           skip rebuilding everything (for
testing/debugging)
  --record                               filename in which to record list of
installed files
  --install-layout                       installation layout to choose (known
values: deb, unix)
  --old-and-unmanageable                 Try not to use this!
  --single-version-externally-managed    used by system package builders to
create 'flat' eggs
usage: setup.py [global_opts] cmd1 [cmd1_opts] [cmd2 [cmd2_opts] ...]
   or: setup.py --help [cmd1 cmd2 ...]
   or: setup.py --help-commands
   or: setup.py cmd --help
```

How to do it...

Let's install Contrail Server Manager in our current directory.

```
$ sudo python setup.py install --root install
```

This will set up the server manager inside a directory called `install` which is inside the current directory.

Now you will be able to see a bunch of Python scripts of the server manager inside the folder `install/usr/local/lib/python2.7/dist-packages/src`:

```
$ cd  install/usr/local/lib/python2.7/dist-packages/src
$ ls
contrail_defaults.py          __init__.pyc
server_mgr_db_convert.py            server_mgr_disk_filesystem_view.pyc
server_mgr_ipmi_monitoring.py    server_mgr_mon_base_plugin.pyc
server_mgr_utils.py
contrail_defaults.pyc         inplace_upgrade.py
server_mgr_db_convert.pyc          server_mgr_docker.py
server_mgr_ipmi_monitoring.pyc   server_mgr_puppet.py
```

```
server_mgr_utils.pyc
create_vm.py                 inplace_upgrade.pyc        server_mgr_db.py
server_mgr_docker.pyc              server_mgr_issu.py
server_mgr_puppet.pyc         server_mgr_validations.py
create_vm.pyc                server_mgr_certs.py        server_mgr_db.pyc
server_mgr_err.py                  server_mgr_issu.pyc
server_mgr_ssh_client.py      server_mgr_validations.pyc
generate_dhcp_template.py    server_mgr_certs.pyc
server_mgr_defaults.py             server_mgr_err.pyc
server_mgr_logger.py          server_mgr_ssh_client.pyc
smgr_dhcp_event.py
generate_dhcp_template.pyc   server_mgr_cert_utils.py
server_mgr_defaults.pyc            server_mgr_exception.py
server_mgr_logger.pyc         server_mgr_status.py
smgr_dhcp_event.pyc
generate_openssl_cfg.py      server_mgr_cert_utils.pyc
server_mgr_discovery.py            server_mgr_exception.pyc
server_mgr_main.py            server_mgr_status.pyc
generate_openssl_cfg.pyc     server_mgr_cobbler.py
server_mgr_discovery.pyc           server_mgr_inventory.py
server_mgr_main.pyc           server_mgr_storage.py
__init__.py                  server_mgr_cobbler.pyc
server_mgr_disk_filesystem_view.py  server_mgr_inventory.pyc
server_mgr_mon_base_plugin.py    server_mgr_storage.pyc
```

How it works...

While Juniper Contrail is a proprietary solution that needs a login to download and use the Contrail Server Manager and other products, these open source python scripts can be used to manage the Juniper Contrail networking cluster.

Configuring OpenContrail controller

OpenContrail (http://www.opencontrail.org/) is an open source network virtualization platform for the cloud from Juniper Networks. In this recipe, we will learn to configure OpenContrail controller, also known as the OpenContrail core project (https://github.co m/Juniper/contrail-controller). This project is developed in C++ and Python.

Getting ready

In this recipe we will configure OpenContrail. We will offer complementary information to the configuration instructions that can be found in `https://github.com/Juniper/contrail-controller/wiki/OpenContrail-bring-up-and-provisioning`. OpenContrail can be executed in a distributed environment consisting of multiple servers for configuration node, analytics node, a control node, and compute node. Each node serves their purpose and they all can be virtualized and installed inside fewer nodes. However, due to their hardware requirements (memory and CPU), it is recommended to run them in individual servers in a cluster, if possible.

How to do it...

You may configure the control node by using the script (`12_4_open_contrail_control_node.sh`):

```
#!/bin/bash
##########################################################################
###
# Python Network Programming Cookbook, Second Edition -- Chapter - 12
# Adopted from
https://github.com/Juniper/contrail-controller/wiki/Install-and-Configure-O
penContrail-1.06
##########################################################################
###

# Configue the Ubuntu repositories.
echo "deb http://ppa.launchpad.net/opencontrail/ppa/ubuntu precise main" |
sudo tee -a /etc/apt/sources.list.d/opencontrail.list
sudo apt-key adv --keyserver keyserver.ubuntu.com --recv-keys
16BD83506839FE77
sudo apt-get update

# Install Contrail Control
sudo apt-get install contrail-control
```

You may execute the script to configure a node as the control node as shown here:

```
$ sh 12_4_open_contrail_control_node.sh
```

Update /etc/contrail/control-node.conf:

```
[DISCOVERY]
port=5998
server=127.0.0.1 # discovery_server IP address

[IFMAP]
password=control
user=control
```

Restart control:

```
$ sudo service contrail-control restart
```

How it works...

The control node orchestrates the OpenContrail cluster. You may receive the registration of control in discovery using the following command:

```
$ curl http://127.0.0.1:5998/services
```

The following command shows the control as a generator in the analytics API:

```
$ curl http://127.0.0.1:8081/analytics/uves/generators | python -mjson.tool
```

Configuring OpenContrail cluster

The OpenContrail cluster requires configuration of an analytics node, configuration node, and a compute node in addition to the controller node that we configured in the previous recipe. In this recipe, we will configure OpenContrail cluster, which is composed of many components and sub-projects. Many of the platform tools and projects of OpenContrail are built in Python.

Important!

The following scripts need to be run in different servers than the controller (each on its own), otherwise they will add the same repository to the sources list multiple times, which may break your Ubuntu update manager. It is highly recommended to test these in virtual machines, unless you are confident of breaking and fixing.

How to do it...

First you need to download and configure the below services for the configuration node:

- Apache ZooKeeper, an open source server for a highly reliable distributed coordination: `https://zookeeper.apache.org/`
- Apache Cassandra, a distributed open source NoSQL database management system: `http://cassandra.apache.org/`
- RabbitMQ message broker: `https://www.rabbitmq.com/`
- **network time protocol** (**NTP**) for time synchronization: `http://www.ntp.org/`

The following script (`12_5_open_contrail_configuration_node.sh`) configures a server as the configuration node:

```
#!/bin/bash
##############################################################################
###
# Python Network Programming Cookbook, Second Edition -- Chapter - 12
# Adopted from
https://github.com/Juniper/contrail-controller/wiki/Install-and-Configure-O
penContrail-1.06
##############################################################################
###

# Download and manually install python-support, as it is dropped from
Ubuntu 16.04.
wget http://launchpadlibrarian.net/109052632/python-support_1.0.15_all.deb
sudo dpkg -i python-support_1.0.15_all.deb

# Configuring the package list.
echo "deb http://ppa.launchpad.net/opencontrail/ppa/ubuntu precise main" |
sudo tee -a /etc/apt/sources.list.d/opencontrail.list
sudo apt-key adv --keyserver keyserver.ubuntu.com --recv-keys
16BD83506839FE77
echo "deb http://debian.datastax.com/community stable main" | sudo tee -a
/etc/apt/sources.list.d/cassandra.sources.list
curl -L http://debian.datastax.com/debian/repo_key | sudo apt-key add -

# Run update
sudo apt-get update

# Install dependencies
sudo apt-get install cassandra=1.2.18 zookeeperd rabbitmq-server ifmap-
server

# Install Contrail Config
```

```
sudo apt-get install contrail-config

# Configre ifmap-server
echo "control:control" | sudo tee -a /etc/ifmap-
server/basicauthusers.properties
sudo service ifmap-server restart
```

Execute the script on a server to configure it as the configuration node:

$ sh 12_5_open_contrail_configuration_node.sh

The updates may leave you with the warnings similar to the following ones:

W:
https://archive.cloudera.com/cm5/ubuntu/trusty/amd64/cm/dists/trusty-cm5.9.
0/InRelease: Signature by key F36A89E33CC1BD0F71079007327574EE02A818DD uses
weak digest algorithm (SHA1)
W:
http://repo.saltstack.com/apt/ubuntu/14.04/amd64/archive/2015.8.11/dists/tr
usty/InRelease: Signature by key 754A1A7AE731F165D5E6D4BD0E08A149DE57BFBE
uses weak digest algorithm (SHA1)

This is because of the weak digest algorithm used by the *Cloudera* and *SaltStack* repositories.

Now we will configure the analytics node with the following script
(12_5_open_contrail_analytics_node.sh):

```
#!/bin/bash
#########################################################################
###
# Python Network Programming Cookbook, Second Edition -- Chapter - 12
# Adopted from
https://github.com/Juniper/contrail-controller/wiki/Install-and-Configure-O
penContrail-1.06
#########################################################################
###

# Get the redis server binary from
http://ftp.ksu.edu.tw/FTP/Linux/ubuntu/ubuntu/pool/universe/r/redis/
# You may use any other working mirror as well.
wget
http://ftp.ksu.edu.tw/FTP/Linux/ubuntu/ubuntu/pool/universe/r/redis/redis-s
erver_2.6.13-1_amd64.deb
sudo apt-get install libjemalloc1

# Install redis server
sudo dpkg -i redis-server_2.6.13-1_amd64.deb
```

```
echo "deb http://ppa.launchpad.net/opencontrail/ppa/ubuntu precise main" |
sudo tee -a /etc/apt/sources.list.d/opencontrail.list
sudo apt-key adv --keyserver keyserver.ubuntu.com --recv-keys
16BD83506839FE77
sudo apt-get update

# Install Contrail Analytics
sudo apt-get install contrail-analytics
```

You may execute the following script to configure a node as the analytics node:

$ sh 12_5_open_contrail_analytics_node.sh

Update the port in /etc/redis/redis.conf from 6379 to 6381 and restart the Redis server:

$ sudo service redis-server restart

Update discovery and Redis settings in /etc/contrail/contrail-collector.conf with that from etc/contrail/contrail-collector.conf in the accompanying source:

```
[DISCOVERY]
port=5998
server=127.0.0.1
[REDIS]
port=6381
server=127.0.0.1
```

Restart the collector.

$ sudo service contrail-collector restart

Update discovery and Redis settings in /etc/contrail/contrail-query-engine.conf shown as follows:

```
[DISCOVERY]
port=5998
server=127.0.0.1
[REDIS]
port=6381
server=127.0.0.1
```

Restart the query engine:

$ sudo service contrail-query-engine restart

Update Redis settings in `/etc/contrail/contrail-analytics-api.conf`:

```
[REDIS]
server=127.0.0.1
redis_server_port=6381
redis_query_port=6381
```

Restart the analytics API server:

```
$ sudo service contrail-analytics-api restart
```

Finally, you may configure the compute node by using the script (`12_5_open_contrail_compute_node.sh`):

```
#!/bin/bash
##############################################################################
###
# Python Network Programming Cookbook, Second Edition -- Chapter - 12
# Adopted from
https://github.com/Juniper/contrail-controller/wiki/Install-and-Configure-O
penContrail-1.06
##############################################################################
###

# Configue the Ubuntu repositories.
echo "deb http://ppa.launchpad.net/opencontrail/ppa/ubuntu precise main" |
sudo tee -a /etc/apt/sources.list.d/opencontrail.list
sudo apt-key adv --keyserver keyserver.ubuntu.com --recv-keys
16BD83506839FE77
sudo apt-get update

# Install Contrail Virtual Rouer Agent
sudo apt-get install contrail-vrouter-agent

sudo modprobe vrouter
echo "vrouter" | sudo tee -a /etc/modules
```

You may run it as follows:

```
$ sh 12_5_open_contrail_compute_node.sh
```

Update `/etc/contrail/contrail-vrouter-agent.conf`:

```
# IP address of discovery server
server=10.8.1.10

[VIRTUAL-HOST-INTERFACE]
# Everything in this section is mandatory
```

```
# name of virtual host interface
name=vhost0

# IP address and prefix in ip/prefix_len format
ip=10.8.1.11/24

# Gateway IP address for virtual host
gateway=10.8.1.254

# Physical interface name to which virtual host interface maps to
physical_interface=eth1
```

Update /etc/network/interfaces:

```
auto eth1
iface eth1 inet static
        address 0.0.0.0
        up ifconfig $IFACE up
        down ifconfig $IFACE down

auto vhost0
iface vhost0 inet static
        pre-up vif --create vhost0 --mac $(cat /sys/class/net/eth1/address)
        pre-up vif --add vhost0 --mac $(cat /sys/class/net/eth1/address) --
vrf 0
        --mode x --type vhost
        pre-up vif --add eth1 --mac $(cat /sys/class/net/eth1/address) --
vrf 0
        --mode x --type physical
        address 10.8.1.11
        netmask 255.255.255.0
        #network 10.8.1.0
        #broadcast 10.8.1.255
        #gateway 10.8.1.254
        # dns-* options are implemented by the resolvconf package, if
installed
        dns-nameservers 8.8.8.8
```

Restart the networking and vRouter agents, and finally restart the compute node:

```
$ sudo service networking restart
$ sudo service contrail-vrouter-agent restart
$ sudo reboot now
```

How it works...

Make sure to set the host names correctly in `/etc/hosts` as you start configuring OpenContrail nodes. Once you have configured the configuration node consisting of the API server, you may receive the list of tenants or projects by querying using the following command:

```
$ curl http://127.0.0.1:8082/projects | python -mjson.tool
```

You may receive the list of services and clients respectively that are consuming the services by the using the following RESTful invocations:

```
$ curl http://127.0.0.1:5998/services
$ curl http://127.0.0.1:5998/clients
```

The analytics node provides the analytics API server. List of Contrail's generators can be found using the following command:

```
$ curl http://127.0.0.1:8081/analytics/generators | python -mjson.tool
```

Compute nodes perform the underlying computations of the Contrail cluster.

Interacting with devices running Cisco IOS XR

Cisco IOS XR (`http://www.cisco.com/c/en/us/products/ios-nx-os-software/ios-xr-software/index.html`) is a distributed network operating system for service providers. It supports many devices to provide a cloud scale networking. It is known as a self-healing distributed networking operating system.

PyIOSXR (`https://github.com/fooelisa/pyiosxr`) is a Python library used to manage the devices that are running IOS XR. In this recipe, we will install `pyIOSXR`, mock a network, and coordinate it with a Python program based on `pyIOSXR`.

Getting ready

First install `pyIOSXR`:

```
$ sudo pip install pyIOSXR
```

How to do it...

Now you may connect to your device using Python as shown by the following code segment:

```
from pyIOSXR import IOSXR
device = IOSXR(hostname='lab001', username='ejasinska', password='passwd',
 port=22, timeout=120)
device.open()
```

You may test `pyIOSXR` without an IOS XR device using the mock scripts provided by the project.

Checkout the source code from the source repository:

```
$ git clone https://github.com/fooelisa/pyiosxr.git
$ cd test
```

Now you may run `test.py` to test the installation:

```
$ python test.py
.........................................
----------------------------------------------
Ran 44 tests in 0.043s
OK
```

How it works...

The `test.py` script gets the mock scripts consisting of `xml` and `cfg` files from the mock folder. `from pyIOSXR import IOSXR` imports the relevant bundles for the management of IOS XR devices from the project. The mock files are converted by the test script to emulate the Cisco IOS XR devices.

Collaborating with Cisco Spark API

Cisco Spark (`https://www.ciscospark.com/products/overview.html`) is a cloud-based collaboration platform from Cisco. It supports communication and collaboration from multiple devices for meetings, messages, and calls.

`ciscosparkapi` (`https://github.com/CiscoDevNet/ciscosparkapi`) is an open source project that offers a simple and compact Python-based API to Cisco Spark where all the operations can easily be performed with simple Python calls. In this recipe, we will configure `ciscosparkapi`.

Cisco Spark is available as a mobile, desktop, and web-based application (`https://web.cis cospark.com/signin?mid=222378440973538330606670057657 98180584`). Following is the web interface of Cisco Spark after signing in:

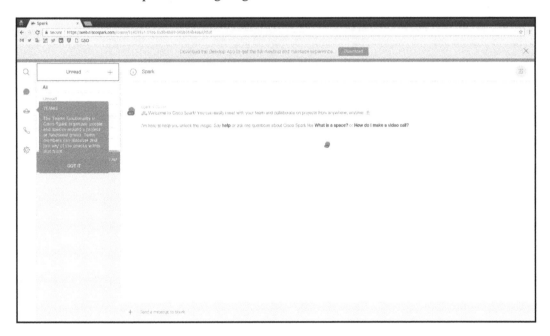

Cisco Spark Dashboard

Getting ready

Install Spark API:

```
$ sudo pip install ciscosparkapi
```

Make sure to export your Spark access token before running this recipe:

```
$ export SPARK_ACCESS_TOKEN="XXXX"
```

If your access token is incorrect, you will receive the following error message:

```
ciscosparkapi.exceptions.SparkApiError: Response Code [401] -
Authentication credentials were missing or incorrect.
```

If you have not set the access token, the following message will be reported:

```
ciscosparkapi.exceptions.ciscosparkapiException: You must provide an Spark
access token to interact with the Cisco Spark APIs, either via a
SPARK_ACCESS_TOKEN environment variable or via the access_token argument.
```

You may copy your access token from the developer portal of Cisco Spark (`https://develo`
`per.ciscospark.com/#`).

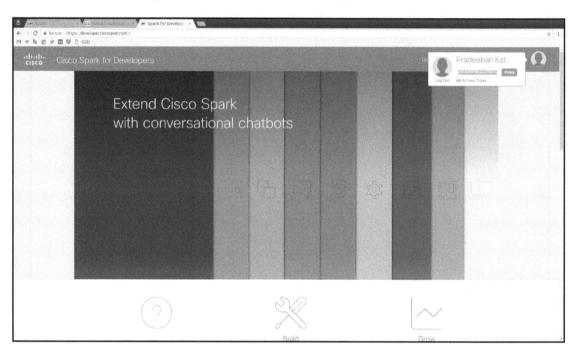

Cisco Spark Developer Portal

How to do it...

Execute the below recipe to create a new room and post a photo to it.

Listing 12.7 gives a simple program that connects to the Cisco Spark cloud, creates a room, shares a textual message as well as a photo as follows:

```
#!/usr/bin/env python
# Python Network Programming Cookbook, Second Edition -- Chapter - 12
# This program is optimized for Python 3.5.2 and Python 2.7.12.
# It may run on any other version with/without modifications.


from ciscosparkapi import CiscoSparkAPI

api = CiscoSparkAPI()

# Create a new demo room
demo_room = api.rooms.create('ciscosparkapi Demonstration')
print('Successfully Created the Room')

# Post a message to the new room, and upload an image from a web url.
api.messages.create(demo_room.id, text="Welcome to the room!",
files=["https://3.bp.blogspot.com/-wWHD9LVAI7c/WVeyurRmeDI/AAAAAAAADXc/CDY1
7VfYBdAMbI4GS6dGm2Tc4pHBvmpngCLcBGAs/
s1600/IMG_4469.JPG"])
print('Successfully Posted the Message and the Image to the Room')
```

This program creates a room called `ciscosparkapi Desmonstration` and posts the message `Welcome to the room!`.

Running the recipe produces the following output in the console and in the Cisco Spark as shown by the following screenshot:

```
$ python 12_7_cisco_spark_api.py
Successfully Created the Room
Successfully Posted the Message and the Image to the Room
```

The output is shown as follows:

Post an Image to the Room

How it works...

`ciscosparkapi` wraps the public API of Spark communication platform to offer a Python-based interface to control and manage it. With the Spark access token, we may create rooms in our channel, delete existing rooms, post to the rooms, add colleagues to the room, and perform more activities—all from the Python program.

13
NFV and Orchestration – A Larger Ecosystem

In this chapter, we will cover the following recipes:

- Building VNFs with OPNFV
- Packet processing with DPDK
- Parsing BMP messages with SNAS.io
- Controlling drones with a wireless network
- Creating PNDA clusters

Introduction

Network softwarization brings software development aspects to networking. We discussed how SDN enables a logically centralized control to the data plane in previous chapters. In this chapter, we will look into the larger ecosystem of **Network Function Virtualization** (**NFV**) and orchestration.

The Linux Foundation leads many open source networking and orchestration projects such as OPNFV, ONAP, PNDA, DPDK, SNAS, ODPi, and FD.io. We will look into how to use Python to extend these projects, and leverage them to build and orchestrate enterprise network solutions. While many of these are built with multiple languages, Python plays an important role in most of these projects as a tool for building and testing, if not as the coding language. We will look into how Python is used in configuring and installing these projects, while addressing common issues faced in configuring these enterprise-grade projects.

The Linux Foundation has a large community bonding effort on bringing various companies and organizations together for a set of open source projects. We looked at a few remarkable projects for NFV and orchestration in the previous recipes of the chapter. In fact, there are many more projects from the Linux Foundation that are worth looking at, and this list keeps growing. You can find a list of active Linux Foundation projects from its website: `https://www.linuxfoundation.org/projects`.

Building VNFs with OPNFV

Open Platform for NFV (OPNFV)
(`http://docs.opnfv.org/en/stable-danube/index.html`) is an open platform from the Linux Foundation to facilitate **Network Functions Virtualization** (**NFV**) across various projects. Various network functions are virtualized and deployed as **Virtual Network Functions** (**VNFs**), with the support of NFV platforms such as OPNFV. OPNFV consists of many projects and features for **Network Function Virtualization Infrastructure** (**NFVI**).

OPNFV can be installed using various installation tools: Compass, Fuel, TripleO from Apex, and Juju. More details on the installation alternatives can be found at `https://www.opnfv.org/software/downloads/release-archives/danube-2-0`. In this recipe, we will look in to installing OPNFV with Compass in detail. As a large-scale cross-layer project with many components, OPNFV is developed in multiple languages. Python is used in OPNFV for many scripts including configuration and installation actions. As we will learn from this recipe, installing and troubleshooting OPNFV requires a Python development environment and extensive experience in Python.

Getting ready

This recipe involves setting up the OPNFV Platform in bare-metal to build VNFs. We have slightly modified the `quickstart` provided by OPNFV for it to work in a single script. This recipe requires downloading a few GB of image files. If you cannot download 20-30 GB in your current data plan, stop executing this recipe. If your disk space is running low, this may exhaust your remaining space with the configuration of OPNFV as well.

This recipe requires around 1 TB of free hard disk space and 64 GB of RAM. Smaller disks may cause issues such as out of space error when the script sets up five hosts for the NFV. Similarly, if you do not have enough memory, starting the domain will fail. This recipe requires you to have the latest version of Python 2 (tested with Python 2.7). OPNFV projects are not yet compatible with Python 3 as a few libraries are incompatible to work with Python 3.

The installation will take around an hour. So be prepared to wait. Make sure to have at least 30 GB hard disk to be spent for this exercise and a stable internet connection for the script to download and configure the repositories. More details on configuring OPNFV can be found at
`http://docs.opnfv.org/en/stable-danube/submodules/compass4nfv/docs/release/inst allation/vmdeploy.html`. The details given here are supplementary information to the installation guides of OPNFV. A complete offline installation is also possible, as described at
`http://docs.opnfv.org/en/stable-danube/submodules/compass4nfv/docs/release/inst allation/offline-deploy.html`.

How to do it...

Install OPNFV in your computer by using the following script:

```
$  sh 13_1_quickstart.sh
```

Listing 13.1 is a script that invokes other commands to build and install OPNFV as follows:

```
#!/bin/bash
################################################
# Python Network Programming Cookbook, Second Edition
   -- Chapter - 13
################################################

sudo apt-get update
sudo apt-get install -y git
# To offer the capability for sys-admins to
  restrict program capabilities
#   with per-program profiles.
sudo apt-get install -y apparmor

# Pyyaml is a required package for the
  configuration scripts.
sudo pip2 install pyyaml

# Cheetah is a required package for the templates and code generation.
```

```
sudo pip2 install cheetah

git clone https://gerrit.opnfv.org/gerrit/compass4nfv

cd compass4nfv

CURRENT_DIR=$PWD
SCENARIO=${SCENARIO:-os-nosdn-nofeature-ha.yml}

# The build script builds the iso file.
# You could also have downloaded the iso file: such as,
# $ wget http://artifacts.opnfv.org/compass4nfv/danube/
    opnfv-2017-07-19_08-55-09.iso
./build.sh

export TAR_URL=file://$CURRENT_DIR/work/building/compass.tar.gz

# Export the below locations.
export DHA=$CURRENT_DIR/deploy/conf/vm_environment/
$SCENARIO
export NETWORK=$CURRENT_DIR/deploy/conf/vm_environment/
network.yml
# Otherwise, your installation will fail with an error
  message similar to the below:
#    + check_input_para
#    + python /home/pradeeban/programs/opnfv/util/
    check_valid.py '' ''
#    DHA file doesn't exist
#    + '[' 1 -ne 0 ']'
#    + exit 1


# If you were following the offline installation, you also
  need to download a jumpshot environment bundle.
# It consists of the dependencies.
# $ wget http://artifacts.opnfv.org/compass4nfv/package/master/
    jh_env_package.tar.gz
# Now export the absolute path for these directions
    (following the below example):
# export ISO_URL=file:///home/compass/compass4nfv.iso
# export JHPKG_URL=file:///home/compass/jh_env_package.tar.gz

# This is the command that is common for both online and
  offline installations.
./deploy.sh
```

This script downloads the *OPNFV Compass* installer project to configure OPNFV. It builds OPNFV through the installer, and deploys it. You may observe the installation progress through the logs.

Install OPNFV

How it works...

If the computer that you run this recipe does not have enough memory, it will produce these following logs during the last few steps:

```
+ sudo virsh start host4
error: Failed to start domain host4
error: internal error: early end of file from monitor,
possible problem: 2017-07-18T16:29:50.376832Z
qemu-system-x86_64: cannot set up guest memory
'pc.ram': Cannot allocate memory
```

This can be confirmed by examining
`compass4nfv/work/deploy/vm/hostN/libvirt.xml`, where `N = [1, 6]`. You will find
the following lines in these files:

```
<memory unit='MiB'>16384</memory>
<currentMemory unit='MiB'>16384</currentMemory>
```

These lines indicate that 16 GB of memory is required for these virtual machines.

Make sure that both your `python` and `pip` commands point to a Python 2 installation. If
both Python 2 and Python 3 are installed, it is likely to have `pip` referring to Python 3 while
python referring to Python 2. For example, see the following scenario:

```
$ pip --version
pip 9.0.1 from /home/pradeeban/.local/lib/python3.5/site-packages (python
3.5)
$ python --version
Python 2.7.12
$ python3 --version
Python 3.5.2
$ pip2 --version
pip 8.1.1 from /usr/lib/python2.7/dist-packages (python 2.7)
```

Here it is obvious that the `pip` and `python` commands are pointing to two different
versions—Python 3 and Python 2. To fix this:

```
$ sudo python3 -m pip install -U --force-reinstall pip
$ sudo python -m pip install -U --force-reinstall pip
```

The preceding commands will ensure that `pip` points to `pip2`, the Python 2 version. You
may confirm this by running the command again:

```
$ pip2 --version
pip 8.1.1 from /usr/lib/python2.7/dist-packages (python 2.7)
$ pip --version
pip 8.1.1 from /usr/lib/python2.7/dist-packages (python 2.7)
$ pip3 --version
pip 9.0.1 from /usr/local/lib/python3.5/dist-packages (python 3.5)
```

If you encounter errors such as the following during the installation:

```
OSError: [Errno 13] Permission denied:
'/home/pradeeban/.ansible/tmp/ansible-local-24931HCfLEe'
+ log_error 'launch_compass failed'
+ echo -e 'launch_compass failed'
launch_compass failed
```

check the permissions to confirm that the root folder `.ansible` can be updated by the current user. If not, change the permissions or delete the folder.

The installation of Python that bundles through `pip` may fail if the locales are not configured properly. You may confirm this through the following command:

```
$ pip2 show virtualenv
Traceback (most recent call last):
  File "/usr/bin/pip2", line 9, in <module>
  load_entry_point('pip==8.1.1', 'console_scripts', 'pip2')()
  File "/usr/lib/python2.7/dist-packages/pip/__init__.py",
  line 215, in main
    locale.setlocale(locale.LC_ALL, '')
  File "/usr/lib/python2.7/locale.py", line 581, in setlocale
    return _setlocale(category, locale)
locale.Error: unsupported locale setting
```

If the output is an error as shown, set the locale through the following commands:

```
export LC_ALL="en_US.UTF-8"
export LC_CTYPE="en_US.UTF-8"
sudo dpkg-reconfigure locales
```

You may of course replace the locale of `en_US.UTF-8` with the language and locale of your preference.

If you run out of space during the final stages of configuration by OPNFV Compass, it will fail with a message similar to the following:

```
changed: [localhost] => (item=compass4nfv/compass-deck)
failed: [localhost] (item=compass4nfv/compass-tasks-osa) => {"changed":
true, "cmd": "docker load -i
\"/dev/opnfv/compass4nfv/work/deploy/installer/compass_dists/compass-tasks-
osa.tar\"", "delta": "0:00:14.055573", "end": "2017-07-19 17:19:13.758734",
"failed": true, "item": "compass4nfv/compass-tasks-osa", "rc": 1, "start":
"2017-07-19 17:18:59.703161", "stderr": "Error processing tar file(exit
status 1): write
/df21d65fec8fc853792311af3739a78e018b098a5aa3b1f6ff67f44b330423b8/layer.tar
: no space left on device", "stderr_lines": ["Error processing tar
file(exit status 1): write
/df21d65fec8fc853792311af3739a78e018b098a5aa3b1f6ff67f44b330423b8/layer.tar
: no space left on device"], "stdout": "", "stdout_lines": []}
```

If your computer does not have the memory or disk space to run this recipe, you may run this in an optimized spot instance such as `r4.8xlarge` in Amazon `Elastic Compute Cloud` (`EC2`). Before launching the instance, increase the storage of the default EBS volume from 8 GB to 1000 GB, so that you won't run out of disk space during the installation of OPNFV.

Many Python extensions have been built around OPNFV. One example is the SDNVPN (`https://wiki.opnfv.org/display/sdnvpn/SDNVPN+project+main+page`) project that seeks to integrate the virtual networking components to provide layer 2/3 **virtual private network** (**VPN**) functionalities in OPNFV. You may clone the source code of SDNVPN from the source code repository to build it with Python:

```
$ git clone https://github.com/opnfv/sdnvpn.git
$ cd sdnvpn/
$ python setup.py build
$ sudo python setup.py install
```

While OPNFV is a complex networking project with clusters of computers involved, we can configure useful and interesting scenarios efficiently using Python on OPNFV.

Packet processing with DPDK

Data Plane Development Kit (**DPDK**) is a Linux Foundation project aimed to offer libraries and drivers for past packet processing for any processor. DPDK libraries can be used to implement `tcpdump`—like packet capture algorithms, and send and receive packets fast and efficiently with usually less than 80 CPU cycles.

True to its name, DPDK limits its focus to the data plane, and does not aim to provide a stack consisting of network functions. Thus, network middlebox actions such as security and firewalls as well as the layer 3 forwarding are not offered by DPDK by design. In this recipe, we will configure DPDK for a fast and efficient packet processing.

DPDK is developed in C language though Python applications have been built on top of it. In this recipe, we will install DPDK and look into a simple Python application built with DPDK.

Getting ready

You may install DPDK in your computer by using the following script:

```
$ sh 13_2_quickstart.sh
```

This script will take a few minutes to configure and install DPDK, and produce the following lines when it completes its successful installation:

```
..
Installation in /usr/local/ complete
DPDK Installation Complete.
```

The content of the script is described in detail in the following steps.

Install `pcap` dependencies, as DPDK depends on `pcap` for the user level packet capture:

```
$ sudo apt-get install libpcap-dev
Failure to have pcap in your system will fail the build with the error
message "dpdk-stable-17.05.1/drivers/net/pcap/rte_eth_pcap.c:39:18: fatal
error: pcap.h: No such file or directory"
```

Download DPDK's latest stable version from `http://dpdk.org/download`:

```
$ wget http://fast.dpdk.org/rel/dpdk-17.05.1.tar.xz
```

Extract and configure DPDK:

```
$ tar -xvf dpdk-17.05.1.tar.xz
$ cd dpdk-stable-17.05.1
$ make config T=x86_64-native-linuxapp-gcc DESTDIR=install
Configuration done
```

Enable `pcap` as the `pcap` headers are required for the capture file format:

```
$ sed -ri 's,(PMD_PCAP=).*,\1y,' build/.config
```

You have two options to build. Option 1 is to build manually using make (which we also have used in our script), and option 2 is to build using the provided `dpdk-setup.sh` script:

- **Option 1:**

```
$ make
..
== Build app/test-crypto-perf
  CC main.o
  CC cperf_ops.o
  CC cperf_options_parsing.o
```

```
CC cperf_test_vectors.o
CC cperf_test_throughput.o
CC cperf_test_latency.o
CC cperf_test_verify.o
CC cperf_test_vector_parsing.o
LD dpdk-test-crypto-perf
INSTALL-APP dpdk-test-crypto-perf
INSTALL-MAP dpdk-test-crypto-perf.map
Build complete [x86_64-native-linuxapp-gcc]
```

* **Option 2**:

```
$ cd usertools
$ ./dpdk-setup.sh
--------------------------------------------------
 Step 1: Select the DPDK environment to build
--------------------------------------------------
[1] arm64-armv8a-linuxapp-gcc
[2] arm64-dpaa2-linuxapp-gcc
[3] arm64-thunderx-linuxapp-gcc
[4] arm64-xgene1-linuxapp-gcc
[5] arm-armv7a-linuxapp-gcc
[6] i686-native-linuxapp-gcc
[7] i686-native-linuxapp-icc
[8] ppc_64-power8-linuxapp-gcc
[9] x86_64-native-bsdapp-clang
[10] x86_64-native-bsdapp-gcc
[11] x86_64-native-linuxapp-clang
[12] x86_64-native-linuxapp-gcc
[13] x86_64-native-linuxapp-icc
[14] x86_x32-native-linuxapp-gcc
. . .
```

Choose one of the preceding fourteen options to build. I have used option 12 for my build. You may set up huge page mappings using options 18 or 19 in the setup script, or use the following commands:

```
$ sudo mkdir -p /mnt/huge
$ sudo mount -t hugetlbfs nodev /mnt/huge
$ sudo su
$ echo 64 >
/sys/devices/system/node/node0/hugepages/hugepages-2048kB/nr_hugepages
```

Now you may install DPDK using the following command:

```
$ sudo make install
```

How to do it...

After the installation, you may test DPDK with the sample applications following the following command:

```
$ make -C examples RTE_SDK=$(pwd) RTE_TARGET=build O=$(pwd)/build/examples
```

`usertools` consists of a few utility bundles written in Python. For example, running `cpu_layout.py` produces the following output in my computer:

```
$ cd usertools
$ python cpu_layout.py
================================================
Core and Socket Information (as reported by '/sys/devices/system/cpu')
================================================
cores =  [0, 1, 2, 3]
sockets =  [0]
        Socket 0
        --------
Core 0 [0, 1]
Core 1 [2, 3]
Core 2 [4, 5]
Core 3 [6, 7]
```

This reports the layout of the quad cores of my laptop. You may receive similar output based on your system.

More networking examples or utility tools can be found inside the folder `build/examples`. More products are built extending or leveraging DPDK. Cisco TRex is a traffic generator developed in C and Python, on top of DPDK. You may configure it locally using the following commands:

```
$ wget http://trex-tgn.cisco.com/trex/release/latest
$ tar -xvf latest
$ cd v2.27/
```

Inside the `v2.27` folder, you will find the Python scripts to execute TRex based on DPDK. For example, you may start the master daemon using Python as follows:

```
$ sudo python master_daemon.py start
Master daemon is started
$ sudo python master_daemon.py show
Master daemon is running
```

How it works...

DPDK is a set of libraries and modules for developing the data plane. It exploits many popular tools and projects such as `pcap` to capture the packets. Many of its user tools and configuration scripts are written in Python, and a few libraries written in Python to extend DPDK. The DPDK example applications found in `build/examples` leverage the core of DPDK to program the data plane.

The bundled example applications are (as named by DPDK) `bond`, `ethtool`, `ip_pipeline`, `kni`, `l2fwd-jobstats`, `l3fwd-acl`, `link_status_interrupt`, `netmap_compat`, `qos_meter`, `rxtx_callbacks`, `tep_termination`, `vmdq`, `cmdline`, `exception_path`, `ipsec-secgw`, `l2fwd`, `l2fwd-keepalive`, `l3fwd-power`, `load_balancer`, `packet_ordering`, `qos_sched`, `server_node_efd`, `timer`, `vmdq_dcb`, `distributor`, `helloworld`, `ipv4_multicast`, `l2fwd-crypto`, `l3fwd`, `l3fwd-vf`, `multi_process`, `performance-thread`, `quota_watermark`, `skeleton`, `vhost`, and `vm_power_manager`.

Parsing BMP messages with SNAS.io

Streaming Network Analytics System (**SNAS**) or commonly known as SNAS.io is a Linux Foundation project that consists of a framework and libraries to track and access a large number of routing objects including routers, peers, and prefixes in real time. Formerly known as OpenBMP, SNAS implements BMP message bus specification. BMP refers to BGP monitoring protocol and by implementing the BMP protocol, SNAS communicates with the BMP devices such as routers.

SNAS has a Python API that lets you develop Python applications on top of SNAS for BMP messages. SNAS also consists of an `mrt2bmp` converter developed in Python, which reads the routers' **MRT** (**Multi-threaded Routing Toolkit**) files and sends BMP messages simultaneously. This SNAS conversion workflow is: **Router | MRT | MRT2BMP | OpenBMP collector | Kafka message bus | MySQL consumer**. You may find more information on these projects at `https://github.com/OpenBMP`.

Getting ready

First install and configure the Apache Kafka and SNAS library for parsing OpenBMP Kafka messages:

```
$ sh 13_3_install.sh
#!/bin/bash
###########################################################
# Python Network Programming Cookbook, Second Edition -- Chapter - 13
###########################################################
# Install Dependencies
sudo apt-get install python-dev python-pip libsnappy-dev
sudo pip install python-snappy kafka-python pyyaml
# Install SNAS Python API
git clone https://github.com/OpenBMP/openbmp-python-api-message.git
cd openbmp-python-api-message
sudo pip install .
# Go back to the root directory.
cd ..
# Download Apache Kafka
wget http://apache.belnet.be/kafka/0.11.0.0/kafka_2.11-0.11.0.0.tgz
tar -xzf kafka_2.11-0.11.0.0.tgz
```

Follow the preceding installation script once to download the dependencies, SNAS, and Kafka. Use the following script to quick-start Kafka Server:

```
$ sh 13_3 quickstart.sh
#!/bin/bash
################################################
# Python Network Programming Cookbook, Second Edition
   -- Chapter - 13
################################################

# Start Zookeeper. To view the logs real time,
   in a terminal: "tail -f zk-server.out".

nohup kafka_2.11-0.11.0.0/bin/zookeeper-server-start.sh
kafka_2.11-0.11.0.0/config/zookeeper.properties >
zk-server.out &
# Start Kafka-Server. To view the logs real time, in a
terminal: "tail -f kafka-server.out".
nohup kafka_2.11-0.11.0.0/bin/kafka-server-start.sh
kafka_2.11-0.11.0.0/config/server.properties >
kafka-server.out &
```

As this script starts Kafka and ZooKeeper as nohup, you need to find and kill these processes when you want to stop them. You may find them by:

```
$ ps -xa | grep java
```

Then kill the process using the following command for the relevant Kafka and ZooKeeper processes:

```
$ kill {process-id}
```

How to do it...

Once you have installed the SNAS BMP message API and started ZooKeeper server and Kafka server as shown previously, you are ready to run a simple listener for the BMP messages.

First, start the Python client of the SNAS message API:

```
$ python 13_3_log_consumer.py
Connecting to kafka... takes a minute to load offsets and topics, please
wait
Now consuming/waiting for messages...

13_3_snas_log_consumer.py is adopted from openbmp-python-api-
message/examples/log_consumer.py.
```

Now, if you run the following from another Terminal and send an empty message using the *Enter* key in your keyboard:

```
$ kafka_2.11-0.11.0.0/bin/kafka-console-producer.sh --broker-list
localhost:9092 --topic openbmp.parsed.router
>
>
```

You will receive the following message:

```
$ python 13_3_snas_log_consumer.py --conf="config.yaml"
Connecting to kafka... takes a minute to load offsets and topics, please
wait
Now consuming/waiting for messages...
Received Message (2017-07-21 12:17:53.536705) : ROUTER(V: 0.0)
[]
```

If you run the following command, you will see a list of topics created for BMP by the
`13_3_snas_log_consumer.py`:

```
$ kafka_2.11-0.11.0.0/bin/kafka-topics.sh --list --zookeeper localhost:2181
__consumer_offsets
openbmp.parsed.bmp_stat
openbmp.parsed.collector
openbmp.parsed.l3vpn
openbmp.parsed.ls_link
openbmp.parsed.ls_node
openbmp.parsed.ls_prefix
openbmp.parsed.peer
openbmp.parsed.router
openbmp.parsed.unicast_prefix
```

Listing 13.3 gives the simple BMP log consumer, adopted from the SNAS examples. This
listing omits a few lines of code for brevity. Check the full code at
`13_3_snas_log_consumer.py`:

```python
#!/usr/bin/env python
# Python Network Programming Cookbook, Second Edition
 -- Chapter - 13
# This program is optimized for Python 2.7.12.
# SNAS Message API Requires Python 2.7 to Run.
# This program may run on any other version with/without
 modifications.
# Adopted from openbmp-python-api-message/examples/
log_consumer.py

import argparse
import yaml
import datetime
import time
import kafka

from openbmp.api.parsed.message import Message
from openbmp.api.parsed.message import BmpStat
from openbmp.api.parsed.message import Collector
from openbmp.api.parsed.message import LsLink
from openbmp.api.parsed.message import LsNode
from openbmp.api.parsed.message import LsPrefix
from openbmp.api.parsed.message import Peer
from openbmp.api.parsed.message import Router
from openbmp.api.parsed.message import UnicastPrefix
from openbmp.api.parsed.message import L3VpnPrefix

def process_message(msg):
    m = Message(msg.value)  # Gets body of kafka message.
```

```
        t = msg.topic  # Gets topic of kafka message.
        m_tag = t.split('.')[2].upper()
        t_stamp = str(datetime.datetime.now())

        # For various cases of BMP message topics. Omitted
            logs for the sake of space.
        if t == "openbmp.parsed.router":
            router = Router(m)
            print ('\n' + 'Received Message (' + t_stamp + ')
             : ' + m_tag + '(V: ' + str(m.version) + ')')
            print (router.to_json_pretty())

        elif t == "openbmp.parsed.peer":
            peer = Peer(m)

        elif t == "openbmp.parsed.collector":
            collector = Collector(m)

        elif t == "openbmp.parsed.bmp_stat":
            bmp_stat = BmpStat(m)

        elif t == "openbmp.parsed.unicast_prefix":
            unicast_prefix = UnicastPrefix(m)

        elif t == "openbmp.parsed.l3vpn":
            l3vpn_prefix = L3VpnPrefix(m)

        elif t == "openbmp.parsed.ls_node":
            ls_node = LsNode(m)

        elif t == "openbmp.parsed.ls_link":
            ls_link = LsLink(m)

        elif t == "openbmp.parsed.ls_prefix":
            ls_prefix = LsPrefix(m)

def main(conf):
    # Enable to topics/feeds
    topics = [
        'openbmp.parsed.router', 'openbmp.parsed.peer',
        'openbmp.parsed.collector',
        'openbmp.parsed.bmp_stat', 'openbmp.parsed.
         unicast_prefix', 'openbmp.parsed.ls_node',
        'openbmp.parsed.ls_link',
       'openbmp.parsed.ls_prefix',
       'openbmp.parsed.l3vpn'
    ]
```

```
# Read config file
with open(conf, 'r') as f:
    config_content = yaml.load(f)

bootstrap_server = config_content['bootstrap_servers']

try:
    # connect and bind to topics
    print ("Connecting to kafka... takes a minute to
    load offsets and topics, please wait")
    consumer = kafka.KafkaConsumer(
        *topics,
        bootstrap_servers=bootstrap_server,
        client_id="dev-testing" + str(time.time()),
        group_id="dev-testing" + str(time.time()),
        enable_auto_commit=True,
        auto_commit_interval_ms=1000,
        auto_offset_reset="largest"
    )
    for m in consumer:
        process_message(m)

except kafka.common.KafkaUnavailableError as err:
    print ("Kafka Error: %s" % str(err))

except KeyboardInterrupt:
    print ("User stop requested")

if __name__ == '__main__':
    parser = argparse.ArgumentParser(description='SNAS
                                     Log Consumer')
    parser.add_argument('--conf', action="store",
    dest="conf",  default="config.yaml")
    given_args = parser.parse_args()
    conf = given_args.conf
    main (conf)
```

A configuration file can be passed by the `--conf` parameter. Default is `config.yaml`, which just points to the default Kafka server location:

bootstrap_servers: localhost:9092

The following screenshot shows the output of the Python program of the SNAS message API and the Kafka broker, along with the list of topics created by the Python program:

SNAS Message API and Kafka Broker

How it works...

First the nine topics of BMP messages are defined and the SNAS log consumer program subscribes to them through the Kafka broker. The BMP parsed messages include notifications of router, peer, collector, bmp_stat, unicast_prefix, l3vpn, ls_node, ls_link, and ls_prefix. Once started, the log consumer waits for messages on one of these nine topics. When you connect kafka-console-producer.sh, you may send messages to the broker. However, the messages will not reach the log consumer unless they are of one of the nine topics. You may emulate the BMP messages by starting the kafka-console-producer.sh with one of the topics, as we did in the example with --topic openbmp.parsed.router flag. The received messages for these subscribed topics are pretty printed using to_json_pretty() in an if-else loop for each of these topics.

Controlling drones with a wireless network

Drones are used more ubiquitously these days with controllers capable to control them from ground through TCP or UDP messages in a wireless network. **Dronecode** offers a platform to control and program drones, with a simulation environment to sandbox the developments. Developed in Python, Dronecode is managed by the Linux Foundation. In this recipe, we will run a simplest of drone simulation. More interesting recipes can be learned by following their website (https://www.dronecode.org).

Getting ready

Dronekit requires Python 2.7 to run. Install the Dronekit and Dronekit **Software in the Loop** (**SITL**) Simulator using Python `pip`:

```
$ pip install dronekit
$ pip install dronekit-sitl
```

How to do it...

In this recipe, we will simulate a simple drone with `dronekit-sitl`. The simulator API is compatible with the Dronekit API that actually controls the drones. Hence, you may develop once and run in simulation and production very easily, as with our previous recipes on Mininet emulation.

First, run the `dronekit-sitl` in a Terminal before running `13_4_dronekit_sitl_simulation.py`:

```
$ dronekit-sitl copter-3.3 --home=-45.12,149.22,544.55,343.55
os: linux, apm: copter, release: 3.3
SITL already Downloaded and Extracted.
Ready to boot.
Execute: /home/pradeeban/.dronekit/sitl/copter-3.3/apm --
home=-45.12,149.22,544.55,343.55 --model=quad
Started model quad at -45.12,149.22,544.55,343.55 at speed 1.0
bind port 5760 for 0
Starting sketch 'ArduCopter'
Serial port 0 on TCP port 5760
Starting SITL input
Waiting for connection ....
```

Listing 13.4 provides a simple simulation of a drone, which can connect to the drone or in our case, a simulation running, through a TCP network connection:

```python
#!/usr/bin/env python
# Python Network Programming Cookbook, Second Edition -- Chapter - 13
# This program is optimized for Python 2.7.12.
# It may run on any other version with/without modifications.

import dronekit_sitl
from dronekit import connect, VehicleMode

# Connect to the default sitl, if not one running.
sitl = dronekit_sitl.start_default()
connection_string = sitl.connection_string()

# Connect to the Vehicle.
print("Connected: %s" % (connection_string))
vehicle = connect(connection_string, wait_ready=True)

print ("GPS: %s" % vehicle.gps_0)
print ("Battery: %s" % vehicle.battery)
print ("Last Heartbeat: %s" % vehicle.last_heartbeat)
print ("Is Armable?: %s" % vehicle.is_armable)
print ("System status: %s" % vehicle.system_status.state)
print ("Mode: %s" % vehicle.mode.name)

# Close vehicle object before exiting script
vehicle.close()

print("Completed")
```

The following code shows the execution of Dronekit:

```
$ python 13_4_dronekit_sitl_simulation.py
Starting copter simulator (SITL)
SITL already Downloaded and Extracted.
Ready to boot.
Connected: tcp:127.0.0.1:5760
>>> APM:Copter V3.3 (d6053245)
>>> Frame: QUAD
>>> Calibrating barometer
>>> Initialising APM...
>>> barometer calibration complete
>>> GROUND START
GPS: GPSInfo:fix=3,num_sat=10
Battery: Battery:voltage=12.587,current=0.0,level=100
Last Heartbeat: 0.862903219997
Is Armable?: False
```

```
System status: STANDBY
Mode: STABILIZE
Completed
```

The following screenshot shows the execution of both the Dronekit and the simulator:

DroneKit and the Simulation

The following lines are printed in the SITL Terminal window, indicating the TCP connection:

```
bind port 5762 for 2
Serial port 2 on TCP port 5762
bind port 5763 for 3
Serial port 3 on TCP port 5763
Closed connection on serial port 0
```

This recipe shows the simulated default values and connects to the SITL with the ports, and closes the execution on its own when it completes.

How it works...

This recipe initializes a simple drone and prints its status. You may execute it to set its parameters and modify its values dynamically. More examples on Dronekit can be found at `http://python.dronekit.io/examples/`.

Creating PNDA clusters

PNDA (`http://pnda.io/`) is a scalable big data analytics platform for networks and services from the Linux Foundation. PNDA requires a cluster to run efficiently. PNDA offers Python scripts (`https://github.com/pndaproject/pnda-aws-templates`) to deploy it over Amazon EC2.

Getting ready

Create an S3 bucket from
`https://s3.console.aws.amazon.com/s3/home?region=eu-west-1`. We are using **EU (Ireland)** as our default region for this recipe. PNDA applications will be hosted in this bucket. Replace the `pnda-apps` with the name of your S3 bucket. Since the bucket names are shared across all the users in the region, you may not be able to use `pnda-apps` as your `Bucket name` as it would already have been used by someone:

```
# S3 container to use for PNDA application packages
PNDA_APPS_CONTAINER: pnda-apps
```

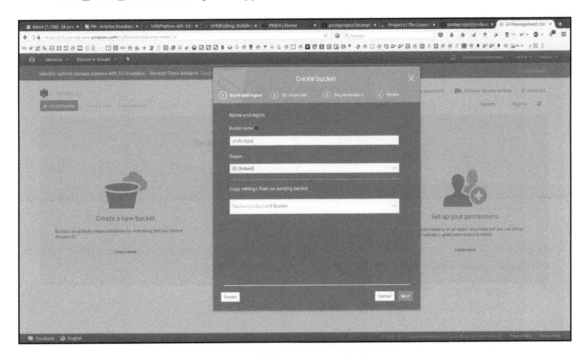

Creating an S3 Bucket for PNDA

Create a key from `https://console.aws.amazon.com/iam/home?#/security_credential`.
Don't forget to download the key (`rootkey.csv`):

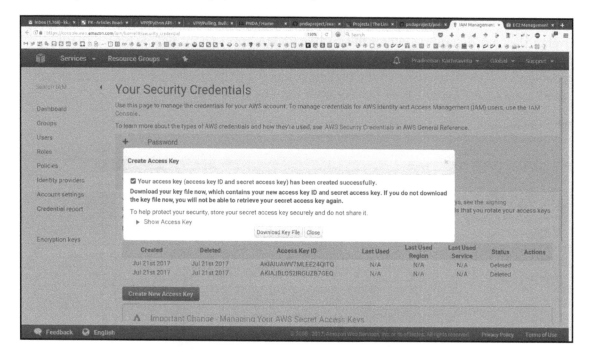

Creating Access Key

Open the `rootkey.csv` and replace the following values in `pnda_env.yaml`. These values appear three times. Make sure to replace all of them accordingly:

```
AWS_ACCESS_KEY_ID: xxxx
AWS_SECRET_ACCESS_KEY: xxxx
```

Replace the value of `PNDA_ARCHIVE_CONTAINER` to something else (more representative and long enough to be unique). However, this bucket will be auto-created.

Create an SSH **Key pair name** named `key`
(`https://eu-west-1.console.aws.amazon.com/ec2/v2/home?region=eu-west-1#KeyPairs`
`:sort=keyName`). Download and save the private key, `key.pem`.

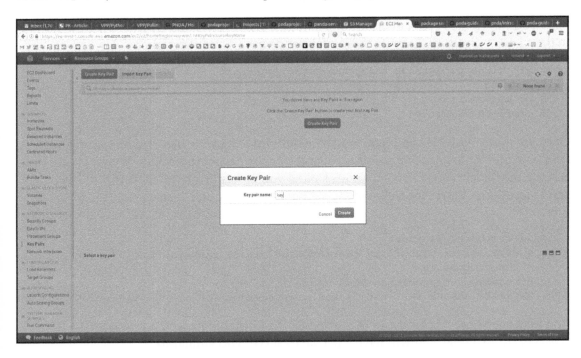

Create and Download the Private Key

Configure the dependencies and AWS templates:

```bash
$ sh 13_5_pnda_aws_setup.sh
#!/bin/bash
###############################################
# Python Network Programming Cookbook, Second Edition -- Chapter - 13
###############################################
# Clone the Platform Salt
git clone https://github.com/pndaproject/platform-salt.git
cd platform-salt
git checkout release/3.4.1
cd ..
# Clone the PNDA AWS Template latest release tag
git clone git@github.com:pndaproject/pnda-aws-templates.git
cd pnda-aws-templates
git checkout release/3.4.1
# Copy the sample pnda_env.yaml to the project after modifying as in the
recipe.
```

```
cp ../pnda_env.yaml pnda_env.yaml
# Install Dependencies
cd cli
sudo pip install -r requirements.txt
```

Now you can create PNDA distribution from the PNDA repository by following the scripts in the `mirror` directory. Execute these commands from your web server:

```
$ git clone git@github.com:pndaproject/pnda.git
$ sudo su
$ cd pnda/mirror
$ ./create_mirror.sh
```

Once the mirror build is complete, move the built folders inside the `mirror-dist` folder (`mirror_anaconda`, `mirror_cloudera`, and `mirror_misc`) to a folder of your choice (we assume the folder name to be `packages`). Now you have mirrored PNDA to your web server location. Change the following URI to indicate this publicly accessible mirror from your site:

```
pnda_component_packages:
  # HTTP server containing the compiled binary packages for
    the components
  # required to provision PNDA
  PACKAGES_SERVER_URI: http://x.x.x.x/packages
```

You may even host this inside an EC2 instance after installing a web server such as Apache2. In that case, you will have a packages server URI similar to, `http://ec2-34-253-229-120.eu-west-1.compute.amazonaws.com/packages/`.

How to do it...

Now you may create a PNDA cluster with the commands:

```
$ cd cli
$ python pnda-cli.py create -e <cluster_name> -s <key_name> -f standard -o
{no-of-tsdb-instances} -n {no-of-hadoop-data-nodes} -k {no-of-kafka-
brokers} -z {no-of-zookeeper-nodes}
```

Replace the names accordingly. For example:

```
$ python pnda-cli.py create -e pnda -s key -f standard -o 2 -n 3 -k 2 -z 3
```

Or with just one instance for each:

```
$ python pnda-cli.py create -e pnda -s key -f standard -o 1 -n 1 -k 1 -z 1
```

Currently pnda-cli.py and the other Python scripts in PNDA do not support Python 3, as they are written for Python 2. It is recommended to use Python 2.7. This will be verbose during the setup, and produce the elapsed time at the end of execution.

How it works...

In this recipe, pnda-cli.py first checks whether the pnda_env.yaml file exists, and reads the parameters from it. It uses boto's EC2 interface (http://boto.cloudhackers.com/en/latest/ec2_tut.html) to run many tasks such as connecting to the region, initializing the EC2 instances, and configuring them. Expect this to take a few minutes, also depending on the connectivity between your mirror and the EC2 instance. Thus it might be a good idea to actually create your PNDA cluster in a region that is closest to you to minimize the latency.

In this recipe, we learned how to configure PNDA in AWS. In this process, we also learned how useful Python can be for such complex configuration tasks as we used it to read the .yaml configuration file and configure an AWS cluster based on our configurations.

14
Programming the Internet

In this chapter, we will cover the following recipes:

- Checking a website status
- Benchmarking BGP implementations with bgperf
- BGP with ExaBGP
- Looking glass implementations with Python
- Understanding the internet ecosystem with Python
- Establishing BGP connections with yabgp

Introduction

Autonomous Systems (ASes) make the internet. Communications between the ASes are handled through implementations of protocols known as **Exterior Gateway Protocols (EGP)**. **Border Gateway Protocol (BGP)** is a standardized EGP, designed for exchanging routing and reachability information between the ASes. In this chapter, we will look into Python libraries for BGP such as `exabgp` and `yabgp`, and how to program the internet with Python.

Checking a website status

A website may be down as its connectivity to the rest of the internet is broken in some way. We start this chapter by checking the status of a website. Though this is a very simple exercise done with just Python, this can be extended as a health monitor application for more complex scenarios on the internet.

Getting ready

This function tests the connectivity of a website by a given address or a **fully qualified domain name (FQDN)** and port (default 80 assumed). When a domain name is passed as an address, the `socket.connect()` method resolves it.

How to do it...

Here we will look into a simple recipe that performs this action, as indicated by listing 14.1:

```python
#!/usr/bin/env python
# Python Network Programming Cookbook, Second Edition
  -- Chapter - 14
# This program is optimized for Python 2.7.12 and
  Python 3.5.2.
# It may run on any other version with/without modifications.
import socket
from sys import stdout
from time import sleep
import argparse
def is_alive(address, port):
    # Create a socket object to connect with
    s = socket.socket()
    # Now try connecting, passing in a tuple with
      address & port
    try:
        s.connect((address, port))
        return True
    except socket.error:
        return False
    finally:
        s.close()

def confirm(addres, port):
    while True:
        if is_alive(address, port):
            stdout.write(address + ":" +
            str(port) + ' is alive\n')
            stdout.flush()
        else:
            stdout.write(address + ":" +
            str(port) + ' is dead\n')
            stdout.flush()
        sleep(10)
```

```
if __name__ == '__main__':
    # setup commandline arguments
    parser = argparse.ArgumentParser
            (description='Health Checker')
    parser.add_argument('--address', action="store",
    dest="address")
    parser.add_argument('--port', action="store",
    dest="port", default=80, type=int)
    # parse arguments
    given_args = parser.parse_args()
    address, port =  given_args.address,
                        given_args.port
    confirm(address, port)
```

The following is the sample output of the program:

```
$ python 14_1_healthcheck.py --address=google.com --port=80
google.com:80 is alive
google.com:80 is alive
```

How it works...

This program checks the website periodically to see if it is up, and prints the log accordingly. If the website is down, it will notify the same, in the time intervals.

Benchmarking BGP implementations with bgperf

In this recipe, we aim to introduce BGP implementations with Python through a simple benchmarking project, as a simple exercise. We will benchmark a few BGP implementations with bgpert, a Python-based benchmarking tool for BGP implementations.

Getting ready

To install bgperf, clone the source code from its source repository:

```
$ git clone https://github.com/pradeeban/bgperf.git
```

For this recipe, we forked `bgperf` and did some minor fixes to make it work with Python 3. The parent project is at `https://github.com/osrg/bgperf`, which is aimed to work with Python 2, and at the time of writing does not support Python 3. A copy of the `pradeeban/bgperf` repository as of now has also been included in the source code bundle of this book in the folder `14_2_benchmark_with_bgperf` for your ease of reference.

Once you have cloned our `bgperf` fork, go to the parent directory of `bgperf`:

```
$ cd bgperf
```

The following command installs the listed requirements. This includes Docker and `pyyaml`:

```
$ sudo pip install -r pip-requirements.txt
```

Now your `bgperf` is ready to benchmark the BGP implementations! Confirm it by running the following command:

```
$ sudo python3 bgperf.py -help
```

Now prepare `bgperf` for benchmarks:

```
$ sudo python3 bgperf.py prepare
```

During this command, `bgperf` downloads the BGP implementations locally. You will be able to observe this from the logs displayed:

```
Removing intermediate container 782c2b5dcecf
Step 5/6 : RUN git clone https://github.com/Exa-Networks/exabgp && (cd
exabgp && git checkout HEAD && pip install six && pip install -r
requirements.txt && python setup.py install)
---> Running in 833e710df9df
Cloning into 'exabgp'...
```

As this command actually downloads and installs many of the BGP implementations, it will take more than an hour to complete. On my laptop, it took me 90 minutes! Nevertheless, the logs will keep you informed and entertained. So you may keep an eye on the logs once in a while, as this progresses.

Eventually, it will succeed with these logs:

```
...
if test -n "birdc" ; then                                              \
     /usr/bin/install -c ../birdc //usr/local/sbin/birdc ; \
fi
if ! test -f //usr/local/etc/bird.conf ; then
\
     /usr/bin/install -c -m 644 ../doc/bird.conf.example
```

```
//usr/local/etc/bird.conf ;          \
else                                 \
        echo "Not overwriting old bird.conf" ;                    \
fi
make[1]: Leaving directory '/root/bird/obj'
---> ad49f9e6f4f0
Removing intermediate container 488a2f8827eb
Successfully built ad49f9e6f4f0
Successfully tagged bgperf/bird:latest
```

Now it is time to finalize the installation of bgperf with the following command:

```
$ sudo python3 bgperf.py doctor
[sudo] password for pradeeban:
docker version ... ok (17.06.0-ce)
bgperf image
... ok
gobgp image
... ok
bird image
... ok
quagga image
... ok
/proc/sys/net/ipv4/neigh/default/gc_thresh3 ... 1024
```

You have bgperf ready in your system now, to benchmark the BGP implementations.

How to do it...

Once you have configured bgperf, you will be able to benchmark the BGP implementations.

For example:

```
$ sudo python3 bgperf.py bench
run tester
tester booting.. (100/100)
run gobgp
elapsed: 16sec, cpu: 0.20%, mem: 580.90MB
elapsed time: 11sec
```

The execution stops only when 100 BGP peers are successfully booted. Further benchmarks can be executed by following the project page.

How it works...

This recipe looks into the common BGP implementations and benchmarks them through the `bgperf` open source project. In the rest of the chapters, we will look at some BGP implementations.

BGP with ExaBGP

ExaBGP (`https://github.com/Exa-Networks/exabgp`) facilitates convenient implementation of SDN by converting BGP messages into plain text or JSON formats.

Getting ready

Install ExaBGP using `pip`:

```
$ sudo pip install exabgp
```

Generate the environment file by using the following command:

```
$ sudo su
$ mkdir /etc/exabgp
$ exabgp --fi >/etc/exabgp/exabgp.env
```

How to do it...

Now you have installed ExaBGP in your computer. You may explore its command using its `help` flag:

```
$ exabgp -help
```

Looking glass implementations with Python

Internet Exchange Points (**IXPs**) are the backbones of the internet, as they offer easy connectivity between the **Autonomous Systems** (**ASes**) of the internet. The **looking glass** (**lg**) implementation is a commonly deployed software in the IXPs. They can be used to trace how an IXP can reach any given IP address on the internet. The lg implementations are made public such that anyone can use it to trace how to connect to a given IP address, thus offering an emulation environment to test the connectivity and performance of an IXP for the service providers before committing to use an IXP for their own connectivity needs.

BIX is an IXP based in Bulgaria. You may access the lg of **Bulgarian Internet Exchange** (**BIX**) at `http://lg.bix.bg/`. For example, see the output of the query from your browser: `http://lg.bix.bg/?query=summary&addr=216.146.35.35&router=rs1.bix.bg+%28IPv6%29` for the IP (IPv6) BGP summary of `216.146.35.35` (`http://dyn.com/labs/dyn-internet-guide/`). The output of this query is shown in the following screenshot:

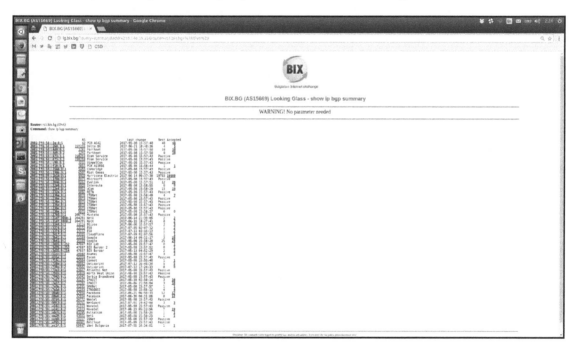

Looking Glass of BIX.bg

You may also run a `traceroute` from the lg (using the web service APIs of the browser) to observe how a given IP is connected through the IXP.

 For example, access `http://lg.bix.bg/?query=trace&addr=216.146.35.35&router=rs1.bix.bg+%28IPv6%29` from your browser.

It will produce the following output in the browser window:

```
Router: rs1.bix.bg (IPv6)
Command: traceroute -w 3 216.146.35.35

traceroute to 216.146.35.35 (216.146.35.35), 30 hops max, 60 byte packets
 1  router.bix.bg (193.169.199.254)  3.600 ms  3.760 ms  3.576 ms
 2  xe-0-2-0--br2.sof.ITDNet.net (212.116.129.29)  0.516 ms  0.532 ms  0.523 ms
 3  br1.sof.ITDNet.net (212.116.133.17)  0.742 ms  0.749 ms  0.747 ms
 4  10ge5-1.core1.sof1.he.net (216.66.85.129)  0.838 ms  0.737 ms  0.926 ms
 5  100ge10-2.core1.buh1.he.net (184.105.65.50)  8.798 ms  8.817 ms  8.843 ms
 6  buca-b1-link.telia.net (62.115.49.165)  26.499 ms  27.758 ms  27.716 ms
 7  ffm-bb3-link.telia.net (62.115.135.250)  40.182 ms ffm-bb3-link.telia.net (62.115.135.242)  39.069 ms ffm-bb3-link.telia.net (62.115.135.234)  39.315 ms
 8  ffm-b1-link.telia.net (62.115.116.160)  32.201 ms ffm-b1-link.telia.net (62.115.121.7)  35.001 ms ffm-b1-link.telia.net (62.115.137.165)  36.025 ms
 9  tata-ic-321348-ffm-b1.c.telia.net (213.248.82.41)  39.816 ms  39.941 ms  44.285 ms
10  if-ae-4-2.tcore1.FR0-Frankfurt.as6453.net (195.219.87.18)  40.336 ms  40.452 ms  44.162 ms
11  195.219.50.186 (195.219.50.186)  40.025 ms  39.887 ms  39.989 ms
12  resolver1.dyndnsinternetguide.com (216.146.35.35)  44.719 ms  40.042 ms  44.152 ms
```

You may notice that the output is different from the same command run from your console, as it will produce the hops from your local network (while the one from the lg produced the output of `traceroute` as seen from the routers of BIX).

The lg can be implemented in Python, and `py-lookingglass` is such an implementation.

You may `install py-lookingglass` through `pip`:

```
$ sudo pip install py-lookingglass
```

Once installed, you may execute the following command to show the options:

```
$ python -m lg -h
usage: lg.py [-h] [-n NAME] [-c [COMMANDS [COMMANDS ...]]]
             [-H [HOSTS [HOSTS ...]]] [-b BIND] [-p PORT]
optional arguments:
  -h, --help            show this help message and exit
  -n NAME, --name NAME  Header name for pages
  -c [COMMANDS [COMMANDS ...]], --commands [COMMANDS [COMMANDS ...]]
Json array for profiles where key is profile name, use %ARG% for substition
of IP/hostname argument. Key in command is display friendly version.
Example:
{
"cisco": {
"Ping": "ping %ARG%",
"BGP Advertised _ARGUMENT_ to Neighbor": "sh ip bgp neighbor %ARG%
```

```
advertised",
"BGP Summary": "sh ip bgp summary",
"Traceroute": "traceroute %ARG%"
},
"juniper": {
"Ping": "ping -c 4 %ARG%",
"BGP Advertised _ARGUMENT_ to Neighbor": "cli -c \"show route advertising-
protocol bgp %ARG%\"",
"BGP Summary": "cli -c \"sh bgp sum\"",
"Traceroute": "traceroute %ARG%"
}
}
-H [HOSTS [HOSTS ...]], --hosts [HOSTS [HOSTS ...]]
 Comma separated profile for router
'password','host_address',port_number,type_of_connection(1 for ssh and 0
for telnet),name,command_profile separated by space.
Example
                                   "password1","192.168.0.1",23,0,"Cisco","cisco"
"login:password2","192.168.1.1",22,0,"Juniper","juniper"
-b BIND, --bind BIND  IP to bind
-p PORT, --port PORT  port to bind
```

Getting ready

There are more Python-based applications that offer a complete DNS looking glass solution. Dyn dns_lg (https://github.com/dyninc/dns_lg) is a DNS looking glass solution that depends on ldns (http://www.linuxfromscratch.org/blfs/view/cvs/basicnet/ldns.html), a fast and efficient DNS library and ldns-python package. ldns depends on SWIG interface compiler (http://www.swig.org) to connect its core modules developed in C and Python code used. Make sure you have SWIG installed on your computer:

1. You may install it using the following command in Ubuntu/Debian-based systems:

   ```
   $ sudo apt-get install swig
   ```

2. Download the source of ldns using the following command:

   ```
   $ wget -nc http://www.nlnetlabs.nl/downloads/
     ldns/ldns-1.7.0.tar.gz
   ```

3. Unzip the archive:

```
$ tar -xzf ldns-1.7.0.tar.gz
```

4. Move to the `ldns` directory:

```
$ cd ldns-1.7.0/
```

5. Now you may install `ldns`:

```
$ ./configure --prefix=/usr        \
              --sysconfdir=/etc        \
              --disable-static        \
              --disable-dane-ta-usage \
              --with-drill \
        --with-pyldns              &&
make
$ sudo make install
```

How to do it...

As you have installed `ldns`, now you may check out the Dyn's `dns_lg` source code from its source code repository:

```
git clone git@github.com:dyninc/dns_lg.git
cd dns_lg/
```

Now, you may run the application simply by executing `api.py`. Running it produces the following output:

```
$ python api.py
* Running on http://0.0.0.0:8185/
  (Press CTRL+C to quit)
```

Now open another console window to run a `curl`:

```
curl http://0.0.0.0:8185/cnn.com/
```

This will output a line to the preceding `api.py` console:

```
127.0.0.1 - - [15/Jul/2017 23:33:40]
"GET /cnn.com/ HTTP/1.1" 200 -
```

The `curl` command produces the following output with the detailed DNS information from the looking glass implementation:

```
$ curl http://0.0.0.0:8185/cnn.com/
{
  "AdditionalSection": [
    {
      "Address": "205.251.192.47",
      "Class": "IN",
      "Name": "ns-47.awsdns-05.com.",
      "TTL": "20545",
      "Type": "A"
    },
    {
      "Address": "205.251.194.64",
      "Class": "IN",
      "Name": "ns-576.awsdns-08.net.",
      "TTL": "20545",
      "Type": "A"
    }
  ],
  "AnswerSection": [],
  "AuthoritySection": [
    {
      "Class": "IN",
      "Name": "cnn.com.",
      "TTL": "20545",
      "Target": "ns-47.awsdns-05.com.",
      "Type": "NS"
    },
    {
      "Class": "IN",
      "Name": "cnn.com.",
      "TTL": "20545",
      "Target": "ns-1086.awsdns-07.org.",
      "Type": "NS"
    },
    {
      "Class": "IN",
      "Name": "cnn.com.",
      "TTL": "20545",
      "Target": "ns-576.awsdns-08.net.",
      "Type": "NS"
    },
    {
      "Class": "IN",
      "Name": "cnn.com.",
      "TTL": "20545",
```

```
            "Target": "ns-1630.awsdns-11.co.uk.",
            "Type": "NS"
        }
    ],
    "None": "true",
    "Query": {
        "Duration": 118,
        "Server": "",
        "ServerIP": "127.0.1.1",
        "Versions": "Dyn DNS Looking Glass 1.0.0"
    },
    "QuestionSection": {
        "Qclass": "IN",
        "Qname": "cnn.com.",
        "Qtype": "A"
    },
    "ReturnCode": "NOERROR"
}
```

The preceding output shows Dyn's `dns_lg` and `curl` in action. Please note that currently Dyn's `dns_lg` works only in Python 2.x. However, with some minor fixes, this can easily be ported to Python 3.x. As we ported `bgperf` to Python 3.x in a previous recipe, this is left as an exercise for those who like to port this to Python 3.x.

How it works...

Looking glass offers you an opportunity to see how you can connect to another part of the internet through the routers of any given IXP. Similar to the functionality of `traceroute`, lg implementations show you the connectivity in the internet scale. They are deployed by the IXPs to demonstrate the IXP performance to the potential customers.

Understanding the internet ecosystem with Python

When network traffic is sent to the internet, it passes through various ASes and IXPs. Tools such as `traceroute` and `tcptraceroute` can be used to trace how a particular network node in the internet can be accessed from your computer through your internet provider. Various tools developed in Python can be used to understand the nature of the internet. traIXroute (`https://pypi.python.org/pypi/traixroute`) is a tool developed on Python 3, which identifies the IXPs on the `traceroute` path.

Getting ready

You may install traIXroute through `pip`:

```
$ sudo pip install traixroute
```

To measure the performance and topologies of the internet, you also need to install scamper (`https://www.caida.org/tools/measurement/scamper/`), a parallel measurement utility for the internet:

```
$ sudo scamper-install
```

Your traIXroute is now ready to analyze the internet connectivity through the IXPs. You may confirm your successful install by running the `--help` command, which will produce the output as follows:

```
$ traixroute --help
usage: traixroute [-h] [-dns] [-asn] [-db] [-rule] [-u] [-m] [-o OUTPUT] [-
v]
                    {probe,ripe,import} ...
positional arguments:
   {probe,ripe,import}
     probe                probe --help
     ripe                 ripe --help
     import               import --help
optional arguments:
  -h, --help              show this help message and exit
  -dns, --enable-dns-print
                          Enables printing the domain name
 of each IP hop in the traceroute path.
  -asn, --enable-asn-print
                          Enables printing the ASN of
 each IP hop in the traceroute path.
      -db, --store-database
                          Enables printing the database information.
      -rule, --enable-rule-print
                          Enables printing the hit IXP detection rule(s)
 in the traceroute path.
      -u, --update        Updates the database with up-to-date datasets.
      -m, --merge         Exports the database to distinct files, the
 ixp_prefixes.txt and ixp_membership.txt.
      -o OUTPUT, --output OUTPUT
                          Specifies the output file name to redirect the
 traIXroute results.
      -v, --version       show program's version number and exit
```

How to do it...

Now you may run `traixroute` to see the IXPs in your path. Running `traixroute` for the first time takes a few minutes, as it has to perform a few initialization actions, downloading the datasets:

```
$ traixroute probe -dest cnn.com -s="-m 12"
Dataset files are missing.
Updating the database...
Started downloading PDB dataset.
Started downloading PCH dataset.
Started downloading RouteViews dataset.
Routeviews has been updated successfully.
PDB dataset has been updated successfully.
PCH dataset has been updated successfully.
Database has been updated successfully.
Imported 13 IXP Detection Rules from /configuration/rules.txt.
Loading from PCH, PDB, Routeviews and additional_info.txt.
traIXroute using scamper with "-m 12" options.
[15:08:06:001] scamper_privsep_init: could not mkdir /var/empty: Permission
denied
Scamper failed. Trying to run with sudo..
[sudo] password for pradeeban:
traIXroute to cnn.com (151.101.1.67).
1)      (62.4.224.1) 15.465 ms
2)      (91.183.241.176) 18.642 ms
3)      (91.183.246.112) 12.178 ms
4)      (62.115.40.97) 20.216 ms
5)      (213.155.136.216) 20.027 ms
6)      (80.91.253.163) 12.127 ms
7)      (*) -
8)      (*) -
9)      (*) -
10)     (*) -
11)     (*) -
```

This did not indicate any IXP in the path between my network and http://edition.cnn.com/. Let's try once more towards `register.bg`:

```
$ sudo traixroute probe -dest register.bg -s="-m 12"
Imported 13 IXP Detection Rules from /configuration/rules.txt.
Loading from Database.
traIXroute using scamper with "-m 12" options.
traIXroute to register.bg (192.92.129.35).
1)      (62.4.224.1) 21.699 ms
2)      (91.183.241.176) 7.769 ms
3)      (91.183.246.114) 8.056 ms
```

```
4)      (BNIX)->AS9002      (194.53.172.71)  7.417 ms
5)      (87.245.234.130)  51.538 ms
6)      (87.245.240.146)  51.324 ms
7)      (178.132.82.126)  44.711 ms
8)      (193.68.0.150)  46.406 ms
9)      (193.68.0.181)  44.492 ms
10)     (192.92.129.35)  44.777 ms
IXP hops:
3) 91.183.246.114 <--- BNIX (BE,Brussels) ---> 4) 194.53.172.71
```

This shows that my request had an `IXP hops` (`BNIX` in `Brussels`) in between. If you repeat the request, you may notice that the `IXP hops` most certainly remained the same while other hops may have changed. You may repeat with other websites to see which IXPs that your network traffic passes through.

How it works...

The `-m` flag indicates the maximum **time-to-live** (**TTL**) between the hops. The * in the output logs indicates failure to trace a node within the given TTL, as no response was received. The `-m` flag dictates the maximum number of hops to be traced. It can be a value between 1 and 255, with 1 producing just 1 hop in between, where 255 produces up to 255 hops towards the end point. However, note that it is unlikely to have such a long path in the internet, and if exists, it is even more unlikely to retrieve the exact IP addresses through `traceroute` or `traixroute` (you will more likely receive * for the latter hops).

Establishing BGP connections with yabgp

Yabgp is a Python implementation for BGP protocol that supports establishing BGP connections from various routers. It can be used for various advanced use cases such as future analysis. In this recipe, we will install `yabgp` using `virtualenv` virtual environment for Python programs.

Getting ready

First, get the sources of `yabgp`:

```
$ git clone https://github.com/smartbgp/yabgp
```

Now to build `yabgp`:

```
$ cd yabgp
```

Install the requirements following this command, and observe the following logs:

```
$ pip install -r requirements.txt
..
Successfully installed Twisted Flask Flask-HTTPAuth netaddr zope.interface
Werkzeug Jinja2 itsdangerous MarkupSafe
Cleaning up...
```

Now you may confirm the correct installation of `yabgpd` by using the following command:

```
$ cd bin
$ python yabgpd -h
```

This will output detailed help information on `yabgpd`.

How to do it...

`yabgpd` is a BGP agent that can orchestrate the BGP routers. You may start the agent as a Python application. Make sure to update the correct values for the BGP local and remote addresses, and the local and remote BGP autonomous system values. The program will print a set of log lines as follows:

```
$ python yabgpd --bgp-local_addr=172.31.0.232 --bgp-local_as=23650 \
--bgp-remote_addr=52.58.130.47 --bgp-remote_as=23650
2017-07-16 16:19:05,837.837 78465 INFO yabgp.agent [-] Log (Re)opened.
2017-07-16 16:19:05,837.837 78465 INFO yabgp.agent [-] Configuration:
2017-07-16 16:19:05,837.837 78465 INFO yabgp.agent [-]
****************************************************
2017-07-16 16:19:05,837.837 78465 INFO yabgp.agent [-] Configuration
options gathered from:
2017-07-16 16:19:05,837.837 78465 INFO yabgp.agent [-] command line args:
['--bgp-local_addr=172.31.0.232', '--bgp-local_as=23650', '--bgp-
remote_addr=10.124.1.245', '--bgp-remote_as=23650']
2017-07-16 16:19:05,837.837 78465 INFO yabgp.agent [-] config files: []
2017-07-16 16:19:05,837.837 78465 INFO yabgp.agent [-]
=====================================================
```

```
....
...
2017-07-16 16:19:05,840.840 78465 INFO yabgp.agent [-] ---remote_as = 23650
2017-07-16 16:19:05,840.840 78465 INFO yabgp.agent [-] ---remote_addr =
10.124.1.245
2017-07-16 16:19:05,840.840 78465 INFO yabgp.agent [-] ---local_as = 23650
2017-07-16 16:19:05,840.840 78465 INFO yabgp.agent [-] ---local_addr =
172.31.0.232
2017-07-16 16:19:05,840.840 78465 INFO yabgp.agent [-] ---capability =
{'remote': {}, 'local': {'cisco_route_refresh': True, 'route_refresh':
True, 'graceful_restart': True, 'cisco_multi_session': True,
'four_bytes_as': True, 'enhanced_route_refresh': True, 'add_path': None}}
2017-07-16 16:19:05,840.840 78465 INFO yabgp.agent [-] ---afi_safi =
['ipv4']
2017-07-16 16:19:05,840.840 78465 INFO yabgp.agent [-] ---md5 = None
2017-07-16 16:19:05,840.840 78465 INFO yabgp.handler.default_handler [-]
Create dir /home/ubuntu/data/bgp/10.124.1.245 for peer 10.124.1.245
2017-07-16 16:19:05,840.840 78465 INFO yabgp.handler.default_handler [-]
BGP message file path is /home/ubuntu/data/bgp/10.124.1.245
2017-07-16 16:19:05,840.840 78465 INFO yabgp.handler.default_handler [-]
get the last bgp message seq for this peer
2017-07-16 16:19:05,840.840 78465 INFO yabgp.handler.default_handler [-]
BGP message file 1500221945.84.msg
2017-07-16 16:19:05,840.840 78465 INFO yabgp.handler.default_handler [-]
The last bgp message seq number is 0
2017-07-16 16:19:05,841.841 78465 INFO yabgp.agent [-] Create BGPPeering
twsited instance
2017-07-16 16:19:05,841.841 78465 INFO yabgp.core.factory [-] Init
BGPPeering for peer 10.124.1.245
2017-07-16 16:19:05,841.841 78465 INFO yabgp.agent [-] Prepare RESTAPI
service
2017-07-16 16:19:05,842.842 78465 INFO yabgp.agent [-] serving RESTAPI on
http://0.0.0.0:8801
2017-07-16 16:19:05,842.842 78465 INFO yabgp.agent [-] Starting BGPPeering
twsited instance
2017-07-16 16:19:05,842.842 78465 INFO yabgp.core.fsm [-] Automatic start
2017-07-16 16:19:05,842.842 78465 INFO yabgp.core.fsm [-] Do not need Idle
Hold, start right now.
2017-07-16 16:19:05,842.842 78465 INFO yabgp.core.fsm [-] Connect retry
counter: 0
2017-07-16 16:19:05,843.843 78465 INFO yabgp.core.fsm [-] Connect retry
timer, time=30
2017-07-16 16:19:05,843.843 78465 INFO yabgp.core.fsm [-]
[10.124.1.245]State is now:CONNECT
2017-07-16 16:19:05,843.843 78465 INFO yabgp.core.factory [-] (Re)connect
to 10.124.1.245
....
```

As can be seen from the logs, the BGP message file is created in the folder, `/home/ubuntu/data/bgp/10.124.1.245`.

By analyzing the logs, you may notice logs are stored from both the remote and local BGP addresses:

```
$ tree /home/ubuntu/data/bgp
/home/ubuntu/data/bgp
├── 10.124.1.245
│   └── msg
│       └── 1500221945.84.msg
└── 52.58.130.47
    └── msg
        └── 1500221444.73.msg
```

How it works...

`yabgpd` is a BGP agent that can establish BGP connections with various routers. The agent receives the BGP messages and is capable of using them for further uses, such as future analysis. Running these applications require access to BGP routers to route traffic between the autonomous systems. These recipes illustrate the capability of Python to build large-scale complex network applications in the internet scale.

Index

Lightning Source UK Ltd.
Milton Keynes UK
UKHW03f2309051018
330000UK00006B/682/P